ROUTLEDGE LIBRARY EDITIONS:
ACCOUNTING

Volume 40



# ACCOUNTING FROM THE OUTSIDE

# ACCOUNTING FROM THE OUTSIDE

## The Collected Papers of Anthony G. Hopwood

Edited with an Introduction by
ANTHONY G. HOPWOOD

Routledge
Taylor & Francis Group
LONDON AND NEW YORK

First published in 1988

This edition first published in 2014
by Routledge
2 Park Square, Milton Park, Abingdon, Oxfordshire OX14 4RN

and by Routledge
711 Third Avenue, New York, NY 10017

*Routledge is an imprint of the Taylor and Francis Group, an informa business*

First issued in paperback 2015



*British Library Cataloguing in Publication Data*
A catalogue record for this book is available from the British Library

ISBN 978-0-415-53081-1 (Set)
eISBN 978-1-315-88628-2 (Set)
ISBN 978-0-415-70299-7 (hbk) (Volume 40)
ISBN 978-1-138-98820-0 (pbk) (Volume 40)
ISBN 978-1-315-88195-9 (ebk) (Volume 40)

**Publisher's Note**
The publisher has gone to great lengths to ensure the quality of this book but points out that some imperfections in the original copies may be apparent.

**Disclaimer**
The publisher has made every effort to trace copyright holders and would welcome correspondence from those they have been unable to trace.

# Accounting from the Outside

*The Collected Papers of Anthony G. Hopwood*

Edited with an Introduction by
ANTHONY G. HOPWOOD

GARLAND PUBLISHING, INC.
NEW YORK & LONDON 1988

**Library of Congress Cataloging-in-Publication Data**

Hopwood, Anthony G.
Accounting from the outside.

(Foundations of Accounting)
Bibliography: p.
1. Accounting. 2. Managerial accounting. 3. Accounting—Social aspects.. I. Title. II. Series.
HF5635.H812 1988 657 88-24496
ISBN 0-4280-6124-1 (alk paper)

Design by Renata Gomes

The volumes in this series are printed on acid-free, 250-year-life paper.

Printed in the United States of America

In memory of
my parents

# Contents

# Acknowledgements

I would like to acknowledge the help provided by all the publishers in obtaining permission to reprint articles, chapters, and other contributions. Reprint conditions require that specific mention be made of the following:

Papers 5, 12, 24, 25, 28, 29, 35, 36, 37, 38, 39, 40, 41, 42, 43, and 44 are reprinted with permission from *Accounting, Organizations and Society*, Pergamon Press plc.

Papers 6 and 17 are reprinted by permission of Philip Allan Publishers Limited.

Paper 13 is reprinted from Kim B. Clark, Robert H. Hayes, and Christopher Lorenz, eds., *The Uneasy Alliance: Managing the Productivity-Technology Dilemma*, Boston: Harvard Business School Press, 1985. Copyright © 1985 by the President and Fellows of Harvard College. Reprinted by permission.

Papers 14, 26, 31, and 32 are reprinted by permission of Pitman Publishing.

Paper 21 first appeared in *Accountancy* (October, 1981). Reprinted with permission.

Paper 22 is reprinted from *New Forms of Work Organization*, Vol.2 (1979), pp.115–145 by permission of the International Labour Organisation. Copyright 1979, International Labour Organisation, Geneva.

Paper 23 is reprinted by permission of the Macmillan Press Limited.

# Observing the Accounting Craft

## AN INTRODUCTION

Accounting has always had a certain fascination for me. As a child, I almost left school on two occasions to enter the accountancy profession. Not doing that, I proceeded to study the subject at the London School of Economics and Political Science. Although thereafter I was one of the few who did not seek to enter professional training, I nevertheless decided to continue my probings into accounting at the University of Chicago, in the process first setting aside the possibility of pursuing research in the area of industrial economics and thereafter in the area of finance. And since that time accounting has become a phenomenon for almost continuous observation, curiosity, and inquiry.

The reasons for the fascination are difficult to appreciate, as they are for many things that provide an element of continuity between one's quite distant past and the here and now. The interest arose during a period of rapid accounting development in the United Kingdom. Its involvement with attempts at industrial and financial reconstruction resulted in a certain prominence in media discussions. Accounting was starting to catch the public eye and I might well have been one of those enticed within its web at that time. Its characterization as a seemingly modern and rational form of knowledge and expertise might have influenced the perceptions of a young grammar school boy, not least when a close family member provided a more immediate exemplar of the accountant in action. I remember what might otherwise have been purely social discussions being peppered with tales of new American methods, accounting's involvement in corporate reorganisation, the early stages of the rise of a new breed of financial executives in the United Kingdom, and, not least in significance, the more questionable implications of this for local manufacturing and employment in a relatively poor region of the North of England.

Just such an ambiguity surrounded many of my initial involvements with accounting. Early attempts to join the profession provided some fascinating insights into the social recruitment criteria used by the agents of a seemingly meritocratic occupation. Through family involvements I had the opportunity to witness some of the personal and organizational tensions, anxieties, and contradictions associated with the economic rationalizing concerns of accountants and the other managerial groups with which they were associated. Not only could parts of a local economy be seen as being more readily incorporated into wider patterns of economic forces, but also the management practices with which accounting was associated were seen in ways that provided some insights into how they could shift patterns of influence and discretion within wider organizational settings. Even at that time accounting started to come across as a more multifaceted phenomenon and one that, however technical its procedures might appear, was not isolated from wider patterns of human and social life. Indeed, as I remember it, I was already starting to be aware of the contradictory nature of the accounting task. Despite the aura of professional neutrality and the articulation of its serving a conception of the public interest, accountants were widely known to be the servants of those wishing to follow the letter rather than the spirit of the legislative intent, not least in the area of taxation. Even quite mundane associations with accounting in practice were starting to create an impression of the equivocality of the accountant's craft, if only in terms of the discretionary nature of a final account. There quite obviously was more at stake in accounting than mere financial arithmetic.

My undergraduate years at the London School of Economics only served to increase such impressions. Under the watchful eye of people like Will Baxter, Harold Edey, and Basil Yamey, accounting started to emerge as a more problematic activity. Although the accounting part of a wider study of the social sciences was not extensive at that time, the economic orientation to the subject that was an important part of the intellectual tradition at the LSE (Dev, 1980), provided a means of confronting the technical practice of accounting with a wider framework for its analysis. Costs and profits were portrayed as multifaceted, complex, and conceptual phenomena whose interpretation required a wider, albeit still economic, appreciation of the contexts in which they functioned and had an effect. Whilst certainly not emphasized, some basis for appreciating how political and social concerns might intermingle with and change modes of economic calculation was nevertheless also provided at the LSE at that time, not least in the context of discussions of approaches to forms of social cost-benefit analysis which were then emerging.

In such ways an interest in studying and understanding accounting developed. A more questioning curiosity about accounting started to emerge, providing the basis for an interest in continuing the study *of* accounting rather than seeking a professional indoctrination *in* the subject. In the mid-1960s, however, it was almost impossible to obtain adequate research training in accounting or indeed most other management subjects in the United Kingdom. The major business schools were just about to be established. The research infrastructure was minimal. Being advised of such constraints, I decided to apply to doctoral programmes in the United States. On these grounds the University of Chicago was to become my intellectual base for the next five years.

## CHICAGO AND THE EXPLORATION OF ACCOUNTING IN USE

Chicago undoubtedly provided the intellectual basis for the development of my interest in the study of accounting in use. Although the focus of that interest was to change a great deal subsequently, the idea of probing into the actual functioning of the accounting craft originated in and was nurtured by the productive academic environment that Chicago provided. The commitment to the sustained and rigorous study of business phenomena that was such an important part of the intellectual life of the Graduate School of Business at the University of Chicago at that time created an intellectual ethos that was exciting, demanding, and, above all, conducive for experimentation.

It was indeed an exciting time to be studying accounting at Chicago. The rise of an interest in empiricism was still occurring, much fostered by David Green and propagated by him in his doctoral seminars and, not least, in the newly established *Journal of Accounting Research*. New interrelationships were being forged between accounting and economics, quantitative methods, and even the behavioral sciences. Research discussions were couched in philosophical terms. Modern finance theory and its empirical basis were being constructed at the School, amongst other places. Even the student community was itself an exceptionally able and innovative one. Bill Beaver, Philip Brown, Joel Demski, and Mel Greenball, for instance, were all ahead of me on the

Doctoral Programme, and Ray Ball and Ross Watts, amongst others, were to join soon afterwards.

In such an environment research, not surprisingly, had a very high profile and priority. For someone recently arrived from the United Kingdom, it was quite obvious that research was perceived as a professional activity rather than a gentlemanly pursuit. Amongst both the faculty and the doctoral students, I think it fair to say, there was a feeling that knowledge itself was in the process of changing. The old was contrasted with the new and the forces driving the new were explicitly discussed and argued.

My own interest in the behavioral and organizational aspects of accounting emerged by chance in an institution devoted to the extension of quite particular conceptions of economic rationality. Forced to take a course on organization theory to satisfy the course distribution requirements of the doctoral programme, that course, so ably and interestingly taught by Paul Goodman (now of Carnegie-Mellon University), provided me with a new vision of how to study accounting. The interest and challenge was such that I restructured my doctoral studies, setting aside a specialization in finance in order to delve further into the behavioral aspects of accounting systems. Of course there were those who thought such a move ill-advised, but the helpful counsels of George Sorter, the director of the doctoral programme at the time, and particularly Dick Hoffman, a social-psychologist who had himself only recently joined the Chicago faculty from the University of Michigan, greatly eased the intellectual transition that was to result in an attempt to forge some understanding of the interrelationship between accounting and the organizational contexts in which it operated.

The dysfunctional consequences of management accounting systems started to be a topic of particular interest to me. Stimulated by Chris Argyris's pioneering study of *The Impact of Budgets on People* (1952), still possibly wondering about my own early exposure to the more equivocal functioning of accounting, certainly influenced by the social-psychological orientation of a great deal of the behavioral science programme at Chicago, and also intrigued by the then emergent contingency formulations of organization theory, I began to think about exploring the factors that influenced the behavioral and organizational consequences of accounting systems, dysfunctional or otherwise.

A commitment to engage in field research also developed at an early stage for reasons now difficult to reconstruct. Perhaps my very early interest in the actual functioning of accounting played some role. I certainly remember holding the view that accounting was an organizational phenomenon and needed to be studied as such. Seen in such terms, I think that there was a quite genuine interest in the development of an action based, more humanistic basis for appreciating the variety of management responses to accounting, with a view to moving towards a more adequate understanding of how accounting functioned as a significant organizational and social practice. I was also quite definitely worried about the validity of laboratory experimentation, a methodology then just starting to be used in accounting research. A trial experiment using friendly subjects reinforced my doubts about the credibility of the exercise as a basis for understanding the functioning of accounting as an organizational practice. By then I was also familiar with and quite worried about a developing body of research on the social psychology of the psychological experiment, work conveniently ignored by the experimental literature. The laboratory appeared to me to be an ever less obvious site for the exploration of accounting in action. Although I was aware of the difficulties of entering the field, not least for a novice Englishman in Chicago, I was nevertheless convinced that this was what I ought to do even though it created a new precedent for accounting research at Chicago and even though there were those who initially did not look on the proposal with favor.

Research access to a suitable organization was far from easy to negotiate, taking nine anxious months in all. As a research orientated institution, the Chicago Business School had relatively few suitable contacts in industrial and commercial circles at that time. I decided I did not wish to study a traditional insurance company, even though access might have been available. However tempting it initially appeared, I also decided that the impracticalities of field work in Florida were too great. And even greater in Chile! Even the efforts of a future Secretary of State failed to get me into one organization. In the end, however, access was gained to a major steel company and Gary, Indiana, amidst its agonising environmental deprivations, was to become a second home for the next couple of years or so.

"You don't need to be a behavioral scientist to understand this lot. You need to be a bloody anthropologist," advised one of my early shop floor contacts. "You're in the jungle now," he went on to add, describing how almost every department in the steel plant had its own ethnic and cultural identity, mirroring the immigration history of the Mid West. The newest arrivals seemingly always started on the shop floor in the dirty and dangerous early processes, slowly being promoted upwards and, over time, moving into the relatively cleaner and safer later processes of steel making. By the time I was around the descendents of the British, the Germans, and the Scandinavians were way down the line and the first black foreman had been appointed in the blast furnaces.

For somewhat different reasons, an anthropologist of sorts I was to become. Entering the field with quite general interests and hypotheses, and almost no prior studies to rely on, a great deal of time was spent on trying to understand how an amazingly complex and quite sophisticated accounting system functioned, how it became involved with wider organizational processes, and how it had the consequences it had. The initial research efforts were exploratory and observational. I worked on the night shift. I had a hole burnt in my jacket in the blast furnace—an initiation of a sort. I spent an amazing amount of time watching, listening, and talking. Later I was to refer to this in terms of tapping into the linguistic culture of the firm. For over time I became increasingly aware of not only the different ways in which the same accounting system was implicated in organizational processes, but also the subtle distinctions in language that both reflected and shaped the patterns of differential use. These distinctions provided a focus for the final study; the linguistic differences were the basis for further exploration by the use of questionnaires. The latter is something that nearly all subsequent users of the research instrument have ignored, merrily but all too ignorantly proceeding with using it in factory-like style.

The form of the doctoral research was influenced not only by the problem and the exploration of the research site. With such field research being all very new in an accounting context, not least at Chicago, it was made quite clear that a more structured approach to the final research design was required. So questionnaire design, distribution, and analysis entered the research process, as did the complexities of nonparametric statistics. So much so, in fact, that in those distant days when field explorations were new and little understood by the accounting research establishment, and when accounting itself was less assured of its intellectual bases, the highly significant exploratory research was purged from the final text, the latter thereby having the appearance of a more structured, anticipated, confident, and seemingly scientific work.

The resultant study, published in its entirety as *An Accounting System and Managerial Behaviour* (Hopwood, 1973; see also the papers in section one of the present collection), provided some insights into the managerial processes through which accounting data acquired an organizational meaning and significance. Focusing on the differing ways in which different managers used the same accounting system, it cast some light on the ways in which organizational factors could mediate and shape the consequences associated with an accounting system, thereby providing a way of appreciating a diversity of effects rather than a set of inevitable ones, anticipated or otherwise. The study also provided a basis for appreciating how factors such as participation in the budgetary process and other organizational circumstances could influence the change the processes at work, thereby creating a whole range of new problems for investigation in further studies. In more contemporary terms, the study also provided some insights into how organizational cultures and managerial philosophies might shape the significance attached to accounting systems and play some role in influencing their effects.

Perhaps more significantly for me, however, the study undertaken in Chicago had demonstrated that it was possible and meaningful to probe into the actual functioning of accounting. Although I was never myself to extend the precise form of that analysis, a basis for a more widespread interest in observing and questioning accounting in use had been created. Rather than focusing on the technical analysis and elaboration of accounting in isolation from its organizational context, I had started along a path of inquiry concerned with the observation of accounting rather than its propagation, with an exploration of its organizational and social bases rather than the presumption of a technical autonomy, and with an attempt to appreciate the actual consequences of accounting rather than the unproblematic acceptance of its stated rationales.

## THE DEVELOPMENT OF AN ORGANIZATIONAL INTEREST

The culture shock on returning to the United Kingdom in 1970 was intellectual as well as social in nature. Having developed my interest in organizational issues in the United States, I had tended to take for granted the social psychological domination of the subject evident at that time and place, and its resulting individualistic orientation (Kassem, 1976). The contrast with a British perspective therefore could not have been more marked, not least with the vibrant organizational research community at the Manchester Business School, which celebrated its links to the substantive disciplines of anthropology, sociology, and even a version of institutional economics. Accordingly I had to set about merging myself in organizational studies afresh, luckily, however, in an environment noted for its excitement, its innovativeness, and its concern with the scholarly, the practical, and the interface between the two.

Working on the text of *Accounting and Human Behaviour* (Hopwood, 1974) provided a most useful way of thinking through what might be at stake with a wider organisational perspective on accounting. It provided a context in which to explore new literatures, to push existing understandings, and to start raising a somewhat different set of questions related to the organizational embeddedness of accounting. Although the text is now a somewhat dated work (albeit one that is still in use), I am still surprised by the apparent novelty of some of the occasional comments and the extent to which it reflected what was then only the beginning of a new way of attempting to perceive the accounting craft. At times even I wonder how I could possibly have thought that way at that time!

A number of influences were starting to reflect themselves in my work. Not only was an expanding interdisciplinary basis evident but also a growing involvement with accounting in practice. Post-experience management teaching was useful in this respect, as were the opportunities that the Manchester Business School provided to work with a mature, ambitious, and intellectually able group of post-graduate students. In a more complex way I was also stimulated by the intellectual agenda created by the Management Control Research Group at the School. Founded by Morris McInnes and Tony Lowe, the group set itself an impossibly ambitious research agenda of both surveying and categorizing the variety of approaches to management control systems functioning in the United Kingdom. At that time there was little prior work to guide such an endeavor. Existing conceptual frameworks and distinctions were woefully inadequate to reflect the diversity of practices in use. And the methodological problems involved in mapping such diversity were very real. Hardly surprisingly the activities of the group generated a fair amount of conflict, an enormous data bank of observations and recordings, and relatively few publications. Be that as it may, the project exposed all of us to the complexities of management accounting in practice and illuminated very forcefully the inadequacies of many existing understandings of the subject. What findings there were pointed to an appreciation of accounting that recognized its involvement with other organizational practices and the ways in which accounting systems were implicated in the construction of organizations as we know them, rather than being mere reflections of the organizational endeavour.

As a result of such experiences a more organizationally grounded appreciation of accounting started to emerge. The technical practice of accounting increasingly came to be related to the organizational and wider contexts in which it functioned. The interrelationships between accounting and organizational structures, aspects of the technological and competitive environments of the enterprise, and the dynamics of the political processes that characterise organizational life started to be explored. Although I was at this time both aware of and influenced by contingent notions of organization developed in the organizational literature, I think that it is fair to say that even then I found such frameworks useful but inadequate, at least as they were then formulated. They provided one way of characterizing the organizational dependency of accounting systems, but they did this in a way that was too deterministic, offered too limited a view of the more complex patterns of interdependency that I increasingly came to see as influencing accounting's functioning in organizations, and ignored the more subtle ways in which flows of accounting information could shift and disturb patterns of influence, power, meaning, and significance within the organizational realm.

Aware of such limitations of more conventional, albeit still emerging, ways of conceiving accounting in an organizational context, a more open personal agenda for probing into the organizational functioning and significance of accounting started to develop. Much interested in the challenge of deriving an approach to teaching in the area, I became increasingly interested in the articulation of quite general but hopefully useful frameworks that might help to improve our understanding of the organizational construction, functioning, and consequences of accounting. Somewhat in contrast but certainly not in conflict, I also developed an interest in both ways of appreciating the quite specific functioning of accounting systems in specific organizations and the research strategies that might result in a more organizationally grounded insight into accounting as it operated. Earlier interests in the "use" of accounting broadened out into interests in the different ways in which accounting systems could be and were caught up in decision and influence processes in organizations. An interest in the micro politics of accounting started to emerge. I became more sensitive to the ways in which accounting changes could influence managerial vocabularies and the articulation of organizational aims, problems, and possibilities. The ways in which accounting got caught up in wider organizational patterns of transformation and change started to become of particular interest. I started at least to talk about the extent to which the elaboration of accounting systems might be a response to organizational crisis. The management of information flows in circumstances characterized by rapid change and disruption became a topic of growing curiosity. The quite complex ways in which accounting could be influenced by organizational restructurings started to enter my research agenda.

Perhaps unfortunately, most of these interests did not result in specific research projects. Rather together they provided a basis for a growing sense of unease with both existing technical appreciations of the accounting craft and the so-called behavioral insights that had emerged by that time. The autonomy attributed to the former and the constrained notions of organizational rationality that were implicit in discussions of them were an increasing source of dissatisfaction, as were the individualistic emphases that were quite explicit in the rise of a behavioral stance in the accounting research community. The inability of the latter to confront a great deal of what I came to see as being at stake in the organizational practice of accounting provided a basis for an intellectual unease with research developments. Increasingly I also put more emphasis on the limitations that such behavioral views had for guiding even pragmatic interests in accounting system design. Perhaps by then the teaching demands evident in a business school environment were making their impact, although not only was I never aware of a conflict between the scholarly and the practical but, in contrast, I became increasingly interested in some of the quite similar demands that both strands of thinking could make on accounting knowledge.

All too clearly, subsequent interests in understanding the dynamics of accounting change were emergent at this time. A focus on grounded inquiry had already been articulated. A multiplicity of rationales for accounting elaboration and development were starting to be appreciated, providing a rich basis for continuing empirical and theoretical inquiries. Although perhaps not quite so well appreciated at that time, an interest in both the scholarly and the practical roles of accounting knowledge was also starting to be made more evident. All told, an agenda for future research, a quite particular theoretical stance, and a perspective on the roles that knowledge might play were all emerging in ways that continued to have a significant influence on the direction of future enthusiasms and inquiries.

## INSTITUTIONAL INVOLVEMENTS

It is most likely quite difficult to appreciate some, at least, of these shifting interests outside of the context of a growing involvement with the institutionalization of accounting research. For reasons that I sense owe more to luck than design, I had the opportunity to become an active contributor to three quite significant advancements in the institutional development of accounting research in the United Kingdom at that time. These were the launching of an accounting research initiative by the then Social Science Research Council, the government funding body for research in the human and social sciences; the development of a programme of European accounting research workshops by the newly established European Institute for Advanced Studies in Management, in Brussels, an activity that subsequently gave rise to the creation of the European Accounting Association; and the establishment of a new specialized international research journal concerned with the behavioral, organizational, and social analyses of accounting, *Accounting, Organizations and Society*. All of these activities consumed a vast amount of my time, and some still do so. Although they considerably constrained my own research and writing endeavors, not only did they not stop them but over the years they also had a very considerable influence upon them.

The development of a European network of accounting researchers brought me into contact with very different research traditions, theoretical ways of appreciating accounting, and strategies for engaging in accounting research. It is always difficult to appreciate and disentangle the influences such awarenesses have had on your own work. They invariably leave few specific residues. But I am very conscious of the cumulative impact, not least with respect to the richness of insight and sheer enthusiasm for grounded organizational inquiry that was such an important part of the Scandinavian, and particularly the Swedish, tradition of research in the areas of accounting and information systems in particular and management more generally. My personal contacts and friendships with Scandinavian researchers provided possibilities for direct theoretical influences; they also prompted a reorientation of my organizational interests, away from a model influenced by the North

American academic community and towards one increasingly open to the quite different intellectual traditions of continental Europe. In ways that would be difficult, if not impossible, to chart with precision, I started to develop into a European academic who increasingly could observe both American work and my own earlier inquiries with interest but from a distance.

The full development of a more European tradition of inquiry will, in all probability, be manifested by a younger group of scholars, rather than by those of us who were privileged to have played some role in the creation of a cross-national network of accounting researchers. But I derive a great deal of pleasure from the part I have been able to play in the establishment of that network and I look forward with pleasure to the days when it might result in understandings and insights different from those I personally have been able to utilize.

Different institutional forms can undoubtedly play some role in changing modes of inquiry and the resultant patterns of knowledge and understanding. Indeed it was with just such a view in mind that I sought to establish a new journal that would be exclusively concerned with the organizational, behavioral, and social analyses of accounting. Although it still has an unfinished agenda for intellectual exploration and change, I like to think that *Accounting, Organizations and Society* has already played some role in opening up new areas for inquiry, legitimizing different scholarly traditions, and creating a more international and open research community amongst those interested in probing into the human and social nature of accounting thought and practice.

The initial idea on which *Accounting, Organizations and Society* was based emerged in an educational context. With other colleagues at the Manchester Business School I had designed a role-playing case study based on the affairs of Pergamon Press, an organization that played a not insignificant role in recent British accounting history. Wanting the students to have the opportunity to question actual participants in the affair rather than rely solely on press reports and official documents, key participants were invited to take part in the teaching of the case study. Robert Maxwell, the founder of Pergamon Press, was one of those individuals and, ever the entrepreneur, Mr. Maxwell used the opportunity to inquire into whether I had any ideas for new research journals!

Well, as it happens, I had. At that time I was becoming increasingly conscious of a gap that existed between the potential for an organizational and social understanding of accounting and the editorial policies and concerns of the existing accounting research journals. That idea of a gap gave rise to a proposal for a new journal and after numerous deliberations and consultations *Accounting, Organizations and Society*, the new journal, was launched in 1976.

In retrospect it is interesting to reflect on the enormous gap between the naiveté of the idea and the reality of the journal's establishment. Even getting agreement on the name of the new journal was problematic. Majority opinion was strongly in favor of it being known as the *Journal of Behavioral and Social Accounting*. I, however, was bothered about the constrained view of what would hopefully become a new research area implicit in such a designation. I wanted something more suggestive of the need to openly explore ways in which accounting functioned in organizational and social settings. Whilst the concerns of the 1970s emphasized the specificities of behavioral and social accounting, I envisioned a journal that would encourage the investigation of wider questions relating to the rise of economic calculation in organizations and society. *Accounting, Organizations and Society* emerged as a title that hopefully suggested the possibilities that the new journal might create, rather than being reflective of, the immediate context out of which it emerged.

Now is not the occasion to review the history of *Accounting, Organizations and Society*. I like to think that it has achieved quite a lot, although I am equally conscious of what remains to be achieved. It certainly has consumed an immense amount of my time and energy, and still does so. But my involvement with the journal has been a reciprocal one. Just as I have at least attempted to steer and influence it, so *Accounting, Organizations and Society* has had a very significant influence on me. I have learnt from what it has published; I have gained from the intellectual agendas it has helped to create; and I am wiser as a result of the new networks of enthusiastic researchers that have been associated with the journal. International in scope, the community of those interested in the organizational and social analysis of accounting has established a tradition of open, friendly, and facilitative interchange that has brought together friendship and intellectual curiosity in ways that have been mutually enriching.

## THE RISE OF A SOCIAL INTEREST

It was whilst *Accounting, Organizations and Society* was still a very new baby, that I moved to what was then the Oxford Centre for Management Studies (now Templeton College, Oxford) with the explicit brief of establishing a programme of accounting research. Although my stay at Oxford was a relatively short one, it was nevertheless a productive and significant one. An active and successful period of fund raising provided the basis for me to plan a more focused programme of research and to recruit a talented team of researchers that included Stuart Burchell, Colin Clubb, John Hughes, and Janine Nahapiet. Freed from many of the pressures of teaching and academic administration, that newly established research group was quickly able to establish a congenial and very productive mode of operation.

The research agenda of the group was explicit, albeit general. We were all interested in pushing further our understandings of what might be at stake in an organizational and social analysis of accounting. Whilst I and others had pointed to the organizational and social bases and consequences of accounting practices, in many ways such appeals had only served to point to the possibilities of a new way of inquiring into the functioning of accounting. The group was all too aware of this; early discussions focused on "what was at stake" with such a view, which ways of characterizing accounting might enrich the task of directly conceiving accounting within the spheres of the organizational and the social, and what were the theoretical and methodological prerequisites for advancing such a view. The research group was also unanimous that a major focus for such inquiries ought to be the study of accounting change. Rather than seeking to directly explore accounting as it was, we viewed that much more might be gained from exploring accounting in the process of becoming, of changing, of becoming what it was not. In such a context, it was thought, more might be seen of the forces that put accounting into motion and of the organizational and social consequences of disruptions in the accounting craft. Whilst we were well aware that change is a relative matter and that we might, as a consequence, have to focus on accounting elaborations rather than more fundamental shifts, we were nevertheless convinced that even such analyses might provide an empirical richness that would stimulate, provoke, and influence our more theoretical explorations of accounting in the process of becoming what it was not.

The specific empirical interests of the research group were influenced by a mixture of pragmatic and intellectual considerations, as is invariably the case. One project focused on the introduction of budgeting systems into a region of the National Health Service. Another aimed to explore the rise of interest in forms of social accounting in a number of European countries, although given the diversity of such initiatives it also sought to understand the social dynamics that gave rise to social accountings and the different nature of the social significances attached to them. A third project was orientated towards organizational studies of accounting system change. Taken together, the projects resulted in a vast amount of rich empirical material, only some of which has been published as of now. Both the diversity and the depth of the empirical findings served as a vital stimulus to theoretical inquiry, raising, as they did, questions about adequate ways of understanding the forces at work and the ways in which accounting changes emerged out of complex configurations of organizational and social circumstances.

The inquiry resulted in a number of more general contributions to the literature, all of which are collected here. Early concerns to probe into, question, and distance ourselves from many conventional understandings of accounting are reflected in "The Roles of Accounting in Organisations and Society." So aware of the possibilities for different ways of interrogating accounting, some initial statements of our research interests and agenda appeared in "The Development of Accounting in its International Context: Past Concerns and Emergent Issues," a paper that now reads as a very preliminary one indeed, and "'A Message From Mars'—and Other Reminiscences from the Past," a paper that reports on some empirical findings that were to serve as a crucial catalyst for more general theorizing. More mature statements of the research position developed in the group are given in "Accounting in Its Social Context: Towards a History of Value Added in the United Kingdom" and, although written and published appreciably later, in "The Archaeology of Accounting Systems."

Other writings pursue and elaborate upon the approach to the organizational and social analysis of accounting developed in those initial papers. Some of the implications for an organizational understanding of accounting are sketched out in "Management Accounting and Organisational Action: An Introduction: and "Accounting and Organisational Action." Questions of a more explicitly social nature are addressed in the rather brief "Economics and the Regime of the Calculative," a paper that reflects my remaining worries about the unproblematic advance of calculative practices, whether they stem from economic or social rationales for action, and in "The Tale of a Committee that Never Reported: Disagreements on Intertwining Accounting with the Social" and "Accounting Research and Accounting Practice: The Ambiguous Relationship Between the Two." Recognizing the potential for the development of accounting in the public sector in the United Kingdom to illuminate some of the more general issues at stake in an organizational and social analysis of accounting, a number of papers have specifically sought to address this area in a tentative way. "Accounting and the Pursuit of Efficiency" and *Accounting and the Domain of the Public: Some Observations on Current Developments* are illustrative examples. Although based on quite extensive contacts with such public sector developments, such analyses nevertheless remain preliminary, not least because of my own equivocality about the role that economic calculation is called upon to play in the reform of organizations seeking to advance quite particular conceptions of the social.

The research perspective addressed in such writings is all too clearly an emergent one. Individually they provide specific illustrations of the issues at stake and the potential offered. Others attempt to sketch out some of the more general implications for social understanding of accounting practice. However, whilst undoubtedly preliminary, the themes developed in the papers hopefully also have a coherence, not least when contrasted with those evident in other organizational and economic perspectives.

Emphasis is placed on both the reflective and constitutive aspects of accounting. Recognizing that accounting is not an autonomous calculative practice, attention is directed towards improving our understanding, not only of how factors external to accounting can impinge upon and change it, but also of how such interminglings can occur and of how accounting can mediate and reflect other organizational and social circumstances. Equally, however, emphasis is placed on the enabling and productive properties of accounting. Explicitly seeking to recognize how accounting can create quite particular and partial patterns of visibility, the analyses hopefully start to provide at least one basis for understanding how accounting can at times disturb and disrupt other organizational and social circumstances. Emphasizing the specificities of the economic categories and linguistic distinctions that infuse accounting in practice, a basis is provided for appreciating some of the ways in which the calculative practices of accounting can permeate and shape patterns of organizational concerns, influencing conceptions of the problematic, the desirable, and the possible.

In these analyses increasing emphasis is placed on the ways in which accounting is implicated in the wider diffusion of economic priorities and concerns. Greater attention is being given to the organizational and social consequences of the calculative rationality that can be associated with the advance of accounting practices. Not unrelated, more attention is being given to the discursive and theoretical conceptions with which accounting is often implicated. Once again recognizing that the technical practices are not independent of notions of their functioning and rationales, although the relationship between them is neither direct nor uniform, some of the papers reflect a growing interest in the knowledges and understandings capable of being advanced and diffused by them.

In all cases the understanding offered of the dynamics of accounting change is quite a complex one. Simple notions of functionality are questioned. Accounting is not seen as being a mere reflection of unproblematic essences or imperatives. A detailed understanding of the specific contexts in which accounting change occurs demonstrates the diversity of influences that can impinge on accounting and its consequences, the often quite complex and shifting circumstances, issues, and practices with which accounting can be associated, and, of equal significance, the roles played by the unintentional and the unanticipated consequences of accounting change.

All too clearly such emerging understandings reflect a combination of theoretical and empirical interests. Increasingly they emerge from a commitment to grounded inquiry and a concern to address and understand the specificities of accounting in use. Consistent with such a view, I still attempt to invest a great deal of time in trying to observe accounting, always trying to maintain an interest in new accountings, major accounting changes and reforms, and pragmatic attempts to articulate new or expanded rationales for accounting practice. The nature of the research task is such that only a small amount of material emerges in public form, although much of the rest influences the intellectual agendas I maintain and develop. Equally the understandings I have of accounting reflect a view that such appreciations are not implicit in the circumstances being observed but reflect the use of an interpretative theoretical lens. There is little doubt that over the years I have attempted to be more theoretically conscious, equally investing an enormous amount of time trying to inform myself of at least some to the theoretical developments in the wider human and social sciences. I also have possibly become more conscious and careful of the criteria that I seek to impose on my own theorizing. Recognizing that such theorizing is a human endeavor, I have become increasingly aware that the particular understandings I seek to develop should attempt to be consistent with the more general notions of knowledge and theory they themselves articulate. I also often say that theorists should always be willing to be subject to their own theories! I am happy to stand by that test, although I know of many theories of the economic, organizational, and social nature of accounting that I, at least, would oppose being subjected to.

## CONCLUSION

Trying to give coherence to a diversity of work is not an easy task. It is equally difficult trying to account for something that so obviously remains open-ended and emergent.

What uniformity there is in the papers that follow reflects a longstanding attempt to delve into accounting, to observe and explore its functioning, to construct a basis for interrogating it in use, and indeed, as I have sometimes said, to account for accounting itself. Rather than accepting accounting, seeking unproblematically to advance its functioning and improve its rationality, I have sought to understand accounting, to appreciate what it is, what it does, and how it does it. My position vis-à-vis accounting has therefore been a more questioning one, always striving to examine it from without rather than from within. Such a stance continues and it therefore still remains appropriate to entitle this collection of papers *Accounting from the Outside*.

*REFERENCES*

Dev,. S., *Accounting and the L.S.E. Tradition* (London School of Economics and Political Science, 1980).

Hopwood, A.G., *Accouting and Human Behavior* (Haymarket, 1975; Prentice Hall, 1976).

Hopwood, A.G., *An Accounting System and Managerial Behavior* (Saxon House, 1973).

Kassem, M.S., "Introduction: European versus American Organisation Theories," in G.H. Hofstede and M.S. Kassem, eds., *European Contributions to Organisation Theory* (Van Gorcum, 1976).

# Getting Started: Exploring Accounting in Use

# An Empirical Study of the Role of Accounting Data in Performance Evaluation

ANTHONY G. HOPWOOD*

2

Accounting systems are often the most important formal sources of information in industrial organizations. They are designed to provide all levels of management with timely and reasonably accurate information to help them make decisions which are in agreement with their organization's goals. It is therefore surprising to find reports that managers, in adapting to accounting systems, deliberately falsify the data and make decisions which may be detrimental to the long-term interests of the organization. Yet there are many such reports in the accounting literature.

Many of the documented examples of falsification and dysfunctional decision making were an outgrowth of attempts to make the accounting reports a more favorable reflection of the manager's or the worker's performance. Whyte has described the ingenious attempts of a group of workers to obtain easier standards when their payments included a bonus based on these standards.[1] Other investigators have noted the tendency of managers to pad their budgets either to make the reported variances more favorable or in anticipation of cuts by either superiors or accountants.[2] Perhaps of even more concern to accountants are the numerous examples in the literature of managers making decisions in response to the accounting system, even though the decisions are contrary to the goals of the

* Lecturer, Manchester Business School.

[1] W. F. Whyte, *Money and Motivation* (New York: Harper and Row, 1955).

[2] See, for instance, L. S. Rosen and R. E. Schneck, "Some Behavioural Consequences of Accounting Measurement Systems," *Cost and Management*, October (1967), pp. 6–16; A. E. Lowe and R. W. Shaw, "An Analysis of Managerial Biasing: Some Evidence from a Company's Budgeting Process," *Journal of Management Studies*, V (1968), 304–15; M. Schiff and A. Y. Lewin, "The Impact of People on Budgets," *The Accounting Review*, XLV (1970), 259–68.

organization.[3] Dearden has reported many such anecdotes in a series of publications.[4] For instance, he tells of a manager who was reluctant to replace equipment, even when it was in the company's economic interest, because of the heavy book losses which would be unfavorably reflected in his current performance reports.

There are many similar examples in the accounting literature, but unfortunately most of them are in the forms of anecdotes and, of more importance, little consideration has been given to the conditions under which such behavior is likely to occur. Yet this type of knowledge is important for accountants who are concerned with system design and change. In particular, it is important to know whether the dysfunctional behavior is a necessary consequence of using the accounting data in performance evaluation or at least of the imperfections in accounting systems or, rather, whether it is dependent upon the precise manner in which the accounting data are used. The issue is a significant one because the various alternative explanations suggest different remedies.

3

## *Some Problems with Accounting Measures of Performance*

Although accounting data can reflect at least some of the important dimensions of managerial performance, accountants are faced with a series of major problems in designing information systems for this purpose. First, not all the relevant dimensions of managerial performance are included in accounting reports since neither accountants nor managers have developed comprehensive measures and standards.[5] Second, even considering the economic aspects of performance, an organization's economic cost function is rarely known with precision and an accounting system can only attempt to approximately represent its complexity. This is a particular problem with highly interdependent patterns of activities. Third, the accounting data are primarily concerned with representing

[3] For instance, F. J. Jasinski, "Use and Misuse of Efficiency Controls," *Harvard Business Review* (July-August, 1956), pp. 105–12; V. F. Ridgway, "Dysfunctional Consequences of Performance Measurements," *Administrative Science Quarterly*, I (1956), 240–47; A. Etzioni and E. W. Lehman, "Some Dangers in 'Valid' Social Measurement," *Annals of the American Academy of Political and Social Science*, CCCLXXIII (1967), 1-15.

[4] J. Dearden, "Problem in Decentralized Profit Responsibility," *Harvard Business Review* (May–June, 1960), pp. 72–80; B. D. Henderson and J. Dearden, "New System for Divisional Control," *Harvard Business Review* (Sept.-Oct., 1966), pp. 144–60.

[5] The development and utilization of human resources is one example, although some preliminary research is now being conducted into ways of measuring the value of human resources. For one line of thought on this issue, see R. L. Brummet, E. G. Flamholtz and W. C. Pyle, "Human Resource Measurement—A Challenge for Accountants," *The Accounting Review*, XLIII (1968), 217–24, and W. C. Pyle, "Monitoring Human Resources 'On Line,'" *Michigan Business Review*, XXII (1970), 19–32. The general topic of more inclusive measures of performance is discussed in the "Report of the Committee on Non-Financial Measures of Effectiveness," *The Accounting Review*, supplement to XLVI (1971), 165–212.

outcomes, while managerial activity is concerned with the detailed process giving rise to the final outcomes. If there are factors which constrain the reported efficiency of the process despite the quality of the manager's performance, the accounting data will be an inadequate reflection of his performance. For a fair evaluation, the controllable component of the reports should be isolated, yet this is a difficult, if not impossible, task.[6] Fourth, the main emphasis of accounting reports is on short-term performance indexes while the evaluation of managerial performance is often concerned with more long-term considerations.[7] Ultimately, of course, the very cost of providing the information is an important constraint on the accuracy and relevance of the data.

In addition, accounting systems are also trying to serve many purposes. Each purpose may ideally necessitate the preparation of a unique set of data, although accountants frequently try to produce general purpose reports which are of some value for at least some of these many purposes. However, in trying to satisfy a series of purposes, the reports may fail to
4 perfectly satisfy the requirements for any single purpose—the appraisal of managerial performance, for instance.

While it is frequently possible to improve an existing accounting performance measurement system, it is often, if not always, impossible to achieve the ideal system. The information provided by an accounting system must therefore usually be used with discretion when evaluations are made on the basis of it. Many accountants realize this and some act accordingly, but the accounting data are also used by other managers who may not use them in an appropriate manner. It was for this reason that the present research was undertaken, in the belief that an understanding of the way in which managers adapt to accounting systems depends upon a more detailed knowledge of how accounting data are used. Particular

[6] In a basic sense the problem may be insoluble. The determination of whether a budget variance, for instance, is due to a manager's efforts or uncontrollable factors in either the internal or external environments of the organization would require a model of the organization and its relationship to the environment. In this way we would certainly be able to measure the influence of a manager but is such a model possible in a world of uncertainty, and even if it existed, might not the role of the manager be radically changed? See K. J. Arrow, "Research in Management Controls: A Critical Synthesis," in *Management Controls: New Directions in Basic Research,* ed. C. P. Bonini, R. K. Jaedicke, and H. M. Wagner (New York: McGraw-Hill, 1964).

[7] Short-term accounting reports may look favorable because decisions have been made to postpone or cancel expenditures as part of a strict cost control program, although the final costs, which may not even be reflected in the cost center reports, may be higher than the cost, at the time, of postponement. This problem is illustrated by Likert's discussion of the more problematic long-term impact of cost control programs despite their apparent short-term success. Although there is the usual tendency to overgeneralize, there is sufficient evidence that the problem is an important one. See R. Likert, *New Patterns of Management* (New York: McGraw-Hill, 1961) and *The Human Organization: Its Management and Value* (New York: McGraw-Hill, 1967).

attention is given in the study to the use of accounting data in managerial performance evaluation, a topic which has been of some concern to both practicing and academic accountants.[8]

## *The Use of Accounting Data in Performance Evaluation*

It is important to recognize that even standard accounting reports can be used in many different ways in performance evaluation. Within the human consciousness, while the accounting data are given, their interpretation and precise use is the outcome of a personal and social process which is sustained by the meanings, systems of belief, pressures and purposes that are brought to bear by the managers using the data. In of necessity providing the data with a personal significance and placing them in their own wider intellectual context, managers are able to use them, perhaps without reflection, in a variety of ways.

Such a process is recognized by many in the social sciences, although, surprisingly, the problem of differential use has not been systematically 5
considered in the accounting literature. So far attention has been primarily focused on the technical design of performance measurement systems and the possibilities for reducing the unanticipated behavioral consequences by changing the indexes used. There is no doubt that this is a necessary concern. It reflects, however, only a partial viewpoint and it is just as necessary to develop a perspective which enables us to distinguish between the plurality of ways in which accounting data can be used to evaluate performance. To this we now turn.

The relative visibility of events within an organization is partly determined by accounting measures of managerial performance since they influence both individual perceptions and the process by which the expectations held by managers at all levels are formulated and revised. While they are designed to mobilize individual energies and motivations to increase the efficiency of an organization's operations, it is possible that at times their presence can lead to a transference of interest from the wider organizational purposes which they were designed to serve on to the specific behavior which is necessary to improve the indexes of performance. Merton has discussed this process in terms of a "displacement of goals" whereby "an instrumental value," in this case an index which is intended to identify areas for investigation and enquiry, "becomes a terminal value" sought for on its own accord.[9]

---

[8] One indication of recent interest in this topic is the symposium held at Ohio State University in 1968. See T. J. Burns, ed., *The Behavioral Aspects of Accounting Data for Performance Evaluation* (Columbus, Ohio: College of Administrative Sciences, Ohio State University, 1970).

[9] R. K. Merton, "The Unanticipated Consequences of Purposive Social Action," *American Sociological Review*, I (1936), 894–904, and *Social Theory and Social Structure* (New York: The Free Press, 1957), pp. 199–200.

The accounting measures of managerial performance are given a meaning and interpretation. In this paper these broad distinctions are used as the basis for distinguishing between ways in which accounting reports which show the actual and budgeted costs for a cost center, and the difference between them, can be used in evaluating the performance of the person responsible for the cost center. Three styles of evaluation which make distinctly different uses of the data are isolated and defined:

1. *Budget Constrained Style.* Despite the many problems in using accounting data as comprehensive measures of managerial performance, the evaluation is primarily based upon the cost center head's ability to continually meet the budget on a short-term basis. This criterion of performance is stressed at the expense of other valued and important criteria and a cost center head will tend to receive an unfavorable evaluation if his actual costs exceed the budgeted costs, regardless of other considerations.

2. *Profit Conscious Style.* The performance of the cost center head is evaluated on the basis of his ability to increase the general effectiveness
6 of his unit's operations in relation to the long-term purposes of the organization. One important aspect of this at the cost center level is his concern with the minimization of long-run costs.[10] For this purpose the accounting data must be used with some care in a rather flexible manner.

3. *Nonaccounting Style.* Accounting data play a relatively unimportant part in the supervisor's evaluation of the cost center head's performance.

While the accounting data clearly indicate whether a person has been successful in meeting the budget, they do not necessarily indicate whether he is behaving so as to minimize long-run costs, let alone influence other determinants of effectiveness. In order to assess this ability, the data may have to be used with discretion and, where necessary, supplemented with information from other sources. Unlike a Budget Constrained evaluation, a Profit Conscious evaluation is therefore concerned with the wider information content, or lack of it, of the accounting data, and not with just a rigid analysis of the direction and magnitude of the reported budget variances.

### *Responses to the Use of Accounting Data in Performance Evaluation*

A study of the manipulations and other dysfunctional behaviors made in response to an accounting based evaluation poses a number of impor-

[10] The idea of cost minimization is overly simple because, in itself, it does not necessarily result in either profit maximization or the attainment of more wide-ranging definitions of organizational effectiveness. However, since production volume was not determined by the persons in charge of the cost centers in the subject company, the objective of minimizing the long-run costs for the specified volume of production is more likely to be congruous with profit maximization. More generally, the idea is used to reflect the direction of concern rather than a constraint.

tant methodological problems. We would expect to find differences between cost centers in both the opportunities for such behavior and its ease of detection. This means that it is difficult to study behavioral responses of this type by the use of survey or data analysis techniques across a large number of cost centers. Instead, they must be investigated through the intensive study of a smaller number of cost centers. However, in order to provide some basis for the selection of cost centers for such an investigation, as well as adding some validity to the findings, concern is given in the study to the specification of a series of concurrent conditions associated with such behavior. In this way a more thorough understanding will be gained of the behavioral responses to the various styles of evaluation.

If the accounting reports are used in a manner consistent with a Profit Conscious style of evaluation, problems associated with using the accounting data in performance evaluation are less important. It may be difficult to isolate the relevant aspects of the data, but the person making the evaluation will at least be aware of the problems. Perhaps of more importance he will know that his own objective of long-term cost minimi- 7
zation is not necessarily consistent with a set of favorable short-term budget variances. Additional information sources must be used to supplement the accounting data.

However, in the case of a Budget Constrained evaluation, the implications for the cost center head are different. Due to the incomplete nature of the accounting data there will be disagreement and conflict between him and his supervisor over the dimensions, and their values, on which the job is described and evaluated. This is capable of resulting in some anxiety since performance evaluations are often an important aspect of the development and maintenance of a person's self-esteem.[11] The cost center head will not gain recognition for his accomplishments on dimensions which he views as important and relevant but which are not reflected in the accounting data, although he might well be evaluated on dimensions which he genuinely considers to be irrelevant.

Furthermore, even if the cost center head tries to improve his performance in terms of the accounting indexes, the behavior which is necessary to achieve this is not always clear if some of the reported costs are not under his control or if the standards are subject to error. His own efforts to improve the performance indexes may be overshadowed by the behavior of other persons who are able to influence his reports. He cannot be sure that a given action will result in a favorable evaluation—a further condition which can contribute to experience of tension and anxiety.[12]

---

[11] S. F. Miyamoto and S. M. Dornbusch, "A Test of Interactionist Hypotheses of Self-Conception," *American Journal of Sociology*, LXI (1956), 399–403.

[12] See, for instance, A. R. Cohen, "Situational Structure, Self-Esteem and Threat Oriented Reactions to Power," in *Studies in Social Power*, ed. D. Cartwright (Ann Arbor, Mich.: Institute for Social Research, University of Michigan, 1959), and R. L. Kahn, *et al.*, *Organizational Stress: Studies in Role Conflict and Ambiguity* (New

The disagreement, biases and uncertainty introduced into the performance evaluation by a Budget Constrained style of evaluation are not only likely to be seen as unjust by the cost center head, but they will also be a source of conflict, tension and anxiety. As a consequence, he is less likely to be satisfied with the supervisor whose style of evaluation poses such a threat to his security.[13]

The cost center head can, however, attempt to relieve the tension associated with a Budget Constrained style of evaluation by engaging in various forms of coping behavior. First, he can try to blame other cost center heads for his own unfavorable variances. He can concentrate on the activities of his own unit, trying to improve the reported budget variances regardless of how this affects the performance of other units. Argyris found that there was the greatest rivalry and competition, and less friendship between colleagues in departments with the highest pressure from management controls.[14] In his earlier study of the budgetary system of four companies, he presents vivid evidence of interdepartmental strife,
8 department centeredness, and blaming other persons when things go wrong.[15] Behavior of this type is hypothesized to be a result of the competitive relationships between the cost center heads in a Budget Constrained department, and the consequent deterioration in their friendship ties, helpfulness and mutual respect.[16] The result is one which is not only uncomfortable for the cost center heads but also dysfunctional to the company since a certain amount of cooperation is essential for achieving

---

York: John Wiley, 1964), pp. 85-86. There is also evidence of a positive relationship between uncontrollability and feelings of tension and anxiety in the specific case where one organization subunit is interdependent with one or more other subunits, whether the interdependence is facilitative or hindering. See M. Deutsch, "An Experimental Study of the Effects of Cooperation and Competition upon Group Process," *Human Relations*, II (1949) 199–231, and E. J. Thomas, "Effects of Facilitative Role Interdependence on Group Functioning," *Human Relations*, X (1957), 347–66.

[13] E. Kay, H. H. Meyer, and J. R. P. French, Jr., "Effects of Threat in a Performance Appraisal Interview," *Journal of Applied Psychology*, XLIX (1956), 311-17. Kahn and his associates have also found that persons who receive conflicting and ambiguous role expectations are less likely to maintain favorable relationships with the persons sending the expectations. See Kahn *et al., op. cit.*, p. 90.

[14] C. Argyris, *Understanding Organizational Behavior* (Homewood, Ill.: The Dorsey Press, 1960).

[15] C. Argyris, *The Impact of Budgets on People*, a study prepared for the Controllership Foundation (Cornell University, School of Business and Public Administration, 1952). H. White has also described a case of interdepartmental conflict due to the specific problems caused by the allocation of costs. See his "Management Conflict and Sociometric Choice," *American Journal of Sociology*, LXVIII (1961), 185–99.

[16] On the relationship between competition and the quality of interpersonal relationships, see Deutsch, *op. cit.*, Thomas, *op. cit.*, and E. Trist and K. Bamforth, "Some Social and Psychological Consequences of the Longwall Method of Goal Getting," *Human Relations*, IV (1951), 3-38.

efficient performance and allowing a flexible response to unusual circumstances.[17]

The cost center head can also attempt to achieve a favorable set of budget variances by manipulating the accounting data. He can falsify the accounting records and make decisions purely on the basis of their effect on the short-term budget reports even when the results are contrary to the long-term interests of the company. Blau found that a group of administrators behaved so as to improve their performance on the basis of the statistical indexes which were used in their evaluation, even if this behavior resulted in dysfunctional consequences for the organization.[18]

The above arguments can be expressed in the following hypotheses which are tested in the study:

> If a cost center head perceives that he is evaluated on the basis of a
> Budget Constrained style he is (a) more likely to experience job
> related tension; (b) more likely to report having poor relations with
> his supervisor; (c) more likely to report having poor relations with 9
> his peers; (d) more likely to engage in falsification of the accounting
> data and dysfunctional decision making, than if he perceives that he
> is evaluated on the basis of either a Profit Conscious or a Non-
> accounting style.

## *Research Site and Methodology*

The study was conducted in one manufacturing division of a large Chicago-based company.[19] The division has a labor force in excess of 20,000 persons and has an annual revenue of several hundred million

[17] See, for instance, B. S. Georgopoulos and A. S. Tannenbaum, "A Study of Organizational Effectiveness." *American Sociological Review*, XX (1957), 534–40. It should be borne in mind, however, that the relationship between both personal and organizational conflict and organizational effectiveness is not straightforward, the outcome depending on the type of conflict, its context, the manner in which it handled one's personal values. See M. Deutsch, "Conflicts: Productive and Destructive," *Journal of Social Issues*, XXV (1969), 7–41.

[18] P. M. Blau, *The Dynamics of Bureaucracy* (University of Chicago Press, 1955), pp. 36–56. The study has been replicated by H. Cohen in his *The Demonics of Bureaucracy: Problems of Change in a Government Agency* (Ames, Iowa: Iowa State University Press, 1965).

[19] The division is divided into a series of areas, departments, and cost centers. Each area includes several departments, and each department is divided into a series of cost centers. There are nine major hierarchical levels in the division: (1) Vice President; (2) General Manager; (3) Assistant General Manager; (4) Area Manager; (5) Departmental Supervisor; (6) Assistant Departmental Supervisor; (7) General Foreman; (8) Foreman; (9) a blue-collar bargaining unit level. Cost centers are usually under the responsibility of a general foreman, although some foremen and assistant departmental supervisors are also in charge of cost centers. One person may be in charge of several cost centers; at the time this study was conducted, there were over 350 cost centers under the responsibility of 193 cost center heads.

dollars. It is a company whose senior management is justifiably proud of its record of good personnel relations and high employee satisfaction.

The division's accounting system, which is a fairly sophisticated one based on flexible budgets and standard costing techniques, was installed a decade ago, and it is now an accepted and important part of the work environment. Monthly reports comparing the actual and budgeted costs for cost centers are issued to all cost center heads and their departmental supervisors,[20] and these are supplemented by daily and weekly reports on such matters as production, labor and supplies, the nature and content of which vary between cost centers. All internal transfers of materials and services are made at a predetermined standard price which is based on the full cost of providing the material or service, and all the reports contain overhead costs allocated from other units in one division.

The study consisted of two phases, a questionnaire phase, the results of which receive primary attention in the present paper, and an interview phase. This research design was selected so as to enable a study of manipulative behavior in a series of carefully selected cost centers, while allowing the other hypotheses to be tested by the use of survey techniques with a larger sample of subjects.

The analysis is based on questionnaires sent to all of the 193 persons in the division who were in charge of cost centers. Where a respondent failed to return the initial questionnaire, up to two follow-up letters were sent to him. The final response rate was very high, namely 87 percent (167 out of the 193). Once the questionnaires had been returned and the basic analysis completed, 20 cost center heads in four departments (two predominantly Budget Constrained, one Profit Conscious and one Nonaccounting) were selected as the focal persons for the interview phase of the study. The statistical analysis of the questionnaire responses is based on nonparametric statistics, namely Kendall's Tau and the Mann-Whitney *U* test.[21]

## *Measurement of the Variables*

### THE SUPERVISOR'S STYLE OF EVALUATION

Information on the supervisor's style of evaluation was obtained from each cost center head. Eight possible criteria of performance were in-

[20] Three monthly reports are prepared for the large production cost centers, namely a Performance Summary, an Operating Statement and a Processing Cost Statement The Performance Summary provides an analysis of the monthly variance and a summary of production data. The Operating Statement accounts for the materials charged to the cost center and the rejected output in both physical quantities and dollars. A statement of the related budget variances is included on the report. Finally, the Processing Cost Statement presents detailed budget and actual cost information on all elements of cost other than the cost of the principal materials. Only the Processing Cost Statement is prepared for the smaller production cost centers and the service cost centers.

[21] S. Siegel, *Nonparametric Statistics* (New York: McGraw-Hill, 1956).

cluded in the questionnaire. A Budget Constrained style of evaluation was represented by the criterion "meeting the budget" and a Profit Conscious style by "concern with costs." These phrases were selected to represent the two styles on the basis of observations made during a series of exploratory interviews on the research site. At the time, it was found that they were used by cost center heads to refer to distinct patterns of behavior which were in agreement with the distinctions described above.[22]

Two measures of the supervisor's style of evaluation were obtained from the questionnaire responses. The principal measure is based on the relative importance of the various criteria. Cost center heads were asked to rank order the three most important criteria in their evaluation. On the basis of the rankings, the following evaluative styles are defined. The number of respondents in each group is shown in parentheses:

(i) Budget Constrained style (BC): meeting the budget, but not concern with costs, ranked among the top three criteria (33).

(ii) Budget-Profit style (BP): both meeting the budget and concern with costs among the top three criteria (17). 11

(iii) Profit Conscious style (PC): concern with costs, but not meeting the budget, ranked among the top three criteria (43).

(iv) Nonaccounting style (NA): neither meeting the budget nor concern with costs ranked among the top three criteria (74).[23]

In addition to these measures based on the relative importance of the various criteria, another series of measures was based upon the cost center head's ratings of the absolute importance of each separate criterion. The ratings were given on a five-point scale varying from "of no importance" to "very important," and there is evidence of consistency between the rankings and the ratings.

### THE DEPENDENT VARIABLES[24]

A 15-item index of job related tension, which has been used extensively in previous research, was used in the study.[25] In addition, a 3-item index

[22] The other performance criteria were cooperation with colleagues, getting along with the boss, effort put into the job, and concern with quality. Also, attitude towards the work and company, and ability to handle the men.

[23] The operational definition of the Nonaccounting style should be interpreted as implying a *low relative importance* to the accounting related criteria.

[24] A complete discussion of the operational definition and characteristics of the dependent variables is included in A. G. Hopwood, "An Accounting System and Managerial Behavior" (unpublished Ph.D. dissertation, University of Chicago, 1971).

[25] See Kahn *et al.*, *op. cit.*, pp. 424–27. In the present study, it is important to investigate the behavioral and attitudinal correlates of tension because in organizational studies, as in personality studies, it cannot be assumed that tension is necessarily dysfunctional to the individual or the organization. Indeed, there is evidence which suggests that certain amounts of tension can be functional to both the individual and the organization, and that the relationship between functional consequences and tension is more like a curvilinear one. See E. P. Torrance, "A Theory of Leadership and Interpersonal Behavior Under Stress," in *Leadership and*

of specific cost tension was developed concerned with the extent to which the cost center head worries about costs, meeting the budget, and feels that this interferes with the rest of his work. The index of specific cost tension is independent of the job related tension index (Tau = 0.07). So as to obtain a comprehensive picture of the state of interpersonal relations, eight indexes of the cost center head's relations with his supervisor and six of his relations with his peers were included in the questionnaire.[26]

## *Results*

The first part of the analysis is based upon the evaluative styles defined in terms of the relative importance of the various performance criteria. An examination of Table 1 reveals that cost center heads who feel that they are being evaluated on the basis of a Budget Constrained style report a significantly higher level of job related tension than those who are eval-
12 uated on the basis of either a Profit Conscious or a Nonaccounting style. There is also a tendency for this to be true even when an attempt is made to combine the Budget Constrained and Profit Conscious styles. However, all of the accounting related styles of evaluation result in a similar level of specific cost tension. A Profit Conscious style does lead to worrying about costs and the budget, but unlike the Budget Constrained style, this does not spread to more general features of the job.

When cost center heads are evaluated on the basis of their ability to continually avoid unfavorable budget variances, success in satisfying this criterion results in lower job related tension. For the combined Budget Constrained and Budget Profit evaluation groups, there is a small but significant negative relationship between the cost center head's success in

*Interpersonal Behavior*, ed. L. Petrullo and B. M. Bass (New York: Holt, Rinehart and Winston, 1961), pp. 100–117, and D. Sirota, "Some Effects of Promotional Frustration on Employees' Understanding of, and Attitudes Toward, Management," *Sociometry*, XXII (1959), 273–78. It is therefore of interest to note that previous studies have found that the index of job related tension used in the present study is correlated with role conflict and ambiguity, and the presence of mild neurotic symptoms. This provides evidence that the index is sensitive to at least some of the dysfunctional aspects of tension. See B. J. Indik, S. E. Seashore and J. Slesinger, "Demographic Correlates of Psychological Strain," *Journal of Abnormal and Social Psychology*, LXIX (1964), 26–38; Kahn *et al.*, *op. cit.*, and J. D. Snoek, "Role Strain in Diversified Role Sets," *American Journal of Sociology*, LXXI (1966), 363–70.

[26] The indexes of relations with the supervisor are trust in the supervisor; respect for the supervisor; the perception of the supervisor's understanding of job problems; the perceived reasonableness of the supervisor's expectations; satisfaction with the supervisor's technical knowledge; satisfaction with the supervisor's administrative ability; satisfaction with the supervisor's human relations skills; general satisfaction with the supervisor. The peer relations indexes are peer supportiveness-achievement; peer supportiveness-affiliation; peer agreement; peer helpfulness; respect for peers; peer friendship. The indexes were developed at the Institute for Social Research at the University of Michigan, and have been extensively used in various studies by members of the Institute.

meeting the budget in the six-month period before the receipt of the questionnaire,[27] and the job related tension which they experience (Tau $= -0.17$; $p < .05$). There is no similar reduction in cost tension (Tau $= -0.04$). Past success is not, however, instrumental in reducing job related tension in either the Profit Conscious or Nonaccounting groups (Tau is 0.04 and 0.03 respectively), an important finding which increases our confidence in the construct validity of the operational definitions of the evaluative styles.[28]

A person who is subject to a Budget Constrained evaluation may have little control over the month-to-month variances, and as a result he is forced to devote a large part of his time and effort to frantic attempts to find some way out of the dilemma. One such cost center head described his difficulties in the following way:

> You have to get yourself out of the woods. It's a process of staying out of the red.
> You have to. It's true, it's true, and it makes a job so much more difficult, There'd
> be times when I could do a good job and save some money by spending a bit 13
> now. But no, the only thing I concentrate on is what I've got forthcoming that's
> going to put me in the red. I've got to concentrate to see . . . there's no more
> money to spend. God, it causes me some problems.

Sometimes it is almost impossible to make the short-term budget variances more favorable, as is the case for the cost center heads whose variances are highly dependent on production volume. "When I'm in the red I start cutting on manpower. Well, I should, but I can't. We've been down on manpower for sometime now. I just have to live on my budget, close to the bone, but you can't, you can't." These frantic and often unsuccessful attempts only result in more problems, more tension and more worry.

Cost center heads who are subject to a Profit Conscious evaluation are

---

[27] The index of past success in meeting the budget is based on the mean of the percentage ratios of budgeted to actual costs for the six months prior to the receipt of the questionnaire. This ratio is the principal form in which the monthly variances are reported in the subject company.

[28] L. J. Cronbach and P. E. Meehl, "Construct Validity in Psychological Tests," *Psychological Bulletin,* LII (1955), 281–302. The finding is important because it provides some independent evidence of the validity of the evaluative classifications. Furthermore, it is not subject to at least the danger of self-consistent responses when the cost center heads supply both the information on the evaluative styles and on some of the dependent variables. In this respect, it is important to note that although the level of general job satisfaction was significantly lower in the BC group than in the PC and NA groups, the overall level of satisfaction in all groups was rather high. With a possible range of 7 to 35, the range of responses on the index of job satisfaction was 18 to 35, with a mean of 30.2 and a standard deviation of 3.9. The level of job satisfaction in the BP group was not significantly different from that in the PC and NA groups. In addition, it is also important to note the subsequent evidence, some of which is based on an analysis of the accounting data, of different decision behaviors associated with the evaluative styles.

not, however, having an easy time, as is shown by the following quotation:[29]

> [The Profit Conscious supervisor] is always asking about costs—all the time. This is basically the heart of it. I guess, costs. Anytime we get together or whenever he gets you its costs, costs, costs. "See if we can cut down." "It's going pretty fast, we'd better talk about it." He's a little bit too strict really. I'm used to discipline, but he runs a tight ship. He does not like us to get sloppy; he gets hot under the collar. He tries to save whatever he can. He just likes to operate that way. He is just that type of person. but to be fair, he applies pressure where it is appropriate.

A Profit Conscious style is seen as a demanding style of evaluation but it is also seen as a fair one. Uncontrollable variances are either not queried or, even if they are queried, they can usually be explained. The cost center heads are able to justify actions which result in long-term cost savings even though they produce unfavorable current budget variances. Indeed it is the ability to explain which plays an important role in avoiding the
14 higher tension and anxiety associated with the Budget Constrained style, a style whose approach is "just don't do it, rather than asking for explanations."

The different uses of the accounting data in performance evaluation affect the cost center heads' perceptions of how justly their performance is evaluated.[30] In Table 2 it can be seen that when there is a tendency to use the accounting data in terms of a Budget Constrained style, the cost center heads feel that their evaluation is less just than those reporting either a Profit Conscious or Nonaccounting style.

The evidence on the effects of the styles of evaluation on relationships with the supervisor is in agreement with hypothesis (b). As can be seen in Table 3, there is a tendency for the cost center heads' perceptions of their relations with the supervisor to deteriorate if he is seen as using a Budget Constrained style or even if he attempts to combine the Budget Constrained and Profit Conscious styles. In contrast, if the supervisor uses a Profit Conscious style, there is a tendency, not sufficient however to reach statistical significance, for the cost center heads to report more favorable relations with him than with even a Nonaccounting supervisor.

A Budget Constrained style of evaluation also results in reports of less favorable relations with peers. The evidence presented in Table 4 is an

[29] There is additional evidence in the questionnaire responses which supports this statement. Cost center heads were asked to rank not only the top three criteria used in their evaluation, but also the three which they would prefer to be used. A comparison of these responses shows that 17 of the 43 (39.5%) respondents who reported that their supervisor used a Profit Conscious style thought that concern with costs should have a lower rank in their evaluation.

[30] Based on responses to the question "How justly do you think your performance is evaluated?" The responses were given on a 5-point scale ranging from "my performance is always evaluated justly" to "my performance is never evaluated justly," and the index has a possible range of 1 to 5.

agreement with hypothesis (c), with the worst reports of peer relationships occurring when the supervisor is perceived as using either a Budget Constrained or a Budget Profit style.[31] When someone is continually asked about budget variances over which he has little or no control, there is a tendency to try to pass on the responsibility by blaming other persons. This is known as "finger pointing" or "passing the buck." The practice is described by a cost center head in a Budget Constrained department:

> There's passing the buck when we're told to cut down, because we have no control. What good is it telling us to cut back. We don't have control. Occasionally there's a noncritical item that I could hold back but, in the main, most conditions of being in the red are things we have no control over. Yet we're still blamed for them. It's a tension reliever to pass it on to someone else.

Not only is there a definite tendency to blame other persons, but also, because each cost center head in this situation is anxiously devoted to the avoidance of unfavorable red variances, he concentrates solely on the activities of his own cost center, failing to be concerned with how this 15
affects the neighboring operations. This can have an important effect on the efficiency of the department's operations, since it results in a sluggish decision process and a constraint on innovation.[32] The arguments and

---

[31] The questionnaire responses cover only certain rather general aspects of the effects of the different evaluative styles on the network of interpersonal relations. In all cases the questions on peer relations, for instance, referred to "the people (or the man) at your level in the company with whom you have to deal in your job." The general reference, while locating important differences between the styles of evaluation, also obscured some of the detailed patterns of response. Some limited forms of task cooperation between cost center heads reporting a Budget Constrained evaluation were noted during the interview phase of the study. There was, however, a very definite preference for this cooperation to be with persons in charge of cost centers in departments other than one's own, particularly the central service units, or with persons in the same department who were in charge of noninterdependent units. The relationships were usually instrumental in nature, being formed for the purpose of mutually improving budget variances, the relationships forming part of a system of reciprocal obligations (see A. W. Gouldner, "The Norm of Reciprocity: A Preliminary Statement," *American Sociological Review*, XXV (1968), 161–78). The findings are similar to those reported by Roy in his "Efficiency and 'the Fix': Informal Intergroup Relations in a Piece Work Machine Shop," *American Journal of Sociology*, LX (1955), 255–66.

[32] The relationship between budgetary systems and innovation has been referred to in the research conducted as part of the Carnegie Project on the Behavioral Theory of the Firm. See R. M. Cyert and J. G. March, *A Behavioral Theory of the Firm* (Englewood Cliffs, N.J.: Prentice-Hall, 1963) and J. P. Crecine, *Governmental Problem Solving: A Computer Simulation of Municipal Budgeting* (Chicago: Rand McNally, 1969). The problem was also raised during the discussions reported in Burns, *op. cit.*, pp. 254–55. In those conference proceedings, Bedford notes, perhaps a little too strongly, the "... complete neglect of the influence of risk on innovation acceptance.... Clearly, any study of the behavioral response to accounting data should include consideration of different types of risks involved in making changes." Burns, *op. cit.*, p. 323.

conflicts in the Budget Constrained departments increase the difficulty of controlling important but highly interdependent aspects of the production process such as delay time. No one wants to take responsibility for a decision, just in case it costs too much or results in an unfavorable budget variance, as is illustrated by the following comments made by a cost center head in a Budget Constrained department:

> We sometimes have problems coming to an agreement. Well, it's the way we talk around here. Discussions can get pretty heated at times. Well, there was one item not too long ago. Whenever a buddy came up with an idea, no one's idea was the same and, as a consequence, we still haven't got it. "No, that wouldn't be worth a damn," that's what the others say. One guy wanted it this way, one guy that way, and as a consequence we still haven't got it. Sometimes there's disagreement on whether to do it at all. That's why I personally like to talk it over with the rest of them so that when it's finished and done they can't come back and say it's not worth a damn.
>
> What do you mean by coming back and saying 'it's not worth a damn'?
>
> 16 ...If the others were against it and it breaks down, then you're just left on your own because they say that it was no damn good to start with. Usually, the trouble is because it would cost too much, and then if it doesn't work 100 percent or if it costs a bit more than you thought, they say it was no damned good in the first place. Well, it's more difficult to blame anyone if you all agree first isn't it?
>
> So other people in the department blame each other for this type of thing?
>
> Yeah, there's finger pointing. Maybe not directly, but you hear about it in a round about way. It always comes back. They go to [the supervisor] on their own. "That's not my idea," that's what they tell him. "I didn't think a damn when it was put in. That was so and so's idea." But they wouldn't come directly and tell you themselves. There is a fair amount of this among the general foremen here, but it's done behind the scene.

On the basis of the intensive study of the selected series of cost centers, it was also found that cost center heads reporting a Budget Constrained style were more likely to engage in manipulative behavior than those evaluated in a Profit Conscious or Nonaccounting manner. The evidence is therefore supportive of hypothesis (d).[33] The manipulation in Budget Constrained departments was found to take three principal forms. First, cost center heads attempted to charge items of cost to other cost centers. This method, which took advantage of the cost center head's role in recording the basic accounting information, was done with some care so as to minimize the chance of detection. The practice was also more likely to occur when the cost center heads had recently received reports of unfavorable budget variances. It was the first frantic response to a stressful situation, and in some cases preceded the design and use of more sophisticated means of manipulation.

Cost over which the cost center heads were able to exercise some discretion as to their timing and amount represented an important focus

[33] A more complete description of the means of manipulation and their comparative incidence is given in Hopwood. *op. cit.*, pp. 118–58.

for manipulative attempts. In the subject company this was particularly true of repairs and maintenance expenditures. To minimize the total costs, including the opportunity costs of interrupted production, such expenditures should ideally be incurred at times of low production. The monthly repairs and maintenance budget, however, was determined on the basis of the month's production volume, resulting in a low budget when the costs should ideally be incurred. Both interview evidence and a statistical analysis of the cost data suggest that the cost center heads who are evaluated on the basis of a Budget Constrained style, unlike those evaluated on the basis of the other styles, tended to time the expenditures in the light of their effects on the short-term variances. They tended to ignore the more long-term implications and the elements of cost which are not reflected in the accounting system.

The correlations between monthly production and monthly expenditures on repairs and maintenance in 1969 were calculated for a series of cost centers.[34] In Table 5 the correlation coefficients are shown for the cost centers in two departments which have a similar technology. One depart- 17
ment is under a Budget Constrained supervisor; the other is under a Profit Conscious supervisor. Three of the six cost centers in the Budget Constrained department have a significantly positive correlation and, in addition, the value of one other coefficient (for cost center B4) approaches significance at the 10 percent level. There is therefore some tendency to do repair work at times of high production when the budget is available, and so avoid red variances. In contrast, none of the coefficients for the eight cost centers in the Profit Conscious department are significantly different from zero; decisions on the timing of repairs and maintenance expenditures are not made in the light of current production volume.

The next analysis is for a single department where the supervisor selectively uses a Budget Constrained style of evaluation. Four of the seven cost center heads in the department report that their supervisor uses this style, the other three reporting another style. In Table 6 it can be seen that for the five cost centers under the responsibility of persons who report a Budget Constrained style, one of the correlations is significantly

[34] The analysis presented a number of problems. First, some cost centers were closed down for a significant portion of the year. Second, repairs and maintenance expenditures are not separately identified for some cost centers. Both these sets of cost centers were excluded from the analysis. Third, different departments have different procedures for accounting for repairs and maintenance expenditures. In some departments such costs are separately charged to the cost center responsible for incurring the cost. In other departments, important portions of such costs are accumulated in a departmental account and then allocated to the separate cost centers on the basis of an engineering estimate of the average expenditures in a predetermined base period. Essentially the portion of the costs so allocated is beyond the control of the cost center head. In the analysis, the basic repairs and maintenance cost data are those directly controlled by the cost center heads; allocated costs are not included.

positive and another (S2) is close to significance at the 10 percent level. The correlations for the six cost centers under the responsibility for persons who did not report a Budget Constrained style are all negative, two reaching a statistically significant level. Again, there is some evidence that the cost center heads use a different decision rule.[35]

A third form of manipulation was available to relatively few persons. Some cost center heads did, however, attempt to influence the volume and type of production. Three ways of doing this were found:

(1) the creation of "pseudo-production" which only exists in the records;

(2) the maintenance of inventory buffers which gave the cost center head greater control over the volume and type of production in a period;[36]

(3) attempts to influence the production scheduling decision itself. Such attempts were instrumental in making the variances more favorable because of the insensitivity with which the accounting system reflected production changes and varying product mixes.

18 In summary, the evidence on the effects of a Budget Constrained style of evaluation, where this is interpreted as a high relative importance being given to a rigid use of the short-term accounting data in performance evaluation, has supported the hypotheses. The use of accounting data in terms of a Profit Conscious style does not, however, result in such unfavorable consequences.

## *The Effects of High Absolute Importance Being Attached to Meeting the Budget and Concern with Costs*

We now discuss the effects of the absolute importance attached to the two accounting related criteria, where absolute importance is defined as the importance attached to a criterion independent of that attached to other criteria. The evidence is contrary to the hypotheses. As can be seen

[35] It is interesting to note one effect this type of manipulation can have on the usefulness of the accounting data for analytical work. As the initial step of a program concerned with achieving a more realistic separation of the fixed and variable elements of cost, members of the company's accounting department performed a statistical analysis of the monthly repairs and maintenance cost data for a series of departments. The analysis was inconclusive. Widely varying patterns of relationships with production volume were found. However, an examination of their findings on the basis of the evaluation groups established in this study suggested that the direction of the relationships with production volume was related to the dominant style of evaluation used in the department. There is a tendency for a Budget Constrained use of the accounting data to reinforce the assumptions built into the accounting system; if some elements of discretionary cost are accounted for as variable costs, a rigid use of the data will insure that they are incurred in this manner.

[36] Thompson has commented on the role of inventories in absorbing uncertainty in organizations. See J. D. Thompson, "Decision-Making, The Firm, and the Market," in *New Perspectives in Organization Research*, ed. W. W Cooper, H. J. Leavitt, and M. W. Shelly (New York: John Wiley & Sons, 1964).

in Table 7, cost center heads who report that their supervisors attach high absolute importance to both meeting the budget and concern with costs are likely to experience relatively low job related tension, although they do tend to worry about specific matters affecting their costs and the budget.

There is also a positive relationship between the ratings of the absolute importance of the two criteria and the cost center heads' reports of their relations with their supervisors. An examination of Table 8 reveals that a high absolute importance of either criteria is associated with greater reported trust, respect and satisfaction with the supervisor. He is seen to be more understanding of the job problems. It would appear however, that the improvement in relations occurs without an easing of job expectations. A similar but weaker pattern of relationships is found for the indexes of peer relations reported in Table 9.

Hence it is only when meeting the budget becomes important in relation to other valued criteria of job performance that unfavorable consequences
occur. Of itself, concern with meeting the budget can result in quite 19
favorable consequences. This might reflect the fact that one purpose of a budget is to clearly set out the objectives for a cost center. While this certainly cannot be done with perfect accuracy, it is possible to carefully and cautiously use the budget for this purpose and thereby add an important element of structure and clarity to the job environment.[37] In Table 10 it can be seen that for the sample as a whole, the perceived absolute importance of meeting the budget is indeed associated with perceptions of greater goal clarity.[38] However, a more detailed examination of the data reveals that the concern with the budget has this effect only if it does not achieve high relative importance in performance evaluation. Significant positive relationships between the absolute importance of meeting the budget and goal clarity occur only in the Profit Conscious and Nonaccounting groups.

A Nonaccounting evaluation, in particular, might be made on the basis of rather vague criteria: attitudes, the way the cost center head handles

[37] French and his colleagues have commented on the advantage of specific job goals. See J. R. P. French, Jr., E. Kay and H. H. Meyer, "Participation and the Appraisal System," *Human Relations*, XIX (1966), 3–19. The literature on the relationship between goal specificity, and organizational and personal variables is reviewed by E. A. Locke, "Toward a Theory of Task Motivation and Incentives," *Organizational Behavior and Human Performance*, III (1968), 157–89, and T. F. Lyons, "Role Clarity, Satisfaction, Tension and Withdrawal," *Organizational Behavior and Human Performance*, VI (1971), 99–110.

[38] The index of perceived goal clarity is based on responses to the question: "Do you know what is expected of you in your job?" Respondents were asked to select one of four responses varying from "I am very sure of what is expected of me" to "I am not at all sure of what is expected of me." In the table, the Budget Constrained and Budget-Profit groups have been combined so as to increase the size of the group for analysis. This is done on the basis of the evidence which suggests that there is no significant difference between the two groups (see footnote 39 below).

his men, and effort. While such criteria are important, they are surrounded by a great deal of uncertainty. It is difficult to clearly specify what constitutes good and bad performance, and a supervisor might find it difficult to determine when improvement occurs. In these circumstances, the budgetary system offers one definite advantage. It attempts to express the units' objectives in a precise manner.

*Discussion*

The important management dilemma which provided the basis for the present study also serves to highlight the relevance of the findings. Although accounting data are often the most important formal sources of information in an organization, attempting to reflect matters which are of vital concern, they are usually incomplete and even biased indicators of managerial performance. A manager may want to make his subordinates aware of the relevant aspects of the data, and yet to use the data in their
20 appraisal is potentially inequitable, and may encourage defensive behavior which is contrary to the very goals of the organization the accounting system was designed to serve.

The study clearly demonstrates the real importance of the manner in which accounting data are used. Accounting data do not in of themselves pose a threat to members of an organization, and their imperfections need not necessarily be seen as unjust when they are used in performance evaluation. A manager is not therefore faced with a simple choice between using or not using the data in performance evaluation. Instead, he can reap many of the benefits of the accounting system by stressing factors which it attempts to measure without this resulting in either emotional costs for the persons being evaluated or defensive behavior which is dysfunctional for the organization. To do so, however, he must, in the terms of the study, use the accounting data in a manner consistent with a Profit Conscious style of evaluation rather than a Budget Constrained style.

The distinction between the two styles is a crucial one.[39] A concern with accounting data, which is often so vital for the efficiency of an organization, is accepted by the cost center heads so long as the data are used with care and the budget variances are not emphasized at the expense of other valued performance criteria. Cost center heads are satisfied with an in-

[39] The evidence suggests that the Budget Constrained and Profit Conscious styles are distinct and that it is not possible to successfully combine them. The Budget Constrained style dominates in the conflicting situation. Seventeen indexes of dependent variables have been presented in Tables 1 to 4. In all cases the values for the Budget Constrained group were not significantly different from the Budget-Profit group. In contrast, in 12 cases the values for this latter group were significantly different from those for the Profit Conscious group. One of the five cases where they did not significantly differ is for the cost tension index. It will be remembered that we noted that all the accounting related styles resulted in high cost tension.

creased absolute importance being attached to both their concern with costs and the extent to which they meet the budget, the latter possibly helping to clarify the job environment and goals. They are satisfied with the Profit Conscious style of evaluation even though it certainly does not result in easier job requirements. It is a demanding style and, as we have seen, produces a high level of cost tension, but it is accepted and respected, and results in significantly less tension, rivalry and ill feelings than the Budget Constrained style.

The Profit Conscious style appears to be one aspect of a problem solving style of management, as distinct from a style which attempts to impose a false measure of cognitive simplicity onto a complex and highly interdependent series of activities. The accounting system is seen as a valuable, although at times imperfect aid to management, and its reports are used in a creative manner, serving as a bias for inquiry and a source of ideas for change. "He throws 'if' into our cost statements. The cost is this or that, so throw an 'if' in and find the cost savings for the year and for a month." The data are not, however, automatically taken at their 21
face value. Rather, the Profit Conscious supervisor probes into their significance and meaning, supplementing them by many other sources of information, both formal and informal, so that the alternatives can be compared and the inconsistencies investigated. All these are processes which allow a continual test of the validity of the accounting data and which help to maintain the healthy, indeed essential element of skepticism in relation to the data.

In contrast, the Budget Constrained style is one in which the evaluation of performance is of primary importance, influencing all aspects of the supervisor's and the cost center head's behavior. Evaluation is not viewed as an ongoing part of the managerial process, interrelated with other important aspects of the job, and just one aspect of the process of influence. Rather, it is seen as a distinct and dominant activity, and the primary source of influence and control, overshadowing other vital elements of the process. The budget becomes not an aid to problem solving but a constraint on it, resulting in short time horizons and a sluggish and inflexible decision process. In the words of one interviewee:

> [A Budget Constrained supervisor] takes the budget to heart, while what [a Profit Conscious supervisor] does is accept it upon himself and if he doesn't agree with it then he'll reject the budget. He's a much tougher guy and it's difficult to argue with him. You have got to have some good arguments, but if he agrees with you then out goes the budget. [The Budget Constrained supervisor] can be stubborn. He aims to stay right on his budget, and that's that.

Although the study has illustrated a number of the important effects of these different ways of using accounting data in performance evaluation, it has not been directly concerned with the overall effects on the final efficiency of operations. This was partly because in the subject company, as in many organizations, the available indexes of efficiency are based on the accounting data and may therefore reflect both real efficiency and successful manipulation of the data. Nevertheless, the issue is both of immediate concern to the manager and of importance in placing the observed effects in a wider organizational context. Accordingly, while the need for further research is recognized, it is worthwhile to briefly review the available evidence which, although incomplete, is suggestive.

While both the Budget Constrained and Profit Conscious styles result in a concern with costs, only the Profit Conscious supervisor achieves this concern without the costly dysfunctional decision making and manipulation of the data. Examples were found of decisions taken in Budget Constrained departments which resulted in higher processing costs, less innovative behavior and a poorer quality service to the customer, and where the manipulation of the data reduced their usefulness for analytical purposes.[40] In addition, the climate of distrust and rivalry which is a consequence of the Budget Constrained style is also of importance because
22 it is known that in many situations such factors can influence long-term performance and success.[41] The presence of the type of tension and conflict observed between members of a Budget Constrained department can often impede the cooperation, mutual help and assistance which are so essential for controlling interdependent activities and maintaining a flexible response to unusual circumstances. These are problems which are nowhere near so prevalent with either a Profit Conscious or Nonaccounting style, a finding which should be borne in mind when the relative advantages and disadvantages of the latter style in particular are being considered.

The evidence is certainly suggestive that a Profit Conscious style is likely to result in a higher general level of efficiency than the Budget Constrained style. Nevertheless, the possibility does remain that it is still better to place at least some emphasis on the accounting data: in other words, some persons could indeed argue that the Budget Constrained style, despite its advantages, results in greater efficiency than the Nonaccounting style.

A number of the issues mentioned above are relevant to this important question, although there obviously remains a need for further research. While the cost associated with the difficulties of controlling interdependent operations, the short-time horizons, the manipulated accounting data and the climate of distrust are often important, their impact on the efficiency of operations will vary from situation to situation. The precise balance of costs and benefits may be different for the control of a stable, technologically simple situation than for the control of an uncertain and highly

[40] Some examples have been referred to above, but for a more complete discussion see Hopwood, *op. cit.*

[41] Georgopoulos and Tennenbaum, *op. cit.*

complex situation. Rather than trying to unnecessarily generalize at this early stage, it is essential that some further attempts be made to isolate the conditions influencing the relative advantages of the various styles of evaluation.

In addition, the Nonaccounting style has been regarded as a residual category in the present study and we have investigated neither its nature and variety nor the implicit assumption behind the design of many accounting systems that efficiency is dependent upon the rather direct use of accounting data in evaluation by supervisors.[42] Yet it is possible that in at least some of the so-called Nonaccounting evaluations, the accounting data may represent an important means of feedback to a cost center head, influencing his self-evaluation and subsequent behavior even though they are relatively unimportant in his superior's evaluation.

Some measure of subordinate defensiveness may be a reaction to all forms of evaluation by a superior. For instance, one group of researchers found that managers' attempts to assist subordinates by indicating areas
for improvement were likely to be seen as a threat by the subordinates 23
and frequently resulted in defensiveness.[43] In which case, the present study has been concerned with differences in the level of threat, and it is possible that even the Profit Conscious style does not represent an optimal solution to the problem. Rather, a greater regard for the cost center head's self-motivation to be concerned with the accounting data may result in both efficient operations and an even lower level of threat.[44]

Such factors represent a significant and important direction for further research. More consideration needs to be given to the precise characteristics of the various styles, their implications for organizational effectiveness and the conditions influencing their relative advantages. While the research findings have suggested the outline of a perspective for viewing the differential use of accounting data in performance evaluation, our knowledge of the subject is still rudimentary. It can, however, best be advanced by further empirical research.

---

[42] E. H. Caplan, "Behavioral Assumptions of Management Accounting," *The Accounting Review*, XLI (1966), 496–509.

[43] E. Kay, H. H. Meyer and J. R. P. French, Jr., "Effects of Threat in a Performance Appraisal Interview," *Journal of Applied Psychology*, XLIX (1965), 311–17. Similar comments are made by N. R. F. Maier in his *The Appraisal Interview: Objectives, Methods and Skills* (New York: John Wiley & Sons, 1958).

[44] Bassett and Meyer found that a self-appraisal prepared by the subordinate resulted in less defensive behavior and a greater perceived improvement in performance than superior-review. See G. A. Bassett and H. H. Meyer, "Performance Appraisal Based on Self-Review," *Personnel Psychology*, XXI (1968), 421–30.

**TABLE 1**

*The Effects of the Style of Evaluation on Job Related Tension and Specific Cost Tension*

| | Style of evaluation | | | | Significance of paired comparisons[a] |
|---|---|---|---|---|---|
| | BC | BP | PC | NA | |
| Job related tension[b] | 2.55 | 2.42 | 2.11 | 2.16 | BC v. PC: $p < .01$ |
| | | | | | BC v. NA: $p < .05$ |
| | | | | | BP v. PC: $p < .05$ |
| Cost tension[b] | 2.81 | 2.78 | 2.81 | 2.42 | BC v. NA: $p < .05$ |
| | | | | | BP v. NA: $p < .05$ |
| | | | | | PC v. NA: $p < .05$ |



[a] Significance tests are based on the Mann-Whitney *U* Test. Unless otherwise stated a paired comparison is not significant at the 5 percent level.

[b] Both indexes have been expressed as values on a 5-point scale ranging from 1 to 5.

**TABLE 2**

*The Effects of the Style of Evaluation on the Perceived Justness of Evaluation*

| | Style of evaluation | | | | Significance of paired comparisons[a] |
|---|---|---|---|---|---|
| | BC | BP | PC | NA | |
| Justness of evaluation[b] | 3.30 | 3.63 | 4.17 | 4.00 | BC v. PC: $p < .01$ |
| | | | | | BC v. NA: $p < .01$ |
| | | | | | BP v. PC: $p < .05$ |

[a] Significance tests are based on the Mann-Whitney *U* Test. Unless otherwise stated, a paired comparison is not significant at the 5 percent level.

[b] The index has a possible range of 1 to 5.

**TABLE 3**

*The Effects of the Style of Evaluation on Reported Relations with the Supervisor*

| Index of relations with the supervisor[a] | Style of evaluation | | | | Significance of paired comparisons[b] |
|---|---|---|---|---|---|
| | BC | BP | PC | NA | |
| Trust in supervisor | 3.26 | 3.06 | 4.24 | 3.98 | BC v. PC: $p < .01$ |
| | | | | | BC v. NA: $p < .05$ |
| | | | | | BP v. PC: $p < .01$ |
| | | | | | BP v. NA: $p < .01$ |
| Respect for supervisor | 3.67 | 3.82 | 4.60 | 4.33 | BC v. PC: $p < .01$ |
| | | | | | BC v. NA: $p < .01$ |
| | | | | | BP v. PC: $p < .01$ |
| | | | | | BP v. NA: $p < .05$ |
| Supervisor's understanding | 3.27 | 3.18 | 4.09 | 3.89 | BC v. PC: $p < .01$ |
| | | | | | BC v. NA: $p < .01$ |
| | | | | | BP v. PC: $p < .01$ |
| | | | | | BP v. NA: $p < .01$ |
| Reasonableness of supervisor's expectations | 3.12 | 3.13 | 3.44 | 3.49 | BC v. NA: $p < .05$ |
| | | | | | BP v. NA: $p < .05$ |
| Satisfaction with supervisor—administrative | 3.36 | 3.53 | 4.40 | 4.11 | BC v. PC: $p < .01$ |
| | | | | | BC v. NA: $p < .01$ |
| | | | | | BP v. PC: $p < .01$ |
| | | | | | BP v. NA: $p < .01$ |
| Satisfaction—technical | 3.42 | 3.75 | 4.42 | 4.21 | BC v. PC: $p < .01$ |
| | | | | | BC v. NA: $p < .01$ |
| | | | | | BP v. PC: $p < .01$ |
| | | | | | BP v. NA: $p < .05$ |
| Satisfaction—human relations | 2.97 | 2.81 | 4.14 | 4.05 | BC v. PC: $p < .01$ |
| | | | | | BC v. NA: $p < .01$ |
| | | | | | BP v. NA: $p < .01$ |
| | | | | | BP v. NA: $p < .01$ |
| Satisfaction—general | 3.33 | 3.47 | 4.58 | 4.38 | BC v. PC: $p < .01$ |
| | | | | | BC v. PC: $p < .01$ |
| | | | | | BP v. PC: $p < .01$ |
| | | | | | BP v. NA: $p < .01$ |

[a] All the indexes have been coded on a scale of 1 to 5 for each case of comparison.

[b] Significance tests are based on the Mann-Whitney $U$ Test. Unless otherwise stated, a paired comparison is not significant at the 5 percent level.

TABLE 4

*The Effects of the Style of Evaluation on Reported Relations with Peers*

| Index of relations with peers[a] | Style of evaluation | | | | Significance of paired comparisons[b] |
|---|---|---|---|---|---|
| | BC | BP | PC | NA | |
| Peer supportiveness—achievement | 3.59 | 3.57 | 3.84 | 3.87 | BC v. PC: $p < .05$<br>BP v. PC: $p < .05$<br>BP v. NA: $p < .05$ |
| Peer supportiveness—affiliation | 3.28 | 3.12 | 3.65 | 3.75 | BC v. PC: $p < .05$<br>BC v. NA: $p < .01$<br>BP v. PC: $p < .01$<br>BP v. NA: $p < .01$ |
| Peer agreement | 3.36 | 3.35 | 3.72 | 3.76 | BC v. PC: $p < .01$<br>BC v. NA: $p < .01$<br>BP v. PC: $p < .05$<br>BP v. NA: $p < .01$ |
| 26 Peer helpfulness | 3.76 | 3.76 | 4.02 | 4.18 | BC v. NA: $p < .01$<br>BP v. NA: $p < .05$ |
| Respect for peers | 3.73 | 4.00 | 4.10 | 4.14 | BC v. PC: $p < .05$<br>BC v. NA: $p < .05$ |
| Peer friendship | 3.31 | 3.40 | 3.71 | 3.65 | BC v. PC: $p < .05$ |

[a] All scales have been coded on a scale of 1 to 5 for ease of comparison.

[b] Significance tests are based on the Mann-Whitney *U* Test. Unless otherwise stated, a paired comparison is not significant at the 5 percent level.

TABLE 5

*Correlations Between Monthly Production and Repairs and Maintenance Expenditures, 1969, for Two Departments*

| Budget Constrained department | | Profit Conscious department | |
|---|---|---|---|
| Cost center code | Correlation between monthly production and R & M expenditures | Cost center code | Correlation between monthly production and R & M expenditures |
| B1 | 0.82* | NB1 | 0.21 |
| B2 | 0.81* | NB2 | 0.13 |
| B3 | 0.61* | NB3 | 0.12 |
| B4 | 0.46 | NB4 | 0.05 |
| B5 | 0.28 | NB5 | −0.13 |
| B6 | 0.02 | NB6 | −0.15 |
| | | NB7 | −0.16 |
| | | NB8 | −0.32 |

* Significant at $p < .05$.

## TABLE 6

*Correlations Between Monthly Production and Repairs and Maintenance Expenditures, 1969, for Cost Centers in a Department Where the Supervisor Selectively Uses a Budget Constrained Style of Evaluation*

| Cost centers where the cost center head reports that the supervisor uses a Budget Constrained style | | Cost centers where the cost center head reports that the supervisor does not use a Budget Constrained style | |
|---|---|---|---|
| Cost center code | Correlation between monthly production and R & M expenditures | Cost center code | Correlation between monthly production and R & M expenditures |
| S1 | 0.52* | S6 | −0.02 |
| S2 | 0.49 | S7 | −0.26 |
| S3 | 0.19 | S8 | −0.36 |
| S4 | 0.01 | S9 | −0.39 |
| S5 | −0.01 | S10 | −0.54* |
| | | S11 | −0.59** |

* Significant at $.05 < p < .10$.
** Significant at $p < .05$.

27

## TABLE 7

*The Relationship Between the Absolute Importance of Meeting the Budget and Concern with Costs, and Job Related Tension and Cost Tension (Kendall's Tau)*

| | The cost center heads' perceptions of the absolute importance of meeting the budget | The cost center heads' perceptions of the absolute importance of concern with costs |
|---|---|---|
| Job related tension | −0.18* | −0.29* |
| Cost tension | 0.31* | 0.31* |

* Significant at $p < .01$.

## TABLE 8

*The Relationship Between the Absolute Importance of Meeting the Budget and Concern with Costs, and Reported Relations with the Supervisor (Kendall's Tau)*

| Index of relations with the supervisor | The cost center heads' perceptions of the absolute importance of meeting the budget | The cost center heads' perceptions of the absolute importance of concern with costs |
|---|---|---|
| Trust in supervisor | 0.29* | 0.27* |
| Respect for supervisor | 0.30* | 0.28* |
| Supervisor's understanding | 0.23* | 0.20* |
| Reasonableness of supervisor's expectations | −0.07 | 0.00 |
| Satisfaction with supervisor—administrative | 0.16* | 0.16* |
| Satisfaction with supervisor—technical | 0.30* | 0.28* |
| Satisfaction with supervisor—human relations | 0.28* | 0.26* |
| Satisfaction with supervisor—general | 0.18* | 0.17* |

* Significant at $p < .01$.

**TABLE 9**

*The Relationship Between the Absolute Importance of Meeting the Budget and Concern with Costs, and Reported Relations with Peers (Kendall's Tau)*

28

| Index of the relations with peers | The cost center heads' perceptions of the absolute importance of meeting the budget | The cost center heads' perceptions of the absolute importance of concern with costs |
|---|---|---|
| Peer supportiveness—achievement | 0.19** | 0.14** |
| Peer supportiveness—affiliation | 0.19** | 0.14** |
| Peer agreement | 0.13** | 0.17** |
| Peer helpfulness | 0.10* | 0.14** |
| Respect for peers | 0.02 | 0.08 |
| Peer friendship | 0.03 | 0.02 |

* Significant at $p < .05$.
** Significant at $p < .01$.

**TABLE 10**

*Relationship Between the Absolute Importance of Meeting the Budget and Perceived Goal Clarity (Kendall's Tau)*

| | Total sample | Evaluation groups | | |
|---|---|---|---|---|
| | | BC & BP | PC | NA |
| Relationship between absolute importance of meeting the budget and goal clarity | 0.17** | 0.10 | 0.21* | 0.22** |

* Significant at $p < .05$.
** Significant at $p < .01$.

# Leadership Climate and the Use of Accounting Data in Performance Evaluation

*Anthony G. Hopwood*

The final effectiveness of any management accounting system is dependent not only upon its design and technical characteristics, but also upon the precise manner in which the resulting data are used. In the extreme, of course, a system contributes little or nothing to the efficiency of an organization's operations if the data are ignored. More generally, however, despite any amount of thought and consideration which may have gone into its design, no management accounting system ever achieves a perfect representation of the underlying structure of economic events. A careful use of the data is always essential to compensate for their many unavoidable inadequacies.

But it remains so much easier naively to acknowledge that the data should be used carefully than to specify what this entails in terms of managerial actions. Yet such an understanding is an essential prerequisite for the intelligent management of change and improvement. The present study was accordingly designed to investigate empirically some of the managerial factors which influence an accounting system's organizational and personal impacts. Particular consideration is given to the relationship between wider managerial behaviors and the use which is made of accounting data in performance evaluation.

## Different Ways of Using Accounting Data in Performance Evaluation 29

The investigation is based upon an analysis of the managerial determinants of the following three distinct styles of using budgeted and actual cost information in performance evaluation.

1. *A Budget Constrained Style.* Despite the many unavoidable problems in using accounting data as comprehensive measures of managerial performance, the manager's performance is primarily evaluated on the basis of his ability continually to meet the short-term budget.

2. *A Profit Conscious Style.* The manager's performance is evaluated on the basis of his ability to increase the long-term effectiveness of his unit in relation to the goals of the organization. The accounting data, although indicating whether the budget has been met, do not necessarily indicate whether long-term effectiveness is being attained. Therefore, while important, they are used with some care in a flexible and creative manner, and where

The author wishes to acknowledge the helpful comments and advice of Professor L. Richard Hoffman ot the University of Chicago.

*Anthony G. Hopwood is at the Administrative Staff College, Henley-on-Thames, England.*

necessary, supplemented by alternative sources of information.

3. *A Nonaccounting Style.* Accounting data play a relatively unimportant part in the evaluation of the manager's performance.

Previous empirical research has demonstrated that these three ways of using accounting data have significantly different organizational and personal effects.[1] Although both the Budget Constrained and Profit Conscious styles resulted in a higher degree of involvement with costs than the Nonaccounting style, only the Profit Conscious style succeeded in attaining this without resulting in either emotional costs
30 for managers or defensive behavior which was dysfunctional for the organization. The Budget Constrained style resulted in a belief that the evaluation was unjust, in widespread tension and worry on the job, and in feelings of distrust and dissatisfaction with the supervisor. Not only were the managers who were evaluated in this way found to manipulate the accounting data and make decisions which resulted in higher long-term processing costs for the company as a whole, but the consequent conflict and rivalry between colleagues impeded the cooperation which was so essential for controlling their interdependent activities. In contrast, the Profit Consious style, while seen as very demanding, was accepted. It resulted in levels of tension and in satisfaction with the supervisor and colleague supportiveness similar to those which prevailed under a Nonaccounting evaluation.

## Factors Influencing the Use Made of Accounting Data

As Argyris noted in this study of the personal impact of budgets in four industrial organizations, the way in which a manager uses budgetary data is only one aspect of his more general approach to the job.

> . . . It became obvious that the way people expressed their interest in budgets, and the way in which they described and used them, were directly related to the pattern of leadership in their daily industrial life.[2]

Many recent studies have made a distinction between the instrumental or task aspects and the socio-emotional aspects of managerial behavior. In this study, these two aspects of behavior are characterized in terms of the two dimensions of the Ohio State University Leadership Behavior Description Questionnaire (LBDQ), namely, Initiation of Structure and Consideration.[3] The Initiation of Structure dimension reflects the extent to which a manager defines both his own work role and those of his subordinates. A high score is indicative of clearly delineated roles and attempts to establish clear channels of communication, patterns of organization, and detailed job instructions. The Consideration dimension reflects the extent to which a manager is friendly, trusting, and respectful of his subordinates. A high score is indicative of a manager who is willing to explain his actions and who tries to maintain warm and personal relationships with his subordinates.

A manager who is seen as using a Budget Constrained style of evaluation is expected to have a leadership style characterized by a high score on the Initiation of Structure dimension of the LBDQ and a low score on the Consideration dimension. Because accounting data have an aura of objectivity and clarity, their use in a rather direct manner should appeal to a manager who is concerned with establish-

[1] A. G. Hopwood, "An Empirical Study of the Role of Accounting Data in Performance Evaluation," *Empirical Research in Accounting: Selected Studies, 1972*, Supplement to Vol. X, *Journal of Accounting Research*.

[2] C. Argyris, *The Impact of Budgets on People* (School of Business and Public Administration, Cornell University, 1952), p. 24.

[3] E. A. Fleishman, "A Leader Behavior Description for Industry," in *Leader Behavior: Its Description and Measurement*, edited by R. M. Stogdill and A. E. Coons (Bureau of Business Research, Ohio State University, 1957), pp. 120–33.

ing well-defined work procedures and means for evaluation.[4] To use the data in such a manner, however, the manager must also be relatively insensitive in his interpersonal relations, being more concerned with the task and goal attainment than with the maintenance of cordial and trusting relations with people. A more considerate supervisor is more likely to have that degree of empathy, and perhaps the open communications with his subordinates, which allow him to see the threat and the subsequent defenses which a rigid concern with the accounting data is capable of creating.[5]

It is, however, impossible to provide any adequate understanding of managerial evaluative behaviors without also considering the complex nature of the interrelationships between different levels of an organizational hierarchy. Since a manager himself is subject to an evaluation which may take on a similar form to those already described, it is necessary to look at the ways in which the demands and pressures are passed down from one level in the hierarchy to the next. In his simulation study of a firm's information and decision systems, Bonini[6] called such a process a "contagion effect," a term which is used in the present context to refer to any tendency for managers to evaluate their subordinates as they themselves are evaluated.

The contagion effect is particularly pertinent for a Budget Constrained style of evaluation because of the additive nature of accounting data. If a manager's superior pays attention to the extent to which the budget is met, the manager can satisfy this objective only by similarly paying attention to the budget variances of his own subordinates.

The above arguments can be summarized in terms of the following hypotheses which are discussed in this paper:

A manager is more likely to be seen as using a Budget Constrained style of evaluation if (a) he has a leadership style which is characterized by low Consideration and high Initiation of Structure; (b) he is himself evaluated on the basis of a Budget Constrained style.

## Research Site

The manufacturing division of a Chicago-based company which served as the site for the study had a labor force in excess of 20,000 persons and an annual revenue of several hundred million dollars. The division's management accounting system had been in operation for over a decade and it was based on flexible budgets, standard costing techniques, and the allocation of certain overhead costs. All 31
levels of management received monthly reports comparing their actual and budgeted costs; these were supplemented by daily and and weekly reports on such matters as production, labor, and supplies.

The division was organized on the basis of a series of areas, departments, and cost centers. Each area included several departments; and each department, a series of cost centers. A simplified organization chart is shown in Figure 1. The cost centers were usually under the responsibility of a general foreman, although some foremen and assistant departmental supervisors also had responsibilities at this level. One person could also be in charge of several cost centers. At the time the study was conducted, there were over 350 cost

[4] P. Weissenberg and L. Grunefeld, "Relationships Among Leadership Dimensions and Cognitive Style," *Journal of Applied Psychology* (October 1966), pp. 392–5.

[5] See E. A. Fleishman and J. A. Slater, "Humanizing Relationships in a Small Business: the Relationship Between the Leader's Behavior and His Empathy Toward Subordinates," *Advanced Management* (March 1961), pp. 18–20.

[6] C. P. Bonini, *Simulation of Information and Decision Systems in the Firm* (Prentice-Hall, 1963). Mann and Baumgartel provided some evidence that a manager's general attitude towards costs influenced his subordinates' concern with them: F. Mann and H. Baumgartel, *The Supervisor's Concern with Costs in an Electric Power Company* (Survey Research Center, Institute for Social Research, University of Michigan, 1953).

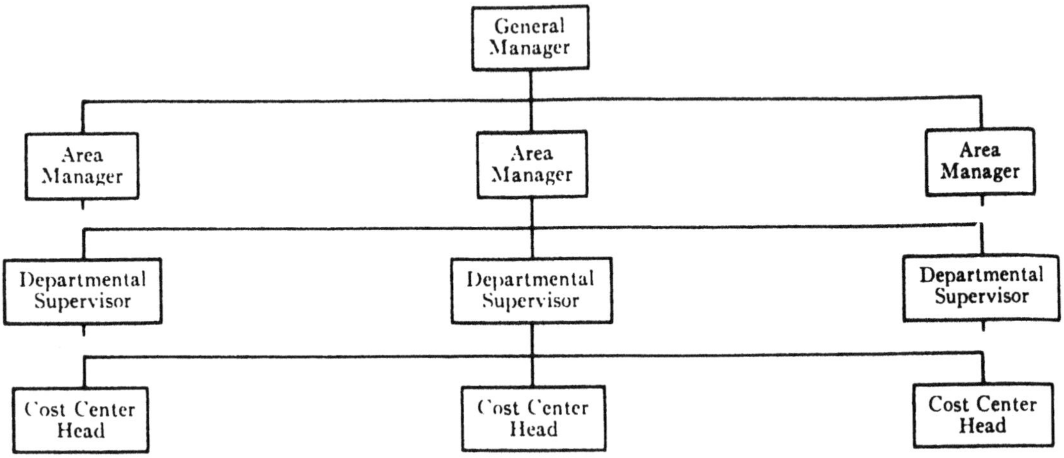


FIGURE 1

32 ORGANIZATION CHART FOR SUBJECT COMPANY

centers under the responsibility of 193 cost center heads.

Questionnaires were sent to 27 departmental supervisors and the 193 cost center heads. When a respondent failed to return the questionnaire two follow-up letters were sent to him. The final response rate was very high: 96% (26 out of 27) for the supervisors and 87% (167 out of 193) for the cost center heads.

## MEASUREMENT OF THE VARIABLES

It was preferable to test for the presence of a contagion effect on the basis of independent reports from at least two levels in the organizational hierarchy so as to avoid any tendency for persons at just one level to report in a consistent manner. Therefore, the departmental supervisors were asked to report on the evaluative styles of the area managers and the cost center heads on the supervisors' styles.

### *The Area Manager's Style of Evaluation*

The major methodological problem confronting the investigation concerned the means for empirically distinguishing among the different styles of using accounting data in performance evaluation. Although a broad set of behaviors had been isolated for each style, their operational definition necessitated an understanding of the meanings which the managers attached to these behaviors and the language which they used to describe them.

During a series of exploratory interviews, it was found that all levels of management referred to patterns of evaluative behaviors which were in agreement with the distinctions described above. In particular, a Budget Constrained orientation was referred to in terms of "meeting the budget" and a Profit Conscious orientation in terms of "concern with costs." These two phrases had distinct meanings which were known to all the managers interviewed, and therefore they were used as the basis for operationally defining the three styles of evaluation.

Each departmental supervisor was presented with a list of eight performance criteria which included both meeting the budget and concern with costs, as well as cooperation with colleagues, getting along with the boss, effort put into the job, concern with quality, attitude towards the work and company, and ability to handle the men. He was asked to rank-order the three factors which he saw as being most important in his own evaluation, and the following operational definitions of the evaluative styles were then defined on the basis of the rankings.[7] The number of respondents in each group is shown in parentheses.

1. *Budget Constrained Style* (BC): meeting the budget ranked among the top three criteria (6).[8]

2. *Profit Conscious Style* (PC): concern with costs, but not meeting the budget, ranked among the top three criteria (10).

3. *Nonaccounting Style* (NA): neither meeting the budget nor concern with costs ranked among the top three criteria (10).[9]

*The Departmental Supervisors' Style of Evaluation*

Although the 167 cost center heads completed an identical series of questions on their supervisors' styles of evaluation, the same operational definitions could obviously not be used because several subordinate cost center heads reported on the style of each of the 27 supervisors. Furthermore, in some departments, as is discussed subsequently, the cost center heads' perceptions were not in agreement. Some means of characterizing the ***dominant*** style reported by the cost center heads in each department was therefore required.

The following operational definitions of the supervisors' styles of evaluation are used in the study. The number of supervisors assigned to each style is shown in parentheses.

1. *Budget Constrained Style:* at least 40% of the cost center heads in a department reported that meeting the budget was one of the three most important criteria in their evaluation (12).

2. *Profit Conscious Style:* at least 40% of the cost center heads reported that concern with costs was one of the three most important criteria used in their evaluation, but less than 40% reported that meeting the budget was similarly important (7).

3. *Nonaccounting Style:* less than 40% of the cost center heads in a department reported that meeting the budget and concern with costs were amonst the three most important criteria in their evaluation (8).

Forty percent was selected since it was the median percentage for the relative importance of concern with costs, and although slightly above the median for the relative importance of meeting the budget, it took advantage of a break in the series.

*The Departmental Supervisors' Leadership Style*

The 48 items of the Ohio State Leadership Behavior Description Questionnaire 33
were included in the questionnaire sent to the cost center heads. The responses were coded to provide scores for the Consideration and Initiation of Structure dimensions of leadership behavior. The totals for all responding cost center heads under a departmental supervisor were then averaged to arrive at values of the dimensions for each supervisor. The range of the values of the Consideration dimension was found to be 50 to 92 (the possible range

[7] A discussion of the evidence on the validity of the operational procedures is given in Hopwood, "An Empirical Study of the Role of Accounting Data in Performance Evaluation."

[8] In an analysis of the cost center heads' perceptions of the departmental supervisors' styles of evaluation which was reported in the previous paper, a distinction was made between a Budget Constrained (BC) and a Budget-Profit (BP) style. The BC style referred to cases where meeting the budget, but not concern with costs, was ranked among the three most important criteria, and the BP style to cases where both the accounting-related criteria were in the top three. Subsequent analysis showed that the BC orientation dominated in the BP situation. There were no significant differences between the effects of the two styles, although the BP style did result in significantly different consequences than the pure PC style. In view of this evidence and the small size of the sample, the pure BC and BP styles are combined into a single Budget Constrained style in this analysis.

[9] The operational definition of the Nonaccounting style should be interpreted as implying a low ***relative*** importance to the accounting related criteria. It neither precludes some importance being attached to them nor their use for nonevaluative purposes.

TABLE 1

RELATIONSHIP BETWEEN THE REPORTED STYLE OF EVALUATION AND THE EXTENT TO WHICH THE COST CENTER HEADS MET THE BUDGET FOR DEPARTMENTS WITH DISAGREEMENT

| *Relationship Between Actual Costs and the Budget for 6-Month Period Prior to Receipt of Questionnaire* | *Cost Center Head Reports a Budget Constrained Style of Evaluation* | *Cost Center Head Does Not Report a Budget Constrained Style of Evaluation* | *N* |
|---|---|---|---|
| On average at least met the budget | 9 | 17 | 26 |
| On average did not meet the budget | 16 | 12 | 28 |
| *N* | 25 | 29 | 54 |

$\chi^2=2.69$; 1 d.f.; $P<0.11$.

was 0–112); the mean value, 75.6; and the standard deviation, 10.6. The range for the Initiation of Structure scores was 30 to 58 (with a possible range of 0–80); the mean value, 46.9; and the standard deviation, 7.0. The two dimensions were found to be independent (Kendall's Tau = −0.04).[10]

## SELECTIVE USE OF A BUDGET CONSTRAINED STYLE

The cost center heads in some departments were not in agreement over whether or not their supervisors used a Budget Constrained style of evaluation. While at least two-thirds of the responding cost center heads in 19 of the 27 departments agreed that their supervisors either did or did not use this style, only 40% to 57% of the cost center heads in the remaining 8 departments reported that he did. Before proceeding with the main analysis, it was important first to investigate whether these differences in opinions were due to inaccurate perceptions or the insensitivity of the measurement procedures or a real selective use of this style by some supervisors. An analysis was therefore made of the factors influencing the style of evaluation reported by the 54 cost center heads employed in the 8 departments where there was substantial disagreement.

The analysis indicated that the cost center heads reporting a Budget Constrained style in these 8 departments tended to have been less successful in meeting their budget. In Table 1 the 54 cost center heads are divided on the basis of (1) whether or not they reported a Budget Constrained evaluation and (2) whether or not they had, on average, met their budget over the 6-month period prior to the receipt of the questionnaire. There is a difference between the two criterion groups, but the difference is only significant at the 11% level.[11]

Prevention might, however, have been seen as being preferable to cure. An analysis was therefore made to see whether the supervisors of these 8 departments focused their Budget Constrained approach on the large cost centers which had the greatest potential to influence the overall departmental results. The cost center heads were divided on the basis of whether or not they were responsible for a cost center or a series of cost centers which dealt with total annual costs above, equal to, or less than the departmental median. From Table 2 it can be seen that these supervisors were more likely to be seen as using a Budget Constrained style by per-

[10] A review of the relationships between the two dimensions of the LBDQ is given by P. Weissenberg and M. J. Kavanagh in "The Independence of Initiating Structure and Consideration: A Review of the Evidence," *Personnel Psychology* (Spring 1972), pp. 119–30.

[11] There was no significant difference between these two criterion groups when the analysis was based on the average performance in the 9-month period prior to the receipt of the questionnaire. For the remaining 19 departments where there was substantial agreement over whether or not the supervisor used a Budget Constrained style, there was no relationship between the reported style and performance in either the 6- or 9-month period

TABLE 2

RELATIONSHIP BETWEEN THE REPORTED STYLE OF EVALUATION AND THE RELATIVE SIZE OF THE COST CENTERS FOR DEPARTMENTS WITH DISAGREEMENT

| *The Total Annual Costs of the Cost Center(s) in Relation to the Median Cost for Its Department* | *Cost Center Head Reports a Budget Constrained Style of Evaluation* | *Cost Center Head Does Not Report a Budget Constrained Style of Evaluation* | *N* |
|---|---|---|---|
| Above the departmental median | 16 | 10 | 26 |
| Equal to or less than the departmental median | 9 | 19 | 28 |
| *N* | 25 | 29 | 54 |

$\chi^2=5.23$; 1 d.f.; $P<0.05$.

TABLE 3

RELATIONSHIP BETWEEN LEADERSHIP STYLE AND THE SUPERVISORS' STYLE OF EVALUATION

35

| | *The Cost Center Heads' Perception of the Supervisors' Dominant Style of Evaluation* | | | |
|---|---|---|---|---|
| *Leadership Style* | *BC* | *PC* | *NA* | *Significance of Paired Comparison*[a] |
| Mean Initiation of Structure | 48.0 | 51.3 | 41.9 | *BC:NA*: $p<0.01$<br>*PC:NA*: $p<0.05$ |
| Mean Consideration | 70.6 | 80.9 | 79.4 | *BC:PC*: $p<0.05$<br>*BC:NA*: $p<0.05$ |
| *N* | 12 | 7 | 8 | |

[a] Significance of paired comparisons is based on the Mann Whitney *U* Test. Unless otherwise stated, a paired comparison is not significant at the 5% level.

sons in charge of the *relatively* large cost centers in a department.[12]

The findings suggest that the supervisors of the 8 departments where there was substantial disagreement over their style of evaluation used the Budget Constrained style with discretion, emphasizing it where it was seen as likely to have the greatest impact on the departmental results. As such, the evidence is in agreement with other studies which have shown that managers do not necessarily use one personal style of management irrespective of their circumstances and subordinates.[13]

## LEADERSHIP STYLE AND THE USE OF ACCOUNTING DATA

As can be seen from an examination of Table 3, both the Budget Constrained and Profit Conscious supervisors were seen as creating a structured job environment geared to the attainment of their perceptions of the organization's goals. The Budget Constrained supervisors, however, were seen as showing significantly less consideration for the feelings and opinions of their cost center heads than either their Profit Conscious or Nonaccounting colleagues. Yet without the maintenance of such a considerate managerial climate, the structured concern with the financial aspects of performance was seen in terms of

[12] There was no relationship between the reported style and the *absolute* size of the cost centers. Also no significant relationship was found between the reported style and either relative or absolute size in the nineteen departments with substantial agreement.

[13] See E. Kay and R. Hastman, *An Evaluation of Work Planning and Goal Setting Discussions* (General Electric Behavioral Research Service, 1966), and A. Lowin and J. R. Craig, "The Influence of Level of Performance on Managerial Style: An Experimental Object Lesson in the Ambiguity of Correlation Data," *Organizational Behavior and Human Performance* (November 1968), pp. 440–58.

a threatening emphasis on the accounting data in isolation of their organizational context. The findings are therefore supportive of hypothesis (a).

### THE CONTAGION EFFECT

The contagion effect was very strong for the Budget Constrained style of evaluation. With supervisors divided on the basis of whether or not their perceptions of the area managers' styles of evaluation were in agreement with their cost center heads' perceptions of their own dominant style, it can be seen in Table 4 that only one of the 6 supervisors who reported a Budget Constrained evaluation did not
36 pass down the same style to his cost center heads.[14] In contrast, there was no evidence of a contagion effect for either the Profit Conscious or Nonaccounting styles. For the Profit Conscious style, however, many of the supervisors maintained a concern with the accounting data, although the concern was just as likely to be rigidly tied to the short-term budget variances as it was to longer-term cost effectiveness. Four of the 10 supervisors who were evaluated on this basis evaluated their cost center heads in a Budget Constrained manner compared with the 3 who maintained the Profit Conscious style.

TABLE 4

RELATIONSHIP BETWEEN THE AREA MANAGERS' AND THE DEPARTMENTAL SUPERVISORS' STYLES OF EVALUATION

| *Relationship between the Cost Center Heads' Perception of the Supervisor's Dominant Style of Evaluation and the Supervisor's Perception of the Area Manager's Style* | *Supervisor's Perception of the Area Manager's Style of Evaluation* | | | |
|---|---|---|---|---|
| | *BC* | *PC* | *NA* | *N* |
| Agreement | 5 | 3 | 4 | 12 |
| Disagreement | 1 | 7 | 6 | 14 |
| *N* | 6 | 10 | 10 | 26 |

Supervisors were seen as passing on a Budget Constrained style even though they *intended* to do otherwise. All the departmental supervisors were asked to report how they thought that they evaluated their cost center heads, the responses being referred to as the supervisor's intended style of evaluation. It can be seen in Table 5 that only 2 of the 6 supervisors who reported being evaluated on the basis of a Budget Constrained style intended to evaluate their cost center heads in the same way. The other 4 supervisors intended to use a Profit Conscious style. In comparison, a majority of the supervisors who were evaluated on the basis of either a Profit Conscious or a Nonaccounting style intended to evaluate their cost center heads in the same manner, although they did not necessarily possess the requisite managerial abilities to put this into effect.[15]

The supervisors whose performance was evaluated upon the basis of their departments' short-term budget variances were in a conflict situation. It was easy for them to feel that it was necessary to evaluate similarly their cost center heads in order to obtain the desired results. Yet from their own experience they knew that this was an unfair evaluation which was likely

[14] While the Budget Constrained style might have been easier to resist if the departmental variances had been consistently favorable, the single supervisor who was the exception to the rule resisted the contagion effect despite having had unfavorable departmental variances for most of the fifteen months prior to the receipt of the questionnaire. His cost center heads saw him as having an average concern with a structured job environment (his Initiation of Structure score of 47 equals the median for the sample of supervisors), but an exceptionally high consideration for their feelings and opinions. His Consideration score of 89 was the second highest in the sample, and compared with the median of 79.

[15] Recent evidence relating self-reported leadership behavior to subordinate descriptions of behavior has also found that the two are not necessarily equivalent. See M. G. Evans, "Leadership Behavior: Demographic Factors and Agreement Between Subordinate and Self-Descriptions," *Personnel Psychology* (Winter 1972), pp. 649–53, and W. K. Graham and T. Olena, "Perceptions of Leader Behavior and Evaluation of Leaders Across Organizational Levels," *Experimental Publications System* (February 1970), p. 144A.

TABLE 5

RELATIONSHIP BETWEEN THE AREA MANAGERS' STYLE OF EVALUATION AND THE DEPARTMENTAL SUPERVISORS' INTENDED STYLE OF EVALUATION

| *Relationship Between the Supervisor's Perception of the Area Manager's Style and the Supervisor's Intended Style* | *Supervisor's Perception of the Area Manager's Style of Evaluation* | | | |
|---|---|---|---|---|
| | *BC* | *PC* | *NA* | *N* |
| Agreement | 2 | 7 | 7 | 16 |
| Disagreement | 4 | 3 | 3 | 10 |
| *N* | 6 | 10 | 10 | 26 |

to result in excessive tension and worry. One of them described his own experiences in the following way:

"When I'm in the red [the Area Manager] will always blame you. I'll get a black eye. Even if I'm not to blame, I'll still get a black eye. I like a good budget to shoot at but when you have obvious discrepancies in the budget, then it's difficult to show what you are doing. A good budget is a good thing, but a bad budget is a bad thing."

Yet he felt that he had to pass on the Budget Constrained style since his own superiors "will generally criticize me if I'm unfavorable, regardless of reason." So for some of his cost center heads, "if they're in the red, I'll probably know why, but I'll ask *them* why and I'll tarpoon [sic] a few things with them." He was, however, aware of the anxiety and undesirable behaviors which this could cause.

"The accounting numbers are a big thing for most of [the cost center heads]. It gets down to personalities; it's bound to. Generally [a cost center head] has to get a reasonable product to get a reasonable result. Well, he may want good relations with those who supply him with [his material], but then he wants to make himself look good, and to do that he makes others look poor."

With such problems in mind, he tried not to evaluate two of his cost center heads on the basis of their short-term budget variances because he thought that their highly skilled subordinates would react to the subsequent pressure by leaving the company. Since the two cost centers were also "low in real dollars," he was prepared to use a different style of evaluation.

All 5 of the superviors who were seen as passing down their own Budget Constrained evaluation used a similar means of resolving the conflict with which they were confronted. They were, in fact, responsible for 5 of the 8 departments where there was disagreement over this aspect of the supervisor's style of evaluation and in which, as we have already seen, the more rigid style was used for the larger cost centers and possibly those with a poor budget record.[16]

## DISCUSSION

37

In supporting the hypotheses, the evidence allows the initial distinctions which were made among the three styles of using accounting data in performance evaluation to be placed in a wider managerial perspective. For the final impact of an accounting system on managerial behavior has been shown to depend on its interaction with the forms of social- and self-controls which are reflected within the various leadership climates and the personal motives and defenses which they activate.

In being responsive to the feelings and opinions of their cost center heads, the Profit Conscious supervisors recognized and responded to the threat which the financial concerns and structured job environment were capable of creating. But, in addition, the supportive organizational climate encouraged the cost center heads to discuss openly their budgetary problems with the supervisor.[17] This might, of

[16] The percentage of cost center heads in the 5 departments reporting a Budget Constrained style were: 40%, 50%, 50%, 50% and 57%.

[17] In a field study conducted in three major industrial organizations Read found that trust in the supervisor resulted in accurate upward communications. See W. H. Read, "Upward Communication in Industrial Hierarchies," *Human Relations* (February 1962), pp. 3–15.

course, be viewed as a means of avoiding responsibility, although this would be an inappropriate description of the situation in these departments. The Profit Conscious supervisors, while listening to explanations, certainly did not readily accept them. In the words of one cost center head:

> "[A Budget Constrained supervisor] takes the budget to heart, while what [a Profit Conscious supervisor] does is to accept it upon himself and if he doesn't agree with it, then he'll reject the budget. He's a real tough guy and it's difficult to argue with him. You have got to have some good arguments, but if he agrees with you, then out goes the budget. [The Budget Constrained supervisor] can be stubborn. He aims to stay right on his budget and that's it."



The budgetary pressures associated with the Profit Conscious style of evaluation were seen, in the words of another cost center head, as being applied "where they [were] appropriate." The cost center heads were aware of both the supervisors' willingness to listen and, in turn, explain the reasons for accepting and rejecting explanations. As a result, the supervisors were provided with the alternative sources of information which enabled them to test continually the validity of the accounting data and keep the job environment devoid of the rigidities of the Budget Constrained approach. In contrast, the cost center heads subject to a Budget Constrained evaluation hardly felt free to offer realistic explanations. One such cost center head described his supervisor's attitude in terms of "just don't do it, rather than asking for explanations."

Unfortunately the study did not directly investigate the relationship among the three styles of using accounting data and the overall effectiveness of operations.[18] The observed leadership style configurations are, however, of interest in this respect since studies using the LBDQ dimensions have found that, although the Initiation of Structure and Consideration scores were designed to be independent, supervisors who are rated high on both dimensions are considered to be more effective by their superiors, as well as favorably influencing their subordinates' morale and improving indices of productivity and labor turnover. Fleishman and Harris,[19] for instance, found that for production supervisors scoring high on both dimensions, the structured job environment was seen as less threatening and had little or no effect on grievances and turnover. That a number of other studies have come to similar conclusions[20] provides some indirect evidence on the potential benefits of the Profit Conscious style, although it should be stressed that such findings are no more than suggestive in the present context.

However, while recognizing the need for further research on the overall effects of the various styles, the findings do point to a number of implications for both accounting practice and the study of the behavioral impact of accounting data. A the very least, they serve to emphasize the importance of the accountant's educational function. With the increasing complexity of management accounting pro-

[18] A review of the evidence on the differential effects of the various styles did provide some basis for concluding that the Profit Conscious style was likely to be more effective than the Budget Constrained style in situations which required a careful consideration of a wide variety of information, a high degree of interunit coordination, a long time horizon, and an ability to respond in a flexible manner to unexpected circumstances: see the discussion in Hopwood, *op. cit.*

[19] E. A. Fleishman and E. F. Harris, "Patterns of Leadership Behavior Related to Employee Grievances and Turnover," *Personnel Psychology* (Spring 1962), pp. 43–56.

[20] E. A. Fleishman and J. Simmons, "Relationship Between Leadership Patterns and Effectiveness Ratings Among Israeli Foremen," *Personnel Psychology* (Summer 1970), pp. 169–72; A. W. Halpin, "The Leader Behavior and Effectiveness of Aircraft Commanders," in Stodgill and Coons; H. Oaklander and E. A. Fleishman, "Patterns of Leadership Related to Organizational Stress in Hospital Settings," *Administrative Science Quarterly* (March 1964), pp. 520–32. A survey of the relationship between the two dimensions of the LBQD and various criteria of organizational effectiveness is given in A. K. Korman, " 'Consideration,' 'Initiating Structure' and Organizational Criteria—A Review," *Personnel Psychology* (Winter 1966), pp. 349–61.

cedures, it is unrealistic to expect managers to use the data in an appropriate manner without adequate preparation and training. But they need to be informed not only of the objectives and advantages of the accounting system, real though they may be, but also of the inadequacies of the data and the consequences of attaching too much importance to the short-term reports—a far more difficult task.

The different ways of using the data were not, however, simply based on ignorance. They were associated with much more widespread differences in managerial attitudes and behaviors, and for the Budget Constrained style, with the evaluative style of the superiors. Even the most carefully designed educational program is unlikely to provide an easy solution to the problem, and it would certainly require the active cooperation of specialists in organizational development. Hence, consideratio ı needs to be given to how the use which is made of the data can be explicitly recognized as a factor in the design of accounting systems. This does not mean that accountants should immediately strive to stifle the undesirable responses by filling the obvious loopholes in their systems. Rather, there is a need for system designs to take account of the constraints and opportunities of their managerial environment in the manner that Wildavsky has contrived to design federal budgeting procedures which are congruent with the political process.[21]

Such a task requires both practical experimentation and systematic research. But, so far, many of the studies of the effects of accounting data on decision behavior have ignored their managerial context. They have all too often merely presented reports based on different accounting methods to samples of financial analysts, managers, and students, and observed whether their decision behaviors were dependent upon the type of data received. The present findings suggest, however, that the relationship between accounting data and decision behavior is moderated by the leadership style and social context of the decision maker. Much greater explicit consideration needs to be given to these factors in further research, although, in so doing, there may be a need to rely less on the abstractions of laboratory experimentation and more on the complexities of field research.[22]

[21] A. Wildavsky, *The Politics of the Budgetary Process* (Little, Brown, 1964) and *Toward a Radical Incrementalism: A Proposal to Aid Congress in Reform of the Budgetary Process* (American Institute for Public Policy Research, 1965).

[22] This is not to deny that some aspects of the problem can be studied in controlled experiments. Lowin and Craig showed the potential for simulating different leadership styles in the laboratory, and among others, Mock *et al.* have recently reported experiments on the effects of cognitive style on decision behavior: See T. J. Mock, T. L. Estrin, and M. A. Vasarhelyi, "Learning Patterns, Decision Approach, and Value of Information," *Journal of Accounting Research* (Spring 1972), pp. 129–53. Nevertheless, there are formidable difficulties in trying to simulate hierarchical patterns and organizational contexts within the analytical and time constraints of the experimental method.

# PROBLEMS WITH USING ACCOUNTING INFORMATION IN PERFORMANCE EVALUATION

*Anthony G. Hopwood, Lecturer in Management Accounting, Manchester Business School, Manchester, Great Britain*

**An Advancing Technical Sophistication . . .**

The last few decades have witnessed an ever expanding basis of knowledge for the design of effective management accounting systems. New areas of expertise have continually provided new insights, opportunities and challenges to the conventional approaches. Perspectives drawn from economic theory have provided a sound basis for selecting information relevant for decision making and the application of mathematical skills has added to our potential for rigorously analysing complex problems. Moreover the advances in computer technology have ensured the means for providing speedy information to the managers who need it. At least in philosophy, therefore, accounting for management needs no longer be seen as merely a reckoning of post events but as a function which has a vital and positive role in encouraging managers to learn from their past experiences and to anticipate the contingencies of their uncertain tasks. 41

**. . . But a Neglect of Use?**

These are signs of real progress. However, while a great deal of attention has been devoted to the different ways of designing management accounting systems, comparatively little consideration has been given to the different ways of using accounting information. Yet the final impact which any accounting system makes on managerial behaviour is dependent not only upon its design and technical characteristics but also upon the precise manner in which the resulting information is used.

In the extreme, of course, even the most sophisticated system can contribute little or nothing to the efficiency of a company's operations if the information is ignored[1]. More generally, however, despite any amount of care and consideration which may have gone into the design of an accounting system, its value may be questionable if managers use the information in an inappropriate manner, attributing either too much or too little validity to it or being unaware of its intended purposes. Few, if any, management accounting systems ever achieve a perfect representation of the underlying structure of economic and financial events, and a careful and considerate use of the information is always essential to compensate for the many unavoidable inadequacies of the system.

---

1 See R. Beresford Dew and K. P. Gee, "Managements' Use of Budgetary Information", *Management Accounting*, March, 1970, pp. 89—92.

However, any appreciation of the different ways of using accounting information must be based upon an understanding of the human context in which the use occurs. While the information might be given, its interpretation is the outcome of a personal and social process which is sustained by the meanings, beliefs, pressures and purposes that are brought to bear by the managers using the information. In of necessity providing it with a personal significance and placing it in their own wider context, managers are able to use the information, perhaps without reflection, in a variety of ways — appropriate and inappropriate.

### Using Accounting Information in Managerial Performance Evaluation

Questions concerning appropriate use are particularly important when accounting information is used in managerial performance evaluation. The many documented examples of manipulation of accounting reports and undesirable decision making which were an outgrowth of attempts to make the reports a more favourable reflection of managerial performance suggest that we clearly have a number of problems in this area[2]. They are, however, problems which are easier to identify than to ensure the means for

their solution.

Although many accounting systems do attempt to reflect at least some of the important dimensions of managerial performance, there are many difficulties in designing reporting systems for this purpose. The means for measuring vital social behaviours have yet to be devised and even the procedures used for measuring the narrowly economic aspects of behaviour are approximate and often biased. And it is impossible to close off all loopholes against manipulation. Sophisticated though present understandings may appear, the final reports are of necessity partial, often including uncontrollable factors and usually geared to reporting short-term outcomes rather than managerial efforts towards attaining longer-term effectiveness. In practice the problem becomes one of gaining the necessary social understandings to ensure the effective use of imperfect but nevertheless valuable information procedures.

Yet intriguing though all the many reports of manipulation and undesirable behaviour may be, they are often little more than anecdotal accounts of particularly inappropriate uses of accounting information. They do little to provide us with the essential understandings of the precise ways in which the information was used, their determinants and full effects. They do not give use the why's and the wherefore's. While the use which any manager makes of accounting information may well be in some senses unique, it is nevertheless necessary to spot uniformities in the patterns of use. As accountants, like other careful investigators, have found in other areas, only such informities provide the insights for appreciating the nature of a problem and the means for moving towards its diagnosis and solution. The present paper reports on a research study which attempted to move in this direction[3].

---

2 See the early reviews by F. J. Jasinski, "Use and Misuse of Efficiency Controls". *Harvard Business Review*, July-August, 1956, pp. 105—112, and V. F. Ridgway, "Dysfunctional Consequences of Performance Measurements", *Administrative Science Quarterly*, I (1956), 240--247.

3 A more detailed report of the methods, statistical analyses and findings is given in the author's *An Accounting System and Managerial Behaviour* (Farnborough: Saxon House, forthcoming).

### Three Styles of Using Budgetary Information

Based upon a review of previous research findings and extensive interviews in one company, three distinct ways of using budgetary information in the evaluation of managerial performance were distinguished.

1. *Budget Constrained Style*
   Despite the many problems with using budgetary information as a comprehensive measure of managerial performance, the manager's performance is primarily evaluated upon the basis of his ability to continually meet the budget on a short-term basis. This criterion of performance is stressed at the expense of other valued and important criteria and the manager will receive unfavourable feedback from his superior if, for instance, his actual costs exceed the budgeted costs, regardless of other considerations.

2. *Profit Conscious Style*
   The manager's performance is evaluated on the basis of his ability to increase the general effectiveness of his unit's operations in relation to the long-term purposes of the organization. For instance, at the cost centre level, one important aspect of this ability concerns the attention which he devotes to reducing long-run costs. For this purpose, however, the budgetary information has to be used with great care in a rather flexible manner.

3. *Nonaccounting Style*
   The budgetary information plays a *relatively* unimportant part in the superior's evaluation of the manager's performance.

While the budgetary information obviously indicates whether or not a manager has succeeded in meeting his current budget, it does not necessarily indicate whether he is behaving in a manner which is consistent with achieving the organization's longer-term effectiveness. Current cost savings can, for instance, be made at longer term expense and some current cost overruns can also ensure lower cost operations in the future. There are many such problems and the budgetary information has not only to be used with care but also supplemented by information drawn from other sources in order to assess the manager's impact on future as well as current operations.

Unlike a Budget Constrained evaluation, a Profit Conscious evaluation is therefore concerned with the wider information content, or lack of it, of the budget reports and not with just a rigid analysis of the direction and magnitude of the reported budget variances. The budget is, in other words, seen as a means to an end rather than an end in itself.

### Measuring the Styles

It is, however, easier to distinguish the styles in such a general sense than move towards defining them in an operational manner. But how are we to know whether any manager uses a Budget Constrained or Profit Conscious or Nonaccounting style? This is of course, the crucial methodological problem faced by all studies of how accounting information is actually used. In this instance, the problem was approached by probing into the meanings developed by a group of managers in one company. They certainly did not use my terms but they did distinguish between their colleagues and superiors on the basis of evaluative behaviours which were in basic agreement with those described above. And the language which *they* used to make such distinctions provided the means for operationally defining the three styles and in turn, determining the style used in the evaluation of each manager.

The Budget Constrained orientation was expressed in terms of "meeting the budget" and the Profit Conscious orientation by "concern with costs". The two phrases had distinctly different meanings. The managers were then asked to rank the three most important criteria used in their evaluation out of a list of eight which included these two accounting related criteria. If "meeting the budget" was included in the top three criteria, the manager was presumed to be subject to a Budget Constrained evaluation[4] and if "concern with costs" but not "meeting the budget" was in the top three, he was categorized as reporting a Profit Conscious evaluation. The remaining managers were defined as reporting a residual Nonaccounting evaluation.

### The Research Site



The manufacturing division of a large Chicago based company served as the site for the study. The division had a labor force in excess of 20,000 persons and an annual revenue of several hundred million dollars. The accounting system was based on flexible budgets and standard costing techniques, and it was an accepted and important part of the work environment, having been installed for over a decade. Monthly reports comparing the actual and budgeted costs for cost centres were sent to all the responsible managers and their departmental supervisors. These were supplemented by daily and weekly reports on such matters as production, labour and supplies, the nature and content of which varied between cost centres.

The present discussion is based upon an analysis of items included in questionnaires which were sent to all the 193 managers in charge of cost centres and their 27 departmental supervisors. The final response was very high, being 87 % (167 out of 193) for the cost centre heads and 96 % (26 out of 27) for the supervisors. Subsequently, a series of intensive interviews were held with 45 managers at all levels in the division.

### The Effects of the Three Styles

The empirical evidence, a summary of which follows, indicated that both the Budget Constrained and Profit Conscious styles resulted in a higher degree of involvement with costs than the Nonaccounting style. Only the Profit Conscious approach, however, succeeded in attaining this involvement without incurring either emotional costs for the managers in charge of the cost centres or defensive behaviour which was undesirable from the company's point of view.

The Budget Constrained style resulted in a belief that the evaluation was unjust and widespread tension and worry on the job. In the words of one manager:

> You have to get yourself out of the woods. It's a process of staying out of the red. You have to. It's true and it makes a job so much more difficult. They'd be

4 In the full analysis a distinction was made between a pure Budget Constrained style where "meeting the budget" but not "concern with costs" was ranked in the top three criteria and a combined Budget-Profit style where both of these criteria were given this high ranking. The empirical evidence indicated that the Budget Constrained orientation dominated the Profit Conscious orientation in the combined style, the pure and combined styles having very similar effects and determinants. Therefore in this report they are treated as one style.

> times when I could do a good job and save some money by spending a bit now. But no, the only thing I concentrate on is what I've got forthcoming that's going to put me in the red. I've got to concentrate to see . . . there's no more money to spend. God, it causes me some problems.

Sometimes it was almost impossible to make the short-term budget variances more favourable.

> When I'm in the red, I start cutting on manpower. Well, I should, but I can't. We've been down on manpower for some time now. I just have to live on my budget, close to the bone. But you can't, you can't.

Such frantic and at times unsuccessful attempts only resulted in more problems, more tension and more worry.

It was hardly surprising that such a single minded concern with the budget was met with manipulation of the accounting reports and even decisions which increased the total processing costs for the company as a whole. Costs were charged to incorrect accounts, repairs delayed until the money was available in the budget despite this resulting in higher costs and, in the words of one manager: 45

> Simply no one will take the decision to spend. Most people in this position try to make themselves look good. They don't want to see negative signs on their reports. They're aiming for promotion without worrying about the future. It's let's look good today, tomorrow I'll get promoted. It's someone else's problem then.

Manipulation and undesirable decision behaviour were not, however, the only means of relieving the tensions created by the Budget Constrained style. The managers' relationships with the Budget Constrained supervisors were allowed to deteriorate. But the rigid emphasis on the short-term budget results also served to highlight the interdependent nature of their tasks and the immediate instrumental concerns easily permeated the patterns of social relationships amongst colleagues in the same department. When the managers were continually asked about budget variances over which they often had little or no control they each went out to improve their own reports regardless of the detrimental effects for the organization of such a narrow parochialism, and if this failed, they then tried to pass on the responsibility by blaming their colleagues. Yet the ensuing rivalry and conflict often impeded the cooperation which was so essential for controlling their interdependent activities.

In contrast, the Profit Conscious style resulted in similar levels of tension, supervisor satisfaction and cooperation amongst colleagues as prevailed under a Nonaccounting style. And there was little or no fiddling of the reports. But while the style was accepted, even respected, it was certainly seen as very demanding. A Profit Conscious supervisor, according to one of the subordinates . . .

> . . . is always asking about costs — all the time. This is basically the heart of it, I guess, costs. Anytime we get together or whenever he gets you it's costs, costs, costs. "See if we can cut down." "It's going pretty fast, we'd better talk about it." He's a little bit too strict really. I'm used to discipline, but he runs a tight ship. He does not like us to get sloppy; he gets hot under the collar. He tries ta save whatever he can. He just likes to operate that way. He is just that type of person, but to be fair, he applies pressure where it is appropriate.

It was far from being an easy style to satisfy but the pressure was seen as being applied fairly rather than along the rigid lines of a Budget Constrained supervisor. The latter's approach was "just don't do it, rather than asking for explanations".

**Table 1**
A Summary of the Effects of the Three Styles of Evaluation

| | Style of Evaluation | | |
|---|---|---|---|
| | Budget Constrained | Profit Conscious | Nonaccounting |
| Involvement with costs | High | High | Low |
| Job Related Tension | High | Medium | Medium |
| Manipulation of the Accounting Reports | Extensive | Little | Little |
| Relations with the Supervisor | Poor | Good | Good |
| Relations with Colleagues | Poor | Good | Good |

A summary of the effects of the three styles of evaluation is given in Table I. Unfortunately it was not possible to directly investigate the overall impact of the different styles on the effectiveness of operations. The presence of extensive manipulation in some cost centres made the accounting information unreliable for this purpose and given the subject of the research, it was difficult to revert to subjective assessments. The fiddling, short-time horizons, distrust, rivalry and parochial attitudes engendered by the Budget Constrained style are nevertheless vital considerations in all companies and the Profit Conscious style avoided these problems while at the same time ensuring an active involvement with the financial aspects of performance.

The costs associated with unreliable accounting records, short-time horizons and the difficulties of controlling interdependent operations will, however, vary from situation to situation. Therefore the precise balance of costs and benefits associated with the three styles might well be very different for the control of a stable technologically simple situation, for instance, than that of an uncertain and highly complex situation. It is essential that further attempts should be made to isolate the conditions influencing the relative advantages of the three styles[5].

## A Choice of Uses?

It is always interesting to document the extent to which human initiative can be motivated to beat the most sophisticated of accouting systems, but many have done this before. What is of far greater significance than viewing the ingenious responses to the Budget Constrained style in isolation, however, is that the contrast between the Budget Constrained and Profit Conscious styles suggests that the accounting information did not in and of itself pose a threat to the managers of the company when it was used in performance evaluation. Both these styles resulted in some type of concern with financial consequences, however different these concerns might have been, although only the former also resulted in the questionable defensive responses. The threat came from the way in which the information was used.

5 Some recent research has addressed itself to closely related problems. See J. V. Baumler, "Defined Criteria of Performance in Organizational Control", *Administrative Science Quarterly*, XVI (1971), 340—350, and W. Murray, *Management Controls in Action*, Human Science in Industry — Study Number 6 (Dublin: Irish National Productivity Committee Development Division, 1970).

A manager is not faced with a simple choice of using or not using accounting information in evaluation and feedback. Instead it would appear that he can reap many of the benefits of an accounting system by stressing factors which it attempts to measure without this resulting in defensive behaviour. To do so, however, consideration must be given to the precise manner in which the information is used. But what are the various styles of evaluation related to? Certainly it is not sufficient to merely acknowledge their presence. It is also necessary to consider the factors determinig the styles because a systematic understanding of their nature is an essential prerequisite for the intelligent management of change and improvement.

## The Determinants of the Styles

No doubt due to the arithmetical nature of accounting reports, the Budget Constrained style was difficult to resist passing down once it had been established at one level in the organizational hierarchy. If a manager was called upon to meet his budget, he could only ensure doing so by making his subordinates do likewise. All but one of the departmental supervisors who were themselves subject to a Budget Constrained evaluation assessed the performance of a significant proportion of their own subordinates on a similar basis.



Neither of the other two styles were passed down from one level to the next. For instance, while many of the supervisors maintained the concern with the budget reports expressed in their own Profit Conscious evaluation, whether this concern was interpreted in a flexible or rigid manner was dependent upon the second factor determining the styles, namely the manager's own capabilities.

The ways in which the accounting information was used were very clearly associated with much more widespread differences in managerial style. Using the well accepted dimensions of managerial style developed at Ohio State University, namely Initiation of Structure and Consideration[6], it was found that both the Budget Constrained and Profit Conscious supervisors, unlike those using a Nonaccounting style, were seen as trying to create a structured job environment. The Profit Conscious supervisors, however, were also seen as maintaining a warm and friendly atmosphere which was supportive and conducive for mutual trust and respect. In this regard they were similar to the Nonaccounting supervisors but very different from the Budget Constrained ones. Without the moderating effect of the considerate attitudes towards the subordinate managers, the concern for the budget reports was seen as threatening and stressful, and served as a trigger for defensive and often undesirable behaviour.

## Problem Solving Versus Evaluative Approaches

The accounting information was one vehicle through which the managers were able to express their more general approaches to the job. The way in which it was used was often, in fact, a good enough indicator of the managerial philosophy and ethos which pervaded any section of the company. The Profit Conscious style, for instance, appeared to be only one aspect of a problem solving approach to management, as distinct

---

6 E. A. Fleishman, "The Description of Supervisory Behaviour", *Journal of Applied Psychology*, XXXVII (1953), 153—158, and "A Leader Behaviour Description for Industry", in *Leader Behaviour: Its Description and Measurement*, edited by R. M. Stogdill and A. E. Coons, (Columbus, Ohio: Bureau of Business Research, Ohio State University, 1957), pp. 120—133.

from an approach which attempted to impose a false measure of simplicity onto a complex and highly interdependent series of activities. The evaluation of performance was itself of primary importance with the Budget Constrained style, influencing all aspects of the managers' behaviours. Evaluation was not viewed as an ongoing part of the managerial process, interrelated with other important aspects of the job, and itself a problematic activity. Rather it was seen as a distinct and dominant activity, and the primary source of influence and control, overshadowing other vital elements of the process. The budget became not an aid to management but a constraint upon it.

### Implications for the Operation of Accounting Systems

The study emphasizes the vital importance of considering the precise manner in which accounting information is *used* by line managers. It is never a simple matter of merely getting them to use the information in any manner. Budgets, like other management accounting procedures, are certainly quite capable of being important means for assessing achievement and helping to gain involvement and concern with the financial aspects of operations. But they also share with all the other procedures the problems of being partial and imprecise. The real challenge comes in trying to achieve an effective utilization of imperfect but nevertheless valuable procedures. Such a challenge is only just being acknowledged in many companies.

Understandably, it is easy for accountants to be defensive about any suggestion that their procedures are imprecise. Many would say that there are already enough problems in gaining the acceptance of accounting systems without adding any more. My comment is not, however, meant to be critical. While the imprecision and partiality may really reflect inadequate efforts in some situations, in many other cases, they simply reflect the current state of the art. Sophisticated though many procedures have become, they still have a long way to go. There is no need to be defensive if the full implications of the problem are recognized.

But one real danger comes in responding to many of the undesirable responses to accounting systems by immediately striving to improve the procedures. Work should indeed be devoted to this end but it must also be recognized that beyond some point, the search for technical perfection will achieve little in the foreseeable future. Of more importance, however, it can so easily lead to a diversion of effort from the identification and diagnosis of other central problems. In particular, the effectiveness of any management accounting system is not determined by its design alone. The design has to be actualized through the efforts of line managers. It has to be used appropriately.

At the very least accountants have an important educational function to serve. With the increasing complexity of management accounting procedures, it is unrealistic to expect managers at any level in a company to use the information in an appropriate manner without adequate preparation and training. But they need to be informed not only of the objectives and advantages of the accounting system, real though they may be, but also of the inadequacies of the information and the consequences of attaching too much importance to the short-term reports — a far more difficult task.

The different styles of using the information were not, however, simply based on ignorance. They were, as we have seen, associated with much more widespread differences in managerial attitudes and behaviours, and for the Budget Constrained style, with the evaluation style of superiors. Even the most carefully designed educational programme is therefore neither an easy nor the only solution to the problem.

The real need is for a view of accounting systems which sees them as a part of a much more complex process of influencing behaviour in organizations. They represent only one means of control and their final effectiveness is dependent upon how they interact with the other approaches to the problem. The behaviours so inadequately reflected within the dimensions of managerial style are, for instance, also trying to influence behaviour. And the effects of just these two approaches, let alone others, certainly do not occur in isolation. It is all too easy to concentrate on separate mechanisms for influencing behaviour, perhaps even achieving some satisfaction in the individual situations, but by not taking an integrated view of them as a whole, still fail to achieve their full potential.



## Conclusion

The problems described in this paper point to the necessity of moving beyond questions of the design of management accounting systems, which have received the major share of attention to date, to gain a real and systematic understanding of this wider human and social factors which influence their effective use in large organizations. The systems are embedded in rich and varied organizational settings. They are designed to serve organizational purposes. Yet all too little is known about how they are used and function within organizations. However, while it is still an area where we have a lot to learn, the paper has tried to suggest that the potential benefits to be derived from empirical studies of the social context of accounting systems are great.

## — Résumé —

# Accounting in its Organisational Context

*Accounting, Organizations and Society*, Vol. 3, No. 1, pp. 3–13.
© Pergamon Press Ltd. 1978. Printed in Great Britain.

0361-3682/78/0301-0003$02.00/0

# TOWARDS AN ORGANIZATIONAL PERSPECTIVE FOR THE STUDY OF ACCOUNTING AND INFORMATION SYSTEMS

ANTHONY G. HOPWOOD

*Oxford Centre for Management Studies*

Many might think that the introduction to a collected series of papers ought to reassure the reader, showing how each sheds light on the others and on the overall accumulation of knowledge, thereby guaranteeing the unity and coherence of the various contributions. Here, however, I believe that it would be unrealistic to attempt an introduction along such lines at this stage of conceptual development. Certainly the following papers, with one exception, were brought together for two workshops at a conference organized in late 1976[1] and all of them focus on the same topic – the relationships between the organization and its accounting and information systems. But the criteria employed in selecting the papers deliberately set out to provide a plurality of theoretical and empirical perspectives. So, it is important to point out right from the beginning that this diversity is not being concealed but, on the contrary, openly stated. It represents, in my opinion at least, not a pathological condition of inquiry into accounting and information systems, but quite the reverse. The diversity of conceptual and research strategies reflects scholarship in action. For understanding in any area of human inquiry has to be constructed through a process of debate, be it explicit or otherwise, between different conceptual systems, reasonings and analytical and methodological approaches. At the very least this collection of papers aims to illustrate the potentiality of such a debate for accounting (and information system) thought and practice.

## PAST TRADITIONS AND CONCERNS

So many of the early studies of the way in which accounting systems operate, or might operate, in organizations have concentrated on gaining a rather static understanding of the more 53
psychological and social psychological aspects of the accounting process. A great deal of consideration, for instance, has been given to the way in which different accounting methods, configurations of data and modes of presentation influence the decision making behaviour and the decision outcomes of individual managers. And this tradition of research now provides the rationale, if not the intellectual basis, for today's increasingly influential and rigorous concerns with the way in which individuals process, interpret and use accounting information. However, it is now being recognized that this and other related research, has tended to study what are admittedly quite crucial aspects of the accounting process in isolation of the ongoing organizational context that provides the very *raison d'être* of the accounting function.

The relationship between individual responses to accounting information and other aspects of the dynamic functioning of the organizations in which individuals manifest their behaviour has rarely been regarded as explicitly problematic. And, in consequence, a great deal of the research on the human processing of accounting information has, of necessity, had to adopt a rather fragmented view of the organizational decision process and the

[1] The original versions of the papers by Bariff & Galbraith, den Hertog and Hedberg & Jönsson were presented at the Workshop on Designing Management Accounting Systems for Organizations in a Changing Environment organized by Anthony Hopwood at the November 10–12, 1976 meetings of the American Institute of Decision Sciences held in San Francisco. The paper by Waterhouse and Tiessen is a revised version of one presented at the Workshop on The Relevance of Modern Organization Theory for the Design of Accounting Systems organized and chaired by Vijay Sathe at the same meetings. A brief report of the latter workshop also appears in this issue.

role which information plays in this. Accordingly emphasis has had to be placed on understanding particular individual responses to particular presentations of information and little consideration has been given to either the more specific role that might be played by ongoing managerial learning, and the resulting shiftings of meanings and concerns, or the more general findings of those studies that have sought to investigate the way in which managers make decisions in organizations and the role that formal information systems, such as accounting systems, might or might not play in this process (March & Olsen, 1976; Mintzberg, 1973, 1975; Pettigrew, 1972, 1973, 1977). Although the resulting rather simple view of organizational, as distinct from individual, behaviour, with its emphasis on pro-active, goal directed behaviour in response to the discrete
54 presentation of information (Atkin, 1978), might be implicit rather than explicit, it is nevertheless real.

Even in cases where accounting has been studied in its organizational context, emphasis still has been placed on gaining a comparatively static understanding of the more individual, or at the most group, aspects of the process. So, for instance, the response of the individual manager or employee to different degrees of budget tightness has been studied, at one time, in a great deal of detail. However, this has been done without any consideration of the known social as well as individual influences on such responses, the effects of individual and organizational learning and of the possible relationship between different budget standards and formats and, for example, the distribution and management of organizational power and influence or alternative strategies for coping with uncertainty, even though it has been recognized that the managerial response to budgets might be as dependent, if not more so, on the organizational rather than the overt technical meanings attributed to them.

Studies of participation in the budgeting process, to cite another substantive body of the literature in this area, have also tended to focus on the static relationships between participation and such factors as managerial orientations to the budgeting system, extrinsic and intrinsic motivations to perform, levels of individual satisfaction and the propensity or not to engage in such protective strategies as 'padding' the budget and 'fiddling' the accounts rather than on attempting to gain an appreciation of the organizational process through which such results are achieved or of the relationship between budgeting and other organizational control structures and strategies. Indeed not only have accounting researchers not investigated such dynamic aspects of the process themselves but they have only made symbolic or little or no use of those pioneering studies by other social scientists that have focused on such matters (Argyris, 1952; Bower, 1970; Pettigrew, 1973; Roy, 1969; Whyte, 1955; Wildavsky, 1964). Related static and individualistic concerns are also evident in many of those studies that have focused on the way in which accounting information is actually used where factors such as managerial style and the characteristics of the manager-subordinate relationship have tended to dominate research perspectives.

After striving to identify the partiality of so much of the past research that has sought to understand the ways in which accounting systems operate it *must* be stated that an emerging area of research inquiry cannot hope to provide a comprehensive view, let alone appreciation, of all aspects of its problematic domain. Not only do choices have to be made, and the resulting partialities and incompleteness accepted, but it is more than likely that such choices should be made if enquiry is to be thorough and cumulative. Nevertheless, whilst respecting the inevitability of specialisation in such an embryonic area, it is still appropriate to retrospectively identify what choices have been made, particularly at a time when there are clear pressures for alternative approaches and domains of inquiry, and it is even more appropriate to ponder on those factors that might have influenced the direction of progress to date.

## SOME INTELLECTUAL INFLUENCES

Firstly, it should be stated that the static and individualistic orientation of research on the behavioural aspects of accounting reflects much more general influences on the development of social science inquiry. Given that virtually all the pioneering studies in the area, and the vast majority of the subsequent work to date, has emanated from the U.S.A., or at least been strongly influenced by U.S. approaches and concerns, it should not be surprising that the conceptual and methodological approaches that characterise behavioural enquiries undertaken in the accounting area should be related to the dominant concerns in substantive areas of American social science. And this would appear to be the case. For although an adequate understanding of the complex social, political, institutional and philosophical factors that influence the development of social science knowledge remains to be achieved, numerous commentators (Hage, 1978; Karpik, 1978; Kassem, 1976; Lammers, 1976; Wilson, 1977) have pointed to the distinct and often divergent social science traditions and concerns in the U.S.A. and Europe with the U.K. for this purpose at least rather ambiguously having a foot on both sides of the intellectual Atlantic!

Such commentators, and particularly Kassem (1976) in his discussion of the contrasting perspectives brought to bear on the study of organizational behaviour, have tended to contrast the more micro American orientation, with its focus on organizational psychology, with the more macro European approaches focusing on questions of organizational sociology. Such comparisons have emphasized the centrality of U.S. concerns with the problems of the individual contributing to the organization, as reflected, for instance, in the human relations movement and the 'radical psychological individualists' (Whitley, 1974) and the consequent study of the organizational mechanisms for relating individual performance, and rewards, to organizational action and goal achievement, whether such mechanisms be seen as ways of increasing organizational rationality or as social and procedural means for managing commitment, motivation and hence achievement. Such pragmatic and functional U.S. concerns have been contrasted with more European interests in the structural and broader environmental influences on organizational processes and actions, which perhaps inevitably, because of the very breadth of the definition of the problematic, have been more oriented towards providing conceptual, interpretative and possibly critical appreciations of the historical and specific influences on organizational action (Hage, 1978; Sandberg, 1976, pp. 29–32).

Broad generalizations of this type are difficult to make for inevitably there are always exceptions, including, in this case, some rather influential ones. In the U.S., for instance, important sociological inquiries have been undertaken, not least the early studies associated with the Chicago School of Sociology, the work of Merton, Gouldner, Blau, Etzioni, Hage, Perrow and others and the more recent contingency formulations. And in Europe exceptions also abound. But the contrasts remain, in general terms, meaningful ones, and particularly in an accounting context if further consideration is given to the filtering processes inherent in the academic system itself. For in many of the major U.S. Business Schools the more micro psychological and social psychological perspectives have been even more dominant than in the social science community at large.

Perhaps related to the above broader intellectual concerns and perhaps, to some extent, independently building on them is another factor which also must be considered when analysing those factors that have influenced the development of research on how accounting systems operate. And this is the view taken of the broader purpose of the research task.

Research can seek to illuminate and elucidate, to provide, thereby, in the hermeneutic tradition (Taylor, 1971) a basis for interpreting and understanding the role played by accounting systems, and accountants, in organizational and social functioning. It can, however, have more pragmatic concerns, immediate or otherwise. Research can be oriented towards improving the functioning of accounting systems as we know them either by aiming to improve the effectiveness of present systems or by providing the basis for the design of accounting systems, possibly moving accounting a little nearer towards what Simon (1969) has called the 'sciences of the artificial'. And lest we forget it, given the present parsity of research, scholarly inquiry can also seek to provide a critical appreciation of the role played by current modes of accounting, questioning, in the process, the role they might play in furthering the influence of economic interests on organizational action, and possibly, on this basis, moving towards the design of alternative accountings.

Different research orientations, and clearly there are others, make very different demands on knowledge. Both the hermeneutic and critical perspectives require a broad appreciation of the social as well as organizational context of accounting, although clearly the critical approach also requires a more thorough insight into the relationship between accounting and social interests and the organizational knowledge that is so essential for any attempt to construct a design orientated perspective, critical or otherwise. Only when research accepts the present body of accounting knowledge as itself being unproblematic in broad outline, merely seeking to improve the effectiveness of present systems, are fewer demands made on knowledge. For with such a research orientation an appreciation of the organizational basis of accounting might be less crucial than understandings of the role played by the more detailed aspects of design, such as formats and modes of presentation, and of those psychological and social psychological processes which mediate the effects of any given system.

A view that as yet the research horizons of a great deal of accounting research might be (perhaps justifiably) constrained by an acceptance of the present functioning of accounting is supported by others (see Jensen, 1976) who have noted the relationship between research orientations and the demands on knowledge and the
56 direction of scholarly inquiry in accounting. Indeed as other areas of accounting research have moved away from more limited research perspectives, shedding, in the process, some of the traditional constraints of accounting givens, in order to provide a basis for understanding the broader organizational, economic or socio-economic role played by accounting, one can witness the process in operation. This is certainly true for investigations into the role played by accounting information in the capital markets, the economic rationale for information and control system design and the more recent inquiries into the socio-political bases for accounting standard setting.

It is likely, however, that the effects of the broader intellectual traditions discussed above exert their influence on the research community indirectly through more specific and immediate aspects of the institutional context in which research takes place. We have, for example, already referred to the possible exaggeration of the individualistic orientation in the specific context of business schools. Research perspectives that orientate themselves more towards the production of immediately pragmatic and hopefully generalizable understandings, and are less questioning of existing approaches, will also be more acceptable in such contexts, as has already been demonstrated in the case of industrial psychology (Baritz, 1960). Then, as Kassem (1976) points out, the more micro organizational orientation to social research is more amenable to methodologies that are both compatible with the research traditions of academic peers in different disciplines and functional areas, and to the speedy production of research results. Both of these factors are important within the context of the reward structure of the academic community, influencing both individual advancement and what is acceptable to the established channels of communication.

## CHANGING INTERESTS AND CONCERNS

However the approaches of a 'normal science' (Kuhn, 1970) carry within themselves the means for their own advancement and eventual succession. So although one can delineate some reasons why past research has focused on certain concerns to the detriment of others, such appreciations do not necessarily provide any basis for thinking that past concerns will continue into the future. Indeed the opposite is more likely to be the case in scientific endeavour. For whilst the institutional embodiment of research perspectives, in terms of reward structures for instance, can be a constraining influence, historical experience provides one with a basis for expecting that many, if not all, of such constraints will be overcome, sometimes with difficulty and delay, but often with amazing facility and speed.

At present there are indications of at least some pressures for change in the behavioural accounting research community. Some of these pressures eminate from within the present, advancing body of knowledge. Others stem from broader, ongoing changes in social science inquiry. Whilst yet other pressures come from the client community, broadly defined; some from the changing interests of existing clients in corporate management and others from the gradual recognition of the legitimacy of the interests of other social groups in accounting knowledge and research.

Certainly the gradual accumulation of psychological and social-psychological understandings of the way in which accounting systems operate in organizational settings has itself provided a basis for regarding more structural and organizational issues as being problematic. Hofstede's (1967) research on the social psychological dimensions of budgeting, for instance, pointed to the role that technological and organizational factors, as reflected in departmental and organizational cost structures, might play in mediating the effectiveness of budgetary procedures. And the comparative analysis of participation in the budgetary process undertaken by Swieringa & Moncur (1975) provided more direct evidence. Even social psychological studies undertaken in single organizational settings are no less suggestive when the differing results of individual studies are set side by side. So, for example, a comparison of the differences, and commonalities, in the findings of Hopwood (1973) and Otley (1978) points to the role that might be played by organizational level differences, particularly when the diverging results are set aside the comparative hypotheses and findings of Baumler (1971).

The presumption that ever more of such pointers will be discovered as empirical research progresses, and it should be remembered that we have precious little as yet, is supported by the findings of those studies that have been more consciously influenced by an organizational rather than an individualistic or group perspective. The early study of the organization of the accounting function undertaken by Simon and his colleagues (1954), which is so frequently cited by textbook writers for its analysis of the alternative modes of using accounting information but just as frequently ignored for its substantive findings, provided a clear indication of the relevance of such an appreciation. And the subsequent studies reported by Khandwalla (1972), Bruns & Waterhouse (1975), Watson (1975), Watson & Baumler (1975) and Hayes (1977), all much more directly influenced by advancing knowledge in the field of organizational behaviour, demonstrate not only the richness, relevance and potential of the approach but also the way in which the gradual development of behavioural accounting research is itself moving towards more explicitly recognizing the importance of understanding organizational questions.

Such an explicit recognition of developments in organizational behaviour research is itself of significance and no doubt we can expect many more explorations of this type. Certainly the emerging pattern of submissions to this and other journals, successful and otherwise, would support such a conclusion. Equally relevant, if not more so, is the growing interest that organizational researchers themselves are taking in questions related to the design and functioning of accounting and information systems. Whilst this is not a new phenomenon, as evidenced by the pioneering and influential studies undertaken by Agyris (1952) and Simon (1954) and the attention given to such issues by Roy (1969), Dalton (1959), Whyte (1955), Blau (1966) and Wildavsky (1964), amongst many others, there is some basis for believing that the critical role played by accounting and information systems in organizations is now being more generally recognized and studied by scholars of organizational behaviour (Pfeffer, 1977; Pettigrew, 1973; Pondy, 1970; Heydebrand, 1977; Connolly, 1977; etc.). If this is indeed the case then it can only add to our understanding of the area, most likely legitimising and encouraging, in the process, the adoption of similar research perspectives and methodologies by accounting scholars.

The pressures for change do not only eminate from within the research community however. For in business and public organizations there is, I think, and here one can only talk in a much more tentative way, drawing on one's own experiences
and impressions, a growing appreciation of the 57
need for a more organizational understanding. In part this reflects, inevitably perhaps, a greater awareness of the limitations of present pragmatic perspectives and approaches (Earl, 1978). More significantly, perhaps, it reflects an increasing recognition of the need for accounting and information system innovation and the role that new knowledge might play in this process.

Until recently the development of accounting and information systems was a very pragmatic affair, prodded, no doubt, by the recognition of the inadequacies of prevailing approaches and the possible relevance of known alternatives. Although change was often real and major (Chandler, 1962; 1977), one can only presume that it was guided by practical wisdom, and on occasions ignorance, and shaped by the rules of experience and the lessons of trial and error. Certainly there is little or no evidence of any systematic research being undertaken, least of all in an academic community.

The results of such processes constitute the substantive bulk of management accounting as we now know it (Gardner, 1954; Parker, 1969; Pollard, 1965). Critical as some researchers might be of it, and at least some of such criticism could be tempered by a greater appreciation of some of the radically innovative and seemingly modern marginal and oft forgotten developments made by our entrepreneurial predecessors, it nevertheless provides the basis on which today's more technical research on topics such as divisional performance measurement, costing methods and capital investment appraisal is conducted.

The increasing pace of change and the growing size and complexity of organizations have created a need for more rapid and more sophisticated accounting and information system developments however. And such increases in organizational complexity, in particular, have increased the relevance of and need for a more explicit understanding of the relationship between information (and accounting) systems and organizational design (Galbraith, 1973). Increasingly, therefore, business and public organizations have turned to outside consultants and researchers for help, sometimes also creating their own specialist developmental teams in the area. The growing sophistication of information system technology provides many examples of such a response, as do the increasing difficulties of costing and controlling both major, long term projects and of
58 deciding upon the production and commercial policies for products with increasingly short life cycles. Similarly, and perhaps more significantly, the complexities of designing the information and control systems, including accounting systems, for the massive modern aerospace and defence organizations have engaged the attention of researchers in both universities and specialized institutes such as the RAND Corporation (Chandler & Sayles, 1971). For in this area in particular the need for the joint design of organizational and information structures and processes was real and recognized.

That few accounting researchers *per se* might have been involved in such innovations does not detract from either their pragmatic or intellectual significance for the development of accounting and information system knowledge, although it might point to the isolation of main stream accounting researchers from matters of major organizational concern. But given that the design and functioning of accounting systems, like other information and control systems, are interrelated with wider aspects of organizational design, and that organizational designs have never been and are unlikely to be static, as witnessed, for example, by the growing relevance today of matrix (Knight, 1977), network and loosely coupled (Weick, 1976) organizations, past isolation by itself is unlikely to remove the continued pressures for new understandings of the organizational basis for accounting system design.

Broader social pressures are also likely to add to such pressures. For as recent research has illustrated (Braverman, 1974; Hales, 1974; Heydebrand, 1977; Marglin, 1974; Whitley, 1974), management practices and structures in organizations, including prevalent accounting and information systems (Mumford & Sackman, 1975), are reflections of wider social structures, institutions and ideologies. Although such aspects of our societies certainly do not change rapidly, there is already evidence of interest in the bases, and at times the reality, of alternative approaches as new social groups gain both power and an understanding of the relevance of managerial insights (Sandberg, 1976). For instance, in Europe research is already under way on the design of either more participative forms of information, accounting and control systems (Magnusson, 1974; Stymme, 1977) or even systems that explicitly aim to further the interests of labour rather than capital (Briefs, 1975; Nygaard & Bergo, 1975). And on both the sides of the Atlantic consideration is being given to the design of information and accounting systems that facilitate the management and assessment of new forms of work organization (Hopwood, forthcoming; Mirvis & Macy, 1976).

## EMERGING POTENTIAL AND PROBLEMS

The pressures for a greater organizationa appreciation of the way in which accountin systems operate are undoubtedly diverse bu nonetheless real. Ranging from those that originate within the context of normal scientific develop ment, through those arising out of the changin needs of existing salient interest groups, to thos that stem from more questioning or even critica perspectives, all are slowly resulting in researc endeavours and new understandings. At this stage however, the diversity of approaches and concern and the relative sparcity of findings, makes an overall assessment a precarious task, and such a assessment certainly is not attempted within th confines of this introductory essay. Already however, the developments do point to a emerging potential and, perhaps of equal impo tance, to some of the problems that might have t be met on the routes ahead.

The first and most obvious advantage is that a organizational perspective provides a way building on research developments that are alread in progress. As we have discussed, some schola have laid a basis for exploring both t organizational processes through which accounti and other information systems effect, or not, the consciousness and actions of members of organizations and those organizational, and even wider environmental, factors that influence, shape and constrain the form that accounting and information systems take and the organizational roles that they perform. The papers by Waterhouse & Tiessen, and Wildavsky, and the report by Sathe, contained in the present issue all highlight such developments and their potential. Furthermore, implicit in such ongoing work, and possibly more explicitly in future concerns, might also be a basis for better understanding some of the differences and contrasts that are now evident when the findings of separate psychologically and social psychologically oriented studies are compared, some examples of which have been mentioned above.

Such developments are important for a number of reasons, not least of which is the potential for achieving an understanding of the accounting function that complements the complexities of accounting in action. Rather than being satisfied with an understanding of accounting that focuses on the generalizations that can be made across organizations, organizational researchers might be able to move towards an understanding that is able to cope with the heterogeneous and changing circumstances that shape the form, significance and effects of accounting in specific organizations and sections of organizations. And, in trying to articulate and substantiate such an understanding, it is also likely that consideration will have to be given to views of the accounting and information function that move beyond today's almost exclusive characterisation in terms of the particular combination of techniques, procedures and technologies in use. For whilst these certainly constitute an important part of the whole, and that part which is most obviously visible, the partiality of such a characterisation will be realised when consideration has to be given to those organizational structures and processes through which the technical aspects of accounting achieve their effect. As Simon and his colleagues sought to illustrate, the organization of the accounting function itself and those organizational linkages through which it relates to the rest of the organization are as essential as the techniques and procedures, and often more problematic in managerial terms. Yet our understanding of the organizational form and locus of the accounting function is minimal and both it and the derivation of a more heterogeneous basis for diagnosing and analysing the functioning of accounting systems can only be advanced if accounting research starts to draw on the perspectives and findings of organizational sociologists and theorists.

Such a closer relationship with wider developments in the social sciences, the potential of which already has been illustrated in other areas of accounting research, would enable the consideration of important topics known to be of significance but so far not systematically investigated.

At present the behavioural understandings so far gained by accounting researchers stand in rather stark contrast with the findings of those other social scientists who have strived to probe into their relationship to the dynamics of the
organizational decision making process (Bonini, 59
1963; Bower, 1970; Crecine, 1971; Pettigrew, 1973; Whyte, 1955; Wildavsky, 1964). The emerging understandings of, for instance, feedback processes (Annett, 1969; Rosenthal & Weiss, 1966), the retrospective interpretations and rationalizations that accompany and shape prospective decision making (March & Olsen, 1976; Weick, 1969), the role of bargaining and negotiation in resource allocation (Bower, 1970; Pondy, 1970; Wildavsky, 1964), the way in which commitments develop and influence both the production and use of information (Bower, 1970; Staw & Ross, 1978) and the relationship between the design of information and accounting systems and the ways in which those with organizational power attempt to manage the attribution of meaning and significance in an organizational context (Jönsson & Lundin, 1977; March & Olsen, 1976; Pettigrew, 1977) are providing interesting and important leads to the understanding of accounting in action. And, as Bariff and Galbraith suggest in this issue, the reemergence of social science inquiry into power and conflict in organizations (Burns & Buckley, 1976; Pfeffer, 1977; Zald, 1970) has obvious relevance for the study of a subject that has overtly recognized its role in organizational control, influence and restrain.

One important aspect of the emerging organizational appreciation, and one that also relates to more immediate pragmatic concerns, is the consequent possibility it offers for moving towards a more explicit design orientation for accounting. For although accounting systems are organizational artifacts (Simon, 1969), consciously designed and adapted, the study of them has tended to focus on generalizable specifics more than either the nature of the design process, and the way in which design choices are constrained, or the manner in which systems are adapted to organizational circumstances. The foundations for a theory of accounting system design, if they do exist, currently remain within the experiential understandings of accounting practitioners and consultants.

But many of the pragmatic pressures for new accounting and information system knowledge require a more explicit appreciation of the factors that influence and constrain system design (Bjørn-Andersen & Hedberg, 1977). In days of moderate change, implicit understandings may suffice. However a more systematic and articulated
60 understanding becomes vital when organizational structures change with increasing regularity, when, as discussed by both den Hertog & Hedberg and Jönsson in the present issue, there is a growing realisation of the constraining influence of past designs and when ever more social interests attempt to influence design options and the design process.

Real though the potential of an organizational appreciation of the accounting function may be however, its achievement will not be unproblematic. For progress will be dependent not only on accounting researchers mastering new methodologies and theoretical perspectives, some, at least, of which will initially be at variance with those which are embodied and valued within the institutions in which such research takes place, but also on the research keeping pace with the evolving nature of organizational thought and research. It is tempting in all interdisciplinary research, to focus on those insights from the neighbouring disciplines that are thought to be firmly established rather than those that are still in the process of being established, or rejected. But however admirable such a tendency might be in theory, in the context of normal let alone revolutionary scientific progress (Kuhn, 1970) the resulting 'citation lag' will not only unnecessarily constrain the development of research but also do little to discourage it from focusing on findings and perspectives that were subsequently questioned, if not discredited. So, for instance, accounting research is starting to investigate the relevance of contingency theories at the very time when their empirical basis and present theoretical formulation is being questioned (Pennings & Tripathi, 1978; Aldrich & Mindlin, 1978; Weick, 1977).

A further difficulty facing organizational research in accounting relates to its very potential for changing our perceptions of the accounting function. Findings related to the relationship between accounting and the management of power and conflict in organizations will be challenging. Evidence of the contingent nature of the accounting system design process will be disturbing to technical universalists. And research oriented towards the specification of accountings that service new values will be regarded as threatening by existing interest groups.

However, even in having to cope with the latter problem as well as the problems stemming from the substantive nature of the research itself, accounting research will be dealing with difficulties that are endemic to most scientific progress.

## CONCLUSION

Accounting and information systems play a vital role in organizational functioning. They have, as a result, responded, and still are responding to changing organizational and environmental circumstances and there is no reason whatsoever for thinking that the future will be different. New knowledge and insights are constantly needed and although research might not have played a major role in the past, it does have at least the potential to influence the future.

Research which is oriented towards understanding the organizational basis for the design and operation of accounting and information systems is particularly important in this respect. For despite the pioneering work that has been done, particularly on information systems *per se* where investigations may have advanced more readily in the absence of either such a well articulated set of techniques and procedures or their professional embodiment, we still have only the barest understanding of the factors which shape either the design of information systems or the processes through which they, in turn, influence the consciousness and actions of organizational participants. The challenge to understand accounting in action remains, in other words, a real one, although, as we have discussed, the pressures for change are equally evident.

Perhaps, outside of such a context, the differences between the articles in this issue of *Accounting, Organizations and Society* may appear more evident than any similarities. Certainly very different intellectual, social and pragmatic bases are evident. But in what might be very different ways they jointly illustrate how research on how accounting and information systems are designed and function is now responding to the challenge of organizational understandings and the pressures and circumstances of wider environmental change.

## BIBLIOGRAPHY

Aldrich, H. & Mindlin, S., Uncertainty and Dependence: Two Perspectives on Environment, in Karpik, L., ed., *Organization and Environment Theory, Issues and Reality* (Sage, 1978).

Annett, J., *Feedback and Human Behaviour* (Penguin, 1969).

Argyris, C., *The Impact of Budgets on People* (School of Business and Public Administration, Cornell University, 1952).

Atkin, R. S., Review of *Information and Control in Organizations, Administrative Science Quarterly* (March, 1978), pp. 168–171.

Baritz, L., *The Servants of Power: A History of the Use of Social Science in American Industry* (Wesleyan University Press, 1960).

Baumler, J. V., Defined Criteria of Performance in Organizational Control, *Administrative Science* 61
*Quarterly* (September, 1971), pp. 340–350.

Bjørn-Andersen, N., and Hedberg, B. L. T. Designing Information Systems in an Organizational Perspective, in Nystrom, P. C. & Starbuck, W. H., *Prescriptive Models in Organizations* (North-Holland, 1977), pp. 125–142.

Blau, P. M., *The Dynamics of Bureaucracy: A Study of Interpersonal Relations in Two Government Agencies* (Chicago University Press, 1966).

Bonini, C. P., *Simulation of Information and Decision Systems in the Firm* (Prentice-Hall, 1963).

Bower, J. L., *Managing the Resource Allocation Process* (Division of Research, Graduate School of Business Administration, Harvard University, 1970).

Braverman, H., *Labor and Monopoly Capital* (Monthly Review Press, 1974).

Briefs, U., The Role of Information Processing Systems in Employee Participation in Managerial Decision-Making, in Mumford, E. & Sackman, H., *Human Choice and Computers* (North-Holland, 1975).

Bruns, W. H. & Waterhouse, J. H., Budgetary Control and Organization Structure, *Journal of Accounting Research* (Autumn 1975), pp. 177–203.

Chandler, A. D., *Strategy and Structure* (MIT Press, 1962).

Chandler, A. D., *The Visible Hand: The Managerial Revolution in American Business* (Harvard University Press, 1977).

Chandler, M. R. & Sayles, L. R., *Managing Large Systems* (Harper & Row, 1971).

Connolly, T., Information Processing and Decision Making in Organizations, in Staw, B. M. and Salancik, G. R., eds., *New Directions in Organizational Behaviour* (St. Clair Press, 1977).

Crecine, J. P., Defense Budgeting: Organizational Adaptation to Environmental Constraints, in Byrne, R. F. *et al., Studied in Budgeting* (North-Holland, 1971), pp. 210–261.

Dalton, M., *Men who Manage* (Wiley, 1959).

Earl, M. J., Prototype Systems for Accounting Information and Control, *Accounting, Organizations and Society*, Vol. 3, No. 2 (1978).

Galbraith, J., *Designing Complex Organizations* (Addison-Wesley, 1973).

Gardner, S. P., *Evolution of Cost Accounting to 1925* (University of Alabama Press, 1954).

Hales, M., Management Science and the 'Second Industrial Revolution', *Radical Science Journal* (January, 1974), pp. 5–28.

Hage, J., Toward a Synthesis of the Dialectic Between Historical-Specific and Sociological-General Models of the Environment, in Karpik, L., ed., *Organization and Environment: Theory, Issues and Reality* (Sage, 1978).

Hayes, D. C., The Contingency Theory of Managerial Accounting, *The Accounting Review* (January, 1977), pp. 22–39.

Heydebrand, W., Organizational Contradictions in Public Bureaucracies, in Benson, J. K., ed., *Organizational Analysis: Critique and Innovation* (Sage, 1977).

Hofstede, G. H., *The Game of Budget Control* (Van Gorcum, 1967).

Hopwood, A. G., *An Accounting System and Managerial Behaviour* (Saxon House, 1973).

Hopwood, A. G., *Towards Assessing the Economic Costs and Benefits of New Forms of Work Organization* (ILO, forthcoming).

Jensen, M., Reflections on the State of Accounting Research and the Regulation of Accounting. Paper presented at the Stanford University Lectures in Accounting, May 1976.

Jönsson, S. A. & Lundin, R. A., Myths and Wishful Thinking as Management Tools, in Nystrom, P. C. & Starbuck, W. H., *Prescriptive Models of Organizations* (North-Holland, 1977).

Karpik, L., *Organization and Environment: Theory, Issues and Reality* (Sage, 1978).

Kassem, M. S., European versus American Organization Theories, in Hofstede, G. H. & Kassem, M. S., *European Contributions to Organization Theory* (Van Gorcum, 1976).

Khandwalla, P. N., The Effects of Different Types of Competition on the Use of Management Controls, *Journal of Accounting Research* (Autumn, 1972), pp. 275-285.

Knight, K., ed., *Matrix Management* (Gower Press, 1977).

Kuhn, T. S., *The Structure of Scientific Revolutions* (2nd edition: University of Chicago Press, 1970).

Lammers, C. J., Towards the Internationalization of the Organization Sciences, in Hofstede, G. H. & Kassem, M. S., *European Contributions to Organization Theory* (Van Gorcum, 1976).

Magnusson, A., Participation and the Company's Information and Decision Systems, Working Paper 6022, Economic Research Institute, Stockholm School of Economics, 1974.

March, J. G., and Olsen, J. P., *Ambiguity and Choice in Organizations* (Universitetforlaget, 1976).

Marglin, S. A., What Do Bosses Do? The Origins and Functions of Hierarchy in Capitalist Production, *Review of Radical Political Economics* (Summer, 1974), pp. 33-60.

Mintzberg, H., *The Nature of Managerial Work* (Harper & Row, 1973).

Mintzberg, H., *Impediments to the Use of Management Information* (N.A.A., 1975).

Mirvis, P. H. & Macy, B. A., Accounting for the Cost and Benefits of Human Resource Development Programs *Accounting, Organizations and Society*, Vol. 1, No. 2/3, (1976), pp. 179-194.

62 Mumford, E. & Sackman, H., *Human Choice and Computers* (North-Holland, 1975).

Nygaard, K. & Bergo, O. T., The Trade Unions – New Users of Research, *Personnel Review* (1975), pp. 5-10.

Otley, D. T., Budget Use and Managerial Performance, *Journal of Accounting Research* (forthcoming, 1978).

Parker, R. H., *Management Accounting: An Historical Perspective* (Macmillan, 1969).

Pennings, J. M. & Tripathi, R. C., The Organization-Environment Relationship: Dimensional Versus Typological Viewpoints, in Karpik, L., *Organization and Environment: Theory, Issues and Reality* (Sage, 1978).

Pettigrew, A. M., Information as a Power Resource, *Sociology* (1972), pp. 187-204.

Pettigrew, A. M., *The Politics of Organizational Decision Making* (Tavistock, 1973).

Pettigrew, A. M., The Creation of Organizational Cultures. Working Paper. European Institute for Advanced Studies in Management, Brussels, 1977.

Pfeffer, J., Power and Resource Allocation in Organizations, in Staw, B. M. & Salancik, G. R., *New Directions in Organizational Behaviour* (St. Clair Press, 1977).

Pfeffer, J. & Salancik, G. R., Organizational Decision Making as a Political Process: The Case of a University Budget, *Administrative Science Quarterly* (1976), pp. 227-245.

Pollard, S., *The Genesis of Modern Management* (Edward Arnold, 1965).

Pondy, L. R., Toward a Theory of Internal Resource-Allocation, in Zald, M., ed., *Power in Organizations* (Vanderbilt University Press, 1970).

Rosenthal, R. A. & Weiss, R. S., Problems of Organizational Feedback Processes, in Bauer, R. A., *Social Indicators* (MIT Press, 1966).

Roy, D., Making-Out: A Counter-System of Workers' Control of Work Situation and Relationships, in Burns, T., ed., *Industrial Man* (Penguin, 1969).

Sandberg, A., *The Limits to Democratic Planning* (LiberForlag, 1976).

Simon, H. A., *The Sciences of the Artificial* (MIT Press, 1969).

Simon, H. A., Guetzkow, H., Kozmetsky, G. & Tyndall, G., *Centralization Versus Decentralization in Organizing the Controller's Department* (Controllership Foundation, 1954).

Staw, B. M., and Ross, J., Commitment to a Policy Decision: A Multi-Theoretical Perspective, *Administrative Science Quarterly* (March, 1978), pp. 40-64.

Stymme, B., To Organize For Participation, Working Paper, Stockholm School of Economics, 1977.

Swieringa, R., and Moncur, R. H., *Some Effects of Participative Budgeting on Managerial Behaviour* (NAA, 1975).

Taylor, C., Interpretation and the Science of Man, *Review of Metaphysics* (1971), pp. 1-45.

Watson, D. J. H., The Structure of Project Teams Facing a Differentiated Environment: An Exploratory Study in Public Accounting Firms, *The Accounting Review* (April, 1975), pp. 259-273.

Watson, D. J. H. & Baumler, J. U., Transfer Pricing: A Behavioural Context, *The Accounting Review* (July 1975), pp. 466-474.

Weick, K. E., *The Social Psychology of Organizing* (Addison-Wesley, 1969).

Weick, K. E., Educational Organizations as Loosely Coupled Systems, *Administrative Science Quarterly* (March, 1976), pp. 1-19.

Weick, K. E., Enactment Processes in Organizations, in Staw, B. M. & Salancik, G. R., *New Directions in Organizational Behaviour* (St. Clair Press, 1977).
Whitley, R. D., Management Research: The Study and Improvement of Forms of Cooperation in changing Socio-Economic Structures, in Roberts, N., ed., *Information Sources in the Social Sciences* (Butterworth, 1974).
Whyte, W. F., *Money and Motivation* (Harper & Row, 1955).
Wildavsky, A., *The Politics of the Budgetary Process* (Little, Brown, 1964).
Wilson, H. T., *The American Ideology: Science, Technology and Organization as Modes of Rationality in Advanced Industrial Societies* (Routledge & Kegan Paul, 1977).
Zald, M., ed., *Power in Organizations* (Vanderbilt University Press, 1970).

# 11

# The Organisational and Behavioural Aspects of Budgeting and Control

ANTHONY G HOPWOOD

*Professor of Accounting and Financial Reporting,*
*London Graduate School of Business Studies* 65

## Introduction

In accounting texts, budgeting and other related procedures of financial control are portrayed as technical phenomena. Emphasis is placed on the rules and calculative procedures by which budgets are formulated and thereafter used to provide means for evaluating the adequacy of actual performance. Consideration is given to the identification of key budgetary constraints, to the alternative mechanisms for assembling and analysing the mass of expectations for the budgetary period, and to the technical possibilities for analysing the variances between budgeted and actual performance. Although such statements of the technical apparatus of budgeting and financial control invariably commence with appeals to the underlying organisational processes and roles which they serve, the detailed discussion of the technical means for their attainment invariably results in a distancing of the technical from the organisational – a distancing which once achieved is often difficult to reverse.

Unfortunately such an emphasis on the technical rather than the organisational has resulted in an appreciation of budgeting which is detached from the organisational setting in which it operates and the ways in which it is implicated in

other organisational processes. Emphasis has been placed on the calculative procedures which give rise to 'the budget' and its subsequent comparison with actual performance, but not on the organisational processes through which budgetary pressures and demands emanate, and as a result of which budgeting achieves its organisational significance. Hardly any consideration has been given in traditional accounting sources to either the competing political processes within organisations which provide the bases for deliberations about an uncertain future, or those processes for organisational evaluation and review which provide the context within which budgetary comparisons are considered and used. Furthermore, in emphasising the calculative and procedural aspects of budgeting, attention has not been given to the ways in which budgeting
66 and other instruments of financial control themselves have shaped the structure and operation of the modern organisation. However, the organisational map of cost centres, profit centres, divisions and programme units, which underlies the structure of budgeting today, bears witness to the roles which mechanisms for financial planning and control have played in reconstituting and, indeed, creating what we now know as the modern organisation. In part, at least, the organisation is now defined in terms of the mechanisms which were introduced to further its control. Moreover, by facilitating the separation of planning and control from action, budgets and other mechanisms for financial control have played a key role in enabling the centralised managerial control of ever larger groupings of activities.

An organisational view of budgeting also highlights the social as well as economic and technical nature of budgetary outcomes, a fact that is well known to practitioners of the craft. 'The budget' is a reflection of the underlying political structure of the organisation, as well as economic constraints and opportunities and the technical procedures out of which it arose. It has a social as well as an economic significance, reflecting the outcomes of debates over organisational power and influence, the social location of uncertainties and constraints within the organisation, and the allocation of organisational resources.

Therefore, in the realm of accounting practice as distinct from that of the accounting textbook, it is difficult, if not impossible, to disentangle the organisational and the technical aspects of budgeting. Both shape each other. The technical components are designed to activate organisational processes, and can themselves help to shape participants' perceptions of the organisational domain. And budgeting, in turn, achieves its significance through those organisational processes which the techniques engender.

To further our understanding of the organisational nature of budgeting, we will consider the many and often conflicting purposes which it serves, the processes which give rise to the practice of budgeting, and the different ways in which budgetary information can be used. We conclude with some speculations on the possible relationships between financial practice and organisational performance.



### Budgeting as a Multi-purpose Activity

Budgeting can serve a variety of roles and purposes, often simultaneously. Even several purposes can enter into the justification and implementation of a budgetary control system, as different managerial groups, or even individuals, emphasise different roles which it can serve. Those in the finance department, for instance, can have interests and needs in mind very different from those in production and marketing, let alone general management; and yet all might agree on the need for an extension of budgetary practice. And the purposes to which budgeting is put also can be very different from those which entered into its original justification. For, once installed, budgetary systems have some measure of autonomy. As the technical apparatus becomes intertwined with the activities of a wider array of organisational participants, it can be used to further a diverse and often conflicting array of organisational and personal ends.

Such a view of budgeting in action suggests that it would be a difficult and rather futile activity to list, in isolation from the organisational context in which they operate, the purposes which budgets and other mechanisms for financial control have come to serve. They are so diverse, and often so idiosyncratic, that very little of general value would be gained from the exercise. Instead, we shall try to understand some of the ways in which the practice of budgeting and financial control can arise out of the interplay of organisational processes, paying particular attention to how they are implicated in the processes of decision making.

### *Different Approaches to Organisational Decision Making*

Decision making in organisations takes place in the context of uncertainty or disagreement over both the objectives and consequences of action. Different participant groups, both within and outside the organisation, have different views of both the desirable and the achievable. Whilst those with financial inclinations, for example, might seek to establish the
68 primacy of economic ends, those interested in the management of the organisation's technical resources might articulate concerns with either more immediate physical indicators of performance, or the organisation's longer-term innovative potential. These, in turn, might well be different from the interests emphasised by marketing and personnel management groups. For the organisation is rarely an assembly of the agreed. Debate and deliberation are almost inevitable features of organisational life. With different interests and perspectives coming together to constitute the organised endeavour, objectives, as such, are rarely pre-given, but rather emerge out of the interplay of organisational pressures, constraints and opportunities. At times there might be a temporary resolution with many, if not all, agreed on the primacy of particular overall concerns. Equally, there might be agreement over the aims of either particular organisational actions or the activities of particular organisational units. At other times, however, discord and debate might well be the only way of characterising the organisational mission.

Views over the consequences of particular organisational actions are subject to no less variation. Where there is considerable investment in past experience and where the environment for action is stable and known, relative certainty may prevail. Organisational participants may then be able to presume that particular sequences of actions are likely to result in certain patterns of consequences. On other occasions, however, the

| | | Uncertainty over the objectives for action | |
|---|---|---|---|
| | | Relative certainty | Relative uncertainty |
| Uncertainty over the consequences of action | Relative certainty | COMPUTATION | BARGAINING |
| | Relative uncertainty | JUDGEMENT | INSPIRATION |

Figure 11.1 *Uncertainty and Decision Making Processes*

consequences of action may be far from predictable. With either limited experience or a volatile and poorly understood environment, they are likely to be subject to disagreement and debate. A whole range of possible consequences will then have to be considered at some stage in the decision making 69
process.

What are the consequences of acknowledging such a variety of uncertainties in decision making? If in any particular instance the objectives for action are clear and undisputed, and if the consequences of action can also be presumed to be known, decision making can then proceed in a computational manner, as illustrated in figure 11.1.[1] In such circumstances it is possible to compute whether the consequences of the action or set of actions being considered will, or will not, satisfy the objectives that have been unambiguously articulated beforehand. As the consequences of action become more uncertain, however, the potential for computation diminishes.

1. The discussion of organisational decision making is based on J.D. Thompson and A. Tuden, Strategies, structures and processes of organisational decision, in J.D. Thompson *et al.* (eds), *Comparative Studies in Administration*, University of Pittsburgh Press 1959. See also J.D. Thompson, *Organisations in Action*, McGraw-Hill 1967. Further discussions of the subsequent extension of this decision making framework to take account of the organisational roles of information and control systems are given in M.J. Earl and A.G. Hopwood, From management information to information management (a paper presented at the IFIP TC8 WG 8.2 Working Conference on the Information Systems Environment, Bonn 1979, to be published in *Organisational Dynamics*) and A.G. Hopwood, Information systems and organisational reality, Occasional Paper No. 5, Thames Valley Regional Management Centre 1980

Decisions then have to be made in a judgmental manner, with organisational participants subjectively appraising the array of possible consequences in the light of the agreed objective or objectives. Just as the introduction of uncertainty into the specification of the consequences of action results in a different approach to decision making, so does the acknowledgement of debate or uncertainty over the objectives themselves. If the consequences of action are presumed to be known, disagreement or uncertainty over objectives results in a political, rather than a computational, rationale for action, as organisational participants seek to further their own particular objectives. A range of interests in action are articulated in such circumstances and decision making, as a result, tends to be characterised by bargaining and compromise. And when
70 even the consequences of action are in dispute, decision processes can be complex indeed, being rather positively characterised in figure 11.1 as of an inspirational nature! With so little known beforehand, rationales for action can emerge in the course of the decision making process itself.

Mechanisms for financial planning and control, like other information and control systems, invariably have been justified in terms of the contribution which they make to organisational decision making. In providing such rationales, the process of decision making has only rarely been considered in social terms, however. Emphasis has repeatedly been placed on the economic and the technical, rather than on the social and the political. If, in contrast, we do try to recognise, not only such a social context, but also the variety of approaches to decision making that can stem from the uncertainties that might be inherent in both the consequences of action and the objectives for action, what insights can we gain into the roles which such mechanisms serve? How, in other words, might interests in budgets and other financial procedures emerge out of organisational decision processes? And what different roles might they serve in the contexts of the computational, the judgmental, the political and the inspirational? To such questions let us now turn.

*Accounting and Computational Practice*

Given low uncertainty over both the consequences and the

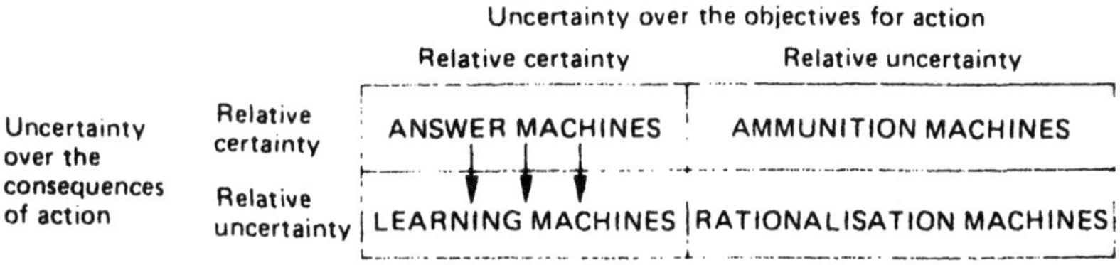


**Figure 11.2** *Uncertainty, Decision Making and the Role of Information and Control Systems*

objectives of organisational action, we approach the management scientist's definition of certainty where algorithms, formulae and rules can be derived to solve problems by computation. Alternatively, this situation may represent what Herbert Simon[2] has called structured decision making, 71
where the intelligence, design and choice phases are all specifiable and programmable. And in case you have not recognised it, this is also the organisational world presumed by many introductory management accounting textbooks!

In all cases a wide variety of management practices, including the mechanisms of financial planning and control, can serve as what in figure 11.2 are termed 'answer machine' aids to decision making. The techniques of budgeting and investment appraisal, for instance, can further the evaluation of proposed actions in the light of agreed financial objectives. By providing a way of comparing the achievable and the desirable, in a world of relative certainty, the computations introduce a powerful element of structure into the decision making process. Similarly, the practice of budgeting can facilitate the co-ordination and integration of organisational activities by computational means. Production and marketing operations can be synthesised, inventory policies evaluated and amended in the light of envisaged organisational circumstances, and the consequences for particular organisational resources, such as cash, calculated and evaluated.

Moreover, some, at least, of the certainties which enable the use of computational approaches can be created by managerial action, rather than having to be implicit within the organisational task. By a judicious management of inventory, for

2. H.A. Simon, *The New Science of Management Decision*, Harper and Row 1960.

instance, production operations can sometimes be temporarily buffered from the uncertainties inherent in the market place. The impact of other uncertainties can be isolated by the availability of surplus capacity and resources. And internal organisational boundaries can be drawn so that the more certain spheres of organisational endeavour can be managed in partial isolation from their more uncertain context. In ways such as these, the organisational and the technical can together create a particular decision making environment. With organisational strategies creating pockets of activities with higher predictability and surer ends, computational approaches to decision making can function and flourish in otherwise alien terrains.

72

### *Accounting and Organisational Learning*

In the context of judgmental decision making, such 'answer machine' approaches are no longer of such direct value. Acknowledging the uncertainties that are inherent in action requires that they be confronted rather than managed.

Of course, many of the procedures created to serve 'answer machine' roles are still used in judgmental contexts. Often, however, this is in spite of, rather than because of, the underlying uncertainties over the consequences of organisational action! So in circumstances which cry out for information to stimulate managerial learning and the exercise of judgement, we find routine financial evaluation and control systems which often assume the very certainties which cannot be found. Indeed, as is illustrated by the arrows in figure 11.2, such procedures have been subjected to enormous increases in technical sophistication as various experts have sought to extend the boundaries of computational practice. The articulation of forms of risk and probabilistic analysis in a budgetary context bears witness to such tendencies.

Often, however, computational procedures are used in a judgmental context, but in very different ways. Rather than directly facilitating the search for answers, they are used to explore problems and to probe into assumptions and the range of possible implications. Serving to stimulate the human mind, they can be used to analyse the analysable before organisational participants finally resort to judgement. In figure 11.2 such approaches are referred to as 'learning machines', in order to emphasise the potential for a more active interplay between the technical and the cognitive.

Sensitivity analyses involving the multiple use of computational procedures are of this type, as is the use of simulation models in budgeting and planning. In both cases the procedures can help organisational participants to appreciate the nature of the decision environment in which they are working. And the iterations to and from departments and organisational levels which characterise the practice of budgeting point to a similar interrelationship between the computational and the judgmental. Indeed, one of the most frequently quoted purposes of budgeting, that of encouraging an active concern with the future, focuses on the learning rather than the mere 73
calculative potential of the process.[3] When seen in this way, the procedures of budgeting can serve to emphasise the need to investigate, albeit if thereafter to constrain, the financial and wider organisational implications of possible future activities. By iteration and deliberation, the discipline and structure which are implicit in the budgetary process can stimulate organisational participants to reflect on at least some of the implications of what they are proposing; to test out their assumptions and estimates, and ascertain whether the necessary resources are likely to be available to the organisation as a whole and its constituent parts.

### *Accounting and Political Processes*

Whilst the roles served by the procedures of financial planning and control in computational and judgmental decision situations have been explicitly discussed in the official literature of accounting, those which are served when the objectives of action are themselves subject to debate have not. In their writings, at least, accountants have tended to assume that the objectives of organised endeavour are given. By now you are all familiar with those seemingly unproblematic

3. A stimulating discussion of the role of planning in organisational and social learning is given in D. Michael, *On Learning to Plan and Planning to Learn*, Jossey-Bass 1973.

assertions that the objectives of a firm are '. . . to maximise profits', '. . . to maximise cash flow', '. . . to maximise shareholder wealth', or whatever. Fortunately or unfortunately, such assertions represent gross abstractions from organisational practice, useful for some purposes perhaps, but of limited value when trying to understand rather than influence the ways in which organised endeavour emerges out of coalitions of interests and concerns. For when objectives are themselves uncertain and decisions characterised by bargaining and debate, financial planning and control practices can arise out of the political processes which permeate organisational life, serving as (in the terminology of figure 11.2) 'ammunition machines' to articulate and promote particular interested positions and values. Rather than being reflective of agreed
74 ends, the mechanisms of financial control seek to articulate and further particular ends.

Indeed, budgeting and other mechanisms for financial control most likely achieved a great deal of their present organisational significance because of the roles which they came to play in furthering the centralised, financially orientated, control of large organisations, whether public or private. In this context, however, it should be stated that financial practices cannot be operated independently of other management practices. They both reinforce and, in turn, enable to operate those practices which establish particular patterns of organisational segmentation: the procedures which delineate management responsibilities, the methods for the regular reporting of performance, and the practices, formal or otherwise, for the evaluation of managerial performance.[4] Seen in such terms, mechanisms for financial control are but one component of the battery of control practices which enabled and assisted the birth of the modern organisation.

In such a constellation of management practices, budgeting and other mechanisms for financial control nevertheless have a

4. For discussions of the organisational origins of management accounting and related practices see A. Chandler and H. Deams, Administrative co-ordination, allocation and monitoring: a comparative analysis of the emergence of accounting and organisation in the USA and Europe, *Accounting, Organisations and Society*, Vol. 4, Nos. 1 and 2, 1979.

number of vital roles to play. Out of the mass of organisational actions and their consequences, they can influence those which become relatively more visible and influential, particularly to senior management groups. And the visibility so established is invariably an asymmetric one: the powerful can observe the less powerful (but not vice versa), as a rather particular mode of surveillance is established. The centralised co-ordination of activities can thereby be facilitated. Equally, however, demands, requirements, pressures and influences can be more readily passed down through the organisation, particularly in the spheres of the financial and the economic, because of the disaggregative arithmetical properties of the accounting art. Budgeting and financial reporting practices together can provide the framework within which a measured and observed delegation of authority can take place. A pattern of expectations can be established, an organisational ethos articulated, and even motivations influenced, as the visibility which is created provides a basis for organisational rewards and sanctions. Moreover, by influencing the accepted language of negotiation and discourse, control and reporting systems can help to shape what is regarded as problematic, what can be deemed to be a credible solution and, perhaps most important of all, the criteria which ought to be used in the selection of a particular solution. Even the more ritualistic roles of budgeting are important in this context.[5] As one senior manager once commented: 'You will never understand the budgetary system in my company unless you realise that it is like a rosary bead: it quite simply makes sure that every manager says profit, cost, cash, working capital, etc. at least a thousand times a year!'

### *Accounting and the Rationalisation of Organisational Action*

However, financial reporting practices are used not only to influence what is to be. Although the realms of the computational, the judgmental and the political can be important, in all organisations they are complemented by the inspirational,

5. An interesting discussion of the ritualistic and mythical roles of accounting is given in T. Gambling, Magic, accounting and morale, *Accounting, Organisations and Society*, Vol. 2, No. 2, 1977.

where actions arise out of the uncertainties of both aims and consequences. And even that particular variety of decision making provides a basis for roles which the mechanisms of financial planning and control can serve. In such circumstances, the roles are related to the justification and legitimation of what has been decided upon. In the terminology of figure 11.2, financial practices serve as 'rationalisation machines' in such a context.

The widespread use of capital budgeting procedures, for instance, has resulted in the availability of justification devices for proposals which have gained early commitment and support, as well as simply providing information (prior to decision making) on those proposals which remain problematic to the end.[6] Having decided on action, organisational parti-
76 cipants can consciously or otherwise manage the calculations which are used for its more official evaluation. Similarly, budgets and plans can be built around what is to be. Particularly in the context of large, complex and highly innovative decisions, organisational knowledge of the preconditions for action can be widely dispersed and plans can serve to provide a more general, albeit retrospectively created, rationale. Even quite complex procedures for evaluation and control can arise out of the need to marshall support for action. The emergent apparatus of social cost–benefit analysis served such purposes in the nineteenth century,[7] let alone today, and many more recent innovations in control system design have originated from the pressures to maintain an organisation's autonomy for action in the face of external pressures and influences.[8]

6. Further insights into the retrospective interpretation of action are given in K. Weick, *The Social Psychology of Organising*, 2nd edn, Addison-Wesley 1979.
7. G. Pringle, The early development of cost benefit analysis, *Journal of Agricultural Economics*, January 1978, pp. 63 71. For a further discussion of the role of accounting in the rationalisation of action see S. Burchell, C. Clubb, A.G. Hopwood, J. Hughes and J. Nahapiet, The roles of accounting in organisations and society, *Accounting, Organisations and Society*, Vol. 4, No. 4, 1979.
8. See J. Meyer and B. Rowan, The structure of educational organisations, in M.W. Meyer *et al.* (eds), *Environments and Organisations*, Jossey-Bass 1978.

Pressures for the practices of financial planning and control therefore arise in many ways. Whilst accounting textbooks continue to emphasise those which reflect a particular computational rationality, other rationales are equally influential in organisational life. For, faced with the uncertainties and complexities of organised action, information is a vital resource. It can serve to constrain and influence in a political context, facilitate the exercise of judgement, and legitimise what has been done, as well as what might be. All such roles, including the computational, have provided organisational bases for the development of the technical practice of budgeting and financial control and, of equal importance, all continue to influence the use which is made of that practice, regardless of its specific organisational origins. Indeed, many of the complexities and dilemmas which characterise budgeting in action stem from the very diversity of the uses which have been, and are, made of it.

## Budgeting and Organisational Action

With such diverse origins and uses, it is hardly surprising that the organisational practice of budgeting and financial control is complex, grounded as it is in the intricacies of organisational processes and politics. Unfortunately, however, all too little is systematically known about the organisational functioning of budgeting and other control practices. Whilst a wealth of experiential insights are potentially available, comparatively few attempts have been made to probe into the underlying organisational processes, the ways in which control practices do and do not interrelate with other management practices, and their significance for organisational performance.[9] Much

9. Some rich and interesting insights into the practice of budgeting in public organisations are given in A. Wildavsky, *The Politics of the Budgetary Process*, 2nd edn, Little, Brown 1974; A. Wildavsky, Policy analysis is what information systems are not, *Accounting, Organisations and Society*, Vol. 3, No. 1, 1978; and H. Heclo and A. Wildavsky, *The Private Government of Public Money*, Macmillan 1974. The last reference is based on British experience, whilst the others are based on US practice. Unfortunately there

of what is known contrasts with the rather stark computational and procedural rationality that has been codified in and propogated by accounting texts. Compared with the economic analytics of the latter, ongoing practice has been seen to be often characterised by bargaining, controversy and debate, and by a rather loose, indeed ill-defined and shifting, relationship with many other management practices; with its consequences being dependent upon the wider organisational processes in which it is embedded and which determine how it is used.

*The Strategies of Budgeting*

Assembling a budget for a large organisation is a massive as
well as contentious endeavour. The persons engaged in the
78 process have, of necessity, to use strategies to reduce both
the uncertainty of the endeavour and the sheer burden of
calculation, as well as to promote particular interests and aims. As a result the process is often an incremental activity. Emphasis is placed on the deviations which might be made from the firmer historical base of either past budgets or past performance. And because of, rather than in spite of, the complexity of the task, budgeting is an activity which is invariably characterised by the use of the simplest rules of thumb.

However, although such approaches reduce the burden of calculation and breadth of debate, these benefits are gained at the expense of focusing the remaining discussion on the areas of particular uncertainty and controversy, namely the changes from one year to the next. 'Is an increase justified?' 'And what of the over-spending on last year's budget?' 'Should this year's budget be the same or higher?' Careful analysis can, of course, provide some assistance, but since the basic problem involves the extrapolation of an uncertain past into an uncertain future, analysis alone cannot solve the problem. Lobbying, exhortation and an array of bargaining and simplifying strategies come into play.

---

are no similar descriptions of business practice, although the interested reader might consult the descriptive studies of capital budgeting reported in J. Bower, *Managing the Resource Allocation Process*, Graduate School of Business Administration, Harvard University 1970.

Where proposed activities are beyond the comprehension of budget officers and senior managers, the final decision may well depend on their impressions of factors which, although relatively minor, are nevertheless within the bounds of their own experience. Financial procedures themselves can also contribute to such simplifying processes, as they are used to force the debate along more predictable lines. Budgetary decisions can also be made within the context of a predetermined amount of resources which are to be allocated. 'How much can we afford?' then becomes more important than the objectives which might be attained, and organisational norms develop to guide the priority to be given to individual requests. A multitude of other similar simplifying strategies may be used; but in the end, if all else fails, the 'big meat-axe' approach (as it was called by one senior manager) may be used to 'just arbitrarily, without logic, dictate a cut of $x$% across the board'.[10]



Such strategies are a response, not only to the uncertainties and complexities which are inherent in the budgetary process, but also to the fact that budget demands reflect individual and group ambitions. Intertwining the logic of both economics and politics, the demands are strategies in an intensely serious game. The ability to estimate 'what will go' is a vital skill. Managers seek out facts and opinions, in order to arrive at an estimate of what they should ask for in the light of what they can expect to get and then, with due 'padding' to allow for anticipated cuts, they seek to market their budgetary demands. The support of others is actively canvassed and demands are packaged in the most appealing way. Tangible results can be given undue weight and complex activities described in either the simplest or the most complex of terms — but not the more understandable mean! Emphasis can be placed on the qualitative rather than the measurable advantages, the forthcoming rather than the current results, and the procedures to be gone through rather than the outcomes to be achieved. Points can be stretched a little, but never so far as can be

10. C.C. Schwarz, The behavioural aspects of accounting data for performance evaluations at industrial nucleonics, in T.J. Burns (ed.), *The Behavioural Aspects of Accounting Data for Performance Evaluation*, College of Administrative Science, The Ohio State University 1970, p. 101.

tested. If some cuts are seen to be inevitable, essential or popular activities can be pruned first, in anticipation of their subsequent restoration. It can even be pleaded that the smallest of cuts could damage an entire programme of activities. For new activities it is often beneficial to emphasise their relationship to the old, and sometimes it is best to demonstrate that they can either 'pay for themselves' or that it is a case of 'spending a bit now to save a lot later'.

The practice of budgeting provides a forum for organisational debate. It can influence what are regarded as viable organisational strategies, and the techniques of budgeting themselves can be used more actively to influence and constrain the political processes which constitute organisational life. In the last resort, however, the technical components of
80 both budgeting and other mechanisms of financial control are only a part of a wider organisational process — a process which combines the technical and the economic with the human and the political.

*Using Budgetary Information*

Very different approaches can be used to disseminate budgetary and other financial information through the organisation. Attempts can be made to ensure its widespread availability, or it can reside in the hands of a few. Many can participate in the processes from which it arises, or it can emanate from the higher realms of corporate authority. It can be integrated with other management practices, particularly those concerned with organisational evaluation and the provision of recognition and reward, or it can remain a rather detached endeavour, only loosely related to other aspects of organisational functioning. Because of such options, the practices of financial control have few automatic and obvious consequences. If there are consequences, they stem from the ways in which the financial controls intertwine with other organisational processes and from the managerial contexts which influence if, and how, they are used.

In the area of performance evaluation, for instance, comparisons of budgeted and actual performance can be used in very different ways. Even in large organisations noted for the

sophistication and rigour of their financial planning and control practices, the data provided by them may have little influence on managerial concerns, if they are seen as being the almost exclusive province of specialist financial experts who are detached from the mainstream of management practice. At the other extreme, a great deal of managerial emphasis can be placed on the data.[11] For instance, data may be taken at their face value and used to influence the distribution of organisational recognition and rewards. Such use, however, can result in explicit concern with the data as such, rather than with the underlying organisational transactions which they (imperfectly) reflect. In such ways perceptions of the intra-organisational boundaries which are implicit within the budgetary framework can be intensified, lateral as well as hierarchical conflicts thereby engendered, 81
and the budgets and accounts subjected to 'padding' and manipulation. In other contexts, however, the data can be used in more problem oriented ways, not being emphasised in their own right but evaluated, questioned and used alongside other pertinent information, both formal and informal.

An appreciation of the different ways in which financial planning and control practices are used in organisations must therefore be based on an understanding of the human and social contexts out of which their use arises. Technical understandings alone are not sufficient. The interpretation and use of the information provided by financial practices, although influenced by the technical characteristics of those practices, is also the outcome of personal and social processes which are sustained by the meanings, beliefs, pressures and purposes that are brought to bear by both organisational participants and external agents. It can be ultimately intertwined with the use of managerial power. External pressures and demands can create particular rationales for the economic and the financial. And in striving to facilitate the decision making process, its use can be influenced by the ways in which organisational participants clarify and define the problematic, the possible and the desirable. In placing the information in their own wider contexts, managers and employees provide

11. For a more comprehensive discussion see A.G. Hopwood, *An Accounting System and Managerial Behaviour*, Saxon House 1973.

the information with a personal and organisational significance. In this way the information can be, and is, used in a variety of ways — and with a variety of consequences.

### *Some Thoughts on the Consequences of Financial Control Practices*

Budgeting and other practices of financial planning and control have been shown to have a complex relationship to organisational functioning. Although invariably introduced in the name of economic efficiency, their origins and functioning have been seen to have as much to do with political and social, as with economic, rationality. Whilst they can, and do, facilitate economic decision making, they can also be
82 used to introduce a particular political order, reinforce patterns of organisational power and segmentation, and provide for the legitimacy and understanding of the organisational past as well as playing a role in the creation of the organisational future. Once introduced into an organisation, the use which is made of financial practices, and thereby the consequences which they have, is shaped by the ways in which they interrelate with other complex organisational processes. Capable of being influenced by a wide variety of pressures, practices and beliefs, they can have a range of possible consequences, only some of which would be deemed to be compatible with the furtherance of economic performance.

In fact, we know very little about the organisational consequences of the practices of financial planning and control. A great deal of their ultimate utility has been taken on faith, despite the all-too-evident differences in investment in them made by different, but apparently equally successful, organisations. Rather than probing into the ways in which they operate and the consequences which they have, analysts have been content to emphasise the adequacy of the economic logic inherent in their construction and technical design. However, as we have seen, the technical can have an ambiguous relationship with the organisational; and the ultimate consequences of even economic rationales can be determined in the spheres of the social and the political as well as the economic – interrelationships which are only partially understood at the organisational level.

Perhaps in the light of these observations it should not be surprising that what evidence is available, which is not very much, points to the rather equivocal relationship between organisational performance and the practices of financial planning and control.[12] On the positive side, there are some insights into the processes through which they can facilitate organisational choice and action by helping to shape patterns of organisational visibility, influencing thereby perceptions of both the problematic and the possible and reinforcing certain sequences of actions and constraining others. Some other evidence is potentially more questioning, however. In part, this might reflect very different approaches to the organisational dissemination of the practices: at least on 83
occasions, even potentially favourable consequences might not be exploited. And on other occasions, the evidence no doubt reflects the fact that poorly performing organisations tend to be the ones which systematically increase their investment in the practices of financial control as they seek, possibly with uncertain effect, to re-establish a particular economic order – a phenomenon which has been termed 'newly poor behaviour'. However, the evidence which remains is still consistent with the possibility that particularly heavy emphases on the rigours of financial planning and control can hinder, rather than facilitate, the achievement of economic ends. For organisations are complex artifacts, the survival and development of which are dependent on the mutual satisfaction of numerous and often conflicting demands, both internal and external to the organisation itself. To focus on any one, without due care, might result in the neglect of others, on which (paradoxically) the achievement of the focal concern can, in turn, depend.

If for no other reason, the equivocality of such findings

12. A very brief discussion of some of the evidence is given in A.G. Hopwood, Criteria of corporate effectiveness, in M. Brodie and R. Bennett (eds), *Perspectives on Managerial Effectiveness*, Thames Valley Regional Management Centre 1979, pp. 81–96.

points to the need for an organisational, as well as technical, appreciation of the financial craft.

## Conclusion

In seeking to demonstrate both the breadth and potential of an organisational and behavioural understanding of the practices of financial planning and control, consideration has been given to how interests in such practices can arise out of organisational processes; and how those processes, in turn, can shape the use which is made of the practices and the consequences which they might have. Our explorations accordingly have taken us into realms that remain implicit within accounting texts. Almost inevitably, many problems have been raised rather than answered. Indeed, even conflicting tendencies have been acknowledged. For rather than focusing on detailed understandings and research findings, emphasis has been placed on illuminating the range of issues where an organisational appreciation can provide not only new, but useful, insights. All too obviously, the arena for such a discussion is enormous, both in scope and potential. Many issues of importance have not been discussed, or have received only fleeting mention. Hopefully, however, those issues which have been considered will stimulate you to think and read about those which have not.[13]



13. A more comprehensive introduction to the area is provided by A.G. Hopwood, *Accounting and Human Behaviour*, Prentice-Hall 1974.

# 14 The design of information systems for matrix organisations

ANTHONY G. HOPWOOD

The design of appropriate information and control systems should be a crucial part of any attempt to develop and implement a matrix organisation. Matrix organisations, like any other management structures, require information to function effectively. Planning procedures, information for decision making and systematic ways of monitoring and controlling performance are an essential part of the management process. Indeed for matrix organisations the need may be all the greater. For the matrix 85
approach is invariably implanted within an existing organisation and there are usually innumerable forces that have the potential to frustrate its success. There is invariably a real need for carefully designed information and control systems that explicitly aim to support the matrix rather than neutralise or even destroy its potential. Yet, on so many occasions, the seemingly obvious need for appropriate information systems is not given the emphasis that it deserves, and matrix structures are left to exist alongside information and control systems orientated towards a previous functional management structure.

In part this reflects a much more general management problem. The complexities facing modern organisations, and their increasing size, have resulted in a fragmentation of not only the actual management task but also the evolving body of management expertise and knowledge. Once started, this fragmentation process develops its own momentum. Technical and functional boundaries become jealously guarded, and, with time, as different management groups respond to differing circumstances and the pressures of their increasingly separate environments, leads and lags, if not stark inconsistencies in managerial practices, become increasingly apparent.

Of course, matrix organisations are intended to provide one way of overcoming these very problems, but the same factors which provide the impetus for their development can also constrain their effective implementation. In no area is this more readily observable than in the design and use of complementary information systems. The technical concerns of the designers of information and control systems, and the behavioural and organisational assumptions that they implicitly make, can easily appear to be, and frequently are, very distant from the concerns and assumptions of those organisational designers who have fostered matrix approaches.

### An illustrative example

That the fragmentation of expertise and efforts certainly has its attendant costs is illustrated by the endeavours of one major company that was experiencing tremendous difficulties in co-ordinating a complex set of highly interrelated activities. Recognising that co-ordination required both an appropriate organisation and more effective information systems, senior managers in the company proceeded to establish two high-level task forces in these areas. Both groups produced what appeared to be emin-
86 ently reasonable recommendations and, with comparatively few changes, these were speedily implemented. But no sooner had this been done than the underlying problems got even worse. For whilst the organisational group had recommended the use of project and product managers to strengthen the co-ordinating role of lateral relationships in the company, the emphasis that the information group placed on clarifying existing responsibilities and producing more comprehensive departmental performance information did little either to highlight the troublesome interdepartmental problems or to help with their solution. Indeed, with the new reports providing more detailed and comprehensive information on the activities within departments, existing departmental loyalties and the power of the vertical patterns of influence were strengthened. As each manager strove to improve the reported results of his own unit, conflict between the units intensified and co-ordination became ever more difficult.

The recommendations of the information group were firmly based on the doctrines of individual responsibility and accountability that are so influential in accounting thought and practice. The group had thought that the previous co-ordination problems were a result of the fact that responsibility for some crucial areas of management activity was far too diffused. From their point of view it appeared that many managers could not be held responsible for all the consequences of their own actions. Hence they had sought to extend the degree of individual accountability and to do this they recognised that an improved information system was an essential requirement. With more comprehensive departmental information systems, they thought that it would be possible to motivate individual managers to achieve specific objectives which were in the interests of the company as a whole and for which they could be held personally responsible.

Within the context of their own separate bodies of expertise, both sets of recommendations had looked reasonable enough, but their orientations and aims conflicted. One had focused on the activities of separate units and their aggregation through the management hierarchy whilst the other had focused on the relationships between units. By making those differences explicit, their combined implementation intensified rather than reduced the difficulties of co-ordinating the company's complex activities. Rather than supporting the move towards more influential lateral relationships, the new and highly visible information and control system helped to undermine both their affective and analytical bases. It strengthened existing departmental loyalties and provided little or no information to improve the quality of interdepartmental decision making.

If, however, the dominant concern is with the effectiveness of the 87
overall enterprise, both organisational structures and information and control systems need to be designed so that they reinforce each other's concerns with the wider ends rather than dissipate each other's potential in the creation of additional conflict. Both, in other words, need to be seen as part of an organisational design endeavour. For, as Galbraith (1973, pp. 4–6) has pointed out, both are means by which enterprises strive to cope with the uncertainties and complexities of the task which they manage. Although the approach in practice may depend on the ends to be fulfilled, the overall need is present whether the aim is to achieve better co-ordination, facilitate organisational responsiveness, promote participation and autonomy or emphasise the significance of organisational outcomes rather than just internal processes.

## Some common problems

Given that there is a frequent tendency to maintain traditional information and control systems alongside a matrix organisation, or only to modify them marginally to deal with the most apparent inconsistencies, it is important to consider the nature of the problems that this can create. Many management information and control systems, and particularly responsibility accounting systems which are so influential in practice, concentrate on reporting the consequences of activities within particular sub-units of an enterprise and on the aggregation of the information vertically through the enterprise. In so doing they reflect not only the need to compile the aggregate information on the enterprise that is required by law, but also the evolving role that such information systems have come to play in facilitating the exercise of authority downwards through the enterprise. In contrast, however, matrix organisation structures frequently aim to facilitiate inter-unit co-ordination through a greater emphasis on lateral decision processes.

In reflecting vertically oriented conceptions of organisational control, such information systems can, if used rigidly, encourage managers to focus too narrowly on the operations internal to their own units to the detriment of their relationships with other interacting units. The structure of the information system can, in other words, itself encourage a fragmentation of managerial perceptions, and as this occurs, the attendant rivalries and conflicts can endanger the very lateral relationships that a matrix structure aims to facilitate.

The dominant role that so many of today's information systems play in
88 enforcing the influence of a vertically oriented power structure also means that they emphasise the production of information for the evaluation and control of subordinates rather than providing the information which is needed for decision making. This is a particularly important problem when traditional information system designs are implemented within matrix organisations. For whilst the need for decision information within the functional management units of the matrix remains, the project managers have additional needs for decision information that can facilitate co-ordination and integration and more generally contribute to the overall decentralisation of power and influence.

The above factors suggest that functionally oriented information and control systems have the potential to frustrate the aims of a matrix organisation. Similarly, however, the implementation of an integrative information and control system without a complementary change in the management structure can also be of no avail. If the underlying objectives of the matrix approach are to be realised, the management structure and the information and control systems must be mutually reinforcing.

## Towards a framework for information systems design

One way of looking at both the problems and the potential of designing information and control systems for matrix organisations is to consider two fundamental dimensions underlying system design. The first dimension relates to whether the system emphasises decision or control information. Information for decision making is oriented towards facilitating the exercise of self control by managers, whilst information for control is oriented towards control by others, especially by hierarchical superiors. The second dimension relates to whether the information system is oriented towards facilitating the management of functional units, with an emphasis on the utilisation of resources, or towards the overall project or programme of activity to which these contribute, with an emphasis on end results. The two dimensions and the resultant information system categories are illustrated in Fig. 14.1.

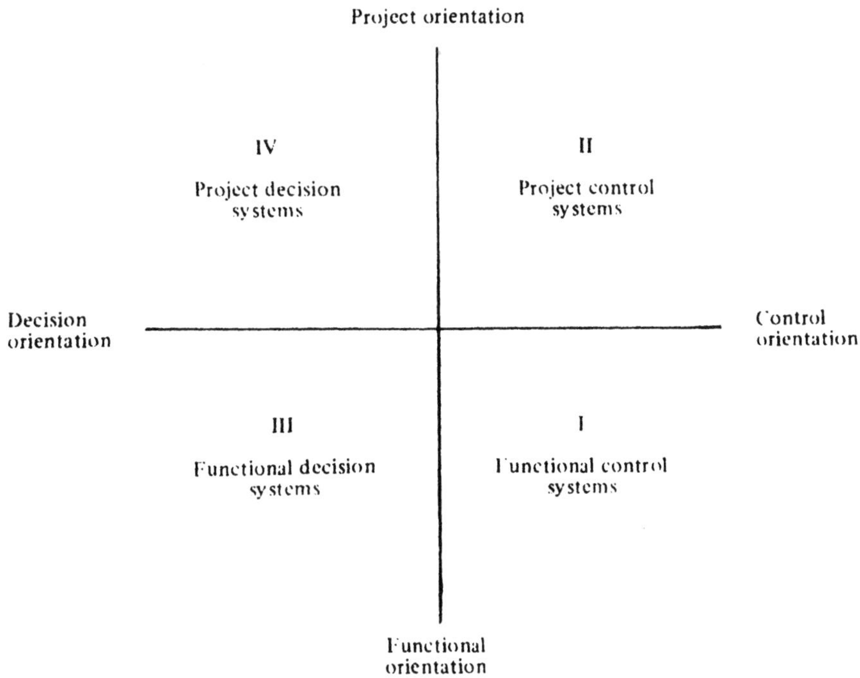


89

Fig. 14.1 A classification of information systems

Type I functional control systems are for monitoring the performance of functional management units. Many, if not most, of today's responsibility accounting systems, budgetary control systems and financial reporting procedures are of this type. Reporting on the utilisation of resources and the associated financial expenditures in areas of functional management responsibility, consideration is generally given to the relationship between financial inputs and outputs only at higher levels of the organisational hierarchy, and often then on a multi-product or project basis. Project control systems of the type II variety, on the other hand, are explicitly oriented towards monitoring the performance of the separate projects and programmes of the enterprise. In contrast with the primary input orientation of the type I systems, type II systems are goal oriented, aiming to reflect the relationship between inputs and outputs at all relevant organisational levels on an ongoing basis.

Information systems for the financial control of projects report on project costs and revenues irrespective of the functional management units in which these have been incurred or realised (Cleland and King, 1975). Engineering, production, distribution and marketing costs are, for instance, related to the anticipated or realised revenues of particular projects. Similar procedures are used for monitoring the performance of contracts in sectors such as the construction and heavy engineering industries. In both of these cases the collection of the information in this way can be used to facilitate the monitoring of progress against time budgets.

90 The ability to express project outcomes in financial terms eases the design of type II control systems. But in the public sector, and also in some increasingly important areas of private sector activity, it is often impossible to express outcomes in financial terms. Nevertheless, some progress has been made on the design and implementation of related programme planning and budgeting systems (Anthony and Herzlinger, 1975). Extending beyond traditional departmental boundaries, such systems aim to relate all expenditures (and other indicators of resource utilisation) on particular programmes of activity to both quantitative and qualitative indices of programme performance. In local government, for instance, attempts have been made to relate expenditures on community health activities incurred within public health, welfare, education, recreation and sanitation departments to an array of indicators of community health including the incidence of diseases, mortality rate and hospitalisation statistics. Control systems of this type are undoubtedly in their early days. Numerous conceptual and practical problems remain to be solved. But this is not to say that they are not useful. If used with appropriate care they can greatly assist the management of complex and important activities.

The basic aim of types III and IV information systems should be to improve the quality of decisions made by individual managers of the enterprise. The type III systems aim to do this for the managers of functional units whilst the type IV systems strive to facilitate the activities of the project managers who are concerned with overall co-ordination and integration. In both cases the information should focus on those aspects of the job where the manager has discretion to act. If the flow of raw materials, for instance, is beyond the control of a particular manager, information that aims to assist in their control is of no practical value to him. But where the flow is within a manager's discretion, information on the quantity, quality and timing of the flows and associated stocks, and more importantly, on the factors that influence these, is of potential value.

The fact that information systems of this type should reflect the nature of the job that they are aimed at assisting makes it difficult to generalise about the nature and scope of functional decision systems in particular. Different jobs have different information requirements and different management styles may also influence the demand for and use of information. Given these problems it should not be surprising that at this stage we know little about the general principles that might underlie such information systems. But this very ignorance is at least suggestive of the way in which they should be designed.

The basic question that should guide the design of functional decision 91
systems should always be: what information do *you* need to do a better job? Any presumption that *we* know better should be viewed with some caution. Managers may have difficulty responding but the fact that so many do design and operate their own personal information systems suggests that the problem is mainly one of asking the right questions. Given that these systems aim to assist individual managers, their design should, as we consider again later, be of a participative nature, actively drawing on the resources and ideas of both information specialists and the ultimate users.

Project decision systems of the type IV variety should aim to facilitate the activities of the project managers who are concerned with overall project co-ordination and control. Although project managers should also be involved in the design of these systems, the integrative nature of the job suggests that type IV systems should at the very least provide two distinct types of information.

As is illustrated in Fig. 14.2, integrative information systems aim to facilitate the overall co-ordination of a project or programme. They place particular emphasis on the way in which the activities of separate management units jointly contribute to the desired outcome. PERT techniques (project evaluation review techniques) are of this type, as are contract, project and programme planning procedures (Cleland and King, 1975). Coupling information systems, on the other hand, aim to facilitate the co-ordination of particular management units. Whilst of necessity operating within the broader content established by the integrative planning systems, their orientation, scope and hence design can be very different. Many stock control procedures and interdepartmental scheduling procedures are of this type, as are information systems which help to co-ordinate the activities of such separate functions as production and marketing.

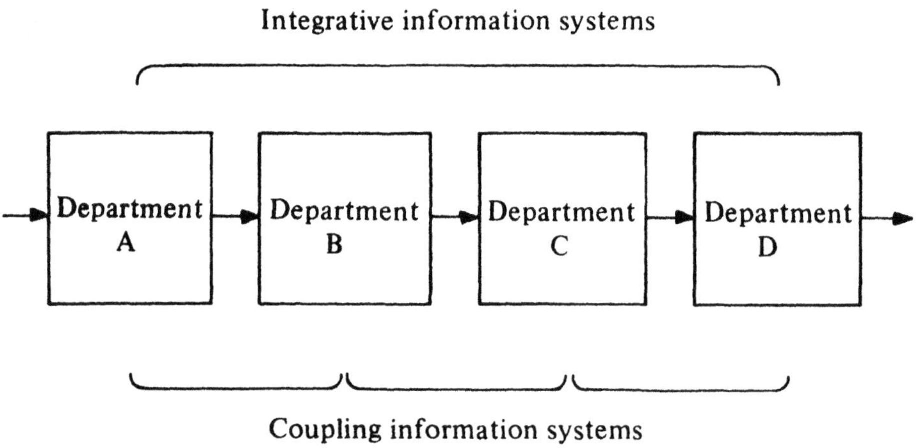


92

Fig. 14.2 Integrative and coupling information systems

Functionally organised enterprises tend to emphasise the need for type I information systems. There is less overt need for the type II and IV project systems, although increasingly it is being recognised that these can play a valuable role, and even functionally oriented information systems for decision making of the type III variety are often weakly developed at the official level. But what are the information system needs of the matrix organisation? What combination of systems is required to support the operation of a management structure that explicitly aims to integrate the often disparate activities of separate management units?

### Information systems for the matrix organisation

It is tempting to think that there might be a single design strategy that would help to identify the information needs of a matrix organisation. Given the emphasis that has been placed on formulating the outline of such a strategy for the functionally managed organisation, surely something similar must be necessary for complementing a matrix structure? However such thinking is misguided. It is increasingly being realised that many of the norms underlying the systematic design of such information systems may not correspond to the realities of organisational life. Several recent investigations have found that high performing enterprises have complex, multi-faceted and even mutually conflicting information systems (Gordon and Miller, 1976; Grinyer and Norburn, 1975). Whilst a concern for simple information system design strategies might meet the designers' needs for clarity, order and tidiness, it is not so obviously related to ensuring organisational effectiveness.

The matrix organisation is complex and multi-faceted. The effectiveness of the whole organisation depends on achieving a continuous balance between vertical and lateral processes. It is this aspect of the matrix approach that provides the clue to its information needs. Rather than looking for a single integrated and tidy information system, it needs to be recognised that to survive and flourish the matrix requires a diversity of information systems. Just as there is a need for both decision and control
information, so both the vertical and lateral processes within the matrix 93
need to be provided with their information support. A matrix structure requires, in other words, types I, II, III and IV information systems.

Ways in which type I and II systems may be combined in an integrated control system for matrix organisation have been suggested by Vancil (1973) and Davis (1973), although little evidence of the actual effect of such strategies exists at present. One possibility is that of treating functional departments as cost centres, products or projects as profit centres, with separate controls on each. A second step is to use transfer pricing to allocate part of the profit to the functional managers and part to projects or products (though the frequent arbitrariness of price determination may engender its own forms of conflict). The third possibility is a system of double counting, with total costs or profits being calculated both vertically and horizontally in an accounting matrix which matches the organisational one (cf. Wilkinson, 1974). What evidence we have on the information and control systems that have been associated with the implementation of matrix organisations, and admittedly this is rather limited at present, tends to support the need for a multiple information system strategy.

In the National Aeronautics and Space Administration, surely one of the most complex of modern organisations, project and functional control systems functioned alongside one another. As Sayles and Chandler (1971, p. 307) comment:

> In the daily course of events, managers have to use and be responsive to the use by others of, a variety of control measures. Some are

> consistent with, and critical to, . . . 'dispersed' responsibilities [where the emphasis is on an entire project, without regard to inter-personal, departmental or organisational boundaries]; others represent the more traditional concern with 'jurisdictional' responsibility (of a functional nature) . . . . In the real world of advanced technology implementation both types of controls are necessary.

However, although important, control information alone was not sufficient for the management of this complex enterprise.

> Unfortunately, most high- and low-level controls try to measure accomplishment: how actual costs, schedules, and performances compare with the original estimates. This can be misleading, in part because such controls assume rigid plans, compartmentalized jurisdictions and responsibilities. ('Our engineers are mesmerized by watching dollars when they should be watching technology and
> 94 people.')

The adaptability and responsiveness of the whole organisation depended on the use of more flexible sources of decision oriented information. Given the dominance of the overall mission of this agency, the managers themselves responded to this problem and provided their own sources of information (Sayles and Chandler, p. 314):

> Rather than emphasising regular reports, managers place importance on random organisational probes designed to identify co-ordination problems. Thus, each . . .. manager concentrates on monitoring the interfaces . . . . These include suppliers of components and sub-systems, the next and preceding work-flow stage, test and control groups.

The initial self-designed information-for-decision systems were of an informal nature. With time, however, such pressing needs for information for decision making resulted in the design and official implementation of coupling information systems of the type IV variety, type IV integrative systems which 'direct the attention of . . . managers to the total system's requirements and to the breakdowns that threaten its performance', and, within the functional management units, supportive information systems of the type III variety.

The descriptions of matrix oriented information systems in other governmental agencies and departments also stress the complementary role of project and functional control systems. The very terminology of programme planning and budgeting systems serves to emphasise the recognised need for, if not the actual attainment of, project information systems which serve both decision making (planning) and control (budgeting) needs.

Within the context of the industrial research laboratory, Wilkinson (1974) outlines how functionally oriented financial control systems can be adapted to provide project and programme control information and also considers, albeit briefly, the need for type IV planning information within the matrix structure. Costs were planned and monitored on the basis of individual research projects and project groupings as well as in relation to overall cost type and functional location. Bergen (1975), on the other hand, discusses the construction and use of a type IV project planning system for new products which identifies resource and time requirements by project, function and specific managerial activity. Complementing the existing functional controls, this planning procedure also had the potential of providing the basis for a subsequent type II
project control system through which actual accomplishments could be 95
compared with the original plan. In a comprehensive, even if not detailed, description of matrix support systems, Goggin (1974) outlines the multi-faceted management systems that are used to support Dow Corning's 'multi-dimensional' structure. MbO, profit reporting and personnel reviews provide the basis for both type I and II control systems whilst corporate planning, economic evaluation and a comprehensive new business planning system constitute systems of the type III and IV decision varieties.

These and the few other descriptions of practice in the area do provide an indication that a variety of information systems are in simultaneous use in matrix organisations. However, with the possible exception of the more thorough review of the National Aeronautics and Space Administration's experiences provided by Sayles and Chandler (1971), they give little indication of either the way in which the systems actually function as against how they are designed to function, or the relative or combined effectiveness of the various approaches. Yet in this area, as in functional organisations, actual practice can, and does, deviate substantially from what is both intended and claimed.

## Problems and potential

Information systems in a matrix organisation should provide flows of information that support the conflicting yet ultimately interrelated pressures that constitute the matrix itself. Yet the very fact that the overall integration of the enterprise is achieved through the use of potentially conflicting means itself provides the basis for some common and important problems.

The different types of information system have different sources of organisational support and different patterns of growth and development. The functional control systems draw their strength from the vertical power hierarchy which they are designed to complement, whilst the use and final impact of the project oriented information systems and particularly the project decision systems depends on the often more fragile patterns of lateral relationships.

To be effective, project control systems need to be associated with an organisational structure and culture that stresses the overriding importance of the goals of the enterprise. Project controls without a project oriented management structure have little effect and whatever may be a particular enterprise's equivalent to 'getting a man on the moon' must be known, visible and well articulated. In order to survive, such systems must
96 be given their own separate existence. Whilst they can, and often should, share a common data base with the functional control systems, project control systems need to be much more than minor extensions of the functional controls. Product costs appended to functional reports or highly summarised project control information alongside detailed functional control information are not sufficient. To be effective, the project control information needs to be at least as visible and well articulated as the functional control information.

If these conditions are fulfilled, however, the use of the type II project control systems is capable of undermining the very different and equally valuable role that can be played by the type IV systems for project decision making. For the planning activities that the type IV systems aim to facilitate can easily be dominated by the anticipation of subsequent evaluation and control on the basis of the type II systems. Where a great deal of emphasis is placed on monitoring actual project performance against the original plans, the plans themselves may be formulated so as to provide easier targets rather than realistic guides to action. Rather than helping to identify potential problem areas, the project planning systems can become mere adjuncts of the control procedures. As the managers seek to establish plans that improve their own performance-potential in an interdependent organisation, the operation of the system can help to create rather than overcome inter-unit conflict.

What is needed is that the decision oriented information systems should become separate from and independent of evaluation oriented control systems, providing local information resources at the operating level (Hedberg, 1975). An increasing number of people are beginning to realise that the involvement of managers in the design of their own decision oriented information systems may be one way of attempting to achieve this. In this way, and particularly if priority is given to the establishment of the decision oriented information systems, both type III and type IV systems might be given a source of independent support. Rather than using the information of 'others' in decision making, managers might be able to establish a sense of ownership over the information that they use. This might provide not only a means of ensuring the viability of these types of information system, but also help to ensure their more effective utilisation.

Ultimately, of course, the final effectiveness of any type of information system or combination of information systems depends on its appropriate use (Hopwood, 1973). It is easy for complex information systems to be either rejected or taken at their face value. But, to have the appropriate effect, they must be used in a careful and considered manner, sometimes
being used but on other occasions being set aside in the light of alternative 97
evidence. How information is used reflects quite general managerial characteristics. To change these is difficult. Certainly educational programmes have a role to play if they aim to help managers understand the rationale, advantages *and* disadvantages of the systems rather than merely present a public relations version of the activities of the information specialists. But real progress might depend on trying to influence how managers actually use information. As information system designers try to do this, their efforts will be related directly to the organisational development activities of those organisational designers who strive to create the social environment in which a matrix structure can survive and flourish.

## Conclusion

The design of information systems for matrix organisations remains an emerging area of concern. Many unknowns and doubts remain and, as yet, many of the early experiments have still to endure the test of practice. At this stage, however, there is reason to think that the appropriate systems will reflect the conflicting but mutually reinforcing pressures of the matrix itself. Rather than constraining the simultaneous exercising of vertical and horizontal influences, such information systems will provide both the means for these influences to function and some of the checks and balances that are so necessary for the enterprise as a whole to function effectively. However alien design principles of this type may be to those information system designers who look for orderliness and simplicity, they do offer the possibility of nurturing and supporting the vital organisational processes that the matrix approach seeks to promote.

## Summary

The effectiveness of matrix organisation is often frustrated by the retention of inappropriate information and control systems based on a previous functional structure. An example is described in which a reorganisation aimed at strengthening lateral co-ordinating links was made ineffective by a new information system which placed greater emphasis on the vertical reporting patterns of separate departments.

To assist in the development of information systems which will support rather than hinder the operation of matrix structures a two-dimensional
98 classification of information systems is proposed, which distinguishes between control and decision oriented information and between functional emphasis on resource utilisation and project emphasis on end results. This results in four types of information system being distinguished. An examination of the needs of matrix organisations suggests that they require the simultaneous existence of all four types of system, rather than a single overriding design strategy. The little evidence which is available tends to support this view.

The danger that decision oriented project information systems may be distorted by being subordinated to evaluation oriented control systems may be avoidable by involving managers in the design of their own decision information systems. This might make it more likely that information systems will be used constructively to increase the effectiveness of matrix organisations.

# 5. CRITERIA OF CORPORATE EFFECTIVENESS*

**Anthony Hopwood****

99

The idea of corporate effectiveness is an illusive, indeed curious one. Despite appearing to be pragmatic in orientation and intent, its all embracing scope makes it virtually impossible to operationalise in any satisfactory way, with its practical definition ranging from the narrowly technical to visionary depictions of corporate potential. It is also a concept that, until recently at least, has not entered into the discourse of corporate management itself. Concerns with survival, profit, growth and market penetration have certainly been articulated by practising managers. Consideration has also been given to product quality, innovative record, if not potential, consumer impact and even public image. And more recently we have heard of the seeming attractions of the socially responsible corporation with the attendent identification of such manifestations of corporate impact as the quality of working life, energy conservation and the contribution to employment, both regional and national. But effectiveness *per se* has rarely, if ever, been articulated as a management aim. Interest in that concept invariably has emanated from those outside the corporation who have or claim to have some interest in it.

Perhaps not too surprisingly the idea of effectiveness has entered

* I acknowledge the stimulation received from my colleagues Stuart Burchell, Colin Clubb and John Hughes at the London Business School and Janine Naphiet of the Oxford Centre for Management Studies.

** Professor of Accountancy and Financial Reporting at the London Graduate School of Business Studies and Professor of Management at the European Institute for Advanced Studies in Management, Brussels.

into the language of those who seek to change corporate actions and performance. Be they management consultants, facilitators or educators, they have readily adopted a concept which can be used to point to unexploited potential and — so some at least of the literature would have us believe — a constantly expanding horizon of the novel and the unknown. And that very same normative orientation has also appealed to an increasing number of both corporate critics and agents for corporate change. Indeed the very ambiguity of the concept has been attractive to those, be they in private interest groups or agencies of the state, who have sought or currently seek to create and legitimise their own interest in the corporation and the means for facilitating their interventionist concerns.

Such a view of corporate effectiveness implies that the idea is neither a self-sufficient nor a unitary one. Concerns with effectiveness presume, at the very least, an interest, a rationale or an intent
100 and often, albeit implicitly rather than explicitly, a particular conception of the nature and functioning of the corporation. Accordingly, there is, I would venture to suggest, no such thing as effectiveness *per se*. Concepts of corporate effectiveness are socially constructed, their meanings and roles stemming from the articulation of particular social concerns, interests and demands and the specific contexts in which the concepts operate. And, as such interests and contexts vary and change over time, so do the prevailing notions of effectiveness.

Indeed it may well be that the current interest in the concept of corporate effectiveness reflects just such underlying pressures for change. For whilst there always have been competing notions of effectiveness, more recent events have added a new dynamism to the debate. Past interests have been reassessed and new concerns have entered the corporate arena. The government, for instance, be it at a national or local level, has certainly been more influential, seeking both to further its own interests and concerns and to act as a more active agent of the public interest. The media and particularly more independent agencies for change have started to examine and question the consequences of corporate behaviour, the organisational processes from which they emanate and the mechanisms for external accountability and review. Thereby the interests of the consumer, for instance, have started to be recognised and endowed with a more substantive legal status and those of labour also have been articulated more clearly and forcefully. And within the corporation itself change has been underway. The emergence of the personnel function (Watson, 1977), in particular, and especially its recent concern with personnel and organisational development, has provided a basis on which long standing notions of economic and technical effectiveness can be and have been elaborated, if not challenged. In ways such as these, accepted notions of corporate effectiveness have been made problematic at the very least. What may have been taken for granted is now being questioned and reassessed.

Of course the social contexts of particular notions of effectiveness, be they new or longstanding, rarely enter into their articulation for invariably that would constrain their acceptance and use. Indeed, as the bases of at least some of our concerns with corporate effectiveness have come to be recognised, it has become even more important for the articulated criteria to appear self-evident and disinterested. As a consequence, in a world where an ever increasing number of interests are being expressed, we are being faced with an ever expanding array of criteria for judging corporate effectiveness, most of which are so stated as to appear universalistic and objective (Pfeffer and Salancik, 1974).



## THE ROLE OF RESEARCH ON CORPORATE EFFECTIVENESS

Such a social view of the interest in corporate effectiveness increases the complexity of understanding the roles which research and scholarly inquiry have and can play. For if notions of effectiveness are socially constructed, the role of research cannot be seen in terms of a simple and unproblematic search for the real and the true or the ideal and the absolute. With concerns with effectiveness being seen as stemming from the articulation of interests and concerns, the relationship which research itself bears to such processes must also be recognised and considered.

Seen in such terms, research can play three main roles within the context of an interest in corporate effectiveness. First it can seek to facilitate the articulation of particular notions of effectiveness by improving their underlying conceptual frameworks, their empirical approximation or the processes through which they gain their organisational significance and impact. Such research may also help to promote those important elements of empirical objectification and contextual neutralisation, the growing need for which already has been mentioned. Secondly research can try to further our appreciation of the social nature of concerns with corporate effectiveness. An interest in effectiveness in such a research context will be seen as a problematic rather than a self-evident phenomenon. The research task then becomes one of understanding the social nature of such interests and the social processes through which they are articulated and change prevailing conceptions of what is or is not regarded as effective corporate performance. Finally research can play a role in increasing our understanding of the effects which particular notions of effectiveness have in organisational terms and the processes through which such impacts are or might be achieved.

To date most research on corporate effectiveness has emphasised the first role. Rather than seeking to establish the social and organisational nature of the interest in particular concepts of corporate effectiveness, researchers have tended to accept at least some basic notion of effectiveness as being unproblematic, trying on this basis to improve its conceptual clarity and its empirical assessment. However, there are now some indications that research interests are starting to expand. Some, at least, of the earlier concerns with the elucidation of universalistic and objective criteria of corporate effectiveness are being set aside, as researchers adopt a more complex view of organisational functioning (Scott, 1978) and the very observation of, if not involvement in, the many recent debates and even conflicts over possible criteria for appraising corporate action has itself encouraged a more questioning and analytical stance. How, some researchers are starting to ask, can we understand the
102 changing orientations? How do they come to be articulated? What meanings and consequences do they have? And through what organisational processes are these achieved?

Such concerns are being reinforced by a number of other research developments. Not least in importance might be the emergence of a more independent tradition of inquiry in organisational research which has started to investigate and even question the prevailing conventional wisdom of corporate action. New rationalities are emerging, for instance, which attach a different significance to goal setting and assessing processes and procedures in organisations (Cohen, March and Olsen, 1972; March and Olsen, 1976; March, 1978; Weick, 1969) and research is starting to inquire into the ways in which meanings in organisations become established and change (Pettigrew, 1977). Also, as research has come to recognise explicitly the pluralistic or even conflicting nature of corporate functioning (Fox, 1966), concerns with effectiveness are being seen in new ways (Benson, 1977; Tribe, Schelling and Voss, 1976; van Gunsteren, 1976), with some researchers, particularly in Scandinavia (Carlsson et al, 1979), trying to help very different groups articulate and assess their own interests and perspectives.

One consequence of such ongoing research developments is that a series of very different perspectives are now being brought to bear on the study of corporate effectiveness. Whilst this might be frustrating, if not challenging, to those who merely want simple answers and improved procedures, some at least of the emergent approaches do offer the possibility of providing a basis for understanding problems which are undoubtedly of real organisational and social significance. For the dominant interest in clarifying and assessing particular notions of corporate effectiveness has resulted in a neglect of the organisational processes through which change might be achieved.

And yet, as any one who has tried to implement a new approach can testify, such processes are far from being unproblematic. On so many occasions a concern with the new has been frustrated in part at least because of our unbalanced understanding of organisational action and achievement.

Some of the ways in which research is starting to throw light on such issues of orgaisational practice are discussed later. Before doing so, however, it is important to gain some further insights into the problematic nature of particular criteria of corporate effectiveness and some of the ways in which concerns with these have developed over time. We can start by focusing, albeit in far too brief a manner, on the recent debates on financial measures of corporate performance, the traditional concern of the accountant, and the more recent questioning both from within corporations and without of the dominance and adequacy of these. For however partial financial criteria measurements may be, there can be little doubt as to their practical significance.



## CORPORATE ACCOUNTING IN A CHANGING WORLD

Accounting in practice, in the past a seeming citadel of traditional orientations and concerns, has gone through, and indeed continues to go through, a period of turmoil in most industrial nations. Unease, at the very least, with many conventional accounting measures of corporate performance and position has been expressed by many traditional users of and commentators upon accounting reports. And, at the same time, a whole array of new social interests and associated perspectives have entered into accounting debates. Public policy issues in the area, for instance, have been articulated with increasing frequency by both state bureaucracies and legislative assemblies, and interest groups, once not concerned with accounting matters, including in many countries the organised labour movement, have started to isolate their own demands for the development of accounting practice and regulation. Moreover, at the same time as accounting debates have grown in both complexity and contentiousness, so many of the institutional mechanisms for considering and introducing change, if not a new order, into the accounting domain have entailed a search for more satisfactory frames of reference and modes of operation.

Such debates have gone a long way towards irreversibly changing the way in which accounting indicators of corporate economic performance are perceived and accounting discourse takes place. Rather than being seen as one of the more stable albeit partial components of an effectiveness repertoire, quite explicit attention has had to have been given to the sheer diversity of accounting procedures (Briloff, 1972) including some newly emergent alternatives, to the many and varied arguments that can be and are marshalled in support of a large number of them, and to the range of their impacts and consequences (May and Sundem, 1976). In the process, consideration also has had to be given to the origins of particular interests in the development of accounting measures of corporate performance and to the varied and often conflicting organisational and social roles that are served by forms of accounting practice.

Not too long ago, a profit was a profit was a profit. Accounting measurements were seen as rather neutral approximations to an underlying economic truth and the role and intent of both research and practice was to further such an empirical approximation. Of course the ultimate could never be achieved, but the potential for improvement was recognised. Either by abstracting from theoretical discourse or by inquiring into what were presumed to be the decision 'models' and economic information 'needs' of the users of account-
104 ing reports (Carsberg, Hope and Scapens, 1974) attempts were made to get ever closer to achieving the accounting ideal.

The impact of an inflationary economic environment resulted in such notions of truth being irreversibly set aside. In such an economic setting, interplay between the adaptive responses of corporate management, the actions of a profession struggling for its continued autonomy and those of a government moving towards discovering the significance of accounting policy for its own economic management concerns, resulted in a whole array of alternative accounting indicators of corporate economic performance entering into practical discourse. The progression, if that is the appropriate word, from the Accounting Standards Steering Committee's Current Purchasing Power Accounting, to Sandiland's Current Cost Accounting, to the Morpeth 'mix', to the Hyde Guidelines, to . . . is now familiar to all. Perhaps less familiar is the fact that as a result of such deliberations accounting has had to be recognised quite explicitly as a conceptual phenomenon, with alternative concepts increasingly having to be evaluated on the basis of both their internal logic and their practical consequences rather than on their approximation to some underlying notion of an economic truth.

Accounting research was strongly orientated towards the former logical task (Baxter, 1976; Chambers, 1966; Lee, 1974; Sterling, 1970). Practical discourse and debate continued to move on, however, as it emphasised the consequences of alternative modes of accounting that might arise in the specifics of a particular economic and social milieu rather than within the abstract confines of a theoretical framework. So some corporations were clearly concerned about the effects that might flow from a very low level of reported profits. Others focused on the dangers in the opposite direction. Yet others, including albeit in a tentative way some representatives of the labour movement, emphasised the fact that in an increasingly bureaucraticised world, where decisions are made by administrative rather than competitive means, accounting had become an even more influential medium. With, for example, allowable price and wage increases in both the private and public sectors and certain forms of government financial assistance being dependent in part on reported profit margins, alternative accountings could and did have different economic consequences. And with past accounts of the utilisation of economic resources so influencing their future availability, accounting debates became even more political in nature (Watts and Zimmerman, 1979). Interests in accounting had become clear and visible.

Once perceived as an approximation of an economic reality, accounting started to be recognised, perhaps implicitly more than explicitly, as a social phenomenon, grounded in the political
economy of the nation and serving a variety of roles within the nexus 105
that links the corporation, the capital markets and increasingly the state and an array of other social interests that relate to them. Indeed, the roles and modes of 'accounting' in such a context are still emergent. Many of the social, institutional and economic changes which are resulting in our changing appreciations of financially orientated modes of accounting are also stimulating an active and more fundamental questioning of the adequacy of financial representations of corporate performance and well-being. Both within the corporation and outside, notions of social accounting, social reporting and social auditing, of social cost-benefit analysis and of social calculation, are being articulated with increasing frequency and interest.

Within the corporation, for instance, factors such as the changing nature of the labour market, the growing power of trade unions and the increasing scope and significance of legal provisions and requirements in the industrial relations area have fostered the development of a more extensive form of internal corporate social administration, manifested in the growing significance of the personnel function in most corporations in recent years. The routine administrative concerns of such a function themselves resulted in the collection and compilation of a growing volume of social information on the activities of the corporation, at least some of which has provided the basis for more extensive developments in social information processing within the context of changing forms of work organisation (Jonson, Jönsson and Svensson, 1979) and the growing recognition of the need to report to employees and trade unions (Dekker, 1977; Page, 1978). And some corporations, particularly in the USA (Epstein, Flamholtz and McDonough, 1976) and Germany (Dierkes, 1978), have given attention to the internal development of wider forms of external reporting. Still varying tremendously in content, scope and form of presentation, the social account or report in the USA started as a response to the criticisms of the social role of the corporation that were a feature of the mid to late 1960s, their German parallels possibly being more attuned to the developing environmental concerns of the State.

Whilst to date internally initiated forms of social accounting have been almost completely absent from the United Kingdom, we have seen a proliferation of interest in and experimentation with broader and more critically orientated criteria of corporate impact by a whole range of external pressure and interest groups. The activities of the Public Interest Research Centre, one of the pioneers in the area, gave rise to the publication of the journal *Social Audit*, the conduct of a number of social audits of both public and private organisations (Medawar, 1976), including that of Avon Rubber
106 (1976), and, on the basis of such experiences, the articulation of a set of concerns and approaches that goes far beyond the group's original basis in the consumer movement (Frankel, 1978; Medawar, 1978). Related, if somewhat more radical concerns have also emanated from Counter-Information Services. The government sponsored Community Development Projects also forged their own approaches to the socio-economic assessment of public and private organisations within the context of urban and industrial change and decline (1974, 1975).

Such experiences have yet to be assessed and incorporated into wider public discourse. In the meantime, however, sections of the trade union movement have started to develop their own perspectives and empirical approaches (Coates, 1978). Often grounded in the specifics of redundancy and unemployment, some at least have nonetheless sought for an appreciation of their situation in terms of wider social and economic criteria. Sometimes this has added little to debates over policy options and alternatives. But on occasions, such as that provided by the Alternative Corporate Plan published by the Lucas Shop Stewards (Cooley, 1978), trade union groups have offered a challenge to all of those who claim to be interested in notions of corporate effectiveness. Just how, if at all, do strategies for, and evaluations of, corporate action based on concepts of value in use rather than value in exchange relate to prevailing concerns in the more conventional literature on corporate effectiveness?

Research, at least as conventionally defined as taking place within the confines of the academy or similar institutions, has played a rather limited role in the search for and assessment of wider, more socially orientated criteria for corporate effectiveness. For the vast majority of initiatives would appear to have been grounded in the development of ongoing practice, be that located within or without the corporation as such.

Internally to the corporation, innovation, where it has occurred, has resulted from the identification of problems which have arisen as management has sought to adapt to the changing nature of and constraints upon the management task. Often with an interest in maintaining an existing order, the specifics of new management practices have been created. Complex in concept and operation, these have necessitated the construction of new flows of information and often from these have stemmed more embracing concepts and methods for assessing aspects of corporate action.

External to the corporation, there has been a similar relationship between the new and the intended. Innovation, where it has occurred, has also been grounded in the specifics of organisational and social reality, often stemming from a desire to change. With an interest in the promotion of new social objectives, or at the very least patterns of social accountability and responsiveness, consideration has been given to the means by which present practice can be assessed, alternative aims articulated and new options suggested.

Indeed, to be honest, the roles that more traditional varieties of 'accounting' research can play in such a socio-political milieu are still emergent. On the one hand, some corporate practitioners and professional associations have started to recognise the tactical role that research can serve in the ongoing political forum of accounting discourse, and some representatives of other interests are now following this lead. All seek to elicit the support of research and the new bodies of knowledge which it can create, in the elaboration, articulation and objectification of their own particular notions of corporate performance and effectiveness. A few researchers, on the other hand, are becoming increasingly interested in trying to understand the complexities of just such accounting deliberations and changes (Moonitz, 1974; Watts and Zimmerman, 1978; 1979; Zeff, 1971). Seeing the former varieties of research as operating *within* a particular accounting context, these latter researchers see themselves as striving for an appreciation *of* accounting and the processes by which it adapts and changes.

Such uncertainties of the research role themselves emphasise the way in which our perceptions of accounting have changed. Here at least, an important component of almost any corporate effectiveness repertoire can be seen to be in a state of flux. Once seemingly grounded on the firm rock of economic reality, the shifting nature of its context and the emergence of new interests in it have shown accounting to be as problematic a form of practice as those which underlie the newer criteria of corporate effectiveness which people with different perspectives of organisational functioning have been trying to articulate. For many, of course, the loss of such a former certainty might be, and indeed will be, disturbing. In the context of the wider debates on corporate effectiveness, however, such a loss may have its advantages if it can point to a view of effectiveness which resides in the realm of ongoing organisational and social practice rather than in that of the ideal and the absolute.

## CRITERIA OF EFFECTIVENESS AND ORGANISATIONAL FUNCTIONING

In fact the relationship between concerns with the measurement and reporting of particular notions of corporate effectiveness and organisational practice has been the focus of another developing body of research. Rather than seeking either to improve the measurements themselves or to explore the social conditions for their existence, such research has tried to inquire into how particular measurements of corporate effectiveness function in organisations, the range of their effects and the processes through which these are achieved. Albeit slowly and cautiously, the research has been building up a body of quite important insights, appreciations and perhaps for the practitioner all too open-ended questions.

Some such studies have explored the potential organisational significance of the identification and dissemination of particular indicators of corporate effectiveness. Conceiving the corporation as an arena where multitudinous activities take place, each having a range of consequences both theoretical and actual, such research has focused on the role that indicators of corporate performance and effectiveness play in creating a selective visibility for particular consequences (Becker and Neuhauser, 1975; Gordon, Tanon and Morse, 1977; Shortell, Becker and Neuhauser, 1977). Do the particular conceptions of effectiveness, which are reflected in the flows of information which permeate the corporation, influence perceptions of the problematic and the possible, and thereby, the patterns of actual achievement? Do they, in other words, succeed in infiltrating and influencing the specifics of organisational practice and action? Perhaps not too surprisingly, the answer provided by research has been a possible 'yes', with the possibility being dependent on the presence of organisational mechanisms and processes through which the particular visibility can be articulated and diffused. Even potentially similar organisations which have implemented different patterns of internal visibility have been shown to follow very different patterns of performance over time.

In a study of insurance companies, for instance, different patterns of visibility for the financial consequences of corporate action themselves explained the major portion of the observed variance in the ratio of profits to assets (Becker and Neuhauser, 1975). And a detailed study of American hospitals illustrated how investments in the measurement and reporting of either the economic or the medical components of performance could result in very different outcome consequences if they were disseminated through the relevant organisational communication and decision processes (Shortell, Becker and Neuhauser, 1977). With such dissemination, hospitals emphasising economic consequences were indeed cheaper whilst those emphasising medical consequences tended to be more innovative in the use of both medical technology and pharmaceuticals (Gordon and Tanon, 1974; Rosner, 1968).

The importance of the organisational utilisation of performance information has been suggested by other bodies of research findings. Recent studies of the use of management accounting information, for example, have demonstrated that the effects of such information are not dependent on either its mere existence or its technical characteristics (Hofstede, 1967; Hopwood, 1973a). The way in which information is used, particularly the way in which the social context of its use influences the meaning which is attributed to it, can and does exert a major influence on the roles which such information is seen as serving and the organisational effects which it has. As I have stated in a previous context (Hopwood, 1973b, p.84):



> 'while the information might be given, its interpretation is the outcome of a personal and social process which is sustained by the meanings, beliefs, pressures and purposes that are brought to bear by the managers using the information. In of necessity providing it with a personal significance and placing it in their own wider context, managers are able to use the information, perhaps without reflection, in a variety of ways — appropriate and inappropriate'.

Rigid uses of accounting information, for instance, can certainly stimulate an active concern with those characteristics of financial performance which are reflected within the reporting system. But such a concern is often achieved at the expense of high degrees of vertical and horizontal conflict in the corporation and the manipulation of the accounting data themselves (Hopwood, 1973a), both being consequences which can constrain organisational achievement more broadly conceived. However more flexible uses of the information can be realised. In a context where both the human and task components of the managerial job are valued and where information of any variety is not valued as an end in itself but as a means to a wider end, research has shown that it is possible to gain many of the advantages which can stem from the availability of a particular information system without this resulting in other damaging organisational consequences.

Other research also has started to demonstrate how particular organisational ends may not necessarily be achieved by a

concentration on their mere assessment. The evidence of the relationship between financial performance, to cite that area yet again, and the presence of detailed mechanisms for financial control and accountability is equivocal at the very best. The 'newly poor' (Olofsson and Svalander, 1975) are often those who invest heavily in the search for internal economic visibility, although often in so doing they may further dislocate themselves from their problematic external environments as they consciously or unconsciously succumb to the demands of their ever more visible internal environments. Financially efficient, they may in other words still walk to their economic grave! And the financially successful, on the other hand, tend, so some tentative research findings (Child, 1973, 1974, 1975; Rosner, 1968; Turcotte, 1974) would suggest, to avoid many of the rigors of contemplating ever further heights of financial effectiveness. Seemingly they revel and flourish within the context of
110 multiple and overlapping flows of information (Grinyer and Norburn, 1975), informal planning and assessment practices (Child, 1974) and continually renegotiated exchanges between organisational participants (Georgiou, 1973). Like the all too effective Japanese motor cycle manufacturers studied by the Boston Consulting Group (1975), which failed to use the detailed financial appraisals so beloved of their unsuccessful British competitors, concentrating instead on indicators of potential market penetration and overall corporate strategy, somehow they got there without too consciously trying to.

According to such studies, at least certain of the concerns with the articulation of criteria of corporate effectiveness would appear to be related to rather particular organisational rationalities and goal orientated, instrumental conceptions of the social functioning of organisations. By probing into the ways in which the interventionist strategies which can so readily emanate from such concerns can constrain rather than facilitate the action sequences which constitute organised endeavour, such research is starting to point to the rather uneasy relationship between our emerging knowledge of the social nature of organisational life and the organisational presumptions which underlie so many of the strategies for change.

Of course it would be pretentious to claim that the emerging body of research on the organisational dimensions of the measurement of corporate effectiveness has succeeded in untangling the complexities that reside in such relationships. It has not and will not for some considerable time to come. Already, however, it looks as though it is starting to move in that direction.

The emphasis which it has placed on the organisational processes through which and by which particular concerns with corporate effectiveness are or are not realised was much needed. By themselves criteria of effectiveness, of whatever variety, certainly have a potential to create particular meanings and understandings of corporate life and thereby influence action. But the realisation of that potentiality is far from being unproblematic. It is dependent on the way in which the articulated criteria interlink with complex and ongoing social and human processes, the functioning of which remains poorly understood in theory and practice. If, for the time being, the research can do no more than to introduce an element of caution and complexity into practice and of renewed vigor into research, it has certainly served its role.

## CONCLUSION

Systematic research into criteria for assessing corporate effectiveness is recent in origin. Until now the vast majority of new perspectives and approaches have emanated from the development of practice. Whether stemming from the concerns of corporate management, or 111
from those who seek to question if not challenge them, notions of effectiveness have been pragmatic in orientation, seeking either to guide and legitimise or to question and change ongoing practice and associated patterns of performance. Slowly, however, the role of research and inquiry has been recognised. Initially, it perhaps inevitably focused on the elaboration and operationalisation of particular notions of effectiveness. More recently, though, at least some research on the criteria of corporate effectiveness has adopted a more questioning and analytical stance, as it has started to delve into the complexities that influence their organisational roles and effects and the social processes of which they are themselves an outcome.

Generalisations from such an emergent body of research do not come easily. However, the above review has sought to emphasise the following points.

1. Criteria of corporate effectiveness are neither self-sufficient nor unitary in nature. Rather they are socially constructed, their roles and meanings stemming from social interests and concerns and the specific contexts in which they operate.
2. Financial criteria of effectiveness are as problematic as many others in both concept and operationalisation. Their dominance in practice is derived from the strength and resilience of the interests on which they rest, rather than from any superior claim to approximate the real and the true.
3. The practical significance of criteria of effectiveness does not stem from their mere existence. In and of themselves, criteria of any variety have little more than the potential to influence corporate action. The realisation of that potential is dependent, however, on the way in which articulated criteria interlink with

the complex social and organisational processes through which they are endowed with a particular meaning and relevance. For those concerned with corporate change, an understanding of such processes is at least as vital as that of the more technical aspects of criteria design and implementation.

4. Once grounded in the specifics of organisational practice, however, criteria of effectiveness can indeed influence organisational action. By helping to shape the patterns of organisational viability, they can influence perceptions of both the problematic and the possible, reinforcing certain sequences of actions and constraining the achievement of others.
5. Intriguingly, however, a predominant concern with a particular criterion of effectiveness may not necessarily result in its achievement. For organisations are complex artifacts, the
112 survival and development of which are dependent on the mutual satisfaction of numerous and often conflicting demands, both internal and external to the organisation itself. To focus on any one, without due care, may result in the neglect of others on which paradoxically the achievement of the focal criteria can in turn depend.
6. Finally, research is starting to explore the varied roles which criteria of effectiveness play in organisational functioning. Whilst acknowledging that in many instances the articulation of criteria precedes action, in other cases it is seeing how criteria can be derived from action itself, helping thereby retrospectively to create meanings and understandings of the dynamic sequence of events which constitutes organised activity. Seen in such terms, the effective organisation might well be the one which knows from whence it came!

Although undoubtedly preliminary in nature, such findings nonetheless constitute a rich and challenging agenda for both practical action and further research.

## REFERENCES

**Baxter, W.T.** *Accounting Values and Inflation*. McGraw-Hill, 1975.

**Becker, S.W. and Neuhauser, D.** *The Efficient Organisation*. Elsevier, 1975.

**Benson, J.K. (ed.)** *Organisational Analysis: Critique and Innovation*. Sage, 1977.

**Boston Consulting Group** *Strategy Alternatives for the British Motor Cycle Industry*. HMSO, 1975.

**Briloff, A.J.** *Unaccountable Accounting*. Harper and Row, 1972.

**Carlsson, J., Ehn, P., Erlander, B., Perby, M-L. and Sandberg, A.** 'Planning and Control from the Perspective of Labour: A Short Presentation of the DEMOS Project', *Accounting, Organisations and Society* 1979, Vol. 3, No. 3/4.

**Carsberg, B.V., Hope, A. and Scapens, R.W.** 'The Objectives of Published Accounting Reports', *Accounting and Business Research*. Summer, 1974.

**Chambers, R.J.** *Accounting, Evaluation and Economic Behaviour*. Prentice-Hall, 1966.
**Child, J.** 'Strategies of Control and Organisation Behaviour', *Administrative Science Quarterly*, 1973, pp.1-17.
**Child, J.** 'Management and Organisational Factors Associated with Company Performance — Part I', *Journal of Management Studies*, 1974, pp.175-189.
**Child, J.** 'Managerial and Organisational Factors Associated with Company Performance — Part II', *Journal of Management Studies*, 1975, pp.12-27.
**Coates, C., ed.** *The Right to Useful Work*. Spokesman, 1978.
**Cohen, M.D., March, J.G. and Olsen, J.P.** 'A Garbage Can Model of Organisational Choice', *Administrative Science Quarterly*, 1972, pp.1-25.
**Cooley, M.** 'Design, Technology and Production for Social Needs', in Coates, 1978.
**Community Development Project Intelligence and Information Unit** *The National Community Development Project*, 1974.
**Community Development Project Intelligence and Information Unit** *National Community Development Project Forward Plan* 1975-6, 1975.
**Dekker, C.** 'Social Reporting in the Netherlands'. Paper presented at the INI Colloquium, Madrid, December, 1977.
**Dierkes, M.** 'Corporate Social Performance in Germany — Conceptual Developments, Practical Experience and Political Interests'. Paper presented at the Academy of Management Meetings, San Francisco, 1978. 113
**Epstein, M., Flamholtz, E. and McDonough, J.J.** 'Corporate Social Accounting in the USA: State of the Art and Future Prospects', *Accounting, Organisations and Society*, 1976, Vol. 1, No. 1, pp.23-42.
**Fox, A.** *Industrial Sociology and Industrial Relations*. HMSO, 1966.
**Frankel, M.** *The Social Audit Pollution Handbook*. Macmillan, 1978.
**Georgiou, P.** 'The Goal Paradigm and Notes Towards A Counter Paradigm', *Administrative Science Quarterly*, 1973, pp.291-310.
**Gordon, G. and Tanon, C.P.** 'Costs, Professional Power and Hospital Structure'. Paper presented to the American Sociological Association, Montreal, 1974.
**Gordon, G., Tanon, C.P. and Morse, E.V.** 'Decision-Making Criteria and Organisation Performance', in *Organisational Research in Hospitals*, ed. by S.M. Shortell. Blue Cross, 1977.
**Grinyer, P. and Norburn, D.** 'Planning for Existing Markets: Perceptions of Executives and Financial Performance', *Journal of the Royal Statistical Society*, Series A, 1975, pp.70-97.
**Hofstede, G.H.** *The Game of Budget Control*. Van Gorcum, 1967.
**Hopwood, A.G.** *An Accounting System and Managerial Behaviour*. Saxon House, 1973a.
**Hopwood, A.G.** 'Problems with Using Accounting Information in Performance Evaluation', *Management International Review*, 1973b, pp.83-91.
**Jonson, L.C., Jönsson, B. and Svensson, G.** 'The Application of Social Accounting to Absenteeism and Personnel Turnover', *Accounting, Organisations and Society*, 1979, Vol. 3, No. 3/4.
**Lee, T.A.** *Income and Value Measurement: Theory and Practice*. Nelson, 1974.
**March, J.G.** 'Bounded Rationality, Ambiguity and the Engineering of Choice', *The Bell Journal of Economics*, Autumn, 1978, pp.587-608.
**March, J.G. and Olsen, J.P.** *Ambiguity and Choice*. Oslo: Universitetsforlaget, 1976.
**May, R.G. and Sundem, G.L.** 'Research for Accounting Policy: an Overview', *The Accounting Review*, October, 1976, pp.747-763.
**Medawar, C.** 'The Social Audit: A Political Review', *Accounting, Organisations and Society*, 1976, Vol. 1, No. 4, pp.389-394.
**Medawar, C.** *The Social Audit Consumer Handbook*. Macmillan, 1978.
**Moonitz, M.** *Obtaining Agreement on Standards in the Accounting Profession*. American Accounting Association, 1974.

**Olofsson, C. and Svalander, P.A.** 'The Medical Services Change Over to a Poor Environment — "New Poor" Behaviour' Unpublished Working Paper, University of Linkoping, 1975.

**Page, G.T.** *An Employer's Guide to Disclosure of Information* Kogan Page, 1978.

**Pettigrew, A.** 'The Creation of Organisational Cultures', Working Paper, European Institute for Advanced Studies in Management, Brussels, 1977

**Pfeffer, J. and Salancik, G.R.** 'Organisational Decision Making as a Political Process: The Case of a University Budget', *Administrative Science Quarterly* 1974, pp.135-151.

**Public Interest Research Group** *Social Audit of Avon Rubber Co Ltd* 1976

**Rosner, M.M.** 'Administrative Controls and Innovation', *Behavioural Science* 1968, pp.36-43.

**Scott, W.R.** 'Effectiveness of Organisational Effectiveness Studies', in P.S. Goodman, J.N. Pennings and Associates, *New Perspectives on Organisational Effectiveness* Jossey-Bass, 1977

**Shortell, S.M., Becker, S.W. and Neuhauser, D.** 'The Effects of Management Practices on Hospital Efficiency and Quality of Care', in S.M. Shortell, ed., *Organisational Research in Hospitals* Blue Cross, 1977

**Sterling, R.** *Theory of the Measurement of the Business Enterprise* University of Kansas Press, 1977.

**Tribe, L.H., Schelling, C.S. and Voss, J.** *When Values Conflict – Essays on Environment Analysis, Discourse and Decision* Wiley, 1976

**Turcotte, W.E.** 'Control Systems, Performance and Satisfaction in Two State Agencies', *Administrative Science Quarterly* 1974, pp 60-73

**Van Gunsteren, H.R.** *The Quest for Control* Wiley, 1976.

**Watson, T.J.** *The Personnel Managers* Routledge and Kegan Paul, 1977.

**Watts, R. and Zimmerman, J.L.** 'Towards a Positive Theory of the Determination of Accounting Standards', *The Accounting Review*, 1978, pp 112-134

**Watts, R. and Zimmerman, J.L.** 'The Supply of and Demand for Accounting Theories. The Market for Excuses', *The Accounting Review* 1979

**Weick, K.** *The Social Psychology of Organising* Addison-Wesley, 1969.

**Zeff, S.** *Forging Accounting Principles in Five Countries: A History and an Analysis* Stipes, 1971

116

# Discussion of "Some Inner Contradictions in Management Information Systems" and "Behavioral Implications of Planning and Control Systems"

ANTHONY G. HOPWOOD

The study of the organizational and behavioral aspects of management accounting now has quite a long, albeit somewhat irregular, history. Stimulated in large part by Chris Argyris' initial study of the behavioral consequences of budgeting,[1] the area has since attracted the attention of both accounting scholars and an array of social psychologists, sociologists and political scientists who have been interested in exploring the part which accounting plays in organizational functioning and control. Although our knowledge must still be regarded as emergent, real understandings nevertheless have been achieved. Moreover the potential importance of the area is now acknowledged by a growing number of both scholars and practitioners, and the insights that are available are even starting to replace those gratuitous and often mythical genuflections to the human and organizational context of the craft that have graced so many management accounting texts.

---

[1] Chris Argyris, *The Impact of Budgets upon People* (New York: The Controllership Foundation, 1952).

Given the current stage of development of the area, the papers by Chris Argyris and Bob Swieringa together provide an interesting basis on which to consider the state of our knowledge of the organizational and behavioral aspects of accounting and the challenges which might lie ahead. To comment on their papers, I shall first briefly review the differing traditions of inquiry which have characterized the area to date. Thereafter, after considering the two papers themselves, I shall attempt to discuss some of the implications which they might have for the future direction of research.

## TWO TRADITIONS OF INQUIRY

Our understandings of the organizational and behavioral aspects of management accounting systems have so far emanated from two rather different traditions of inquiry. On the one hand, a number of 117 sociologists, social psychologists, political scientists, and other scholars of the social have been fascinated, yet puzzled, by the organizational significance which accounting has achieved. Just what roles do management accounting systems play in organizations? How do they really function? And what consequences do they have? With no commitment to the prevailing procedures of the craft, they have sought to delve into the seeming mysteries of accounting in action, in the process providing us with a rich, illuminating and challenging array of insights into the accounting condition.[2] On the other hand, we have a growing number of inquiries undertaken by accounting researchers themselves. Although sometimes stimulated by the findings of their social science colleagues, the perspectives which have influenced their inquiries have often been very different, for rather than seeking to gain an appreciation of management accounting's wider organizational context and significance, until recently accountants have tended to adopt a more instrumental approach. How, they often have asked, can we overcome the resistance to the accounting craft? Which accountings are likely to have more impact? And just what roles can different organizational and behavioral approaches play? Accepting the preordained imperatives of the accounting mission and the conventional conceptions of the instrumentality of the craft, many accounting scholars of the behavioral have sought to increase its effectiveness by behavioral means. Rather than venturing to appreciate, let alone question, accounting in action, they have continued to seek new ways of influencing its outcomes.

[2]Particular note should be made of the works listed in Appendix A.

Hardly surprising, the two traditions of inquiry have remained rather detached. Many, although by no means all, of the social scientists who have been interested in the accounting endeavor have not chosen to use their understandings to influence the process of accounting itself. Equally, however, their studies have only rarely been cited in the accounting literature. Although occasionally used to legitimize an area of inquiry, until recently the substantive findings and perspectives have had little or no impact on the studies undertaken by accountants. Leads for further research have remained unexplored and accounting scholars have repeatedly failed to draw on either the theoretical or methodological contributions and insights.



With the traditions of the appreciative and the applied remaining so separate, accounting scholars of the behavioral have forged their own separate lines of investigation. Rather than delving into the complexities of accounting as it is practised, so often they have preferred to rely on the possibilities of the psychological laboratory. Indeed it is difficult to name more than a handful of inquiries that have been undertaken within the factory gate—or even outside the college wall. The world of accounting as it is has been largely ignored. Seemingly questions of internal validity have been emphasized to the almost complete neglect of external validity. Almost invariably, emphasis has been placed on methodological rather than theoretial sophistication and on the rigors of hypothesis testing rather than theory generation.[3] So, few attempts have been made to analyze directly the processes of accounting development and change, the interplay between accounting and other features of organizational life, and the consequences which accounting might or might not have for organizational action. Apparently it has been deemed to be sufficient to theorize in the armchair, to borrow a neat theory here and there,[4] and to so construct a basis for a tightly controlled excursion into a specifically constructed unknown. The net result of such a tradition of inquiry is a rather fragmented set of insights, however, many of which have a largely unknown and possibly equivocal relationship to accounting in action.

The reasons for such a research tradition are numerous.[5] The intel-

[3]See C. Tomkins, D. Rosenberg, and I. Colville, "The Social Process of Research: Some Reflections on Developing a Multi-Disciplinary Accounting Project," *Accounting, Organizations and Society* (1980).

[4]R. E. Jense, "Empirical Evidence from the Behavioral Sciences: Fish Out of Water," *Accounting Review* (July 1970): 502-8

[5]A. G. Hopwood, *An Accounting System and Managerial Behavior* (London: Saxon House, 1973); idem., "Towards an Organizational Perspective for the Study of Ac-

lectual traditions which have been deemed acceptable in schools of business no doubt have had a major role to play. So has an academic reward structure which has emphasized speedy, low-risk research having readily visible signs of rigorous inquiry. Also of importance, however, has been the accounting tradition itself, for while social scientists outside it have been prepared to take a less committed look at accounting as it is practiced, many accounting scholars of the behavioral have chosen to accept more readily the preordained canons of the accounting mission. Rather than trying to construct a view of what is, they have tried to shape what might be. Even when accountants have ventured into the world of practice, appreciative inquiries into the functioning of accounting have been rarer than attempts to provide more directly bases for improving the accounting endeavor. So while we have seen research oriented toward increasing accounting's motivational potential, analyses of the interplay be- 119
tween accounting and the political and the powerful have been rare indeed.

Such divergent research traditions of the past provide a fascinating context for considering the papers by Argyris and Swieringa, for to some extent the authors are seemingly engaged in a process of role reversal! Although Chris Argyris draws on a vast accumulation of insights into accounting and information systems as they are, he nevertheless seeks to provide some pointers as to how they might be. Bob Swieringa, on the other hand, not only critically points to the presumptions of the accounting past, but also seeks to draw upon and promote traditions of organizationally grounded inquiry which are oriented towards illuminating what is.

### ORGANIZATIONAL CONTRADICTIONS AND THE ROLE OF MANAGEMENT INFORMATION SYSTEMS

I agree with many of the points raised by Chris Argyris. Like him, I also have been confronted repeatedly with the frustrations which managers, and other organizational participants, I might add, can experience as a result of trying to cope with conventional management information and accounting systems. In such circumstances I, like him, find it difficult not to be aware of the constraining and disabilitating consequences which they can have at the individual level, the organizational consequences of which must be real and profound. So I can not only sympathize but also join in with his

counting and Information Systems." *Accounting, Organizations and Society* (1978): 3-14; and Tomkins, Rosenberg, and Colville, "Accounting Project."

strong concluding plea for a body of knowledge on the basis of which we might be able to design information flows which can engender learning and adaptation rather than frustration and disillusionment at both the individual and organizational level.

In the course of his discussion, Argyris provides us with a rich insight into the relationships between the instruments of official management practice and the complexity of the social processes which influence how management information systems emerge, develop, and function, and the consequences which they can have. I particularly approve of the emphasis which he gives to the constraints which are placed on the ability of organizational participants to articulate and thereby learn from and build upon *their* knowledge of the reality of information practice. So much of that reality is taboo in today's organizations. The limitations of official practice are
120 known to many, as are the richness and relevance of the unofficial information underworld. Yet such perceptions of the world of action invariably must be distanced from the language of management. So often the existence of what invariably are essential parts of organizational functioning is officially denied. They do not enter into the language of management and, as a consequence, they cannot influence the possibilities for change and development. With what "might be" thereby being shaped by rather limited conceptions of "what is," official practice becomes ever more influenced by particular and highly abstract notions of both action and order.

Argyris points to the dynamic consequences of such a situation. On the one hand, we see the emergence of central pressures for further system elaboration and development. In the continual "quest for control,"[6] systems are "tightened," gaps are plugged so that the systems might become even more "tamper proof," and renewed searches are made for ever further precision. And although Argyris emphasizes the internal origins of such tendencies, we should not forget that pressures external to the organization also can give rise to the same phenomenon. Olafsson and Svalander have illustrated the interests which the "newly poor" have in control system elaboration in constrained economic circumstances,[7] and Meyer, among others, has pointed to the roles which management and information practices can play in the creation of a symbolic order between those within the organization and external parties, such as the State, which have an

[6] H. R. van Gunsteren, *The Quest for Control: A Critique of the Rational Central-Rule Approach in Public Affairs* (London: Wiley & Sons, 1976).
[7] C. Olafsson and P. A. Svalander, "The Medical Services Changeover to a Poor Environment—'New Poor' Behavior" (University of Linköping, 1975).

interest in it.[8] On the other hand, as Argyris points out, the refinement and yet further abstraction of the official and centralized information practices results in the development of a range of informal, ad hoc and often idiosyncratic modes of information processing—his local MIS. Organizational participants increase their investment in their own approaches to information processing. "Black books"[9] and "just-in-case files"[10] are elaborated, and the power and significance of more tacit ways of managing information increased.

The description which Argyris provides of such conflicting tendencies in information practice is a useful one. However, as Argyris recognizes by his own rather cautious and ambivalent discussion of the possibilities for change, care should be exercized in discussing the implications which such a state of affairs might have for both organizational and information system development and change. My
own grounds for emphasizing the need for such caution are both 121
organizational and social in nature.

At the organizational level, we should remember that it might well be that at least some of the tendencies which Argyris outlines are exaggerated by particular ways of using official management information systems, for despite a growing body of research on differential system use and its individual and organizational consequences,[11] comparatively little consideration has been given to its implications for organizational change. That, however, is a small point. More importantly, we need to explicitly recognize that complex and dynamic organizations require a vibrant mix of different approaches to information processing.[12] Official information systems do have limitations. They can only service particular needs for organizational learning and control, having constraints on their ability to con-

---

[8] J. Meyer, "Environmental and Internal Origins of Symbolic Structure in Organizations" (Paper presented at the Seminar on Organizations as Ideological Systems, Stockholm, 1979).

[9] Simon et al., *Centralization vs. Decentralization in Organizing the Controller's Department* (New York: The Controllership Foundation, 1954).

[10] Argyris, *The Impact of Budgets*.

[11] Becker and Newheuser, *Efficient Organization* (Amsterdam: North-Holland, 1975); C. Cammann, "Effects of the Use of Control Systems," *Accounting, Organizations and Society* (1976): 301-13; S. M. Shortell and M. Brown, eds., *Organizational Research in Hospitals* (Blue Cross, 1976); Hopwood, *Managerial Behavior*; and M. Rahman and A. M. McCash, "The Influence of Organizational and Personal Factors on the Use of Accounting Information: An Empirical Study," *Accounting, Organizations and Society* (1976): 339-55.

[12] M. E. Earl and A. G. Hopwood, "From Management Information to Information Management" (Paper presented at the IFIP TC8-WG8.2 Working Conference on the Information System Environment, Bonn, 1979); and J. Galbraith, *Designing Complex Organizations* (Reading, Mass.: Addison-Wesley, 1973).

tinually adapt to the novel and the new.[13] So while we can contrast the characteristics of local and central approaches to the management of information flows, such contrasts should not prevent us from seeing the very different roles which the different approaches might serve. Perhaps in today's organizations, the central cannot assume the characteristics of the local; perhaps very different "conceptions of order" should exist; perhaps, therefore, the local and the central need to coexist in the complex and changing organizations which we have today. Indeed, it may well be that the effectiveness of official management information systems depends on their ambiguous and questioned existence and use. In circumstances where the need for information is changing and cannot be completely anticipated, the systemic and the preplanned might need to have a "loosely coupled"[14] relationship to ongoing management practice. The of-

ficial and the central might need to be complemented by the unofficial and the local. Indeed, I think that we are now starting to realize the role which ambiguity and redundancy can play in organizational functioning. As a review of the development of innovative management practices in the National Aeronautics and Space Administration (NASA) indicated,[15] their effectiveness might well have been dependent upon the loose, entrepreneurial, and irreverent manner in which they were used. Although such a perspective undoubtedly increases the difficulty of system change and implementation, I think that we should recognize both that official information systems may need to be used, but not believed, and we should acknowledge the potential facilitating roles served by unofficial, local and other modes of information processing. I would have liked to have seen Argyris giving some consideration to this yet further set of organizational paradoxes and contradictions.

Our recognition of the difficulties of gaining improvement and change in the information system area might be even further increased if we consider in greater detail the organizational and social roles which they serve. Argyris emphasizes the learning potential of management information systems, quite rightly contrasting, however, the roles which they might play in self-learning with the roles which they do play in facilitating the learning of others. In this way, he places the design and use of management information systems

[13]W. H. Starbuck, "Information Systems in Organizations of the Future," in *Information Systems and Organizational Structure*, ed. E. Grochla and N. Szyperski (New York: de Gruyter, 1975).

[14]K. E. Weick, "Educational Organizations as Loosely Coupled Systems," *Administrative Science Quarterly* (1976): 1-19.

[15]R. L. Chapman, *Project Management in NASA* (NASA, 1973).

firmly within the context of the management of the modern hierarchical organization, seeing much of present information-system practice as being oriented towards increasing unilateral patterns of hierarchical control. However, having done that, I do not think that Argyris goes on to extract and discuss the full consequences and implications of such an organizational positioning, despite the fact that this could provide a host of further insights into the origins and consequences of the organizational contradictions on which he focuses his subsequent discussion.

To the extent that information systems are implicated in the management of the hierarchical relationships on which the modern organization is grounded, as Argyris himself points out, they are not and cannot be considered as being apart from the organization. Forming part of the micro apparatus of power on the basis of which
organized activity is ordered, information systems, like other forms of 123
conventional management practice, are constitutive of the organization as we know it. In other words, not only are information systems influenced by the organization, but they, in turn, influence the form which the organization takes. Reflecting pressures that have been put on the organization as well as the processes of internal management and control, information systems are involved in both the definition of the organization itself and the constituent parts of it. They are implicated in the delineation of those who shall be considered within and without it, and vital processes of organizational segmentation and integration are based at least in part on the categories of organized endeavor reflected in the official flows of information. Providing mechanisms for planning and control, they not only facilitate but enable the separation of planning and control from the execution of the task—a key characteristic of the modern organization. Plans can be grounded on the specifics of organizational practice but thereafter readily aggregated to centralized decision making and control. Objectives for specific organizational activities can be distributed throughout the organization, with information systems then providing a selective pattern of organizational visibility on the basis of which achievement can be monitored at a distance and the distribution of organizational rewards attuned to particular forms of accomplishment. In ways such as these information systems create and propagate a particular form of organizational visibility and consciousness, they help to shape participants' views of the organization itself and what is to be regarded as both problematic and desirable, and they provide one basis on which power and influence can be gained and exercised. Today's information systems are, in other

words, centrally implicated in the creation and functioning of the hierarchical organization as we now know it.[16]

Such a view of the organizational and social context of information systems provides a rich basis on which to appreciate the full implications of the contradictions inherent in information system practice which are highlighted by Argyris' discussion. In such a context, "learning about others' performance in order to control their performance" may well "inhibit learning" by the subject of attention. Indeed, some even have gone so far as to suggest that this may often be the intention.[17] At the very least, an awareness of the roles which official information systems play in the separation of planning and control from the execution of the task helps us to appreciate just what might be at stake in the contradictions which Argyris emphasizes. Equally a more critical social insight into the organizational bases of information systems functioning places us in a better position to appreciate the difference between "a map for understanding" and "a map for taking action" and how the use of information flows in order to manage "a system" under control can "create conditions of injustice," for such concerns point to the very real possibility that the practices of information management rest upon the surer bases of concerns with the direction of organizational power and influence. However, Argyris' suggestion that the "tightening up" (of) MIS in order to "get a performance under control" may inhibit the achievement of this objective more directly suggests that such contradictions are not "inner" to the condition of management information systems themselves but are reflective of more basic contradictions which characterize modern organizational and social life. Equally suggestive in this respect is his statement that "Model I theories-in-use do not make it possible for people to have problem solving skills that question the governing values of theories-in-use."

When viewed in such a way, one can well appreciate why so much

[16]Indeed M. Foucalt, in *Discipline and Punish* (London: Allen Lane, 1975), would maintain that information systems now constitute a key feature of the "disciplinary mode of domination" which is characteristic of much organized endeavor today. For at the centre of such a mode of domination or control "lies a distinctive organization of observation. Discipline is based on the perpetual surveillance of its subjects, as well as on its own administrators: on a surveillance that is public in the sense that everyone knows of their constant subjection to its gaze; on a surveillance that is non-reciprocal, in that its subjects can neither know nor influence when they are being observed, or what the content and effect of their observation is; on a surveillance that is asymmetrical, in that its subjects are not in a position themselves to survey their surveyors." B. Fine, "Struggles against Discipline: The Theory and Politics of Michael Facault," *Capital and Class* (1979): 75-96.

[17]H. Braverman, *Labor and Monoply Capital* (New York: Monthly Review Press, 1974).

of the reality of information practice in organizations might remain taboo. Its revelation would be threatening to both the powerful and the controlled, for in such a contested context, to illuminate the multiplicity of information worlds which characterize organizational life would illustrate the partiality of official practice and might stimulate changes in it over which the providers of any insights might have little or no influence.

Illustrative of both the search for control and the resistances to it, the management of information flows can never stand in isolation of more all-embracing and thereby contentious questions of organizational design and influence. The creation of patterns of organizational visibility, be they official or otherwise, is inextricably bound up with the formation of modes of organizational operation and control, and the propagation of organizational rationales. Information system change, therefore, is a complex and difficult endeavor. 125
Certainly there are most likely few occasions on which information flows can be changed without influencing other aspects of organizational functioning. The informational invariably intersects with the organizational. And because of such interrelationships, it may well be that the radical information system changes which Argyris points to in his paper will require complementary organizational changes of an equally profound nature.

By emphasizing the relevance and interconnectedness of such issues, Argyris' paper serves an important purpose: it provides a basis for a questioning appreciation of the information and management accounting system craft. Equally, however, it, like my own comments, illustrates the extent of what is not known about the roles and operation of management information systems. For although we have a whole array of insights into the technical possibilities for information and accounting system design and at least some appreciation of the social nature of the modern organization, we still have comparatively little appreciation of the interrelationship between the two and the ways in which one might serve the other. One can only hope that it stimulates others to contribute to that broader basis for the design and operation of management information systems which is so central to Chris Argyris' concerns.

## ORGANIZATIONAL AMBIGUITY AND THE STUDY OF ACCOUNTING IN ACTION

Bob Swieringa provides us with a rather different appreciation of the management accounting (and implicitly, the MIS) craft. Emphasizing the complexity of illuminating "what is," he explicitly avoids any consideration of the accounting that "might be." Nevertheless Bob's is a valuable paper. Unlike so many in the behavioral accounting repertoire, it focuses on at least some of the moving frontiers of organizational thought. More significantly perhaps, he chooses not to prioritize a particular conception of the organizational world, but rather illustrates a number of organizational perspectives, including that which is implicit in the management accounting texts with which we are all so familiar.

The result of Swieringa's multiple analysis of the Birch Paper case is illuminating and rich in possibilities, not least because it begins to focus our attention on some elements of the social construction of organizational observation and the implications which that can have for the appreciation of the accounting craft. The analyses illustrate the relationship between theory and observation. They point to the
126 possibility of diverse conceptions of the real, even within an organization itself. By together emphasizing the multiple, overlapping, and possibly inconsistent uses to which accounting is both put and seen to be put, they illustrate the heterogeneous nature of the ways in which accounting enters into organizational discourse and debate, and even some of the ways in which the contradictions noted by Chris Argyris might emerge. In these respects, Swieringa's contribution is both useful and important providing a basis in the management accounting area for moving beyond those rather simple searches for the real and the true which have tended to dominate many of our inquiries to date.[18]

At what is undoubtedly an early stage in the recognition of the importance of such issues, we should not be too concerned about the fact that Swieringa has sought to describe and utilize a number of alternative theoretical perspectives on organizational functioning rather than to critically evaluate them either in terms of their general theoretical status or their potential relevance for illuminating particular aspects of the accounting craft. Hopefuly, however, subsequent scholars will attempt to provide that more critical review.

[18]Similar questionings of the nature of accounting knowledge and practice have been evident in the financial accounting domain for sometime now. See for example, R. Watts and J. L. Zimmerman, "The Demand for and the Supply of Accounting Theories: The Market for Excuses," *Accounting Review* (April 1979): 273-305. No doubt stimulated by both the theoretical diversity and political contentiousness of recent policy debates, they are resulting in a more appreciative and critical analysis of financial accounting deliberation and practice. Unlike some of his financial accounting colleagues however, Swieringa chooses not to prioritize a particular conception of the true on the basis of which to politize the status of alternative and competing conceptions.

However useful the behavioral theory of the firm, for instance, might be, we should remember that it provides a relatively static apprecia-tion of the organizational world. Accepting so much of the social and organizational context as given, it provides a rather constrained view of the processes of organizational change and those conflicts for power and influence which underlie the contradictions of informa-tion and organizational practice which were emphasized by Argyris. In other words, the behavioral theory, and many of the theoretical perspectives which have been derived from it, tell us little about either how organizations and the information and accounting systems which function within them have come to be what they are or how they might change. Equally, we should remember that the apparently more challenging conceptions inherent in the garbage can and organizing models also tend to be based on rather micro and short-
term analyses of organized endeavor. While they can illuminate some 127
of the paradoxes and contradictions of organizational life, they too provide only limited insights into the processes of organizational change, taking as given many of the constraints, relationships, and filters which currently influence what organizations are.

Swieringa has drawn on only some of the available understandings of organizational behavior, emphasizing the insights which can be derived from theories which tend to accept the organizational context as we now know it. As such, his analyses consider micro rather than macro processes of change and individual and organizational as distinct from social influences on behavior. Let me make it clear that I do not criticize him for this; there are very real limits on what can be done within the confines of a single paper, theoretical preferences also vary, and what has been done is illuminating, useful, and im-portant. However, I think that the partiality of the analyses should be pointed out so that others might be encouraged both to explore other competing views of the organizational world and to be both con-scious and critical of the status, potential, and limitations of the perspectives which are or might become available.

Another implication of Swieringa's selective utilization of organi-zational theories is that he has emphasized the need to understand accounting as it is, rather than as it has become and as it might be. However, I still find myself intrigued as to what he might see as being the implications which his analyses hold for the practice as well as the study of the accounting craft. One personal reason for this is that I have my own uncertainties (rather than doubts) about the practical directions in which the garbage can and organizing theories might take us! By providing such illuminating and provocative insights into the complexities of what is, do they also encourage us to accept that status quo? More particularly, if it is useful to conceive of organizations as "organized anarchies,"[19] are we to resign ourselves to the fact that information and accounting practice might have to focus on the organizing elements while other practices stimulate the anarchical? Are we really to lose out on all the fun? Or are there real possibilities for "designing" (in an anarchical and loosely coupling manner, of course!) information flows which can promote the anarchical as well as the organized, and the loose as well as the tightly coupled? Can we really think in terms of designing "semi-confusing information systems"[20] and "foolish" information technologies?[21] And if we can, just who is to set the parameters for confusion and foolishness? Who, in other words, is to do the fooling, and who is to be fooled? Admittedly, such questions are posed in a jocular manner. However, I think that they point to serious issues underlying any attempt to relate the appreciative to the applied, particularly when the appreciative does relatively little to explicate the underlying presumptions of organizational and social life that may be implicit within it.[22]

Such concerns set an agenda for the future, however. In the meantime, the radical questioning of the "tenets of the (accounting) faith" which is so central a part of Swieringa's paper must be welcomed. For so long, such imperatives of the accounting mission have remained supreme, all be they amazingly detached from the practice of accounting in action. By discussing how the uses to which accounting is put can be emergent rather than pregiven, how accounting practice can further be diverse and far from consistent ends, and how the rationalities implicit in action can be shaped by the accounting craft as well as influencing the impacts which it in turn has, Swieringa has provided a useful stimulus for further inquiry. One can only hope that other scholars will be encouraged to delve further into the issues which he raises. Hopefully, such inquiries will also shed some light on the equally intriguing question of why those

---

[19] M. D. Cohen and J. G. March, *Leadership and Ambiguity: The American College President* (New York: McGraw-Hill, 1974).

[20] B. Hedberg and S. Jönsson, "Designing Semi-Confusing Information Systems for Organizations in Changing Environments," *Accounting, Organizations and Society* (1978): 47-64.

[21] J. G. March, "The Technology of Foolishness," in *Ambiguity and Choice in Organizations*, ed. J. G. March and J. P. Olsen (Bergen: Universitetsforlaget, 1976).

[22] What may be at stake with such concerns can be illustrated by the comment made by one of my students after he had read a number of works by one of the authors cited in Swieringa's paper: "This guy is really serious about foolishness!"

tenets of the accounting faith have remained so unquestioned and supreme for so long.[23]

## SOME IMPLICATIONS FOR FURTHER INQUIRY

Both Chris Argyris and Bob Swieringa point to the complex ways in which management information and accounting systems are implicated in organizational functioning. While as accountants many of us continue to propogate the absolute virtues of the craft, the analyses of Argyris and Swieringa illustrate that the consequences and impacts which it has in practice are the result of the ways in which the calculative technologies intersect with a diverse variety of other organizational practices and processes. Considerations of organizational power and influence, the ways in which the organization as we now know it has emerged, and the processes underlying organiza- 129
tional action and change all have a profound effect on what management accounting is perceived to be and the consequences which it does and might have. As both papers repeatedly demonstrate, albeit in very different ways, management accounting is a phenomenon which needs to be understood in organizational terms.

However, both papers also demonstrate how little we currently know of the organizational aspects of the management accounting and information system crafts. Argyris concludes his analysis with a plea for an alternative body of knowledge on the basis of which we might seek to change at least some of their individual and organizational consequences; and Swieringa explicitly seeks to demonstrate the potential of alternative organizational perspectives which as yet have not been applied within the accounting arena. Albeit in different ways, both point to the need for further inquiry. However, just what type of research is now required in the so-called behavioral accounting area? What perspectives and approaches are most likely to enrich our understandings of accounting both as it is and as it might be?

Put quite simply, my own view is that accounting researchers need

[23] In the meantime, inquiries into the latter question could well commence within the academy itself. In his paper Swieringa notes that so much of the teaching of management accounting continues to propagate the tenets of the faith, in the process often denying the relevance of the rich appreciation of organizational functioning and accounting in action that might be present in the student body. Indeed on occasions students are encouraged to deny their own perceptions of that richer reality. As the introduction to a "solution" in the instructor's guide for an accounting text stated: "Students will often want to emphasise the organizational aspects of this case. This should be discouraged. This should start by focusing on the accounting alternatives. . . !"

to get inside the factory gate or the office door. There is, I think, an urgent need for observational studies of accounting in action, and I think that this would be the opinion of both Argyris and Swieringa. We need to study how accounting systems function, how accounting information is and is not used, how accounting does or does not permeate other organizational processes, and the consequences which accounting does or does not have at both the individual and the organizational level. We need to ascertain just what the relevant variables for understanding the accounting craft are, rather than presuming them beforehand, and we need to ascertain precisely how different organizational perspectives can enrich our understandings of accounting as it is. In fact, I find myself repeatedly amazed that such work has not been done. Surely, one tends to think, and many of my nonaccounting colleagues do think, scholars with such applied
130 instincts as accountants would revel in the complexities of accounting in action. Well, revel they might; but apparently they have not, for we have so few studies of the organizational functioning of accounting. Just what have been the pressures for accounting change? Have they emanated from within the organization or without? What organizational significances have been attributed to the craft, and in what circumstances? What have been the relationships between accounting and other forms of organizational practice? Just what roles has accounting played in the emergence of the modern hierarchical organization? When, for instance, have organizations invested heavily in accounting? And of equal significance, when have they continued to function quite adequately without the assistance of such sophisticated forms of control?

Such latter forms of inquiry also point to the need for inquiries into alternative forms of accounting and accounting as it might be. What accountings, for instance, have been associated with organizations claiming to have very different modes of operation and forms of governance? Are there ways of reducing rather than increasing an organization's dependence on the craft? Just why do some organizations seem so peculiarly accounting intensive while others invest in alternative modes of control? Rather than so readily presuming any functional imperative for the accounting craft as we now know it, I think that we, as researchers, should be prepared to take a less committed stance, on occasions seeking to problematize "what is" so that we might gain some rather different appreciations of "what might be."

Such organizational and historical investigations would be very different from what is now done in the name of management accounting research, even be it of an organizational and behavioral variety. For that reason alone, there are a host of reasons why such studies will not be done. Yet that should not delude us from recognizing that if we are to build on the richness of Argyris' and Swieringa's insights, very different research perspectives and strategies will be required in the management information and accounting system area.

## APPENDIX A

Argyris, Chris. "Management Information Systems: The Challenge to Rationality and Emotionality." *Management Science* (1971): B275-92; idem., "Organizational Learning and Management Information Systems." *Accounting, Organizations and Society* (1977): 113-23; Simon, H. et al. *Centralization Versus Decentralization in Organizing the Controller's Department*. New York: The Controllership Foundation, 1954; Whyte, W. F. *Money and* 131
*Motivation*. New York: Harper and Row, 1955; Ray, D. "Efficiency and 'The Fix': Information Intergroup Relations in a Piecework Machine Shop." *American Journal of Sociology* (1955): 255-66; Dalton, M. *Men Who Manage*. New York: Wiley, 1959; and P. M. Blau. *The Dynamics of Bureaucracy*. Chicago: University of Chicago Press, 1955. For the contributions of the Carnegie Project on the Behavioral Theory of the Firm, see Cyert, R. M. and March, J. G. *A Behavioral Theory of the Firm*. Englewood Cliffs, N.J.: Prentice-Hall, 1963; Bonini, C. P. *Simulation of the Information and Decision Systems in the Firm*. Englewood Cliffs, N.J.: Prentice-Hall, 1963; Clarkson, G. P. *Portfolio Selection: A Simulation of Trust Investment*. Englewood Cliffs, N.J.: Prentice-Hall, 1962; Crecine, J. P. "Defense Budgeting: Organizational Adaptation to Environmental Constraints." in *Studies in Budgeting*, ed. R. F. Byrne et al. Amsterdam: North-Holland, 1971; idem. *Governmental Problem Solving: A Computer Simulation of Municipal Budgeting*. Chicago: Rand McNally, 1969; and Williamson, D. F. *The Economics of Discretionary Behavior*. Englewood Cliffs, N.J.: Prentice-Hall, 1964. Also refer to Wilkavsky, A. *The Politics of the Budgetary Process*. Boston: Little, Brown, 1964; idem. "Policy Analysis Is What Information Systems Are Not." *Accounting, Organizations and Society* (1978): 77-88; idem. and Hammand, A. "Comprehensive Versus Incremental Budgeting in the Department of Agriculture." *Administrative Science Quarterly* (1965): 321-46; Heclo, H. and Wildavsky, A. *The Private Government of Public Money*. London: Macmillan, 1974; Hofstede, G. H., "People and Techniques in Budgeting." in *Quantitative Methods in Budgeting*, ed. C. B. Tilanus. Leiden: Martinus Nijhoff, 1976; idem., *The Game of Budget Control*. Van Gorcum, 1967; Bower, J. *Managing the Resource Allocation Process*. Graduate School of Business, Harvard University, 1970; Ackerman, R. W. "Influence of Integration and Diversity on the Investment Process." *Administrative Science Quarterly* (1970): 341-52; Pettigrew, A. M. *The Politics of Organizational Decision Making*. London: Tavistock, 1973; and Michael, D. *On Learning to Plan and Planning to Learn*. London: Jossey-Bass, 1973. At a more organizational level of analysis, see the work of Chandler, A. *Strategy and Structure*. Cambridge, Mass.: MIT Press, 1963; idem. and Deams, H.

"Administrative Co-ordination, Allocation and Monitoring: A Comparative Analysis of the Emergence of Accounting and Organization in the USA and Europe." *Accounting, Organizations and Society* (1979): 3-20; Litterer, J. A. "Systematic Management: The Search for Order and Integration." *Business History Review* (1961); and idem. "Systematic Management: Design for Organizational Recoupling in American Manufactauring Firms." *Business History Review* (1963): 369-91; and Galbraith, J. *Designing Complex Organizations*. Reading, Mass.: Addison-Wesley, 1973. The interest of social scientists in information and accounting systems continue in the work of Becker, S. W. and Neuheuser, D. *The Efficient Organization*. Amsterdam: North-Holland, 1975; Shortell, S. M. and Brown, M., eds. *Organizational Research in Hospitals*. Blue Cross, 1976; Ouchi, W. G. "The Transmission of Control through Organizational Hierarchy." *Academy of Management Journal* (1978): 173-92; Pfeffer, J. "Power and Resource Allocation in Organizations," in *New Directions in Organizational Behavior*, ed. B. M. Shaw and G. R. Salancik. Chicago: St. Clair Press, 1977; idem. *Organizational Design*. Arlington Heights, Ill.: AHM Publishing, 1978; Salancik, G.
132 R. and Pfeffer, J. "Organizational Decision Making as a Political Process: The Case of a University Budget." *Administrative Science Quarterly* (1974): 135-51; and Fox, F. V. and Staw, B. M. "The Trapped Administrator: Effects of Job Insecurity and Policy Resistance on Commitment to a Course of Action." *Administrative Science Quarterly* (1979): 449-71.

*The Information Systems Environment*
*Lucas, Land, Lincoln, Supper (Editors)*
*North-Holland Publishing Company*


# FROM MANAGEMENT INFORMATION TO INFORMATION MANAGEMENT

Michael J. Earl
Oxford Centre for Management Studies

and

Anthony G. Hopwood
London Graduate School of Business Studies

Systems designers, managers and researchers increasingly recognize that there are problems in the development and operation of MIS. Frequently lack of management support and involvement are cited as causes of inadequate MIS and calls are made for managing information as a resource.

In this paper the authors argue that a new perspective is required, from a concern with management information as a technical phenomenon to a concern with information management as a substantive organizational phenomenon. Such a re-direction may depend on new metaphors, language and frameworks being derived first.



Among both researchers and managers there is an increasing realization of problems in the management information area. A recurring theme in the literature is that MIS have been disappointing in so far as they commonly have failed to meet expectations (Argyris 1977). In management courses, sessions on MIS rarely want for lively discussion, heated debate and general concern. Managers frequently complain of information overload on the one hand and an information gap on the other. The professional information providers - systems analysts, accountants and management scientists - proudly describe their achievements and earnestly explain their current plans. The information users listen with mixed feelings ranging from hope to scepticism, from commitment to antagonism and from understanding to incomprehension. There are problems in the current state of MIS.

Meanwhile substantial sums of money continue to be spent on information processing. Companies commonly claim that their data processing budgets consume 2% of sales turnover. One major multinational company has estimated that 10% of its world-wide corporate turnover is spent on information processing. Ten percent of net assets on world-wide balance sheets are thought to be explained by hardware investment and a UK multinational's data processing budget is currently growing by 30% per annum compound. Top management understandably is becoming concerned with "value for money".

Gibson and Nolan (1974) have suggested that DP budgets follow an S-shaped curve characterized by increasing management attention to planning and control of the computer resource. Concern with efficiency of information processing is expressed by productivity audits, performance monitoring and proliferation of controls. Effectiveness is emphasized by the introduction of steering committees, attempts at cost benefit analyses and charging for computer services. Maturity, they suggest, is reached only when the computer resource is fully integrated into everyday management practice and thinking. Our evidence would suggest that such a maturity has yet to be achieved however. While continual thinking and concern may be evident, it would appear that we are a long way from gaining the full integration of the computer resource into management practice.

Meanwhile information processing technology continues to advance. Mainframes and mass storage continue to approximate to Grosch's Law providing more power for less money. Minicomputers, and now microcomputers, threaten to change the shape of data-processing and perhaps of MIS. "Convergence" of computing, data communication and word processing will extend the scope of formal information processing. Managers and specialists are both excited and alarmed. The specialist contemplates new techniques and new applications. The DP manager sees new options and new anxieties. Managers wonder whether an opportunity has arrived to regain control or, more frequently perhaps, whether the technology will finally leave them stranded.

Yet despite some of the fundamental questions posed by these trends, investment in formal MIS continues. With the persuasiveness of so many interested parties, particularly the information providers, the appeal of sophisticated technology and the felt need to keep up with others, it is easy to justify ever more information systems. There is always an information need, the system always needs improving and incremental growth is generally invisible. Indeed MIS perpetuate themselves: they are necessary because they are there. Professions and disciplines such as accounting, computer science and cybernetics are built around them. Other seemingly successful organizations have MIS and publicize them. Yet in transferring systems from other organizations we fail to examine the context in
134 which they originally operated, often implementing misfits as a result. Finally, we seek spin-offs, trying to satisfy management information needs on the basis of existing data-orientated systems (Zani 1970). In short, MIS are assumed to be good for us. After all, or so it is frequently claimed, is not information the raw material of decision making, the *sine qua non* of planning and control and the life blood of organizations?

Increasingly however the existence of any *a priori* relationship between formal MIS as commonly conceived and effective organizational performance is being questioned. In a planning context, for instance, Grinyer and Norburn (1975) found no significant relationship between formal information systems and financial performance. Instead they found use of both informal channels of communication and informal decision-making processes was associated with success. Lorsch and Allen (1973) found that complexity of management control information systems facilitated upward information flows, but not downward flows. However both downward and upward flows were found to be associated with favorable financial performance with alternatives to formal MIS appearing to be essential.

Indeed it is the "newly poor" (Olofsson and Svalander, 1975) that invest heavily in additional mechanisms for internal visibility and control, although often in so doing they may further dislocate themselves from their problematic external environments as they consciously or unconsciously succumb to the demands of their ever more visible internal environments. Financially efficient, they may still walk to their economic grave (Hopwood, 1979). And the financially successful, on the other hand, tend to avoid many of the rigors of ever more sophisticated information and control systems (Child, 1973, 1974, 1975; Rosner, 1968; Turcotte, 1974). Seemingly they revel and flourish within the context of informal planning and assessment practices (Child, 1974), multiple and overlapping flows of information (Grinyer and Norburn, 1975) and continually renegotiated exchanges between organizational participants (Georgiou, 1973). Indeed the hearsay evidence of many managers suggests that the information they use in critical decisions does not emanate from the formal MIS. As Mintzberg (1972) discovered, top managers select and prefer informal information processing in most of their work.

Thus with the past disappointments with information systems which explicitly have claimed to facilitate the process of management, the growth of expenditure on information processing and the newly emergent technological developments, pressures on both MIS designers and users are undoubtedly increasing. Concerns and dissatisfactions are being expressed and at least some are starting to probe for alternatives.

The theme of our paper is that a major constraint on both current practice and the delineation of alternatives is that information processing is viewed in too narrow and technical a manner. Information is still seen as a technical phenomenon, a "thing" that has a seemingly problematic relationship to the intricacies of organizational processes and practices. And, as a consequence, our underlying information concepts and language tend to encourage the formalization, bureaucratization, standardization and mechanization of information processes - the very things which the recent studies quoted above suggest neither fit nor suit the realities of organizational activity. If this is the case, and we think that it is, then the alternatives to present practice may not be recognized because our existing MIS perspectives are outdated and not descriptive of even present organizational practice.

In this paper we argue for a new perspective, from a concern with management information as a technical phenomenon to a concern with information management as a substantive organizational phenomenon. Our theme is not just a play on words or a mere evangelical call to put management back into information systems. The perspective which we seek is one that is concerned with a broader appreciation of information processing in organizations. We are urgently in need of some new and very different metaphors for considering the roles which information does, can and might play in organizational functioning. To illustrate this we start by examining the variety of ways in which organizations process information.



## THE INFORMATION PROCESSING MIX IN ORGANIZATIONS

Despite the emphasis which has been placed on MIS, organizations have invested and continually do invest in a multitude of ways of processing information. One way of looking at the variety of approaches used in practice is to distinguish between routine and non-routine and official and unofficial modes of information processing. The resulting array of information possibilities is depicted in Figure 1.

| | Routine | Non-Routine |
|---|---|---|
| Official | MIS<br>Management Accounting Systems;<br>Production Control Systems | Access Facilities;<br>Task Forces;<br>Liaison Roles |
| Unofficial | Black-books;<br>Just in Case Files | The Grape Vine;<br>Lunch Table Chats |

Figure 1. The Information Processing Mix

The official, routine information processing box contains the MIS which have been emphasized so much. They are often the operational systems upon which our organizations depend from day to day. In some businesses they have even become a substantial part of the business itself; for example air-line reservation systems, production control systems in the engineering sector and transactions systems in banking.

The unofficial, routine category of information processing contains systems which serve local needs. In some cases these strive to compensate for the inadequacies of the routine systems; in other cases they are maintained as defensive information against attack from superiors and peers. It is evident from research (Hopwood

1973; Simon et al., 1954) and from discussions with managers that such informal, but nonetheless routine, approaches to information processing are ubiquitous. Hedberg and Johnson (1978) saw them as having value in creating and maintaining subcultures to question and challenge the status quo and stability. Also they suggested that they often provide more flexibility and discretion to managers than the official counterparts. Argyris (1977) suggests that unofficial, routine systems often represent actuality, provide concrete descriptions of unique situations, indicate true causality and provide private and tacit views. Earl (1978a) suggests that they may be attractive because they are simple and may serve as unofficial prototypes for subsequent official routinization.

The non-routine, official category includes purposive approaches to facilitating the processing of information such as investments in the capability to provide ad hoc information and mechanisms for furthering access to information. Also included in this category are those structural approaches to information processing which are effective because they are based on managerial actions and interpersonal activities through which "things get done" and by which we can learn from experience. Such structural mechanisms provide means for crossing intra-organizational boundaries, for transcending levels of authority and influencing others by discourse and persuasion. Meetings, conferences and task forces provide channels of lateral

and downward communication when often the routine MIS are predominantly upward. By being less formal and structured, non-routine and official "information systems" may also help achieve "control with" rather than "control over". They may perhaps offer top management a means of keeping "in touch", when the formal and official MIS no longer represent the reality they once measured. Finally they can often be created quickly and then killed when their purpose has been satisfied. Conversely the routine, official forms of information processing take a long time to create and may never die.

The unofficial, non-routine category comprises many of the informal information systems upon which managers depend. These devices carry news quickly, convey nuances, and can process qualitative information. To discover what is important, one joins the grape-vine. To influence some-one or break down the system one sits at the right lunch-table. To try and make sense of complexity we share the problem and construct our organization and world through and with each other. These forms of information processing are personal and private and accordingly fulfill purposes which the official or routine system could never attempt.

The reality of information processing in organizations is the vibrant and varied mix depicted by this framework. Organizations both have and require a balance of complementary information processing forms, including the more personal and structural varieties. However it seems to us that so much of this reality does not influence or enter into legitimate professional discourse in the MIS area, and this may well be a major constraint on organizational adaptation or change. Investing heavily in routine, official MIS we often forget and exclude investment in, and development of, competing, counter-balancing, overlapping and reinforcing information flows and processes. Just why does the emphasis on the formal and routine continue? What is at stake with the development of MIS as we now know them? What organizational roles do they really serve? To address such questions, let us consider further a key aspect of the interface between information and organization, namely the roles which information plays in decision-making. How is the development of MIS implicated in the very different types of decision-making processes which constitute organizational life?

## INFORMATION AND DECISION

Many writers have seen MIS as servants of decision making and several authorities have devised decision-orientated strategies for MIS design (Ackoff 1967; Zani 1970; Mason 1969). The relationship between information and decision making has been an influential basis for the analysis, development and articulation of normative MIS "solutions". Indeed some have even described MIS as Decision Support

Systems (Gorry and Scott-Morton 1971).

However, one problem with the use of the decision-making perspective for the analysis of both information needs and information systems is that the relationship between information and decision has rarely been critically examined. The link has, in other words, been presumed rather than described and analyzed. A particular view of human rationality and the attendant relationship between information and decision-making has been uncritically adopted. We have tended to presume, for instance, that the specification and analysis of information preceeds decision-making, that the roles played by information in decision-making are invariate across a multitude of different decision situations. Information is there to facilitate and ease rather than more actively influence, if indeed not frustrate, the decision-making process. Such presumptions are however little more than abstractions from the complex reality of information processing in organizations. While they might simplify the information system design process, their relationship to the realities of organizational life is questionable.

One way of looking at the relationship between information and decision-making in more detail can be based on the analysis of Thompson and Tuden (1959) which adds to the traditional view of the link between decision-making and uncertainty by classifying various states of uncertainty and different types of decision-making processes. As can be seen in Figure 2, they distinguish between uncertainty (or disagreement, for that is the same at the organizational level) over organizational objectives and the uncertainty over the cause and effect relationships which are embodied in particular organizational actions. When objectives are clear and undisputed, and cause and effect certain, Thompson and Tuden highlighted the potential for decision-making by computation. As cause and effect relationships become uncertain, however, that potential diminishes and decisions start to be made in a judgemental manner. If the focus of uncertainty resides in the specification of objectives, however, decisions tend to be the result of compromise when cause and effect relationships are certain, and of a more "inspirational" nature when even that clarity disappears.



| | | Uncertainty of Objectives | |
|---|---|---|---|
| | | Low | High |
| Uncertainty of Cause and Effect | Low | Decision by Computation | Decision by Compromise |
| | High | Decision by Judgement | Decision by Inspiration |

Figure 2. Decision-Making and Uncertainty

By being based on a more detailed characterization of the ways in which uncertainties are perceived and located in organizations, we believe that such an array of decision possibilities is of real significance in trying to understand the emergence and functioning of information systems in organizations. Moreover the framework relates to the views of those who have seen information processing as a means of uncertainty reduction (Galbraith, 1973) and information value as the degree to which uncertainty is reduced. However rather than presuming the link between information and uncertainty, let us consider the roles which information processing and information systems might and do play in the different decision situations described by Thompson and Tuden.

First we strive to articulate a normative view. Using an all too unsatisfactory "machine" analogy, Figure 3 outlines the orientations which information systems perhaps might adopt in the best of all possible worlds. Given low uncertainty on each dimension, we approach the management scientists' definition of certainty, where algorithms, formulae and rules can be derived to solve the problem by computation. Alternatively it may represent Simon's structured decisions (1960) where the intelligence, design and choice phases are all programmable. In either case stock control systems, credit control routines and linear programming models are all examples of what we call "answer machines".

| | | Uncertainty about Objectives: Low | Uncertainty about Objectives: High |
|---|---|---|---|
| Uncertainty of Cause and Effect | Low | Answer Machines | Dialogue Machines |
| | High | Learning Machines | Idea Machines |



Figure 3. A Normative View of the Relationship

Between Information Systems and Uncertainty

Given clear objectives but uncertain causation, we need to explore problems, ask questions, analyze the analyzable and finally resort to judgement. Here MIS cannot provide the answer but they can go part of the way, providing assistance through what Gorry and Scott-Morton (1971) would call decision support systems, Mason and Mitroff (1973) might call dialectical systems and Churchman (1971) calls inquiring systems. Examples of what we refer to as "learning machines" are enquiry facilities, sensitivity analysis and what-if models.

Given uncertainty or disagreement over objectives but relative certainty on causation, then values, principles, perspectives and interests conflict. In a rapidly changing economic, social and political environment, such bargaining situations may be increasing. Here political processes are important where often the vital tasks include discussion, intelligence and problem-sharing to gather different points of view, seek conflict resolution or just keep talking. Examples of relevant information processing here might include 'think-tanks', information centers, consultative and participative processes, retreats and the like - all examples of what we refer to as "dialogue machines". The orientation is towards freeing channels of opinion and communication and toward polemics and debate, with the value of information being measured by the number of consistent points of view that can be persuasively argued with the data and within the context provided by the information system (Boland 1979).

Finally given uncertainty in both dimensions, or decision by inspiration, we seek "idea machines". Here the formal MIS may provide multiple streams of thought which Koestler (1964) suggests triggers creativity. Other information processing forms may include the semi-confusing information systems suggested by Hedberg and Jonsson (1978) and the use of creativity techniques, such as Delphi processes or brainstorming. They will also include experience sharing and contact with other organizations or related thinkers. Certainly fluid or organismic organization design will be advantageous, encouraging boundaries to be crossed and the fertilization of ideas (Burns and Stalker, 1961).

Most people will not argue with this exposition. When presented in such terms they are prepared to acknowledge the variety of roles which information systems might serve and even the consequent variety of approaches to information system design and operation. However although the analysis may be acceptable, it describes, we would venture to suggest, a set of circumstances which is very different than the reality of the relationship between information and decision-making which exists in many organizations. That reality which is so fundamental to our argument is illustrated in Figure 4.

| | | Uncertainty about Objectives | |
|---|---|---|---|
| | | Low | High |
| Uncertainty of Cause and Effect | Low | Answer Machines | Ammunition Machines |
| | High | Answer Machines | Rationalization Machines |

Figure 4. Uncertainty Decision-Making and the Roles of Information Systems



On the whole we have learned how to develop MIS for decision by computation. While some problems may remain, quite successful "answer machines" are in widespread use. Thereafter, however, organizational reality starts to diverge from the normative and all too appealing set of circumstances outlined in Figure 3. Rather than using "learning machines" to confront the uncertainties inherent in cause and effect relationships, information system designers have sought to reduce or even camouflage them. Uncertainty, it would appear, is seen as a threatening rather than inevitable state of the world, which rather than being exploited for what it is, needs to be masked by an enormous investment in tidy minded systems and in pushing down the boundaries of computational practice. So in circumstances which cry out for information which can stimulate learning and the exercise of judgement, we find routine MIS which often assume the very certainties which cannot be found.

The management scientist seeks to develop optimizing models where descriptive models can only be appropriate. The same specialist promotes the use of probability models and modes of risk analysis where a sensitive use of deterministic models may better facilitate the exercise of judgement. The systems analyst prescribes enquiry systems which have specified answers rather than interrogation facilities for the user to select and develop, and the modeller seeks solutions as answers rather than frameworks for decision-making. All the above assume a certainty which the user has never readily experienced. Designers simply forget how much prior knowledge and insight their procedures require, or impute, and by so doing they are rarely, if ever, able to come to terms with the "wicked" (Mason and Mitroff 1973) problems which constitute an important part of management practice.

In emphasising the more technical mechanisms for the improvement of information, designers so often ignore the complementary but equally essential investments which need to be made in interpretative and decision skills. In other words our parent disciplines of computing, accounting and management science have sought for answers where they cannot always be specified, aiming for technocratic solutions regardless of the context of either the user or the organizational environment.

Such approaches result in the presumption of states of quasi-certainty which do not exist and the use of particular forms of economic and scientific rationality which bear little or no relationship to those which are implicit in the processes of management decision-making.

Then as we also suggest in Figure 4, far from creating a basis for dialogue and interchange, MIS tend to be used as "ammunition machines" in decisions by compromise. By the use of this perhaps emotive term, we wish to point to the ways in which information systems serve to promote and articulate particular interested positions and values. Political processes in organizations give rise to the emergence and elaboration of information systems as one party or interested group seeks to influence others. For as Bariff and Galbraith (1978) point out, information systems may be used to perpetuate or modify decision-making processes and social structures. By influencing the accepted language of negotiation, such systems can help to shape what is regarded as problematic, what can be deemed to be a credible solution and, most important of all, the criteria which are used in their selection. In ways such as these, traditional management accounting systems and mechanisms for financial appraisal can be used to reduce the complexity of a decision environment into a simple uni-goal economic system that has a life of its own divorced from the broader realities of organizational functioning. As one manager put it: "given a sensitive strategic decision (for example divestment) the information on the table is generally financial. Once the decision is made and we discuss its implementation other information is used, such as engineering, marketing or personnel considerations".

The "idea machine" we suggested for decision by inspiration may appear to be the only contribution that MIS can make in the context of such extreme uncertainty. However we suspect that that very uncertainty creates the need for other roles which they can and do serve. Rather than seeking to promote the creativity, inspiration and entrepreneurship which is so vital in such strategic contexts, MIS may more often than not operate as "rationalization machines" seeking to legitimize and justify actions that have been decided upon. As Bower (1970) discovered, and as many managers have described to us, the widespread adoption of capital budgeting procedures has resulted in the availability of justification devices rather than the simple and unproblematic provision of information for, and prior to, decision-making.

We do not seek the question the necessity for rationalization machines, for organizations require mechanisms through which they can legitimize what is to be done and retrospectively create a rationale for action. What we do suggest is that the information processing which is typical of such procedures be recognized for what it is, and that more active acknowledgement be given to the fact that the creativity and inspiration, which are so necessary in such contexts, are more likely to spring out of socially interactive forms of information processing.

By introducing our rather strong metaphors for information and decision, we are calling for a re-orientation away from the exclusive emphasis on technocratic and bureaucratic forms of information processing which is so characteristic of today's information system practice. There is, we think, an urgent need to acknowledge the reality of information practice in its full diversity; to see, in other words, the processes which create the roles for information processing and give rise to information systems in their wider organizational context. Such metaphors point to both the present existence of, and extended future possibilities for, MIS designs which acknowledge the uncertainties of organizational life. Hedberg and Jonsson (1978) in prescribing semi-confusing information systems called for a similar re-orientation. Like them, we advocate a move to a process view of MIS rather than the structured view which has been prevalent hitherto. Such a view would be dynamic rather than static, emphasizing the roles which information processing plays on the actions and interactions through which and by which managers make sense of their environments and cope with uncertainty.

## TOWARDS INFORMATION MANAGEMENT

In summary, we can state that many MIS specialists adopt a partial and rather idiosyncratic view of the role which information processing does and can serve in organizations. Emphasizing the importance of formal and systemic approaches, they invest heavily in a perspective and approach which can be, and often is, radically at variance with the way in which managers in their own organizations engage in the active and influential processing of information. Indeed we frequently get the impression that the MIS function is increasingly operating in a rather isolated, albeit comfortable, organizational niche. That is not to say that it lacks influence. Isolated though it may sometimes be from the more active processing of information in organizations, it can nonetheless have an important influence on the delineation of the desirable and the possible. However that influence stems not from the appropriateness of the MIS designs, but from the way in which the resultant information is taken up and used by those managers who strive to personally influence ongoing processes of organizational control. So, in the last resort, it may well be that it is the managers, or at least some of them, who put the management into MIS!

If these claims are valid, it becomes apparent that information management which emphasizes the development of conventional MIS in isolation from their organizational context will only at best yield marginal gain. At worst it might be dysfunctional for it can perpetuate and strengthen information processing forms which neither represent the social reality of organizations nor the real complexity and uncertainty of the organization and its environment. Indeed it is by no menas unlikely that such a limited view of information processing may be impairing organizational performance and threatening organizational survival.



However, we should not overlook the fact that today's organizations do contain a mix of vibrant and varied information flows and processes. The routine co-exists with the non-routine, the official with the unofficial and despite the massive investment in formal MIS and the application of limited information-decision concepts, the undercurrents of the non-routine and unofficial have survived. Indeed we would like at least to acknowledge the possibility that their survival is the result of under-emphasis and inattention. It could well be that if we attempt to plan, organize and control them too much, we may kill the very spontaneity, flexibility and informality on which their effectiveness depends. This is indeed a real possibility. Nevertheless we are still convinced that if information management is to offer something of real benefit to organizations, it has to have a framework that can at least place the formal within its wider context. Otherwise a continued focus on the narrow, technical aspects of information processing may not only ultimately drive out these very necessary complements and counterparts, but also we may fail to fully exploit the real possibilities for the organizational processing of information which emerging technologies may offer (Earl, 1978b).

The wider, alternative and complementary forms of information processing which currently co-exist in organizations must therefore start to enter into the discourse of MIS designers, managers and even users. Indeed a vital task of information management needs to be the explication of a broader framework for the consideration of information processing in organizations and an understanding of its implications for MIS analysis and design.

We can summarize our own, albeit tentative, suggestions for the outline of such a framework in the following way:

* New frameworks and metaphors are required to re-orient our information thinking.

* A major goal of such frameworks and metaphors is to explicate social reality and challenge technocratic wisdoms.

* Information problems do not necessarily require information systems; alternative forms of information processing can, do and should exist in organizations.

* Investment in organizational processes and structural forms of information processing are required to complement the MIS.

* We need to improve our understanding of how organizational decision-making and control is achieved, before major advances in MIS will be possible.

* Many MIS will need to generate frameworks rather than providing mere solutions.

With such a broader organizational perspective, tasks and responsibilities of **information management** will take on a very different form.

With the technical so explicitly linked to the organizational, no one management function can be, or should be, responsible for the whole of information processing. The role of the information specialist therefore will need to become that of a catalyst for change. The user in contrast will need to have the confidence to
142 explicate and describe his own information environment, processing and problems. In such a context progress in information management therefore will depend on *us*, as managers and users as much as, if not more than, on *them* as specialists.

## REFERENCES


(1) Ackoff, R.L., Management Misinformation Systems, Management Science, Dec. (1967), 147-156.

(2) Argyris, C., Organisational Learning and Management Information Systems. Accounting, Organisations and Society, Vol.2. No.2. (1977), 113-123.

(3) Bariff, M.L., and Galbraith, J.R., Intraorganisational Power Considerations for Designing Information Systems. Accounting, Organisations and Society, Vol.3. No.1. (1978), 15-28.

(4) Boland, R.J., Control, Causality and Information System Requirements, Accounting, Organisations and Society, Vol. 4. No.4. (1979), forthcoming.

(5) Bower, J., Managing the Resource Allocation Process (Division of Research, Graduate School of Business Administration, Harvard University, 1970).

(6) Burns, T., and Stalker, G.M., The Management of Innovation. (London, Tavistock, 1961).

(7) Child, J., Strategies of Control and Organisation Behaviour. Administrative Science Quarterly, (1973), 1-17.

(8) Child, J., Management and Organisational Factors Associated with Company Performance, Part 1. Journal of Management Studies (1974), 175-189.

(9) Child, J., Managerial and Organisational Factors Associated with Company Performance - Part 2. Journal of Management Studies, (1975), 12-27.

(10) Churchman, W., The Design of Inquiring Systems. (Basic Books, New York, 1971).

(11) Earl, M.J., Prototype Systems for Accounting, Information and Control, Accounting, Orgnisations and Society, Vol.3. No.2. (1978a), 168-172.

(12) Earl, M.J., What Microprocessors Mean. Management Today, December (1978b), 67-74.

(13) Galbraith, J., Designing Complex Organisations (Addison-Wesley, 1973).

(14) Gibson, C.F., and Nolan, R.L., Managing the Four Stages of EDP Growth. Harvard Business Review, (Jan.-Feb. 1974), 76-88.

(15) Gorry, G.A., and Scott-Morton, M.S., A Framework for Management Information Systems, Sloan Management Review, (Fall, 1971), 56-70.

(16) Georgiou, P., The Goal Paradigm and Notes Towards a Counter Paradigm. Administrative Science Quarterly. (1973), 291-310.

(17) Grinyer, P., and Norburn, D., Planning for Existing Markets: Perceptions of Executives and Financial Performance. Journal of the Royal Statistical Society, Series A, (1975), 70-97.

(18) Hedberg, B., and Jonsson, S., Designing Semi-Confusing Information Systems for Organisations in Changing Environments, Accounting, Organisations and Society, Vol. 3., No.1 (1978), 47-64.

(19) Hopwood, A.G., Criteria of Corporate Effectiveness, in Brodie, M., and Bennet, R., (Eds.) Managerial Effectiveness, (Thames Valley Regional Management Centre, 1979). 143

(20) Hopwood, A.G., An Accounting System and Managerial Behaviour, (Saxon House, 1973).

(21) Koestler, A., The Act of Creation, (Hutchinson,London, 1964).

(22) Lorsch, J., and Allen, S., III, Managing Diversity and Independence, (Division of Research, Graduate School of Business, Harvard University, 1973).

(23) Mason, R.O., Basic Concepts for Designing Management Information Systems, (AIS Research Paper No. 8. Graduate School of Business Administration, University of California, Los Angeles, October, 1969).

(24) Mason, R.O., and Mitroff, I.M., A Program for Research on MIS. Management Science, (Jan. 1973), 475-487.

(25) Mintzberg, H., The Myths of MIS. California Management Review. (Fall, 1972) 92-97.

(26) Oloffson, C. and Svalander, P.A., The Medical Services Change Over to a Poor Environment - "New Poor" Behaviour. Unpublished Working Paper, University of Linkoping. (1975).

(27) Simon, H.A., Guetzkow, G., Kozmetsky, G., and Tyndall, G., Centralisation v. Decentralisation in Organising the Controller's Department. (New York, Controllership Foundation Inc. 1954).

(28) Thompson, J.D., and Tuden, A., Strategies, Structures and Processes of Organisational Decision, in Thompson, J.D., et.al. (Eds.), Comparative Studies in Administration, (University of Pittsburgh Press, 1959).

(29) Turcotte, W.E., Control Systems, Performance and Satisfaction in Two State Agencies. Administrative Science Quarterly, (1974), 60-73.

(30) Zani, W.M., Blueprint for MIS. Harvard Business Review, (Nov.-Dec.1970), 95-100.

# CHAPTER 2: EVALUATING THE REAL BENEFITS

*Anthony G. Hopwood*

## INTRODUCTION

Computer-based information systems can have pervasive effects on organizational life, including many which do not enter into the original justification of the system. They not only have the potential to alter the nature of work, employment levels, cost structures and the efficiency of 145
operations directly, but can also have major indirect impacts on the whole functioning and performance of the organization over a long period of time.

The remainder of this book examines in detail the consequences of information-system changes for individuals and organizations. This chapter uses many practical examples to provide an overview of key problem areas that have been encountered during such changes. It illustrates the narrow scope and short time focus that often characterizes evaluations of information systems, and suggests a basis for making wider, more strategic assessments that take into account the political nature of the decision-making processes involved.

## THE ROLE OF INFORMATION IN ORGANIZATIONAL LIFE

The evaluation of computer-based information systems is a complex endeavour because information plays a key role in most activities in modern organizations. Information is gathered and analyzed to make decisions at all levels. Information delineates organizational structures, the responsibilities of particular units, the nature of managerial authority and associated spheres of discretion and influence. Flows of information disseminate organizational goals and missions, forge the linkages between organizational units and assist the co-ordination and integration of the complicated interactions between specialized tasks.

Information therefore creates perceptions of organizational reality and is actively involved in supporting and effecting work activities. It is neither a static nor a self-contained phenomenon but permeates all functions. A new information system can influence and sometimes radically alter the environments that need to be managed. Yet many computer-based information systems are introduced on the basis of limited administrative, economic and technical analyses and expectations.

*Organizational flexibility*

An information system can hinder or help an organization's ability to adapt to meet new challenges. For example[1], after introducing the extensive use of automated control processes and robotics, a large motor manufacturer realized that it had successfully automated the traditional concept of an assembly line, building in all the rigidities of the old process.
146 About the same time, a key competitor had introduced new systems only after a more fundamental evaluation of the potential of information technologies which questioned the need to maintain the previous manufacturing rigidities. The competitor's resultant system was much more flexible, even though it employed similar technological components. This flexibility gave the competitor considerable strategic and economic advantage when the automobile market became volatile and unpredictable.

Similarly, an insurance company planned to introduce a new type of policy. To promote it, the company wanted to identify all of their existing policy-holders, between certain ages, who did not have the relevant cover. This is an ideal task for an integrated computerized database management system but the relevant information within the company was on different files. While these files were being integrated, at great expense and with difficulty, a competitor launched a similar policy. 'We lost out because our information systems had just about set like concrete,' commented the Managing Director.

*Organizational control*

Information systems reinforce or change relationships between central authorities and local departments and agents. A manufacturing company operating through subsidiaries around the world, for example, reinforced centralized control by introducing a global computerized system which gave direct, updated reports on cash and fund flows directly to corporate headquarters. This provided a mechanism to implement effectively the management policy of having each subsidiary responsible for generating profits against an annual plan and contributing to an annual dividend in cash to corporate funds.

On the other hand, a government department used an information system to devolve management control, by introducing new office technology to facilitate the collection of information in its geographically remote regions. This enabled regional managers to have more direct control over local costs. It also implied a passing of authority to the regions to initiate actions which previously required central sanction. This led to a backlash from some officers at the centre who felt their authority and status had been eroded.

*Indirect impacts*

The implications of a new information system often extend into areas outside the context for which they were initially introduced. For example, a central information system implemented by a credit card company changed the company's marketing strategy. Previously, advertising had to be selective and upmarket as a means of controlling who was allowed to use its card. However, the new information system could provide up-to-date monitoring of the transactions made by card holders as a means of management control. The advertising policy could therefore be changed to be less selective.



Labour relations are often brought into the development and operation of new information systems (see Chapter 9). For example, when a retail chain installed new 'point of sale' equipment at checkouts, the union asked for the operators' jobs to be upgraded because they were now responsible for providing input into corporate systems. In a British company, the union asked for access to personnel records, which they were entitled to under collective bargaining legislation. From this, the union could tell the labour rates at various plants, which influenced its bargaining position.

A computer-based system can change job functions, which makes a significant difference to an individual's motivation and job satisfaction (see Chapters 8 and 11). For example, when a bank computerized its local branch operations, the main aim was to automate the cashier's work. It also altered the manager's function by shifting much of the accounting and control of branch operations to the head office. As a result, many managers complained that they had become merely 'salesmen' selling central services rather than influential figures in the local business community.

## MISTAKES IN EVALUATING COMPUTER-BASED INFORMATION SYSTEMS

Computer-based information technology has the potential to improve many processes involved in managing information. In practice, however, many problems have been encountered in trying to fulfil that potential. The techniques which have traditionally been used to set objectives have tended to look at mainly technical and short-term quantifiable economic criteria. This has been satisfactory for identifying the technical problems that arise from the rapid rate of innovation, but it is inadequate as a means of pinpointing and managing the broader — and crucial — human and organizational aspects.

148 Despite the massive growth in routine information provision by computer-based systems, many organizations have found that demands for information are still unmet, particularly when faced with newly turbulent environments. Systems based on formal organizational procedures (see Chapter 6) reflect the problems and crises of the past rather than the present 'need-to-know'; unfortunately, such formal systems are the bases for many computer-based information services.

Different evaluation strategies are needed to relate new office technology developments to the whole spectrum of real-world requirements. It must remain important to consider technical, administrative and quantifiable economic elements which have been emphasized in the past. The relationships which information flows have to other aspects of organizational functioning suggest, however, that consideration of these factors is insufficient to comprehend the complexities of the information problems of today's organizations. The main mistakes that have been made in setting objectives and evaluating implementations have been:

- Placing the primary emphasis on short-term economic consequences;
- Evaluating the information system in isolation from organizational functions which they serve — often ignoring human and social consequences or, when they are considered, placing an overemphasis on individualistic needs and physical ergonomics;
- Failing to relate economic and social perspectives;
- Recognizing uncertainties in the future but not giving sufficient priority to providing flexibility in the system to adapt to changes;

—Viewing information in a partial way;

—Taking a limited view of the roles served by information systems in organizations.

The following sections examine the experiences which have brought these problems to light.

*Too much short-term economics*

When considering investments in new information systems, there is a tendency, as in other investment decisions, to emphasize the relationship between the initial capital costs of the project and the net operating savings. Instead of giving high priority to *value-added* aims, the ways in which the new system can add value to various organizational activities, a dominant position is given to the *cost-substitution* assessment. This calculates savings in personnel costs and financial gains from improved operational activities, such as more efficient inventory control and speedier decisions. The savings are compared to the costs of the new system's capital, operational and development expenditure and related personnel training. In most cases, the primary problems confronted are of a technical and forecasting nature. The image of the change process created by this concentration on short-term economics invariably requires that little consideration is given to other closely related aspects of organizational functioning and to longer-term economic aspects. Attention is focused on those economic factors which can be identified at the time the decision is taken to introduce a new system. This in itself is a complex process and has sometimes missed important practical considerations, such as the support and maintenance costs for the equipment.



Even when care has been taken to try and look deeper than straight cost-substitution analysis, mistakes have been made. A leading European car manufacturer, for example, introduced a vehicle inventory recording system throughout its network of main dealers, enabling each dealer as well as the company to know the location of all stock via immediate direct computing access to the data. A thorough economic appraisal of the system seemed to demonstrate that it could be cost effective, assisting dealers' sales efforts and giving more efficient management of the manufacturer's inventories. Unfortunately, the major economic consequence of the system was not anticipated: the ease of access to inventory information inadvertently induced dealers to reduce their own stocks. Why keep large stocks of cars, they asked, when they could satisfy customers' needs by finding the nearest location of a suitable model at the press of a button? This meant that the manufacturer had to increase its own stocks, which significantly added to its costs.

Another manufacturing company was faced with a sudden increase in competitive pressures. It ordered a complete review of its information systems strategies after finding that the information produced by the computer was mainly oriented towards internal, short-term problems whereas the company's real problems were external and long-term.

*Isolating the information system*

The calculation and acceptance of short-term economic criteria are simplified if the information system is regarded as a self-contained entity. Growing technological complexities and the increasing influence of technical professionals has meant that such false simplifications have
150 often caused the information function to become isolated from other organizational activities. Lip-service may be paid to concepts like 'information as a corporate resource' but, in practice, information systems can become an almost autonomous development.

The characteristics of the information itself and the information system are emphasized rather than the consequences that these might have. What is needed is a more detailed charting of the specific implications for key activities such as marketing strategies, production options, labour relations and financial structures. In the next chapter, Peter Keen recommends a strategy to handle new office technology products which effectively integrates all aspects.

An example of what can go wrong is the experience of a large oil company which had a sophisticated long-range plan for computer developments. Unfortunately, the strategy had been created separately from product and market development plans and was not updated in phase with changes in the business environment. Eventually, a crisis occurred when there was a fundamental shift in marketing policy. 'We are tending to revert to manual systems to meet the urgent, rapid changes in data needs,' the Chief Executive commented ruefully.

The inward-looking nature of many information systems institutionalize internal management processes and perceptions at a time when increasingly interdependent and volatile world economic, industrial and technological activities mean that more problems come from external sources. The Marketing Director of a major European consumer electronics firm, for example, succeeded in initiating a major review of corporate information system after discovering that it could not cope adequately with changes in the life cycles of products. The average product life cycle had been cut from 7 to 8 years to 1.5 to 2 years. A major management problem was therefore to develop strategies which would span across life cycles but the information system was optimized to handle within-life-cycle performance.

*Inadequate attention to human and social consequences*

During the first phase of commercial computing in the 1960s and early 1970s, hardly any attention was given to the human and social consequences of computing. Most users of the systems were given special training to handle generally complex and difficult-to-use systems. When microelectronics caused computing to come closer to real working environments, such as the office, increasing attention was paid to the individual's use of systems (see Chapters 10 and 11).



Research was carried out, particularly into the physical ergonomic design of systems to make them safe, comfortable and easy to use. The nature of the software interaction between user and system and the impact of the system on individuals' motivation and productivity also began to be regarded by managers as a significant factor in information system changes. This concern was sharpened by laws on ergonomics introduced in some West European countries and by pressure from trade unions (see Chapter 9). The interest in these aspects was a step in the right direction but its partial nature should be noted. The emphasis has been individualistic rather than on the broader organizational ramifications.

The emphasis on individualistic and ergonomic aspects can be made compatible with the narrow short-term economic and technical perspectives discussed above. The advocates of ergonomics usually regard themselves as being in a more 'human' tradition than the rationalist school of 'scientific management' which dominated production-line automation (see Enid Mumford's comparison of Taylorism and socio-technical techniques in Chapter 4). Somewhat paradoxically, however, quantifiable ergonomic standards have often been used by management to reinforce a scientific management approach that would be opposed by many who are sympathetic to the ergonomic approach.

*Failing to relate social and economic perspectives*

Given that social issues themselves have generally been treated in a partial and haphazard way, it is not surprising that it has been rare for social and economic evaluations to be related. It has also been rare for a social analysis to be used as a way of determining the nature of the economic goals or for economics to be used explicitly to constrain the assessment of the social environment. Prevailing practices have maintained the autonomy of these two aspects despite the fact that repeated evaluations of information system changes illustrate the limitation of doing this.

The kind of problems which result from this separation were highlighted by the experience of a major North American manufacturing company. It invested in a massive centralized computer-based information service to support key decisions and facilitate planning and scheduling of marketing and production. The same information, however, was also used to set targets to motivate managers. Being aware of its evaluative uses, the managers biased many of the key information flows. The resultant optimistic forecasts led to increased expenditures on unnecessarily high inventories and production line work-in-progress and made for a lack of
152 flexibility in co-ordinating marketing and production activities.

*Inability to adapt to the future*

When evaluating the consequences of information systems attention is usually given to the improvement of forecasting methods, probabilistic assessments and other techniques which try to decipher future uncertainties. It is less common for recognition and priority to be given to the more fundamental, unpredictable discontinuities which characterize the future. Despite a theoretical genuflection towards the need for information systems to respond to the unexpected, in practice emphasis has usually been placed on the need to identify the most efficient way of responding to what is perceived as a known future.

As the quotation from the Managing Director of the insurance company indicated, the result is that many systems have been 'set in concrete'. Little attention has been given to creating systems which are flexible, responsive and adaptive. In addition to the earlier examples given of the inflexibility of some computer-based systems, an evaluation exercise by an important manufacturing company highlights the far-reaching negative impact of an over-shortsighted design. The company found that its information system had detracted from, rather than enhanced, its operational flexibility, management processes had been made more complex and time consuming, investment in rapid access to *ad-hoc* information had been neglected and management defensiveness had increased.

*Over-emphasizing formal information flows*

There has been a tendency to stress the official routine flows of information when designing computer-based systems, despite the fact that many studies of the way organizations work stress the significance of the diversity of other information channels[2]. A summary of the main type of information flows is given in Figure 2.1. Computer-based systems have provided an explosion of 'official-routine' information in activities such as personnel, materials management, inventory control, production control and many other management and administrative functions. This is supplemented by unofficial but still routine information kept in 'black books' or 'in the desk drawer', which individuals feel they need to make decisions. 'Just-in-case' files contain routine but unofficial information, which an individual feels could be used in defence of decisions and actions.

| | Routine | Non-routine |
|---|---|---|
| Official | Computer-based information systems | *Ad hoc* queries<br>Direct access to data<br>Task forces |
| Unofficial | Black books<br>Just-in-case files | The 'grapevine'<br>Lunch-table chats |

**Figures 2.1.** Types of information flow

Informal information flows play an important role in all organizations. These are passed via the grapevines and *ad hoc* chats which permeate managerial, office and shop floor circles and are facilitated by close personal proximity or by membership of clubs and outside organizations. Even official computer-based systems can be used to provide non-routine *ad hoc* enquiries or to give direct access to a database. Structural changes are also made in the organization, such as the setting up of task forces to improve communications channels.

Computer-based systems are primarily used in — and emphasize — official information routines, although the unofficial, alternative information flows are known to play strategic roles in organizational activities. These important unofficial communications can be endangered unless the partial role played by official information is recognized and active steps taken to understand and cater for the complex informal sources of information which contribute to organizational performance.

The dangers of failing to investigate the organizational impact of unofficial information was dramatically illustrated by the experiences of a

British company. It had emerged as the only large company in its sector to survive a turbulent period, although it was in a lean and financially insecure state. Management initiated rationalizations, including the dispersal of two-thirds of head office staff to a suburban site, and expansion of the existing computer-based system to provide 'better information on management efficiency'. Shortly before implementing these plans, a consultant undertook a survey of information flows, which led to the abandonment of the move. The consultant found that the company had survived the crisis that had hit the industry primarily because of the close physical proximity of key organizational members. This enabled messages from the volatile outside world to be transmitted through the company and acted on very quickly. That role had not been recognized in the original plan.

154 Another example of the problems with partial information occurred in a hospital which intended to introduce new office technology. One aim was to 'rationalize' the information flows, which had been shown to include a substantial amount of 'redundant' information which was either duplicated or unused. Instead of producing the expected cost savings, the change was a painful process, with many key organizational processes grinding to a halt. The reason was that no consideration had been given to the important role of the 'redundant' information in assisting staff motivation and the co-ordination of activities. Although it did not help senior management to monitor lower level performance, it did help local managers to understand what was going on in their own areas. Eventually that so-called redundant information had to be provided again, at a higher cost than with the original system.

*Ignoring the political role of information*

Most evaluations of computer-based information systems give primacy to the 'rational' role which such systems are deemed to service, such as 'facilitating decision making, providing 'quicker, more accurate and relevant' information or assisting in the 'efficient' allocation of resources. Participants in the organization, however, realize that this is a limited view of the real role of information.

Information system requirements are closely related to organizational power and emerge from essentially political processes which characterize organizational life[4]. Although official evaluations attempt to suggest that new systems are neutral technical artifacts, there is strong grassroots awareness that this 'rational' perception is a very partial representation of reality. Based on the work of two American sociologists, Michael Earl and I have categorized the different roles that the same information system can take within an organization (see Figure 2.2)[3]. The important elements, which they believe determine the role of the information system, are the degree of certainty/uncertainty that applies to the objectives of actions and to the cause and effect relationships underlying organizational processes.

| | | Objectives: Certain | Objectives: Uncertain |
|---|---|---|---|
| Cause and effect relationships | Certain | Answer Machine | Ammunition Machine |
| | Uncertain | Learning Machine | Rationalization Machine |



**Figure 2.2.** Various roles of information systems

When the cause and effect and objectives are both certain, decisions tend to be made in a computational manner, using the information system as a mechanistic 'answer machine', within a highly structured and well understood decision-making process. With increasing uncertainty of the cause and effect relationship, the information system can assist the decision-maker to exercise subjective judgements. It acts as a 'learning machine', which helps the user to understand the context in which he or she is operating and to find out about some of the uncertainties involved.

Where there is uncertainty about objectives but the underlying cause and effects of decisions are certain, demands for information arise from the process of managing an environment characterized by conflict and bargaining; Information systems in this context serve as 'ammunition machines' used to support a particular case or to shape a picture of 'reality'. If all certainty disappears, 'inspirational' decision-making has to be used. In this case, information is marshalled by a retrospective 'rationalization machine' to legitimate actions already taken.

The roles of information systems as answering or learning machines are the main substance of official computer system designs and evaluations. Information specialists are reluctant to be associated with the more 'political' roles because it is threatening to them. They like to use the traditional and partial approaches criticized earlier in this chapter to provide partial and short-term ammunition and rationalizations to defend their supposedly neutral technology.

## EVALUATION AS A SOCIAL PROCESS

This chapter has illustrated some of the mistakes in making narrow and shortsighted evaluations of computer-based information systems. It is possible, however, to extend the horizons of economic assessments to include, at least in qualitative form, organizational considerations of a more strategic nature. The remainder of this book examines methods of implementing such broader perspectives, in particular by explicitly integrating human, organizational and social consequences with technical and economic considerations.

156

Such techniques, however, will merely serve to provide better and more refined 'answer' and 'learning machines' unless there is a recognition of the political context in which the information system has a key role. Evaluations should take into account the political interests of various groups with different interests and concerns. This would sharpen the perceptions of problems, influence the options available for action and assist in adapting the resultant system to real requirements. There is no magic formula, however, which can solve what is intrinsically a complex and unpredictable task. As Rob Kling analyzes in Chapter 13, information system planning and design must satisfy pluralistic and often conflicting demands. Issues that need to be decided range far beyond purely technical considerations or factors which can be simplified in terms of isolated applications of the technology. Typical questions that arise include: Should decision processes be centralized or decentralized? Will changes create more or less social interaction? Will organizational flexibility be lost or will information systems enable the organization to cope more effectively with a volatile environment? Does the system increase the efficiency of social surveillance and control? Can computer-based systems replicate the subtle, informal, personal communications on which all organizations depend? How can society in general cope with the employment and training implications of information technology?

Technical and short-term economic aspects cannot be separated from the social dimensions of these impacts. The only way to resolve questions such as these is explicitly to recognize the political aspects of decision making. One way of doing this has been for some interest groups to press for legislation and to negotiate agreements which provide staff with rights to participate in taking decisions which influence the direction of technological change. Generally, however, the technically-oriented approach has predominated because it is based on relatively well-developed methodologies (although there are many difficult unsolved technical problems) and tends to reinforce the existing and well established power structures.

Both the technical and political perspectives of new office technology require a great deal of live practical experience before they can provide a mature understanding of exactly how to manage the total process of technological change to take account of the multiplicity of interactions and implications. A first step in that direction is at least to recognize that evaluations of information systems should face up to the whole spectrum of human and organizational aspects which has been highlighted in this chapter and is further examined in the rest of the book.



## RECOMMENDATIONS

1 Acknowledge that the setting of goals and evaluation of information systems is a political process involving many groups and individuals with vested interests.

2 Seek to illuminate the various interests and their consequence for the eventual evaluation process.

3 Examine the mechanisms for the representation of different interests, the institutional means by which divergent evaluations can be discussed and the ability of different groups to have access to informed opinion and relevant data regarding the options available.

4 Recognize that evaluations can take place from different perspectives — the individual, the group, the organization and the social.

5 Give active consideration to the ways in which new information systems will influence the diversity of official and unofficial information flows.

6 Never evaluate an information system in isolation from its organizational context and consider the ramifications of information system developments for the operation, performance and integration of various functions in the organization.

7 Consider the importance of ensuring that the information system is

flexible and adaptive, particularly in a world characterized by uncertainty and the occurrence of the unexpected.

8 Avoid evaluations that divorce social aspects from economic factors.

9 Question the apparent certainties of short-term evaluative exercises and probe the assumptions of simple, short-term cost-benefit justifications of new systems.

10 Be aware that the evaluation exercise is itself a complex information processing activity, subject to all the problems and opportunities which characterize this area.

158 **REFERENCES**

1 Examples in this chapter are taken from a number of sources, including Tricker, R.I., *Effective Information Management*, Beaumont Executive Press, Oxford, UK, 1982.

2 Minzberg, H., *How Managers Manage*, Harper & Row, New York, 1974.

3 Earl, M., Hopwood, A.G., 'From Management Information to Information Management' in Lucas, H.F. *et al* (eds) '*The Information System Environment*, North-Holland, Amsterdam, 1980.

4 Burchell, S., Clubb, C., Hopwood, A.G., Hughes, J., Nahapet, J., 'The Role of Accounting in Organizations and Society', *Accounting, Organizations and Society*, Vol 5, No 2, 1980.

*Accounting, Organizations and Society*, Vol. 8, No. 2/3, pp. 287–305, 1983.
Printed in Great Britain.

0361–3682/83 $3.00 + .00
Pergamon Press Ltd.

# ON TRYING TO STUDY ACCOUNTING IN THE CONTEXTS IN WHICH IT OPERATES

ANTHONY G. HOPWOOD
*London Graduate School of Business Studies*

Accounting has come to be seen as playing a key role in organizational functioning. Concerned, as it now is, with such activities as assessing the costs and benefits of organizational actions, the setting of financial standards and norms, the representation and reporting of organizational performance, and financial planning and control, accounting has been used to cast important aspects of the functioning of the modern organization into economic terms. By offering particular economic representations of organizational activities and outcomes to both internal participants and interested external parties, it has come to be involved in the creation of a quite specific organizational order and mission. Accounting is now associated with particular ways of seeing and trying to shape organizational processes and actions, with the maintenance of certain forms of organizational segmentation, hierarchy and control, and with the furtherance of an economic rationale for action (Batstone, 1979). Indeed in many cases the forms taken by decision processes, the structuring of organizational activities and even the specification of an organizational boundary are not independent of the accounting representation of them. Modes of accounting have become not only important and valued management practices but also ones whose existence and consequences are difficult to disentangle from the functioning of organizations as we know them. 159
Accounting, in other words, has become centrally implicated in the modern form of organizing.

With accounting so intertwined with organizational functioning it is surprising that so little is known of the organizational nature of accounting practice. That, however, is the case. Although early studies of accounting in action focused on trying to understand its organizational roles and consequences, many more recent investigations have detached accounting from its organizational setting, preferring instead to study the consequences which it has at the individual rather than the organizational level.[1] Admittedly such studies are providing us with many interesting and useful insights into both the interpretation of accounting information and ways of trying to facilitate its use in decision making situations. Be that as it may, they do not explicitly aim to help us to understand what is at stake in the organizational

[1] Some of the reasons for this are discussed elsewhere (Hopwood, 1976; 1978). An interesting discussion of the general problem is given in Gowler & Legge (1981). Given the relative recency of research into the behavioural and organizational aspects of accounting, the latter's citation of Platt (1976, p. 42) is particularly interesting:

> . . . there are strong insitutional forces pulling people towards distinct disciplinary approaches; the pressure to disciplinary conformity is probably particularly strongly felt by younger people who do not yet have a securely established base or identity in a particular field. To the extent that this is so, the effects of different patterns of intellectual training and socialisation are reinforced by personal needs . . .

I think that a case could be made that such a situation has prevailed in the behavioural study of accounting, the assessment becoming even more appealing when the situation in management accounting is contrasted with that prevailing in the financial accounting area where legitimacy has been provided to institutional (i.e. market) rather than individual level studies.

practice of accounting, even though it is the latter which provides so many of the rationales for the accounting craft. Studies at the individual level can neither illuminate the ways in which accounting intersects with other organizational practices, decision processes and power structures nor the factors which both give rise to the accounting phenomenon and induce it to change.[2]

Together the papers collected here aim to provide some perspectives on accounting in an organizational context. As such, they aim to build upon earlier collections (see, for example, *Accounting, Organizations and Society*, Vol. 3, No. 1 (1976)) and contributions to show both the potential of an organizational perspective for the study of accounting practice and some of the range of
160 approaches which might be included within it. However, before trying to summarise some of the key concerns of the papers and the more informal discussions which they stimulated, it is useful to attempt to delineate both some of the distinguishing features of an organizational level interest in accounting and the reasons for its significance.

## SOME RATIONALES FOR AN ORGANIZATIONAL FOCUS

Individual level studies of accounting invariably take the accounting phenomenon for granted. Accounting, as such, is not the problematic issue. The primary concerns are with understanding and improving the interpretations which are made of it, with these insights frequently being seen as providing a basis for fine tuning rather than more fundamentally reforming the practice and technology of accounting. Moreover in the vast majority of such studies this emphasis enables accounting to be detached from both its organizational setting and other organizational practices. Accounting is seen to be a relatively independent art, having its roles and consequences primarily moderated by the cognitive properties of its immediate users rather than the setting in which it is placed. Indeed on many occasions the exclusive focus on the cognitive mediation of accounting justifies transferring the settings in which this can be studied to the college classroom and the psychological laboratory.

A more organizational approach would not deny the significance of such cognitive mediation. Indeed, the ways in which accounting influences individual action are a central part of its concern. However, rather than detaching accounting from its organizational setting, organizational researchers aim to understand the meanings which are given to accounting in particular settings, emphasising not the interpretation of an accounting given but the more active ways in which a particular account can shape, mould and even play a role in constructing the setting of which it forms a part. Accounting, to the organizational theorist, cannot be isolated from the processes which give rise either to its presence or to its present significance, be those within or without the particular setting or even organization in which it plays a role.

For the cognitive theorist accounting is primarily an independent variable, although, on the basis of the understandings which are gained from observing the responses to it, he or she also might seek to change, indeed to improve, the accounting representation of what is seen as being an independent organizational reality. The organizational theorist, on the other hand, can see accounting as both a dependent and an independent phenomenon. Some organizational scholars of accounting seek to emphasise the contingent nature of the accounting craft, aiming to provide an understanding of how particular accountings emerge from organizational and social settings. Such theorists do not necessarily remain content with offering an explanation of a particular accounting manifestation, however. Together with those other scholars of the organizational who place primary emphasis on the ways in which accounting both influences and is constrained by the meanings given to the organizational setting in which it operates, they seek to explore the social processes through which accounts of organizational action influence both the meanings and actions which constitute

[2] For interesting discussions of these and similar points see the papers by Connolly, March & Shapira, Cummings, Pondy and Weick in Ungson and Braunstein (1982).

organizational life.

Such distinctions, however, provide only a relatively superficial view of an organizational level interest in accounting. Given the significance of the contrast, not least in the context of the present studies, it is worthwhile to explore in some more detail the ways in which an organizational perspective might view the accounting phenomenon, appealing both to the studies which are collected here and others which are now available.

*Accounting repeatedly becomes what it was not*

Accounting is neither a static nor a homogeneous phenomenon. Over time, all forms of accounting have changed, repeatedly becoming what they were not. Accounting, moreover, is not a homogeneous craft. Both management and financial accounts are characterised by an amazing diversity, both within a national culture and even more so across different national contexts (Horovitz, 1980). All too apparently accounting is a phenomenon which is what it isn't and can become what it wasn't!

Unfortunately we have a very limited understanding of the forces that either influence accounting change or help to shape the different forms that the accounting craft can take. Although a great deal of work has been done on the history of accounting, many of the studies that are available have adopted a rather technical perspective, seeking not only to emphasise the developments that have occurred rather than also probing into the rationales for them (Hopwood *et al.*, 1980) but also, even when raising questions about the underlying forces at work, all too readily presuming a functionalist and even progressive interest. Indeed, until recently, both historical and comparative analyses of the accounting phenomenon have adopted a most atheoretical stance, only rarely seeking to relate their insights to broader understandings of the development of the corporate form, its social and economic setting, and the roles which organizational accounts might have played in the emergence of both the organization as we know it now and the relationships which it has to other bodies and interests.

These questions are now starting to be addressed by accounting and other scholars however, as the papers and comments by Johnson (1983), D. Flamholtz (1983), Meyer (1983) and Tiessen & Waterhouse (1983) illustrate.

On the historical side, studies of accounting development are beginning to utilise more theoretical analyses of the emergence of the corporate form and the particular roles which procedures for both internal control and the maintenance of external legitimacy have played. Interestingly, scholars from other social science disciplines also have started to be intrigued by the processes underlying the growing significance of the accounting craft and the roles which it may have served in the emergence of modern institutional forms. Consideration has been given to the roles played by economic record keeping in the construction of forms of organizational visibility which can further particular organizational interests, to the ways in which accounting and other forms of management practices became implicated in the resolution of the conflicts which characterised the emergence of today's organizational forms, and to the contribution which accounting has made to the articulation and propagation of a legitimate myth of disinterested administrative rationality and order.

From an organizational perspective, studies of accounting diversity have drawn on the precarious but nevertheless useful understandings available from contingency theory (Otley, 1980). Consideration has been given to the implications which organizational environments, technologies and tasks and management structures have had for the development of accounting practice. Illuminating though such perspectives have been, however, there is now an increasing recognition of the need to move beyond the restrictive static and often functionalist presumptions which have characterised past forms of contingent analysis. More direct interest is now being expressed in trying to understand the nature of the organizational processes through which accounting becomes what it was not. Albeit slowly, there are signs that consideration is being given to appreciating the ways in which both other management practices and external phenomenon intersect with accounting practices to create pressures for change and the difficulties raised by attempts to understand the implications for accounting of the multiple contingencies which characterise organizational life. Attention is also slowly being given to how accounting can be changed in the context of organizational and social conflicts and debates in order to create different but still persuasive images of organizational aims and achievements. Not least in significance, there are signs that the roles which accounting plays in shaping its own development also are being recognised, be these seen in terms of the implications stemming from the professionalisation of the body of knowledge that has emerged around the practice of the craft or of the ways in which accounting actively shapes the perception of and salience attached to some of the very phenomena which are supposed to put pressures on it to change.

Interestingly, questions related to the emergence of organizational forms and the controls which go with them now attract the attention of the economist as well. Rather than being content to view the organization as an unproblematic "black box", economists have started to explore some of the rationales that may be implicit in prevailing organizational forms, appealing to both the comparative advantages of markets, hierarchies and other organizational forms, and the ways in which modes of organization can moderate and further patterns of economic interest and accountability. As Johnson (1983), Tiessen & Waterhouse (1983) and others (Baiman, 1982; Spicer & Bellew, 1983) illustrate, both of these perspectives emphasise the important roles that procedures for monitoring and control can play, helping, thereby, to cast some light on some of the origins of the accounting function. As of yet, however, most of this work has emphasised the role of technical and economic interests. In contrast to historical and organizational inquiries, economists, to date, have given little or no attention to either the ways in which the economic intersects with the social and the political or the more particular questions involved in how accounting itself may have come to be involved in the very specification of those economic interests in the name of which it is changed.

At present all such explorations of the rationales that might be implicit in the accounting craft remain at an early stage of development. The perspectives of the historical, the organizational and the economic remain largely independent, each tending to offer relatively self-contained explanations of the emergence of organizational accountings and the pressures for them to change, and few studies have been made of the emergence and development of particular modes of accounting practice. Nevertheless such attempts to understand the processes of accounting change are of significance, not least because of their potential to provide us with a very different perspective, or more likely, series of perspectives, for understanding what might be at stake in the accounting endeavour.

Conventional understandings of accounting view it from a relatively unproblematic technical perspective. It is presumed that accountings are there to facilitate organizational and social action (see Burchell *et al.*, 1980 for a further discussion of this point). Only rarely, if ever, is the nature of that facilitation and the ends that might be so served examined. Although notions of cost, profit and other indices of financial performance may not be seen as being unproblematic, the difficulties which they give rise to stem, according to such a conventional view, from the problems of operationalizing pre-given aspects of organizational and social reality and achievement. Accounting, so conceived, is essentially a revelatory endeavour, aiming merely to reflect rather than more actively to construct a view of organizational reality and ends. Seeking, albeit often with difficulty, to explicate and make visible an unproblematic view of the means for organizational achievement, accounting is seen as a phenomenon divorced from the social, as distinct from technical, struggles and innovations that have resulted in its emergence.

All too clearly alternative views of the accounting endeavour will not be appealing to those who have invested in articulating and propagating such a conventional perspective. However for those who are willing to consider them, they offer at least the potential of a way of understanding accounting and its problems that is consonant with the historical conditions which have resulted in its emergence and development and those current organizational forces which contribute to its significance.

*Accounting and organizational action*

Accounting gains much of its contemporary significance from the ways in which it helps to shape and guide organizational processes and actions. However although accounting texts, pronouncements and recommendations repeatedly emphasise the ways in which it contributes to organizational efficiency, the improvement of managerial and employee motivation and performance, and the more effective allocation of resources, little is known of if and how such ends are achieved. Compared with the extent of the technical edifice of accounting, very little is known of the organizational processes which this seeks to activate and through which the technical achieves its potential.

What roles does accounting play in the construction of organizational participants' views of the desirable and the possible? Does accounting get implicated in the creation of particular conceptions of organizational time? And if so, with what effects? How and when do accountings of organizational performance provide an incentive for action? How does accounting contribute to the articulation of an organizational mission and through what means do the particular and very partial patterns of organizational visibility that accounting creates facilitate the achievement of control within the organization, be that seen in either social or technical terms? How does the routinized provision of information which accounting emphasises relate to the multitude of informal decision arenas which characterise organizational life? Just how, in other words, does accounting achieve and maintain a position of organizational significance?

Such questioning could be extended. For although a great deal of effort has been invested in extending and refining the technical basis of accounting in the name of its organizational roles and consequences, very little is known about the ways in which the potential which is claimed on behalf of accounting is realised. For some, at least, that is a paradoxical situation for a craft that has continually sought to emphasise the pragmatic organizational implications of its technical endeavours.

An organizational view of accounting has enormous potential to illuminate some of the more problematic aspects of the accounting craft. For instance, it could help us to understand the roles which accounting plays in the creation of particular patterns of organizational segmentation and the consequences which this has, not least in those circumstances where the requirements of the task point to the provision of lateral flows of information which are at variance with the vertical ones which accounting more usually emphasises. Equally, greater insights into the ways in which accounts of organizational performance provide particular mappings of both the organizational environment and its internal processes and outcomes could help those concerned with the design of more effective information provision in times of change and discontinuity. Many also would find it helpful to understand the roles which different, and often conflicting, assessments of organizational performance, both past and prospective, play in the determination of decisions and the allocation of scarce resources. Just how does accounting's emphasis on the economic relate to the interests and practices of those who seek to extend the visibility of the technical, the human and the wider environmental characterisation of organizational performance? And how does accounting's commitment to the detached, analytical consideration of the new relate to the need to generate the commitment which may play a determining role in the realisation of the actual? Together insights of this nature could provide at least a basis for trying to ground the technical apparatus of the accounting craft in the specifics of organizational action, thereby hopefully trying to realise the pragmatic potential that is so frequently claimed on accounting's behalf. At present, however, such insights reside in the realm of experience, only rarely being set aside the abstract and highly generalised claims that grace the manuals of technical accounting practice.

*Accounting and the achievement of the accounting mission*

Conventional discussions of accounting invariably presume that the craft is capable of achieving the claims that are made on its behalf. Accounting, so we are told, is capable of enhancing organizational efficiency and performance (forgetting, of course, the role that it also plays in the definition of the very ends it is trying to further). It can play a positive role in increasing managerial and employee motivations to perform. And accounting can provide the type of information that can facilitate managerial decision making, not least in environments characterised by uncertainty and doubt.

Increasingly, however, some, at least, of such highly generalised claims are being compared with the more equivocal impressions emerging from both research and pratice.

164 There is a long tradition of scholarly inquiry which has sought to illuminate the dysfunctional as well as functional consequences, both latent and manifest, of the accounting craft. More recently, there have been studies which at least have pointed to the ways in which accountings appear to proliferate amidst concerns with organizational crisis and decline rather than in the less problematic days of growth and success. Sometimes such research even has pointed to the ways in which the consequent desire for greater control can result in organizational procedures which detract from rather than enhance the flexibility of managerial response in such conditions.

Such concerns with the actual rather than the claimed achievements of accounting now have started to be articulated by some of the practitioners of the accounting craft. Faced with economic restraint and often with increased competitive pressures, such practitioners have started to become concerned about the limitations of the routinized flows of information which accounting so often provides.

Sometimes seeing how accountings of the present reflect crises of the past, such practitioners have come to appreciate the need for new understandings of how accounting systems emerge in practice rather than in theory and the potential, or otherwise, which they offer for managerial decision making. Although such worries, let alone their causes, have yet to be systematically documented, it is not unusual for such people to express their concerns over the rigidities which routinized controls endow to organizational processes and the contracted time horizons which conventional accountings can often instil. Many also are worried about the problems which result from accounting's almost exclusive emphasis on the economic and the financial, and it is not unusual to hear even quite conventional practitioners articulate their concern for the inefficiencies which might have been legitimised by repeated annual cycles of budgetary reveiw and authorisation. At a more general level, there are now some organizations that are starting to express concern over the full range of implications that might have stemmed from the ways in which accounting and other control practices have resulted in an abstract process of control removed and often distanced from the practice of the task that is being controlled.

All too clearly such concerns are not the worry of the average practitioner. Whilst often concentrated in large organizations, an era of very real economic restraint nevertheless has resulted in at least some accounting practitioners and their managerial colleagues probing into what their investment in accounting has and has not achieved. Although rarely, if ever, expressed in ways other than the immediate set of implications for their own organizations, such questionings have resulted in a new awareness of the interdependency between the technology of the accounting craft and the human and social processes through which the objectives which are set for it are achieved. Moreover that awareness is often expressed in much more subtle terms than those used by the academic practitioners of accounting who have come to see behavioural and organizational studies as providing only a base for their more esoteric colleagues who only deem it worthwhile to worry about the icing on top of the accounting cake.

Unfortunately research on the organizational aspects of accounting is presently not in a position to fully address such practitioner worries. What studies are available have tended to focus on particular aspects of the accounting domain, often seeking to further the missions of accounting as conventionally defined rather than provide a more questioning account of accounting's consequences. Only rarely has research on the behavioural and organizational aspects of accounting concerned itself with investigating those wider linkages between accounting and other organizational processes and practices that provide the basis for some, at least, of the concerns currently emanating from practice.

Be that as it may, an organizational perspective can provide a basis for appreciating the practitioners' worries. It can contrast, for instance, the conventional organizational rationales for accounting which are detached from other organizational processes and concerns with a much more interactive view of organizational life (Ashton, 1976). From the latter perspective, the consequences of interventions in the name of one practice can be seen to be dependent on factors other than the intentions and means of organizational action which are consciously articulated and mobilised. It can be seen that actual outcomes also depend on the practical capacity of accounting procedures to encapsulate, penetrate and then influence the complex fabric of modern organizations, on the ways in which they intersect with both other organizational practices and the wider aims and actions of organizational participants, and, in the latter respect, on the resistances which specific attempts to mobilise one set of organizational practices induce. When seen in such terms there is at least the potential for the aims of any particular intervention in organizational life, be it of an accounting or any other nature, to remain partly or even totally unfulfilled (indeed even resulting in consequences which were wholly unanticipated) since the eventual outcomes are influenced by phenomena which did not enter into its original justification (Merton, 1936; Boudon, 1982). In the words of Hindess (1982, p. 498):

> Outcomes . . . may or may not conform to the intentions or objectives of any of the agents concerned. They are produced in the course of practices which take place under definite conditions and which confront definite obstacles, including the practices of others.[3]

Perhaps when seen in such a light it is not surprising that some consideration is now starting to be given to the circumstances under which accounting does and does not realise the aims that are articulated on behalf of it. The organizationally detached discourses that permeate accounting texts and manuals are being compared with the ways in which accounting has to relate to the practices and underlying bodies of knowledge of other approaches to organizational control. Accounting is being related to questions of organizational design and consideration is being given to how it functions alongside the interrelated practices of production, personnel and even financial management. Finally the resistances to accounting also are now being investigated, be they seen in terms of the behavioural processes which determine the actual use of the accounting craft or the social struggles within the organization in which accounting becomes intertwined. Be that as it may, it must be recognised that an organizational view of accounting in action is still emergent. There remains a very real need for further reflection and inquiry if we are to understand those processes through which accounting achieves the consequences which it both seeks to have and does in fact have.

## AN ORGANIZATIONAL AGENDA

No doubt numerous other rationales could have been provided for an interest in the organizational nature of accounting practice. More emphasis could have been placed on the ways in which accounting becomes implicated in the construction of prevailing conceptions of organizational power and the furtherance of particular organizational interests. Greater consideration could have been given to the nature of the organizational order

[3] Hindess (1982) goes on to argue that "the securing of outcomes should always be seen as problematic, that it is subject to definite and specifiable conditions in at least two respects. First, the means of action of agents are dependent on conditions that are not in their hands. Secondly, the deployment of these means of action invariably confronts obstacles, which often include the opposing practices of others. Success in overcoming those obstacles cannot in general be guaranteed" (p. 501). He concludes his argument by suggesting the need to take "seriously the particular conditions in which these practices and struggles take place and in which their outcomes are produced" (p. 509).

which accounting attempts to maintain and the roles which it plays in creating a particular pattern of economic and financial visibility within the enterprise. Equally, more stress could have been placed on the need for organizationally orientated accounting research to facilitate the decision roles of information within the organization, with consideration even being given to the need to construct new organizational accounts which can positively illuminate different aspects of organizational functioning. In part, at least, such additional factors have been alluded to. More importantly, the discussion of the organizational nature of accounting has sought only to provide a basis for a different view of the accounting craft. Even
166 though it may be partial, it nevertheless has hopefully outlined an area that is of some significance to all interested in the accounting endeavour and an area that is in urgent need of further study and inquiry. Indeed the conference itself was designed to help pursue this latter aim.

The papers presented at the conference focused on a number of different issues, drawing, in the process, on a range of very different organizational perspectives. Rather than striving to attempt to present *an* organizational view, a conscious aim of the conference was to provide an opportunity for the presentation and discussion of a number of different ways of analysing and trying to understand the organizational world in which accounting is embedded.

Together Johnson (1983), D. Flamholtz (1983), as discussant and Tiessen & Waterhouse (1983) provided a number of different perspectives on the processes by which accounting has become what it now is. Attempting to relate both social and economic views of the organization, they provided some bases for appreciating how accounting has become implicated in the construction of the modern business organization and how, in so doing, accounting has provided one means by which the organization can be related to wider economic and social interests, including, in the context of D. Flamholtz's remarks, those of the State. However, although the aims might be related, the approaches adopted by Johnson and Tiessen & Waterhouse are very different. Johnson presents a historical view of the ways in which accounting contributed to the emergence of the modern business enterprise. In part, at least, such a historical perspective provides us with an opportunity for seeing how accounting is both influenced by and in turn shapes the organizational form adopted by the enterprise. Tiessen & Waterhouse, in contrast, attempt to build upon a contingent view of management accounting by seeking to understand how accounting is used to construct a calculative interface between organizational management and those outside the enterprise who seek to pursue an interest in it. By appealing to economic conceptions of organizational rationality, they show how accounting plays a role by making visible a particular view of economic order. Johnson, on the other hand, at least points to the possibility that the resultant order is as much constructed as it is revealed by accounting means. From such a perspective it is possible to see the internally controlled domain of opportunities that is the firm as being a product of both the historical struggles out of which such domains emerged and the present as well as past use of management practices, such as accounting, for their preservation and development.

The papers by Birnberg *et al.* (1983), E. Flamholtz (1983) (and his discussant Kerr, 1983), Boland & Pondy (1983), Markus & Pfeffer (1983) and Hayes (1983) focus on ways of trying to understand how accounting is implicated in the ongoing processes of organizational functioning. In some respects this group of papers is notable for its diversity rather than for its convergence on any single viewpoint or issue. Indeed Hayes explicitly aims to present a number of different ways of accounting for the organizational significance of the accounting phenomenon. However beneath the seeming diversity a number of themes emerge.

Albeit in very different ways, both E. Flamholtz and Markus & Pfeffer discuss accounting's relationship to the bases of organizational power. Indeed in both papers not only the fact of that relationship but also the legitimacy of the present mode of articulation is accepted. With Flamholtz, however, accounting's contribution to mobilizing the powerful and power based organization is accepted implicitly, this seemingly being an unproblematic part of the accounting task. The challenge is to forge sufficient organizational linkages for the power potential of accounting to be realised. Whilst appearing to accept the ways in which accounting (and other forms of information and control systems) further particular conceptions of organizational power, Markus & Pfeffer explicitly discuss, although do little to appraise, the plurality of the bases of power in organizations, the ways in which accountings relate to the exercise of power and the strategies which an explicit recognition of this suggests for the design and implementation of new accounting and information and control systems. So although the organization is seen as having some aspects of a "contested terraine" (Edwards, 1979), strategies seemingly are available to further the contribution which accounting can make to the exercise of a particular powerful interest. Both papers therefore recognise that the accounting endeavour cannot be seen in purely technical terms. Equally, both suggest how the organizational might be mobilized in the name of the technical.

The tension between the technical and the organizational bases of the accounting task is a theme which pervades other papers. Birnberg and his colleagues contrast the stated aims of accounting with some aspects of its organizational achievements. Hayes seeks to ground the artifacts of accounting in the context of the symbolic, linguistic and legitimising roles which they serve. A more direct discussion is provided by Boland & Pondy, however, in terms of the perspectives of the rational and the natural, the former being related to the technical view of an objective accounting that permeates conventional discussions of the subject whilst the latter focuses on the ways in which accountings arise out of processes of social interaction, both reflecting and creating the symbolic structures that give meaning and significance to organizational life. Although outlining two very different views of how accounting is implicated in organizational functioning, Boland & Pondy nevertheless seek to demonstrate the utility of both perspectives. They consciously aim to illustrate how the rational provides a framework for the natural and how the natural can serve as a basis for the emergence and elaboration of the rational. Indeed, by so doing, they focus quite explicitly on the very real tensions that can be created by the juxtaposition of the two; tensions which create the very basis for the development of the accounting craft and the attribution of meanings to it.

Reflecting on such discussions, both Meyer (1983) and Cooper (1983) point to some of the wider issues involved. Meyer focuses on the symbolic domain that is created by accounting fictions, a domain that is important for creating the type of legitimate and seemingly coherent entities that are demanded by the agencies of the modern world. Although acknowledging the ways in which the rational domain so constructed is sometimes only loosely related to the ongoing processes of organizational life, Meyer nevertheless emphasises how the abstract fictions that permeate the accounting craft can nevertheless have a very real impact on organizational decision making and action. Not only does the symbolic define the real, but the reality so created can be and often is changed in the name of the symbolic. With what might initially appear to be the loosely coupled thereby having a very real possibility of becoming quite tightly coupled, Meyer therefore not only asks for a greater understanding of the processes through which this takes place but also suggests the very real need for a greater appreciation of the broader social and ideological factors that are implicated in these processes. Cooper also emphasises this latter point. He too is aware that the technical and the rational can come to be seen as natural; that, in other words, a new view of a seemingly natural order can be created in the name of the technical. However to Cooper, and indeed increasingly to others, such new organizational orders are neither unproblematic nor fully understandable in terms of the technical. Like Meyer, Cooper emphasises how important it is for accounting research both to recognise the wider social nature of the technical and the organizational world that it can in part create. He asks us to analyse much more consciously and systematically than has been the case in the past the social, institutional and ideological factors that are implicated in the emergence of particular conceptions of the technical and the rational, and the implications which they have for organizational and social functioning.

Although such wider debates only had an indirect relationship to the final group of papers presented at the conference, the interests of both Mirvis & Lawler (1983) and Mitroff & Mason (1983) were in part at least mobilised by their dissatisfaction with both the prevailing rationalities incorporated into the accounting craft and some of the organizational consequences of today's accounts. Mitroff & Mason emphasise the dilemmas facing the designers of information and accounting systems in an increasingly complex and uncertain world. Unhappy with the unitary logic which structures today's accounts of organizational action and performance, they argue for an approach to system design which more consciously
168 attempts to map the contradictions, tensions and dilemmas which characterise organizational life. Like Mirvis & Lawler, however, they recognise the resistance which seemingly faces their new organizational order. For Mitroff & Mason such resistance resides in the realms of the cultural, the psychological and the social, all sources, apparently, of an irrational response to the different rationality which they seek to instil. Mirvis & Lawler, on the other hand, at least start to probe into the wider organizational forces which might be implicated in the resilience of the old organizational order which they initially sought to reform – the very same resilience which provided the basis for the wider questionings of both Meyer and Cooper.

By any stretch of the imagination the papers presented at the conference on "Accounting in Its Organizational Context" provided a rich insight into some of the issues that might be at stake in analysing the accounting phenomenon from an organizational perspective. Given this, in the above remarks I have not attempted to provide an overview of all that was said or even the most important things that were on the agenda. I merely have sought to emphasise some similarities, differences, trends and implications from a personal point of view. The task of conducting a detailed assessment remains in the hands of the reader.

## SOME EMERGENT ISSUES

The value of almost any conference rests not only on the papers that are formally prepared and presented but also on the informal discussions which these stimulate. This conference was no exception. It therefore might be useful to conclude with a brief presentation of some of the issues, worries, concerns and possibilities that emerged during the course of the conference deliberations.

### *Accounting as a changing phenomenon*

Repeatedly consideration was given to how accounting had become what it now is and to the strategies that might be used for changing it. Stimulated no doubt by the historical perspectives offered by both Johnson (1983) and D. Flamholtz (1983), and by the socio-economic approach of Tiessen & Waterhouse (1983), the conference discussions often tended to focus on the changing nature of both the accounting domain and the accounting craft – on both what was accounted for and the means through which that was achieved. There was an ever conscious awareness of the fact that accounting changes: it becomes what it was not. Equally, however, there was a recognition of the paucity of our understandings of the processes through which this takes place, the broader issues that might be at stake and the consequences of the changes that do occur. Not only was the latter seen in terms of our own inadequate basis for accounting as we now know it, but also, and more generally, the discussions often emphasised our present inability to confront what might be at stake, both in terms of its antecedents and its consequences, in the seemingly ever increasing pervasiveness of the accounting phenomenon.

Dissatisfaction was voiced over the ability of conventional analyses of accounting history to address such questions. Seemingly it was more concerned with documenting the changing accounting phenomenon and the technologies that are at its deployment than providing an insight into the underlying social, institutional, economic and political forces at work. Indeed it was recognised that a great deal of research into accounting history had adopted, consciously or otherwise, a very atheoretical stance, ignoring, in the process, the problems involved in trying to provide an adequate social understanding of the accounting craft. The roles of accounting had been seen in relatively unproblematic and often very contemporary terms. The juxtaposition of accounting innovations in the *nexi* of relationships between the organization, the markets for both labour and capital, and the State had not been emphasised. And accounting scholars of the historical had seemingly distanced themselves from the concerns of both social theorists of the corporation and the corporate state and more recent theoretical advances in historical inquiry.

Equally, dissatisfaction was expressed with organizational attempts to account for accounting change. Although it was recognised that contingency approaches had provided some insights into the nature of accounting diversity, the relatively static and functionalist presumptions of such perspectives also were discussed. Contingency theory had difficulty confronting the dynamics of organizational and accounting change. In adopting a narrowly organizational perspective, it restricted the range of factors which it could consider in its pursuit of the origins of both difference and change. And its concern with more unitary conceptions of organizational aims and achievement foreclosed too many possibilities for inquiring into how organizational accounts emerged from political processes endemic to the organization rather than from the dictates of a more rational economic order.

In criticising the efforts of the past, and it should be said, the present as well, conference participants were aware of the very real conceptual and empirical difficulties involved in trying to provide more adequate and illuminating insights into the processes of accounting change. Indeed it was quite explicitly recognised that the issues involved reside at the frontiers of scholarly inquiries in the social sciences generally. Even so, although aware that research into accounting was not necessarily backward or too far behind that in other social science disciplines, it nevertheless was thought that much could be gained if accounting scholars were prepared to recognise more explicitly the organizational and social issues at stake and the range of theoretical perspectives that are at least available. It was thought that at the very least such a reorientation in perspective might encourage them to undertake a more sustained series of analyses of the emergence and development of accounting systems and practices. These, in turn, might provide a richer empirical basis for reflecting on those factors that might be implicated in accounting change and the processes through which this takes place.

*Accounting as a heterogeneous phenomenon*

Similar discussions also focused on the diverse nature of the accounting craft, particularly in respect of the practices of management accounting. Not only was there an awareness of the enormous range of technical practices in use (summarised by one participant in the terms of "you name it; somebody is using it!") but also consideration was given to the diversity of those organizational linkages which ground accounting and other information and control systems into the ongoing processes of organizational life. Accounting and control departments are variously organized. Planning, budgeting and performance monitoring procedures operate at different organizational levels, are subject to different degrees of participation, have different expectations and practices for their revision, and even can consider very different time periods. Accounting systems also serve to establish very different patterns of organizational segmentation and relate to the practices for the management of organizational interdependence in a variety of ways. From these and many other viewpoints the accounting domain was seen to exhibit a diversity that seemingly was at odds with the myth of a more generalised phenomenon that permeates accounting texts and those manuals that seek to guide accounting change and reform.

Yet again consideration was given to the inadequate state of our understanding of not only the factors underlying such diversity but also the implications that this might, and perhaps should, have for both the evaluation and change of accounting practice.

Perhaps in this context more sympathy was expressed with at least the aims of contingency approaches. In discussions of the heterogeneous accounting domain at least the contingent nature of the practices was recognised. The roles played by differing technologies, environments, management structures, corporate cultures and other factors were all alluded to. However it was recognised that not only had research from this perspective not progressed as far as it might but also that not sufficient consideration had been given to some of those difficulties of contingent approaches which already have been discussed. The problems raised by multiple contingencies were seen to be important; concern was expressed about the rather deterministic nature of present contingency theories; attention was focused on the need to understand the interplay between management choices and whatever constraints might be deemed to be imposed by the organizational context; and some, at least, wanted research to address more directly the interactive nature of the accounting craft by recognising not only how accounting might be shaped by its context but also how at least some aspects of that very same context might in turn be shaped by accounting itself.

More generally it was recognised that research which could provide insights into both accounting diversity and change had a very real potential to illuminate many key problems of accounting in practice. For the issues which such questions raise about the relationship of accounting to the context in which it operates are ones that are high on the problem agendas of accounting practitioners and consultants. By trying to disentangle the processes by which particular accountings arise, function and change, such research offers the potential to relate knowledge to the specifics of the accounting condition with which such practitioners have to deal.

*Competing accounts of the organizational terrain*

Albeit less explicitly, consideration nevertheless was given to the diverse accounts which seek to characterise organizational life and its outcomes. At the individual level, all organizational participants construct their own maps of the organizational terrain, delineating the significant, the problematic and the possible, accounting in their own terms for significant organizational boundaries, what they see to be the centres of power and influence, and those rationales which they think do and ought to influence choices and actions. Even in the sphere of rationalised systems of information and management, a multitude of accounts pervade organizational life. Physical and technical mappings are provided by engineers and production management; their systems also seek to shape and influence the physical reality of the organization in terms of volumes, flows, qualities, stocks and tolerances for performance. The personnel, marketing, financial and distribution functions (and others) also all impose their own accounts on the organization. Like the accountant, these practitioners also have invested in complex procedures for delineating the organizational world which they seek to manage and change, for recording those attributes which they have assigned to it and for influencing the cognitions and social behaviours of other organizational participants. Therefore the accountant's *Account* is merely one of many that attempt to make visible and salient particular aspects of organizational life and the constraints that are deemed to apply to it. Rather than existing in isolation, *Accounting* was seen as being in a state of tension with the multitude of other organizational accounts, seeking to impose a particular perspective, order and mission on a domain that is characterised not by the absence of maps for its exploration and explitation but rather by the sheer richness of the competing surveys of its problematic terrain.

When the accounting phenomenon was seen in such terms it invariably raised questions about the means through which a particular account had become enshrined as *Accounting* practice. Questions also were asked about the interplay of the diverse accountings, those factors that might have influenced their relative power, their differential consequences and the relationship which the mobilisation of particular accounts had to the patterns of organizational choice and action over time.

To date accounting research has adopted all too parochial a perspective. A very special significance has been attached to the economic and financial mappings provided by the professionalised practitioners of the accounting craft. As a result, a particular account has been accepted as *the Account*. W ilst there are good reasons for some specialisation of interest (not least in a world characterised by increasing system diversity, complexity and technical sophistication), the unproblematic acceptance of the priority accorded to such a partial ordering of organizational life undoubtedly has not only restricted the nature of the inquiries undertaken into the organizational nature of accounting practice and the problems which it faces but also, and perhaps more fundamentally, prevented people from exploring the organizational and the wider social factors which have resulted in one account being attributed with so much significance and power – in the world of action as well as in that of scholarly inquiry. It was thought that at least some investigations of the latter set of issues might help to illuminate some key aspects of the accounting condition, those organizational roles which accounting is expected to serve and the tensions which its implementation and use so often engender.

*The tension between organizational order and disorder*

Such a perspective of competing organizational accounts helped to focus attention on the often precarious nature of the organizational order which accounting seeks to create. Only rarely, if ever, is accounting elaboration and change an unproblematic endeavour of charting an organization anew. More frequently, organizational participants already hold their own views of the significant and the desirable, and usually these have been shaped by the practices of other practitioners who have sought to change the organization in the name of their own particular missions and aims. Accounting, accordingly, enters into a disputed terrain. Its consequences have to be achieved by contesting the dominance of pre-existing conceptions of organizational order and purpose. Accounting therefore can be characterised not only in terms of the aims that are attributed to it but also in terms of the resistances which it engenders. Indeed it is just such resistances which already have stimulated behavioural inquiries and the concerns and worries of those practitioners of the accounting craft who have reflected on the consequences which it has not achieved as well as those which it has achieved but which did not enter into its original justification.

The organizational world in which accounting operates therefore can be seen in terms of the order which accounting seeks to implement and the disorder which its implementation both confronts and, in part, engenders. Moreover both dimensions of such a perspective can be elaborated in terms of what might over simplistically be called the vertical and the horizontal axes of organizational action. Operating vertically, accounting seeks to reinforce a particular conception of organizational power. It aims to create a partial but influential pattern of visibility which can facilitate the operation of the organizational hierarchy by creating a form of organizational segmentation, by channelling down through that an objective for action and subsequently by monitoring actual performance. Seen in such terms, accounting is a tool in the hands of the powerful. Viewed horizontally, accounting also can be seen as being implicated in the propogation of a financial and economic rationale for action, seeking either to contest those alternative conceptions of organizational mission that can be advanced in the name of the technical, the market, the social and whatever or to serve as a means for converting (and invariably modifying in the process) such aims into the language of the economic. On both axes of organizational life accounting can be seen as trying to create a particular conception of organizational order. Equally, however, on both axes that conception of order is invariably contested and challenged, albeit with differing degrees of effectiveness.

In emphasising only the order which accounting seeks to advance rather than the contexts in which it operates there is an ever present danger that accounting scholars of the behavioural merely seek to expose the defects in the present apparatus of accounting and move towards its reform without appreciating the diverse and contested nature of the organizational regime in which accounting operates.

Perhaps somewhat paradoxically, attention also was focused on those circumstances in which accounting had succeeded in imposing its own particular order. Rather than greeting this achievement with acclaimation, however, at least some conference participants were concerned with the organizational consequences which might result, with the latter seen in terms of both more general notions of organizational effectiveness and the particular regimes of power that accounting serves to reinforce.

Concerns were expressed about the potential problems which might stem from trying to guide and manage a complex and diverse organization on the basis of a single perspective. In part such worries reflected an awareness of the dangers of the bureaucratic rigidity which could result from a singular emphasis on the routinised procedures for inducing a particular organizational visibility which are so often associated with the accounting craft. In addition, however, the discussions of the organizational context in which accounting operates had resulted in a recognition of the need for a diversity of accounts to map into the organization the very different but equally salient aspects of both its external and internal environments. Even an approximation towards a singular informational order was seen as too narrowly restricting the messages, the options and, thereby, the actions that were available to organizational members. Thought therefore was given to the need for a more organizationally grounded view of accounting that would be compatible with a role as a complementary rather than over-reaching information and control system – a view that would be content with the disorders as well as with the ordering of organizational life.

Of course the concerns with the power potential of accounting also questioned such notions of a unitary organizational order. Accounting, when seen from such a perspective, was centrally implicated in the construction of particular notions of organizational ends and achievements. Rather than merely reflecting in a neutral manner the constraints and imperatives that impinge on organizations as we now know them, accounting was seen as being involved in the specification and articulation of a specific organizational mission. As such, it could not be seen as a disinterested endeavour. Accounting was at least related to the propogation of a particular set of interests, even though that relationship may be moderated by some aspects of the autonomous nature of the craft, the complex of institutional structures in which its practice is embedded and the diverse agents which call upon its practices and procedures. According to this view a questioning of accounting would necessitate an examination of the interests in the name of which it is mobilised, its effectiveness to serve these ends and the strategies that might be available if other interests wished either to challenge or themselves to utilise the accounting craft.

Conceptions of order and disorder therefore were seen to be far from unproblematic terms, appealing both to views of organizational achievement and those political regimes which might underlie accounting practice. Different though they may be, however, it was recognised that both viewpoints had had little impact on accounting inquiry.

### *The reflective and constitutive role of accounting*

To date organizational research in accounting has emphasised the ways in which accounting systems reflect other aspects of the environments in which they are embedded. As has been indicated already, consideration has been given to the impact which technologies and markets have on accounting, to the relationship between organizational structure and the design and use of accounting systems, and some initial interest has been expressed in examining the broader cultural influences on the form taken by accounting and other types of control systems. In such ways accounting has been shown to be a contingent phenomenon, designed and used in the context of other important features of the organizational environment.

Although concern has been expressed about the adequacy of our present conceptual and empirical skills for handling such contingent relationships, the general notion of an interdependent accounting has not been contested. At the conference it was seen to be a partial view however. For although accounting plays a role in mapping into the organization other salient aspects of the managerial, task and external environments, it also has the power to shape and influence organizational life on its own accord.

The environments that are mapped into the organization can become defined in accounting terms. They can become "profitable" or "costly", "cash cows" or "rising stars". Similarly the organization structures which impinge on accounting practice invariably do not have a manifestation that is completely independent of their accounting reflection. Modes of organizational decentralization are defined in terms of cost, profit and investment centres; organizational units have accounting as well as managerial boundaries; and accounting mechanisms for the monitoring of subunit performance help to make real the powerful potential that is reflected within the organization chart. Equally, accounting plays a role not only in shaping the visible map of what is known of organizational functioning but also in expressing and thereby influencing the objectives that are stated for organized action. An operational definition of profit has been a particularly powerful notion. However consideration must also be given to the mobilising potential of concepts such as cash, working capital, assets and, not least, cost. All provide illustrations of where accounting has made operational, and therefore powerful, more abstract notions of economic discourse.

In ways such as these accounting has come to play a positive role in creating our present conceptions of organized endeavour. Whilst in part reflecting many other parameters of organizational life, accounting also has played a more active role in constructing the organizational world in which it is now embedded, shaping views of both the constraints on organized action and the ends which it seeks to serve. There is, in other words, a complex interplay between the reflective and the constitutive roles of accounting,[4] the former serving to create accounting's dependency on the organizations in which it is embedded and the latter often constraining organizations in the name of the possibilities and potentialities of the accounting craft.

*The external origins of internal accounts*

The conference had explicitly aimed to focus on the organizational nature of the accounting craft. The objective had been to provide some bases for appreciating how accounting was implicated with other aspects of organizational functioning.

At an early stage in the proceedings, however, such an aim was seen to be a partial one. Just as accounting could not be disentangled from the organizational, so the organizational could not be disassociated from the wider social context in which it in turn was embedded. Accounting, thereby, increasingly came to be seen as a phenomenon subject to the influences of both the particular organization and the wider social fabric in which it functioned.

Many of the organizational influences on accounting were seen to be specific manifestations of social influences, pressures and tensions. The State, for instance, in trying to further its own missions had repeatedly provided a basis for the elaboration of calculative endeavours within the enterprise. Its strategies for the control of prices and wages had resulted in the furtherance of those accounting procedures which sought to define, examine, restrain and plan within the organization those phenomenon which had a macro-economic significance at the national level. In the name of both economic crisis and growth the State had sought to further a regime of economic awareness within both organizations and those constituencies, such as the labour movement, which were deemed to have an interest in them. Calling upon conceptions of economic efficiency and effectiveness (and more recently "value for money"), the State repeatedly had tried to reform both its own administrative apparatus and the management practices of those organizations which were thought to play a significant role in the national economy.

Wider social agencies, including those of the State, the media and the professional institutions of the accounting craft, also could play a significant role in establishing a view of both the prevailing technical state of the accounting art and those managerial practices which were regarded as legitimate and in order. A view of the current, the modern, the desirable and the achievable could be propogated with some autonomy from the particular needs and histories of specific organizations. Accounting, particularly when professionalised,



[4] A further discussion of the reflective and constitutive roles of accounting is contained in Burchell *et al.* (forthcoming).

could achieve, and indeed had achieved, some degree of independent action. Solutions could indeed hunt for problems. The craft itself could influence the organizational. Equally significantly, organizations seeking to respond to the pressures of their environments could seek to utilise particular accounting and management practices in the name of the external legitimacy they could endow rather than on the basis of any presumed internal consequences. Indeed with the social thereby becoming the organizational, management might even uncouple their internal procedures and actions from the externally orientated practices of a rational management regime. So although influenced by the social, the organizational might even live in a state of flux with it.

The internal tensions and conflicts within organizations also cannot be detached from broader social movements. Concerns with the humanization of management practices in particular organizations have rarely existed in isolation of social movements which have provided a basis for their rhetoric and aims. The emphasis on the social in accounting itself has been a manifestation of the broader mobilisation of attempts to construct the organization in different terms. Equally, the ways in which accounting has sought to further a particular hierarchical order within organizations cannot be seen outside of the context of the conflicts between different social groups. In this sense accounting has both mirrored the context in which it has operated and enabled it to function in the ways it has. Only certain phenomenon have been regarded as costly. Particular conceptions of time have been emphasised. The benefits that have been incorporated into accounting calculations have not occurred in isolation of the socio-economic fabric to which they seek to relate. Accounting, in other words, has played a not insignificant role in embedding the social into the organizational. Accordingly its practice can never be seen in purely organizational terms.

Such a conclusion is a paradoxical one to emerge from a conference dedicated to exploring the organizational nature of the accounting craft. It reflects, however, the highly interdependent nature of our social world and the complex ways in which accounting has come to be embedded in our everyday lives. The social is not and cannot be isolated from the organizational. Indeed, in part at least, the social is manifest in the organizational and the organizational, in turn, constitutes a significant part of the social. It might even be useful to see the social as passing through the organizational, with both wider and more localised concerns calling upon practices such as accounting to create an ambiguous but nevertheless tethered conception of reality.

*The methodologies of accounting research*

The paucity of empirical studies of accounting in action was a major constraint on the conference deliberations. Repeatedly it had to be recognised how little was known of the accounting endeavour.

Our organizational colleagues had assumed that accounting researchers would be applied social scientists, committed to exploring the intricacies of accounting in practice. They had presumed that by now behavioural and organizational enquiries would have resulted in a mass of insights into the ways in which accounting was related to the fabric of organizational life. Indeed they had come to be illuminated on the relationship of accounting to the organizational, the strategic and the social. Those expectations could not be met however. The simple fact is that accounting research has tended to isolate itself from accounting in practice, if not accounting practice. The vast majority of efforts have been devoted to furthering the technical edifice of the accounting craft rather than seeking to illuminate the ways in which accounting intersects with the organizational and comes to have the significance it now has.

All too clearly if accounting researchers are to advance our understanding of the accounting context very different methodological perspectives will be required. There is a very real need for theoretically informed studies of both the use and design of accounting systems. Much more needs to be known of the ways in which accounting reflects, reinforces or even constrains the strategic postures adopted by particular organizations and of the ways in which accounting relates to the structures that are created for ensuring a coherent and vertically responsible organization. Studies of accounting changes also could do much to illustrate the nature of the diverse forces, both internal and external to the organization, that are operating on the accounting craft. Such studies also might help to cast some light on the ways in which the ambiguities that so often pervade accounting practice might play a positive role on bridging different, if not conflicting, pressures on accounting to change.

Of course all such investigations require the very commitment that is missing in accounting research to-date – a commitment to study, analyse and interpret accounting in the contexts in which it operates. The fact that so little of this work has been done suggests that change will not be easy. The constraints on organizational empirical inquiry must be very real indeed. To-date the difficulties of access and the inexperience of accounting researchers have been important factors. More significant, however, may be those pressures of the academic reward structure which push for speedy and voluminous research, the very low legitimacy which somewhat paradoxically has been given to grounded empirical inquiry, and the marginal commitment which many academic accountants have to the research endeavour. Unfortunate though these constraints may be, they nevertheless are very real ones. Accordingly change will not occur by mere ennunciation. Demonstration is a much more likely route. We can only hope that slowly, but surely, new precedents can be established by adventurous researchers seeking to explore what lies behind today's accounting condition.

## CONCLUSION

Organizational inquiry remains a new area of investigation for accounting research. Despite accounting being given an organizational rationale, we have few insights into the factors which influence accounting systems in the contexts in which they operate.

When one reviews the organizational research on accounting that has been undertaken to-date, it is clear that much of it has been limited in scope, fragmentary and essentially atheoretical. The primary concerns often have tended to be the the laudable but nevertheless constraining ones of exposing defects in the accounting craft and seeking a basis for the reform of prevailing practice. Useful though such inquiries often may be, there nevertheless is a very real danger that if too fragmentary in nature they can serve to perpetuate or even to foster myths about the organizational practice of accounting. What is needed are more substantive investigations orientated towards providing bases for understanding or explaining the workings of accounting in action. Yet it is precisely such studies that have been neglected to-date.

However, as the studies collected in this issue illustrate, there are signs of an emergence of interest in the organizational nature of accounting. The origins of this are diverse, spanning economics, organization theory and sociology. Frequently non-accountants have taken the lead. Economists, for instance, have started to probe into the roles served by accounting in the construction of modern organizational forms and their links to external agents. Organization theorists recetly have become much more interested in questions of information and control, in the process exploring into not only the taken for granted roles which such practices are presumed to serve but also the symbolic and even political aspects of organizational life with which they can become intertwined. And sociologists too have started to recognise the research potential offered by the accounting craft, asking questions about how accounting might be related to the more general elaboration of calculative practices in modern society, the ways in which accounts have provided a powerful calculus for forging a new visibility which can facilitate specific modes of control within the business enterprise in particular, and the more legitimising functions of the accounting craft.

Most of these influences are reflected in the present collection. The result is an impression of an area in motion. Together the papers (and the discussant's remarks) provide both a useful insight into research in progress and a helpful agenda for future inquiries.

## BIBLIOGRAPHY


Ashton, R. H., Deviation-Amplifying Feedback and Unintended Consequences of Management Accounting Systems, *Accounting, Organizations and Society* (1976) pp. 289–300.

Baiman, S., Agency Theory in Management Accounting: A Survey, *Journal of Accounting Literature* (Spring 1982) pp. 154–213.

Batstone, E., Systems of Domination, Accommodation, and Industrial Democracy, in Burns, T.R., Karlsson, L.E. & Rus, V. (eds.) *Work and Power. The Liberation of Work and Control of Political Power*, pp. 249–272 (London: Sage, 1979).

Birnberg, J. C., Turpolec, L. & Young, S. M., The Organizational Context of Accounting, *Accounting, Organizations and Society* (1983) pp. 111–129.

Boland, R. J. & Pondy, L. R., Accounting In Organizations: A Union of Natural and Rational Perspectives, *Accounting, Organizations and Society* (1983) pp. 223–224.

Burchell, S., Clubb, C., Hopwood, A., Hughes, J. & Nahapiet, J., The Roles of Accounting in Organizations and Society, *Accounting, Organizations and Society* (1980) pp. 5–27.

Burchell, S., Hopwood, A. G. & Clubb, C., Accounting in its Social Context: Towards a History of Value Added in the UK, *Accounting, Organizations and Society* (forthcoming).

176

Connolly, T., On Taking Action Seriously: Cognitive Fixation in Behavioural Decision Theory, in Ungson, G. R. & Braunstein, D. N. (eds.) *Decision Making: An Interdisciplinary Inquiry* pp. 42–47 (Kent, 1982).

Cooper, D., Tidiness, Muddle and Things: Commonalities and Divergencies in Two Approaches to Management Accounting Research, *Accounting, Organizations and Society* (1983) pp. 269–286.

Cummings, L. L., A Framework for Decision Analysis and Critique, in Ungson, G. R. & Braunstein, D. N. (eds.) *Decision Making: An Interdisciplinary Inquiry* pp. 298–308 (Kent, 1982).

Edwards, R., Contested Terrain: *The Transformation of the Workplace in the Twentieth Century* (New York: Basic Books, 1979).

Flamholtz, D., The Markets and Hierarchies Framework: A Critique of the Models Applicability to Accounting and Economic Development, *Accounting, Organizations and Society* (1983) pp. 147–151.

Flamholtz, E., Accounting, Budgeting and Control Systems in Their Organizational Context: Theoretical and Empirical Perspectives, *Accounting, Organizations and Society* (1983) pp. 153–169.

Gowler, D. & Legge, K., The Integration of Disciplinary Perspectives and Levels of Analysis in Problem Oriented Organizational Research, Working Paper 81/3, Oxford Centre for Management Studies (1981).

Hayes, D. C., Accounting for Accounting: A Story about Managerial Accounting, *Accounting, Organizations and Society* (1983) pp. 241–249.

Hindess, B., Power, Interests and the Outcomes of Struggles, *Sociology* (November 1982) pp. 498–511.

Hopwood, A. G., The Path Ahead, *Accounting, Organizations and Society* (1976) pp. 1–4.

Hopwood, A. G., Towards an Organizational Perspective for the Study of Accounting and Information Systems, *Accounting, Organizations and Society* (1978) pp. 3–13.

Hopwood, A. G., Burchell, S. & Clubb, C., The Development of Accounting in Its International Context: Past Concerns and Emergent Issues, in Roberts, A. (ed.) *A Historical and Contemporary Review of the Development of International Accounting* (Georgia State University, 1980).

Horovitz, J. H., *Top Management Control in Europe* (London: Macmillan, 1980).

Johnson, T., The Search for Gain in Markets and Firms: A Review of the Historical Emergence of Management Accounting Systems, *Accounting, Organizations and Society* (1983) pp. 139–146.

Kerr, S., Accounting, Budgeting and Control Systems in Their Organizational Context: Comments by The Discussant, *Accounting, Organizations and Society* (1983) pp. 171–174.

March, J. G. & Shapra, Z., Behavioural Decision Theory and Organizational Decision Theory, in Ungson, G. R. & Braunstein, D. N. (eds.) *Decision Making: An Interdisciplinary Inquiry*, pp. 92–115 (Kent, 1982).

Markus, M. L. & Pfeffer, J., Power and the Design and Implementation of Accounting and Control Systems, *Accounting, Organizations and Society* (1983) pp. 205–218.

Merton, R., The Unanticipated Consequences of Purposive Social Action, *American Sociological Review* (1936) pp. 894–904.

Meyer, J. W., On the Celebration of Rationality: Some Comments on Boland and Pondy, *Accounting, Organizations and Society* (1983) pp. 235–240.

Mirvis, P. H. & Lauter, E. E. III, Systems are not Solutions: Issues in Creating Information Systems that Account for the Human Organization, *Accounting, Organizations and Society* (1983) pp. 175–190.

Mitroff, I. I. & Mason, R. O., Can We Design Systems for Managing Messes? Or, Why So Many Management Information Systems are Uninformative, *Accounting, Organizations and Society* (1983) pp. 195–203.

Otley, D. T., The Contingency Theory of Management Accounting: Achievements and Prognosis, *Accounting, Organizations and Society* (1980) pp. 413–428.

Platt, J., *Realities of Social Research: An Empirical Study of British Sociologists* (London: Sussex University Press and Chatto and Windus, 1976).

Pondy, L., On Real Decisions, in Ungson, G. R. & Braunstein, D. N. (eds.) *Decision Making: An Interdisciplinary Inquiry*, pp. 309–311 (Kent, 1982).

Spicer, B. H. & Ballew, V., Management Accounting Systems and the Economics of Internal Organization, *Accounting, Organizations and Society* (1983) pp. 73–96.

Tiessen, P. & Waterhouse, J. H., Towards a Descriptive Theory of Management Accounting, *Accounting, Organizations and Society* (1983) pp. 251–267.

Weick, K. E., Rethinking Research on Decision Making, in Ungson, G. R. & Braunstein, D. N. (eds.) *Decision Making: An Interdisciplinary Inquiry*, pp. 325–332 (Kent, 1982).

# Commentary
# The Growth of "Worrying" about Management Accounting

Anthony G. Hopwood

Until recently it has been rare for accounting to be interrogated in the name of either its organizational functioning or its precise organizational effects. Accounting discourse has remained a purely technical 179
one. Little effort has been invested in exploring the ways in which it intersects with other organizational processes, the actual consequences which it has, and the implications of these for organizational performance. The justifications given for accounting practice, both contemporary and prospective, not only have continued to reside in the technical domain but also have been content to draw on presumptions of its organizational desirability rather than a more pragmatic concern with its actual effects. The result is that accounting, although undoubtedly an influential part of organizational practice, nevertheless has remained an isolated craft, with its normative presuppositions only rarely tested against the very practical contexts that its practitioners somewhat paradoxically continue to emphasize.

Now, however, there are some encouraging signs that these manifestations of the accounting past are slowly starting to change in both the worlds of academic inquiry and practice.

Professor Kaplan's chapter is both symptomatic of, and a significant contribution to, the changes that are taking place in management accounting research. Rather than being content with designing, at a distance, ever more sophisticated technical procedures that seemingly have the potential to improve organizational decision making and control, researchers increasingly have become more interested in understanding management accounting as it is, the factors that influence the forms it takes and the organizational consequences it actually has. Albeit slowly, management accounting research is starting to confront management accounting practice.

Of course, this development is manifested in many and various ways. Accounting practice is being interrogated from a number of very different perspectives. There are those who seek to understand its economic rationality in organizational terms. Others place the emphasis directly on the organizational or social or even political nature of accounting practice. More significantly, perhaps, even the newer variety of management accounting researchers seemingly are content to remain theorists of the accounting craft. Despite the growing concern with confronting practice that is implicit in a number of the new approaches, very few have sought to directly observe management accounting in practice. Kaplan is one of these few and, because of this, his contribution is even more significant.

Kaplan's arguments also are interesting because they are reflective of a growing realization that management accounting not only is not what it should be but also might even be having effects that it
180 shouldn't have. Of course the later realization that practice is subject to unanticipated dysfunctional consequences certainly is not a new one, not least in the research community. Until recently, however, it is fair to say that it has been possible to presume that, although present, the undesirable "side effects" did not prevent the achievement of the main management accounting task. The icing, in other words, was perhaps starting to deteriorate but the cake itself was still regarded as wholesome. Such a presumption, however, is now being questioned. A more radical view that something "might," but only might, be more fundamentally astray with the management accounting craft interestingly started to emerge in the corporation rather than in the academy and Kaplan has provided the first research statement of this growing focus of "corporate worrying."

The history of the development of worrying about management accounting has not been documented as yet. Indeed I sense that much of it has been masked as corporations have simply introduced other management strategies and techniques that complement the increasingly limited and rigid practices of accounting. Other control techniques have been made to operate alongside management accounting, as Kaplan notes. Lateral overlays of information have been introduced to provide the integration that has become more important in organizations segmented by the vertically oriented influence of accounting practice. Other management disciplines even have started to confront the problems involved in the control of cost structures very different from those that both accompanied management accounting's birth and underlie many of the pronouncements made in the textbooks and manuals of the craft. However, despite these important complementary developments, there nevertheless is now a more direct history of practical worrying about management accounting.

The organizational rigidities that were furthered by many management accounting practices were of concern to those who sought to implement more flexible forms of work organization in the late 1960s and early 1970s. The limited notions of costliness incorporated into traditional systems were clearly identified at the same time. At a more general level, a number of major manufacturing organizations started to realize how their existing management information and control systems, including the management accounting systems, might be implicated in the narrowing of management attention onto the purely economic; in the construction of far too short conceptions in time; in a rigidity of organizational structures that was clearly dysfunctional in an era of uncertainty and change; and in a costly regime of suboptimal decision making. 181

In the early 1970s Philips was one of the earliest corporations to specifically identify this disease. In subsequent years other major corporations came to a similar realization, particularly as a result of an intensification in their competitive environment which highlighted the organizational costliness of their cost accounting systems. The rise of strategic notions of corporate management only served to further the perception of a problem as management strategists grappled with the difficulty of relating traditional short-term, accounting-based oriented management information systems to the needs of a more aggressive formulation and monitoring of corporate strategy.

The net result of these developments was a slowly growing corporate awareness of the types of problems discussed in Kaplan's chapter. Some organizations established working parties and study groups in the area. One even restricted any changes in its financial control systems until it had a better idea of where it was going. The Ford "After Japan" ("AJ") program was seen to have implications for their massive existing commitment to financial control systems. In numerous other organizations the traditional accounting information flows are being supplemented, particularly in the name of the vocabulary of "strategy."

Still, however, traditional notions of the management accounting craft are firmly entrenched, as Kaplan's chapter makes clear. As someone from the United Kingdom, surely one of the most accounting-intensive countries in the Western world, I have to agree with his view that accounting is still about accounting. In most of its manifestations it appears to remain an organizational practice rather loosely connected with changes occurring in other organizational arenas. Its emphasis is still on the narrowly financial, the short term, and the organizationally constraining. Although there are some signs of change, these are slow to emerge, contained within relatively few organizations and very poorly known and understood.

Kaplan seeks to account for the seeming permanence of the old in terms of organizational lag and traditionalism. Again, coming from the United Kingdom, I cannot disagree with many of the points he makes in this respect. Management accounting as we now know it did arise amidst the very specific cost structures and control problems that characterized manufacturing organizations of the past. Accounting system reform does appear to be an unknown art. Financial accounting has had a dominant influence, and one that might still be increasing. Textbooks, in particular, and the accounting education process, more
182 generally, are still firmly grounded in the traditions of the past. Until recently, information processing technologies have provided a very constraining influence. And few, if any, alternative conceptions of accounting have been, or even are now being articulated. Accounting still is accounting.

However, although I share Kaplan's view that these factors are implicated to a significant extent in the conservatism that pervades accounting practice, I am far less convinced that together they give an adequate account of accounting as it is. I admit the problems of articulating alternative explanations: Accounting practice is an inadequately researched domain. It is even difficult to isolate the full variety of forms that it takes, let alone outline the factors that lie behind its development and the linkages that it has with other organizational practices. Be that as it may, other considerations are involved in accounting as it is. Some of them, at least, might help us to understand why senior corporate management has not sought to grapple with the problems of accounting practice in the ways that Kaplan might have expected.

The first such factor relates to some of the diverse and conflicting influences that have an impact on accounting practice. Kaplan emphasizes the needs of new manufacturing processes, their attendant cost structures and control needs, and a more competitive environment. But the very same competitive environment that has highlighted the importance of flexibility, noneconomic competitive advantages, and the significance of a more strategic, longer term perspective, also have reinforced the relevance of the immediate and the traditionally economic. Budgets have not only been tightened but revised much more frequently. Standards have been cut. Cash controls have been introduced to complement cost controls. A renewed emphasis has been placed on financial responsibility, accountability, and control. In many organizations these complementary factors have resulted in a vast increase in the regime of economic calculation that pervades organizational life.

So, not only is accounting alive and well, but so is a concern with many of its traditional emphases. The short term has been of significance alongside the longer term. The economic has been emphasized alongside the noneconomic. The very real requirements for flexibility have had to compete with a renewed interest in the constraining and the specific. In other words, all the accoutrements of what has been provocatively called "newly poor behavior" (Olofsson and Svalander 1975), in which accounting traditionally has been implicated, have been very actively competing for organizational space, visibility, and significance with what might be seen as the very different manage- 183
ment practices associated with the rise of the strategic and its less direct concerns with the economic. And no doubt a lot of the balancing of these competing pressures has been done by practitioners firmly grounded in the concerns of the past.

It would have been illuminating if Kaplan had specifically sought to identify the positive interests that there might have been in the accountings of the past rather than just confronting the difficulties faced by the emergence of the new. Further research most definitely needs to confront the variety of current organizational forces influencing accounting. Accounting needs to be seen as emerging and functioning in a conflicting domain with divergent interests, needs, and perspectives seeking to attach themselves to its technical procedures.

A second factor lying behind accounting practice as it is might reside in the diversity of roles that accounting serves in organizations. In part, Kaplan points to this when he contrasts the needs of the new with management accounting's present domination by the dictates of an increasingly regulated corporate financial accounting. Of course the two need not be so tightly coupled. They were not in the past and they are not in some other national contexts. However, one would like to know more about what is at stake in the intertwining that we see today. Rather than too readily labeling it as a manifestation of lag or ignorance or both, one might probe more into the roles that perhaps are being asked of accounting practice in organizations.

In saying this I draw on a view of the roles that accounting serves that go beyond the directly decision-facilitating ones that are implicit not only in Kaplan's paper but in much of the contemporary accounting literature (Burchell et al. 1980). Although the reformist rationales that underlie that decision-facilitating role are valuable, they should be complemented with a much more explicit appreciation of how accounting has been involved in the construction and furtherance of organizational power structures, in the creation and propagation of the goals of organized endeavors, and in the establishment of a dominant pattern of economic visibility that pervades the organization.

When seen in such terms, accounting is involved with much more than directly facilitating managerial action. It is concerned with making visible and thereby governable the detailed work processes of an organization. It provides for both aggregating and disaggregating organizational actions and outcomes—a powerful tool in the hands of organizational managers. It is involved with the establishment of a language of organizational motive, with rendering into the domain of the economic important aspects of the physical and task reality of the
184 organization. And it is quite centrally involved in the construction of operational concepts of accountability, responsibility, and even performance which play a significant role in the creation of a manageable organizational regime.

Such wider organizational roles provide an important basis for understanding not only the development and present functioning of accounting but also the paradoxes and seeming inadequacies of its practice which Kaplan so acutely observes. Although accounting's involvement with facilitating operational decision making is important, not least in the management of change and improvement, that alone cannot provide anywhere near a complete basis for appreciating accounting as it is, the conflicting nature of the organizational pressures on it, and the effects that it actually has. The language of motives, power, and control must be utilized alongside that of decision making. Accounting has to be seen as an influential organizational ritual and an instrument of control and governance as well as a decision aid. The metaphors of acccounting as an "ammunication" and "rationalization machine" need to complement those of the "answer" and "learning machines" that characterize so much of official accounting discourse (Burchell et al. 1980).

A third factor lying behind the present practice of accounting is the professional competition that pervades the management arena. Organizations may need to be managed and controlled, but that can be done in a multiplicity of different ways. Different organizations have invested in different regimes of control. Control practices and emphases have changed over time. And of particular importance in the present context, different occupational and professional groups have competed for the right to control the corporate arena (Armstrong, 1985).

When seen in such terms, a reliance on accounting controls cannot be dissociated from the rise to power of the corporate accountant and financial manager as compared with, for instance, the engineer or the personnel manager. This is not the place to discuss what might have been at stake in the growing significance of industrial accountants and the techniques and procedures that they brought into the organizational arena. Suffice it to say that the conflict for control of the management of the corporation has been resolved in different ways in different contexts. The accountant as a corporate manager is very much a phenomenon of the Atlantic fringe countries of the United States, the United Kingdom and, possibly, the Netherlands—all countries that are playing a leading role in the worrying that is taking place over the adequacy of management accounting practice. As 185
Horovitz (1980) makes clear in his comparative study of management control practices in European countries, not only are financial management practices less well developed in continental European countries but also a much greater investment has been made in the creation of alternative visibilities in the organization. There appears to be a more active competition for management attention between the visibilities of the technical, the human, the financial, and the marketplace.

Comparative and historical studies may play an important role in helping us understand the factors implicated in the accounting practices of today. Equally, but somewhat more provocatively, they might well show how the imperatives and justifications that are so often associated with different management practices emerge from, as well as result in, the practices that we observe today.

One final factor is of importance in understanding management accounting as it is. Most justifications and indeed studies of accounting practice emphasize its internal organizational roles. Kaplan's chapter has adopted this viewpoint, as has this commentary so far. However, further insights into both the practice and functioning of accounting, not least in manufacturing organizations, can be gained from an appreciation of how it came to be involved in the social as well as the organizational management of the corporation.

The discussion so far has been suggestive of this point. This commentary has emphasized the potential of accounting for furthering particular conceptions of organizational power. Attention has been given to the regime of economic visibility created by accounting practices. Accounting's involvement in the construction of governable organizations has been highlighted. And accounting's dependency on a significant professionalized body of practitioners has at least been considered. All of these points provide a basis for understanding the significant linkages between the organizational and the social practice of accounting.

Accounting, when seen in such terms, is more than a mere technical organizational practice oriented to the furtherance of pregiven conceptions of organizational efficiency and achievement. It is a practice that has come to play a significant role in the very articulation and furtherance of the concepts on which it is grounded. Operating, as it does, in organizations where the elucidation of both the ends and the means of organized endeavor resides in a contested domain rather than in one that is subject to the dictates of a pregiven rationale, accounting can be seen as having the characteristics of an interested practice that is
186 concerned with creating and quite actively mobilizing, rather than merely facilitating, the context that it is used to regulate.

Such a perspective is particularly useful when comparative understandings are needed of accounting practice—not an insignificant stimulus for the present questioning. In some contexts the corporation may have been a less significant site for social control. Organizational participants may have already been inculcated into the norms appropriate for the operation of a manageable organizational regime. Accounting then may well have been able to concentrate on its organizational roles. Elsewhere, however, any such presumption may not have been in order. With the corporation itself being a very active site for social action, investments were made in organizational practices that sought to create a more disciplined and controllable work force, an economic vocabulary of organizational motive, and a legitimacy for organizational authority and influence as well as an effective management process. In many Western countries accounting was created and often still functions at just such an intersection of the organizational and the social. It is doubtful whether its development, present functioning, effects, and the contradictions to which it is subjected can be understood outside of this context.

On this basis I therefore conclude these comments by emphasizing that a recognition of accounting as being such a multifaceted practice is important for understanding many of the problems with today's practices. Residing in the realms of both the organizational and the social, they are subjected to both the demands of control and decision making. While undoubtedly influenced by the dictates of traditionalism, accounting also has been shaped by occupational competition, very diverse organizational demands, and even conflicting contemporary pressures. So although often treated as an isolated and purely technical organizational phenomenon, the history of the emergence of accounting as we now know it, its present organizational functioning, and its specific consequences and effects, cannot be understood in such isolated terms. Any accounting of accounting, be it to use the accounting language, historical or current, must be based on a wider appreciation of the contexts in which it emerged and the very diverse expectations that are held of it.

Such a perspective is helpful for understanding the dilemmas, undesirable effects, and even lags identified by Kaplan. It can provide a way of understanding the contradictions currently faced by accounting practice. It can illuminate the factors that both mobilize and constrain accounting developments. And it can provide a basis for appreciating the changing pressures that are impinging on accounting as we know it. For the corporate arena is not a stable one. The salience of past 187
needs can change. The expectations that are held of particular management practices can be volatile, and different occupational groups can seek to renegotiate the interests and influence they have in corporate control.

When seen in such terms, Kaplan has provided us with some significant insights. His chapter provides us with a rich, provocative, and illuminating start on a wider exploration of the accounting craft. His contribution has served to problematize the accounting craft. That has not been done so succinctly and pertinently before. Not only has Kaplan usefully questioned the effects that accounting has, but he has also highlighted the very real need for research to confront the specifics of accounting as it is. I share Bob Kaplan's view of a new, more organizationally grounded appreciation of accounting. Equally, however, I share his view of the sheer magnitude of the steps that are needed to create a different accounting future. A considerable organizational and intellectual distance still needs to be traversed.

## References

Armstrong, Peter. "Changing Management Control Strategies: The Role of Competition Between Accountancy and Other Organizational Professions." *Accounting, Organizations and Society*, 1985.

Burchell, Stuart, Colin Clubb, Anthony Hopwood, John Hughes, and Janine Naphapiet. "The Roles of Accounting in Organizations and Society." *Accounting, Organizations and Society*, 1980, 5–27.

Horovitz, Jacques H. *Top Management Control in Europe*. London: Macmillan, 1980.

Olofsson, C., and P. A. Svalander. "The Medical Services Change Over to a Poor Environment." University of Linkoping Working Paper, 1975.

# 1 Management accounting and organizational action: an introduction

Anthony G. Hopwood
*London School of Economics and Political Science*

Now is an opportune time to appraise the state of management accounting research. Some important aspects of the technical practice of the subject are in the process of being re-examined by practitioners and, for somewhat different reasons, research perspectives are also starting to be questioned and slowly changed. A body of knowledge that until recently seemed adequate is now 189
entering into a period of flux. The taken-for-granted is starting to be seen as more problematic; organizational assumptions, linkages and consequences that for long have remained implicit in the design and functioning of management accounting systems are now being made explicit; and, as a result, a very different array of questions are being asked of both management accounting concepts and practice.

Such a re-examination partly reflects the fact that accounting practices designed to serve the organizations of the past are now in the process of confronting the different contingencies of the present. Different approaches to organizational structuring are creating different information needs for decision-making and control. Greater emphasis is being placed on the need to service both local and central management needs for information (Hopwood, 1982); the roles which accounting information can play in facilitating co-ordination in integrated organizations are becoming more important (Galbraith, 1973; Hopwood, 1977); and the more diverse information needs of semi-autonomous business units being created within the framework of larger organizations are now recognized. The language of strategy has entered into the managerial vocabulary, providing, in the process, a different basis on which to appraise the adequacy of present information flows and a different perspective for shaping the accounting practices of the future (Goold, 1986; Simmonds, 1983). Accounting is also being called upon to play a quite explicit role in the mobilization of organizational change. No longer seen as a mere passive reckoning of the economics of the past, accounting systems are now being implicated in the design of different approaches to the management of organizational visibility and different incentives for organizational action. And although there are those who wish for still further change, accounting is already starting to become much more involved with the articulation of more economic-orientated vocabularies of managerial concerns. Related to the latter, the advance of an economic rationale for action into different sectors of society than those traditionally subject to a regime of economic calculation is also creating new pressures for the elaboration and reform of accounting practice. Most obviously, accounting is being used as one means to infuse the public sector with the language, organizational practices and managerial concerns of the private (Hopwood, 1984a; Plowden, 1986). At the same time, changing task technologies in organizations are starting to create different economic structures for which to account (Kaplan, 1983, 1986) and developments in information-processing technology are creating a seemingly ever expanding array of new possibilities for designing, structuring and managing the information flows of the present and the future (Kaplan, 1986; McCosh, 1986).

All of these changes are now in the process of adding to the body of management accounting practice and knowledge. However, current developments are also more directly undermining the adequacy of the management accounting practices of the past. Although many traditional concerns with the economic control of the organization continue, a more turbulent, competitive
190 and changing environment has placed an ever greater premium on the need for relevant information, rapidly available and expressed in terms which are compatible with increasingly strategic conceptions of management. As a result, past emphases on the provision of routine, short-term information are starting to be appraised in different terms. The demand for *ad hoc* decision-specific information is growing (Earl and Hopwood, 1980). The wider organizational implications of rigid information structures are being recognized and a flexibility of information response is now at a premium. More active consideration is being given to the incorporation into accounting practice of models which can provide a more sympathetic and useful mapping of the contingencies and uncertainties of the present business world. And, for very similar reasons, attention is also being given to the ways in which accounting can constrain management perceptions of time. The debilitating effects of a continual emphasis on the short term are now seen to be problematic.

Although often having only an ambiguous relationship to the practice of the management accounting craft (Hopwood, 1984b), research in the area is also starting to go through a process of re-examination. Not only is it slowly starting to be influenced by the changing agenda of practice (Kaplan, 1983) but it is also independently adopting different perspectives from which to investigate the management accounting domain (Scapens and Arnold, 1986; Dent, 1986). Rather than being content merely to further the technical rationality of the craft, rather belatedly the research community is in the process of adopting a more appreciative stance. A diverse set of questions are now being asked of the organizational rationales for economic information flows (Aiken and Covaleski, 1986; Baiman, 1982; Burchell *et al.*, 1980; Cooper, 1981; Meyer, 1986), the ways in which management accounts permeate and modify organizational processes for decision-making and control (Dent, 1986; Hopwood, 1986), and, once again, the precise organizational consequences which stem from the use of the craft. No longer taking for granted either management accounting as it is or the roles which traditionally have been attributed to it, consideration is being given to the organizational origins of accounting as we now know it (Johnson, 1986), to the ways in which its emergence has been enmeshed with the design and development of other approaches to the governance of the enterprise and to how such other strategies for organizational regulation and control have both impacted upon and, in turn, been themselves enabled by the developments in the regime of internal economic visibility that has been created by management accounting systems. Although such approaches remain preliminary and diverse (contrast, for example, Scapens and Arnold (1986), and Birnberg and Sadhu (1986), Dent (1986) and Johnson (1986)), much more attention nevertheless is being given to management accounting as it is and designs for its reform are starting to be moderated by an awareness of the practicalities of accounting in action. Management accounting is now starting to be questioned, examined and interrogated in the name of its organizational functioning. Members of the research community are becoming more interested in what organizations are doing and the rationales that might be implicit in this. An account of accounting is beginning to be compiled. In the USA, the UK and continental Europe the specificities, complexities and actual rather than envisaged consequences of the craft are now in the process of becoming the foci of research.[1]

It is these processes of both conceptual and practical re-examination which provide the context for the present book. The subsequent chapters focus on some of the changes occurring in the sphere of management accounting practice, the changing nature of research in the area and a number of significant current pressures for continued change.

After Horngren's introductory review of the changes that have occurred, and are still occurring, in management accounting research, Allen and Kirwan provide two views of the area from the perspective of practice, one from the viewpoint of a senior corporate financial executive and the other drawing on the experiences of a leading management consultant in the area. Thereafter, the detailed research reviews are organized around the contributions made by different disciplinary perspectives.

Johnson focuses on the changing nature of historical inquiries in the area, emphasizing how they are starting to throw more light on the emerging organizational roles played by cost and management accounting systems rather than merely document a story of isolated technical elaboration and advancement. The organizational embeddedness of accounting is also emphasized in Scapens and Arnold's discussion of the developments taking place in economic

1 Although there are examples of prior investigations into the organizational functioning of accounting by other social scientists (e.g. Argyris, 1952; Simon *et al.*, 1954; Whyte, 1955; Wildavsky, 1964), the concern of US accounting researchers with organizationally grounded inquiry is relatively recent (see Kaplan, 1983, 1986; Merchant and Simons, 1985). Interest in the UK and northern Europe emerged somewhat earlier (for the UK see the reviews of Colville (1981), Cooper (1977, 1981), Hopwood (1978), Hopwood and Bromwich (1984) and Otley (1984); discussions of the relevant Scandinavian literature appear in Lukka *et al.* (1984), Madsen and Polesie (1984), Ostman (1984), Samuelson (1986) and Hagg *et al.*, (1983)). For a more general discussion of differences in North American and European research in a closely allied discipline see Hofstede and Kassem (1976).

research. Contrasting an earlier emphasis on exploring and improving the economic rationality of technical accounting practices with more recent research on the economic roles served by management accounting systems in organizational monitoring and control, they show how such research is starting to provide a more adequate appreciation of the current state of practice and some of the factors that can induce it to change. Kaplan's review of the quantitative tradition of research also documents a process of re-examination and change. Aware of the rather equivocal relationship between practice and the technical sophistication of past quantitative research, he discusses some of the practical pressures which are questioning existing research emphases and creating new agendas for investigation.

Research into the organizational practice of the management accounting craft is explicitly discussed by Birnberg and Sadhu, and Dent. Concentrating on the growing body of research on the psychological and social-psychological aspects of the functioning of management accounting in action, Birnberg and Sadhu demonstrate how it is increasingly relating to issues of some significance for both understanding and improving the practical effectiveness of the craft. Dent thereafter reviews more recent research conducted into the organizational nature and functioning of accounting. He shows how a research perspective is emerging that is striving to relate management accounting systems to their wider organizational context. The relationships which they have to important aspects of organizational structure, strategy and process are reviewed from the perspective of current research and particular emphasis is given to the nature of the new research agenda that is starting to be created in this area.

In the final group of chapters consideration is given to some of the continuing pressures for management accounting change. Goold discusses the different needs for information which arise from a more strategic conception of management decision-making. The consequences of changes in information technology are discussed by McCosh and a British perspective on the developing interest in accounting for the public sector, a phenomenon evident in many countries at the present time, is provided by Plowden.

As Bromwich makes clear in his final review, together the contributions provide a view of an area in motion with the realms of both the practical and the scholarly being in the process of re-examining what hitherto has been taken for granted. By way of a preface to these contributions, the subsequent discussion aims to identify a number of issues which are relevant for an appreciation of the present context of management accounting. Consideration is given to some of the factors implicated in the development and current functioning of the craft, those of their consequences which have provided the basis for the current questioning of practice, and the implications which changing conceptions of management accounting might have for the conduct of research in the area.

## The creation of management accounting as it is

Management accounting has not had a regular path of development. Born amidst the organizing upheavals which accompanied the emergence of the industrial system, from what we can gather, in the early days accounting within the enterprise was unevenly practised (Pollard, 1965). Identifying a strategic need for information, some entrepreneurs developed the rudiments of systems for costing and internal control (see Johnson, 1984, 1986, for a review). In such contexts a basis was started to be created for internal accountings to be related to the control and restructuring of the manufacturing process, the provision of economic incentives for action, and pricing and output decisions (Hopwood, 1987). Elsewhere, however, other firms relied on a market calculus and perceived no reason to devise elaborate accounting procedures.

The subsequent development of internal accountings demonstrated the importance of the mutual relationship between accounting and modes of 193
organizing – a factor also of some significance when trying to appreciate the different patterns of development in the USA and the UK. In the USA the advance of management accounting seems to have been influenced by the rise of large vertically integrated and geographically dispersed enterprises which could no longer rely on market prices or external rules to guide economic action (Chandler, 1962, 1977; Chandler and Daems, 1979; Johnson, 1983). Accounting systems were devised and elaborated in order to provide a basis for internal processes of control and decision-making. Alongside the rise of a specialized managerial cadre, accounting appears to have created one of the important prerequisites for a managed internal economy within the enterprise. Even more extensive developments accompanied the rise of an interest in organizational efficiency and the role which what were seen as more scientific forms of management could play in this (Epstein, 1978; Wells, 1978). In the UK, in contrast, manufacturing enterprises were smaller, there were many fewer examples of mass production, and the process of rationalizing production was much slower (Hannah, 1976). The British class structure was not so conducive to the emergence of a new middle class of management professionals who would encourage such developments (Merkle, 1980), and industrial partnerships and family-owned firms remained the typical bases of organization and ownership in most types of manufacturing (Hannah, 1976). As a consequence, conditions in the UK were much less favourable to the widespread development of elaborated systems of cost accounting and internal financial control. Even so, some developments did occur. With growing international competition, a prolonged period of recession and increasing industrial concentration, a basis was provided for asking more precise questions of the economic functioning of the enterprise. An increasingly turbulent work force also enhanced the significance of obtaining economic control of the labour process (Littler, 1982) and articulating a more explicit economic rationale for action that could permeate into the inner workings of the enterprise (Batstone, 1979). Albeit slowly, the language and practices of costs and costliness did start to gain a greater managerial

significance. However, it was the interventionist activities of a wartime government concerned with economic regulation and the control of prices and profits that provided a much more explicit incentive for the advancement of a more comprehensive regime of internal economic calculation in the UK (Loft, 1986). In the context of the First World War not only was a relevance created for advances in cost accounting but also the practice of the craft was endowed with a wider legitimacy. That and continued economic restraint appears to have provided an influential basis for the subsequent expansion of the craft in the UK (Armstrong, 1985, forthcoming).

Albeit in a number of different ways, a mutual relationship between internal accounting and modern modes of organizing, and social, as well as economic, management, nevertheless was born. In part, at least, the business enterprise started to be managed and controlled on the basis of the accounts of it. A particular regime of internal visibility started to become influential. Accounting developments, in turn, not only reflected the continuing paths of organizing

developments but also started to play a much more active role in facilitating and enabling these to take place. The modern interrelationship of accounting and the management of the enterprise was in the process of being forged.

Although there are enormous dangers in abstracting from the specific contexts of management accounting's emergence, it nevertheless is useful to consider some of the more general processes implicated in the rise of management accounting systems as we now know them. Recognizing that these always functioned in the diverse contexts of particular organizations and were always influenced by their specific contingencies and trajectories of development, there are still advantages to be gained from more critically examining some of the organizational tendencies underlying the advance of the craft and the ways in which it has come to function within organizations.

**The penetrating accounting eye**

Accounting provides a way of making visible the internal functioning of an organizational economy. It enables management to probe into the inner workings of the organization, to observe the processes of work, to assign to the physical nature of the organization an economic significance, and to both aggregate and, thereafter, again disaggregate in economic terms the mass of separate events which constitute organizational life. Where physical distance or architectural forms constrain managerial observation, an accounting system can provide a silent means of seeing. The otherwise unknown can be translated into an organizational record. The specific and the diverse can be generalized into economic terms. The accounting eye, although often itself unseen, can nevertheless render the organizational terrain not only visible but also, because of that, manageable and potentially controllable.

The visibility so created by accounting is not, however, a mere recording of what is otherwise there. The facts which enter into the organizational accounting are not merely collected but more actively created by the accounting craft

(Crawford, 1984). The categories of cost, profit, efficiency and capital are imposed onto the physical flows which constitute the organization. The activities of the human being are transformed into the language of the human resource. Organizational diversity is reduced and rendered meaningful in economic terms by its assimilation into accounting's categories. Rather than being merely revealed, a coherent organizational economy is a creation of the accounting craft. Not obviously flowing from the specifics of the organization as it is, the more standardized facts of organizational life are forged by the accounting of it.

The facts so created provide only a partial portrayal of organizational functioning, however. Their significance stems not only from what they emphasize and endow with a significance and an impression of reality but also from what they thereby exclude from the organizational record (Foucault, 1971). For in understanding the management accounting craft, it is as important to seek to appreciate where the accounting eye does not penetrate as it is to understand where it does. What organizational processes remain in the dark? What consequences of organized endeavour never enter into the organizational  records? And with what effects? What concerns can be furthered by their incorporation into the archive? Equally, what is not transposed into the domain of the economic? What concerns must remain implicit, unknown and perhaps even illicit, remaining, as they do, unrecognized in the world of organizational facts?

So wrenching a partial domain of the observable from the complexities of organizational life, accounting provides an influential means for the governance and control of the enterprise. Rules, regulations and incentives can be mobilized around the domain of the purported factual. The detail of organizational action can be rendered meaningful in terms of overall organizational objectives and goals. The specific can thereby start to be more precisely reformed in the name of the general. The organization can become not only a less opaque concern but also one that can be more actively regulated, planned and controlled.

The will to know (Sheridan, 1980) in accounting terms has had numerous origins. Faced with the contingencies of an uncertain environment, management has striven to influence the inner workings of the enterprise (Hopwood, 1987). As questions have been asked of both the organizational actual and possible, investments have been made in rendering visible a particular and legitimate organizational terrain. Equally, the desire to regulate and control the internal labour process of the organization has also provided an influential incentive to penetrate into the organization, making visible the detailed workings of its technical core (Clawson, 1980). Human performance thereby has been brought into the domain of facts, enabling economics to become intertwined with the personal. And, finally, as is discussed below, agents external to the organization have also had an influential role to play in the expansion of the accounting eye. Whether they be agents of the state or the capital markets, their regulatory intentions and requests for information have served to expand significantly the activities which are enshrined within the organizational record.

By whatever means they arise, the facts of organizational life quickly become abstracted from the detailed functioning of the organization. The organizational record is physically, linguistically and managerially detached from the context from which it emerged and, as a result, the organization can come to be seen, known and managed in the name of the facts so established. They develop a significance and autonomy of their own. Rather than being seen as having a complex and often ambiguous relationship to the processes which they seek to represent, organizational accounts and records start to constitute a new truth, in the name of which the organization can itself be changed and reformed. The accounting eye can thereby start to be seen as the organization itself, providing a new reality on which to base organizational management and control.

### Management accounting and the celebration of the present

The facts created by management accounting enable the organizational past to be continually brought into the organizational present (Crawford, 1984). Often
196 divorced from the contingencies and uncertainties which were implicated in the circumstances from which they arose, a specific and a precise past can always be rendered into the here and now. With accounting, an organizational record is available for accessing. A more orderly past can thus be interrogated, analysed and compared. The immediate can be contrasted with the distant. A whole new reality of averages, ranks and relationships can be created. So detached from the specifics which gave it an original meaning, the stark factual past can more readily be endowed with a contemporary significance.

The techniques of accounting enable an active intervention in the processes of time. Indeed, their application can create a temporal fluidity as the practices of accounting for the past are also applied to bring forward the future into the present. So abstracted from its own temporal domain, the future can be examined as if it were a greater certainty in the present. By way of budgets and plans, what-might-be is given a current significance, being examined, analysed and decided upon as if it is. The future, thereby, like the past, can be made to be always with us.

Not only can managerial perceptions of uncertainty thereby be radically transformed but also the clinical act of assessing the future as if it were the present frequently ignores the power of human agency which is required to forge and create that future. As is now starting to be realized in a practical context, by focusing exclusively on its contemporary analysis, such a technology for managing the future does little to create the organizational conditions and processes out of which that future can be realized.

Nowhere is this more readily observable than in the area of investment analysis. The accounting telescope not only gazes into the future but also, by using the technology of discounting, wrenches it into the present for analysis and decision. Being so largely detached from the contingencies which will inevitably accompany it, the future-in-the-present can be subjected to detailed and detached analysis and evaluation. Desirable as this at times may be, it nevertheless ignores the role which such an orchestrated process of organizational detachment might play in constraining the mobilization of the very commitments and enthusiasms out of which a future can be made.

Accounting's celebration of the present is still a far too little appreciated but immensely important aspect of its functioning. Deriving, as it does, from its ability to create a domain of the factual which is divorced from the contexts out of which it either arises or will arise, it is one which can play a very significant role in organizational management, enabling the control of not only the immediate but also of both conceptions of the past and intentions for the future.

**A normative intent**

Management accounting is not only implicated in creating observations. Its practices also enable a more pro-active management of the organizational world. Arising initially out of the power of accounting to provide a basis for comparing and analysing across both time and space, the selective facts of organizational life instilled a concern with differences and with strategies for normalization 197
(Foucault, 1977). The unproductive could be identified by its comparison with the productive, the inefficient with the efficient, the costly with the less costly, and the profitable with the loss-making. A whole new domain of organizational reality thereby emerged and one which stimulated an active search for strategies to eliminate the inferior and to enhance the superior. Not only could lessons be learnt from favourable circumstances but the requirements of the latter could start to be imposed upon the organization as a whole. Organizational life could not only be observed but accounting could also be implicated in strategies for its improvement. The organization could start to be mobilized in a much more detailed way. Standards, budgets and plans could be established in ways which could penetrate the specifics of the organization. The world of what is could thereby be constantly compared with what could and should be (Miller and O'Leary, 1987).

Such strategies of normalization are now a prevalent feature of organizations. Management accounting has become a dual activity. Bringing the facts of the past into the present to be compared with the norms which had been set in the past for the future which is today, it provides a powerful basis for the mobilization of the specifics of the organization in the name of the general. At one and the same time accounting can impose a normalizing intention upon the organization while bringing to attention the individual differences which are identified by that (Foucault, 1977).

**Management accounting and the creation of an organizational order**

Accounting is involved with the creation of a more orderly and manageable organization in a number of very different ways.

Organizational hierarchies are endowed with a greater significance and force by the delineation of responsibilities which accompany the use of the accounting craft and the subsequent processes of monitoring and performance review. The exercising of management authority thereafter can be more constrained, more legitimate and more effective. Formal managerial expectations can be more readily diffused through the organizational hierarchy. Performance can be subjected to a more meticulous review. Questioning can be related to prior plans. The use of power need no longer be general and diffuse as it focuses on the detailed representation of organizational activities which is cast in the accounts. A new enabling force can be given to the vertical mobilization of the organization.

Accounting is no less significant for facilitating the ordering and control of the spatial dimensions of organizational life. Implicated in the mapping of the organization into a more managerial space, it helps to give a very particular meaning to the patterns of segmentation which are imposed on the organizational terrain. Cost centres, profit centres, investment centres, strategic business units and subsidiaries all receive much of their significance from the accounting representation of them. Organizational events are thereby more easily attributed to particular managerial responsibilities. Recognized sequences of consequences are more readily confined within the intra-organizational boundaries. Accounting helps to isolate a realm of manageable organizational spaces.



Moreover, management accounting is also involved with the integration of the lateral and vertical orderings of the organization. Through budgets, plans and the subsequent processes of monitoring and review, one can be related to the other. A powerful basis for task co-ordination is created. Of equal significance, the local can be mobilized in the name of the whole. By the transformation of the diverse details of organizational activities by aggregated and subsequently disaggregated information, a powerful ability in itself, the specific can be related to overall objectives and plans. The language, categories and concerns of a financial motive can thereby infuse and change the detailed operational and technical functioning of the organization. A basis for a new economic order can be created.

The ordering potential of accounting also impacts upon the temporal dimension of organizational life. Time is not only made into a more fluid and seemingly more manageable factor in organizational functioning, as has already been discussed, but it itself is also ordered into distinct periods. Although stemming from wider social forces and involving other technologies (Landes, 1983), accounting nevertheless powerfully reinforces the salience of the year, the month and the day. Through accounting, moreover, time can be re-ordered as the temporality of financial transactions is related to different schemes of organizational events. And rather than facing an open-ended future, by plans, budgets and performance reports the organization can be made to focus on specific periods of time. Opportunities can be created for management to come to the end of one period of time before considering the activities associated with another.

## The external origins of internal accounts

Management accounting has arisen to satisfy more than the internal task needs of management. The activities of external agencies and wider social movements have also left a significant impact on the flow of economic information which now pervades organizational life.

The regulatory activities of the state have been particularly influential in this respect. The emergence of corporate taxation served to increase both the regime of economic calculation within the enterprise and the cadre of organizational specialists associated with it. Wartime control of prices and profits has been equally influential, not only implanting in organizations more detailed systems of costing but also endowing these and the specialists associated with them with a greater social legitimacy and acceptability (Crawford, 1984; Loft, 1986). In more recent times, national strategies for macro-economic management have left important residues in the management accounting systems of organizations (Hopwood *et al.*, 1980). Policies for price control have reinforced the salience of cost information. Attempts to regulate profits have even resulted in a recognition of the revenue-enhancing potential of legitimate financial information. Wage-control policies have served to extend further the sphere of detailed economic 199
calculation around the human resource (Burchell *et al.*, 1985). More generally, the state has frequently been a more direct catalyst for management accounting change, particularly in the UK (Armstrong, forthcoming). Associating the presence and use of accounting systems and procedures for the economic evaluation of investment opportunities with a competitive and profitable organizational stance, the furtherance of such systems has often been explicitly incorporated into national economic policies.

Managerial accounting also has been implicated in the control of wider social forces passing through the organization. Attempts to discipline and regulate a newly industrialized work force resulted in the development of management regulatory practices, including those of accounting. The growth of an organized labour movement provided an important incentive for a managerial interest in making visible the detailed work process of the organization, standardizing patterns of work behaviour, and using information systems to try to instil an economic incentive for action. Even more recently, changes in the relative power of the labour movement at times have resulted in an expansion of the domain of economic calculation in the enterprise. Accounting information has been more widely diffused to employees and their trade union representatives. More directly related to conventional views of management accounting, attempts have been made to relate internal modes of financial reporting to more detailed representation of the economic functioning of the production process through the use of categories such as value added (Burchell *et al.*, 1985). On occasions, experiments have also been made to provide a more comprehensive account of the employment relationship (Flamholtz, 1974; European Foundation for the Improvement of Living and Working Conditions, 1982; Hopwood, 1979a).

Management accounting has also been involved with the creation of a wider external legitimacy for the enterprise. As systems of budgeting, planning and financial performances assessment have become associated with organizational efficiency and effectiveness, at times they have been implemented because of the greater organizational legitimacy which such functional claims might be able to create.[2] Rather than being directly advanced in the name of internal management processes, management accounting has come to be seen as a cultural rather than a purely technical symbol of modernity and rational organizational functioning (Meyer and Rowan, 1977; Meyer, 1983; DiMaggio and Powell, 1983). Although management accountings having such origins can still become internally significant, not least because of the new interior visibility and management linkages which they create, the relationship which they have to the functioning of the organization is a question for empirical assessment rather than automatic presumption.

So, although invariably justified in terms of their internal management roles, management accounting systems can also reflect the wider social and environmental contexts in which they operate. While technically functioning within the organization, both their orientation and consequences can be external as well as internal.



### Accounting and the practitioners of the accounting craft

One final tendency is worth explicit consideration. Along with the development and expansion of the management accounting domain a cadre of practitioners of the craft has arisen. Indeed, sometimes the activity has resulted in a distinct occupation (Loft, 1986), a factor which itself can introduce a new dynamic into the patterns of management accounting changes.

International comparisons suggest that such developments should not be endowed with any presumption of necessity, however. Different occupational claims to the area and different patterns of occupational specialization have emerged in different countries. When seen in such terms, it needs to be recognized that organizational control is itself a sphere for occupational competition (Armstrong, 1985), with accountants only sometimes becoming more influential than other control practitioners. The procedures of the management accounting craft can be and are designed, implemented and operated by business economists and analysts, industrial engineers and information system technologists, as well as by accountants *per se*. Indeed, this is an area where change is currently taking place as new bodies of management knowledge emerge, new management occupational groups arise and new demands are made for different organizational linkages between economic information systems and other aspects of organizational functioning.

2 Management accounting systems can also be involved with the direct management of external interests. Such uses might not be unusual in nationalized enterprises in the UK where, until recently, at least, planning and financial reporting procedures may have been orientated as much toward sponsoring civil service departments and political constituencies as to internal management operations. See Berry *et al.* (1985).

## The organizational practice of management accounting

The path of management accounting's development has been neither a simple nor a linear one. A diverse array of factors have impinged on the domain of organizational economic calculation. Moreover, by playing a positive role in actively shaping the organizational forms we now know, management accounting has also provided some of the preconditions for its own subsequent development, often in ways that were not anticipated in the original formulation of any particular system. Indeed, the rise and growing recognition of such unanticipated consequences is one of the main elements in the contemporary development of 'worrying about management accounting' (Hopwood, 1985). We now turn to a consideration of some of these important implications of the underlying organizational tendencies associated with management accounting.



### A diverse craft

The varied circumstances which have impinged on management accounting's development have resulted in a very diverse set of practices in the area. Not only are there significant national differences (Horovitz, 1980) but, within any single country, management accounting practices also vary from company to company, even within the same industrial or commercial sector (Dent, 1986). Seemingly, the state of practice reflects not only environmental, market and technological factors, which one might expect to result in some uniformity within a sector, but also the vagaries of particular organizational cultures, patterns of power and influence, and the specifics of the company history. Furthermore, within a single enterprise, the so-called management accounting system usually consists of only a partially integrated set of practices and procedures, many of which, to the rational observer, might appear to be in conflict with one another. Often reflecting the different historical junctures at which they were implemented, the different managerial and other interests prevailing upon them, and the changing fashions of the managerial world, as well as a poorly articulated body of accounting knowledge, the world of management accounting in practice often appears to be at odds with the myth of a more coherent and integrated phenomenon that permeates accounting texts and those manuals that seek to guide accounting change and reform.

Diversity also pervades the organizational linkages which ground accounting and other information and control systems into the processes of organizational life. Accounting and control departments are variously organized. Planning, budgeting and performance monitoring procedures operate at different organizational levels, are subject to different degrees of participation, have different expectations associated with them and different practices for their revision, and can even consider very different time periods. Accounting systems also serve to establish very different patterns of organizational segmentation and relate to the practices for the management of organizational interdependence in a variety of ways.

All told, the management accounting area is diverse, complex and even messy. At the very least, the state of practice bears only a loose relationship to the more generalized body of knowledge that seeks to embrace it. Although that might be an understandable implication of the varied factors that have impinged on the development of practices in the area, it nevertheless represents a significant problem for both practitioners and scholars who aim to have some more adequate appreciation of management accounting as it is.

**A constitutive accounting**

Although management accounting plays a significant role in mapping salient aspects of both the managerial task and the external environment into the organization, it also has the power to shape and influence organizational life on its own.

The environments that are mapped into the organization can become defined
202 in accounting terms. From a positive point of view they can become 'profitable' or 'costly', 'cash cows' or 'rising stars'. More negatively perceived, the accounting mappings are only partial ones, with the accounting representations being as significant for what they exclude as for what they include for managerial attention.

Similarly, the organization structures which impinge on accounting practice do not have a manifestation that is independent of their accounting representation. Modes of organizational decentralization are defined in terms of cost, profit and investment centres; organizational units have accounting as well as management boundaries; and accounting mechanisms for the monitoring of subunit performance help to make real the powerful potential that is implicit within the organization chart. Equally, as we have discussed, accounting plays a significant role not only in shaping the visible map of what is known of organizational functioning but also in expressing and thereby influencing the objectives that are stated for organized action. An operational definition of profit has been a particularly powerful notion and consideration must also be given to the mobilizing potential of concepts such as cash, working capital, assets and, not least, cost. All provide illustrations of where accounting has made operational and therefore powerful within the organization more abstract notions of economic discourse. Finally, as we have seen, salient notions of time in organizations are invariably influenced by the accounting of them (Cooley, 1985).

In ways such as these accounting has come to play a positive role in creating our present conceptions of organized endeavour. While in part reflecting many other parameters of organizational life, accounting has also played a more active role in constructing the organizational world in which it is now embedded, shaping views of the constraints on organized action, the ends which it seeks to serve and the pragmatic means through which these can be achieved. There is, in other words, a complex interplay between the reflective and constitutive roles of accounting (Burchell *et al.*, 1985; Hopwood, 1985), the former serving to create accounting's dependency on the organizations in which it is embedded and the latter often constraining organizations in the name of the possibilities and potentialities of the accounting craft.

Such an interplay presents dilemmas to both the practitioner and the scholar. For the latter, the process of understanding the pattern of management accounting's development and its current functioning within the organization becomes a much more complex one, requiring more subtle frameworks for appreciating the practice of the craft. For the practitioner, the interplay can constrain the process of management accounting development. As accounting can both reflect and create the contexts in which it operates, it not only plays some role in shaping the preconditions for its own developments but also results in organizations which are not independent of, and therefore dependent upon, the accounting of the organizational past (Hopwood, 1987). In such circumstances management accounting change becomes a much more complex art – a factor that is now recognized by those worried about the adequacy of their present accountings. 203

**Management accounting and that which happens in its name**[3]

Conventional discussions of management accounting invariably presume that the craft is capable of achieving the claims that are made on its behalf. Management accounting, so we are told, is capable of enhancing organizational efficiency and performance. It can play a positive role in increasing managerial and employee motivations to perform. And management accounting can provide the type of information that can facilitate managerial decision-making, not least in environments characterized by uncertainty and doubt.

Increasingly, however, some, at least, of such highly generalized claims are being compared with the more equivocal impressions emerging from both research and practice.

A long tradition of scholarly inquiry has sought to illustrate the dysfunctional as well as functional consequences, both latent and manifest, of the management accounting craft (Argyris, 1952; Hayes and Abernathy, 1980; Hopwood, 1973, 1979b; Jasinski, 1956; Merchant, 1985; Ridgway, 1956). There have also been studies which have pointed to the ways in which accountings appear to proliferate amidst concerns with organizational crisis and decline rather than in the less problematic days of growth and success (Khandwalla, 1978; Olofsson and Svalander, 1975). Sometimes such research has even suggested ways in which the consequent desire for greater control can result in organizational practices which detract from rather than enhance the flexibility of managerial responses in such conditions (Starbuck *et al.*, 1978).

As we have already discussed, not unrelated concerns with the actual rather than the claimed achievements of accounting have now started to be articulated by some practitioners. Faced with economic restraint and often with increased competitive pressures, such practitioners have started to become concerned about the limitations of the routinized flows of information which accounting so often provides. Although rarely, if ever, expressed in ways other than the immediate set of implications for their own organizations, such questionings have resulted in a new awareness of the interdependency between management accounting and the human and social processes through which the objectives which are set for it are achieved.

Some of the factors implicated in such questioning can be appreciated in terms of the tendencies underlying the development of the craft that have been outlined above. The creation of a partial visibility can be seen to be problematic when organizational circumstances change. Management accounting's celebration of the present at times can be seen to constrain the development of a more future responsive stance. The diverse organizational and social roles served by the craft can be seen as being capable of resulting in organizational disorder rather than order as they become intertwined with the exercising of power and influence. The organizational rigidities which can follow from the constitutive roles of
204 management accounting can be better understood. It can be appreciated that the consequences of interventions in the organization in the name of management accounting are dependent on factors other than the intentions and means of organizational action which are specifically mobilized. A recognition can develop that actual outcomes also depend on the practical capacity of management accounting systems to encapsulate, penetrate and then influence the complex fabric of modern organizations, on the ways in which they intersect with both other organizational practices and the wider aims and actions of organizational participants, and, in the latter respect, on the resistances which specific attempts to mobilize one set of organizational practices induce.

When seen in such terms, there is at least the potential for the aims of management accounting to remain partially or even totally unfilled. Indeed, they can even result in consequences which were wholly unanticipated, since eventual outcomes are influenced by phenomena which did not enter into the original system specification or justification.

It is not surprising therefore that more research consideration is now starting to be given to the actual practice of management accounting. Questions are being asked of the circumstances under which it does or does not realize the aims that are articulated on behalf of it. In such ways the organizationally detached discourses that permeate accounting texts and manuals are slowly being compared with the ways in which management accounting relates to the functioning of actual organizations and the practices and underlying bodies of knowledge of other approaches to organizational control.

## The agenda for research

Such emergent concerns are evident in all of the contributions to this book, be they by academics or practitioners. From the latter perspective, both Allen and Kirwan portray a body of practical knowledge that is currently in motion, trying to adapt to the pressures of new demands that are being made on it. The research surveys are possibly even more suggestive of the changes underway, however. All of them illustrate in their own very different ways the changing foci of management accounting research discussed by Horngren. As Johnson makes clear, historical inquiry is becoming much more concerned with understanding the interdependency between management accounting and other organizational practices, and the factors which induce accounting systems to change. According to Scapens and Arnold, and Kaplan, both economic and quantitative traditions of research in the area are now becoming increasingly concerned with explicitly addressing questions of organizational complexity, with understanding the organizational functions and implications of practice, with adopting a richer view of economic and technical rationality, and with adopting a more cautious and organizationally grounded approach to technical change. The rise of a behavioural and organizational research interest in management accounting was itself an early reflection of the changing perspectives on the craft. Although progress to date has been slow, both Birnberg and Sadhu, and Dent illustrate how the research agendas in the behavioural and organizational areas have changed so as to illuminate the actual functioning of management accounting systems. Not surprisingly, given their remit to focus on some important current pressures for change, the final three chapters by Goold, McCosh and Plowden further reinforce the salience of the new practical and research agendas.

Such emergent concerns are encouraging. For, at present, relatively little is systematically known of the practice of management accounting. Its contours and parameters have not been documented. The pressures for it to change are not well understood. Albeit that present research is being conducted from a variety of different and, indeed, conflicting perspectives, at the very least it can help to illustrate technical diversity, highlight the particular and varying features of specific kinds of management accounting systems and their patterns of change, and thereby hopefully enrich our appreciation of management accounting as an organizational and social practice. If nothing else, research of this type can play an important role in stimulating the asking of new questions and the search for alternative ways of conceiving the management accounting craft. What is more, such research, if well conducted, can at least start to provide a view of the management accounting domain as one that is not subject to a unified *a priori* pattern of rational development or a set of procedures reflecting some abstract essence of the craft. Instead, a better understanding might be gained of how organizations have chosen, or even stumbled into, varying patterns of accounting development in the past and how such earlier choices, in turn, both limit and open up alternative possibilities for further change. Such research at least has the possibility of helping us to make better sense of the unfolding of unintended as well as intended consequences of the management accounting craft.

However, as such an outline should make clear, description *per se* is only a part of the process of gaining more adequate understanding of management accounting in action. Although a positive role can be played by attempts to document management accounting as it is, it must be recognized that all description involves a process of categorization, labelling and analysis. If not done explicitly, the resultant descriptions are almost invariably conducted within the implicit framework of existing notions of management accounting, imposing traditional technical rationalities, functional claims and wider organizational presumptions onto the seemingly purely technical account. These still might provide useful stimuli to other researchers, but in and of themselves they can offer few possibilities for appreciating the contextual and dynamic aspects of management accounting in action that have provided the rationales for the new agenda of both scholarly inquiry and practical action.

When seen in such terms, the challenge for the research community resides in the need to develop new conceptual appreciations of management accounting as it functions. While the technical aspects of the craft must not be ignored, for that is one of the ultimate rationales for accounting research, perspectives are needed which can ground the technical in wider organizational and social processes and patterns of transformation. For only through such conceptual and theoretical developments can sense be made of both the technical and organizational contradictions and paradoxes which are a prevalent and now much more frequently recognized feature of the craft.

Although the contributions to this book suggest that some progress is now starting to be made, they also point to the significance of the research agenda remaining for the future. For not only is further progress needed if sense is to be made of existing understandings of the craft but that progress is also a vital precondition for any attempt to improve, from whatever interest or perspective, the practice of the craft in ways that are sympathetic to the human, organizational and social contexts in which it operates.

## References


Aiken, M. and Covaleski, M., 'Accounting and Theories of Organizations: Some Preliminary Considerations', *Accounting, Organizations and Society* (1986).

Argyris, C., *The Impact of Budgets on People*, The Controllership Foundation (1952).

Armstrong, P., 'Changing Management Control Strategies: The Role of Competition Between Accounting and Other Organizational Professions', *Accounting, Organizations and Society* (1985), pp. 129–148.

Armstrong, P., 'The Rise of Accounting Controls in British Capitalist Enterprises', *Accounting, Organizations and Society* (forthcoming).

Baiman, S., 'Agency Research in Management Accounting: A Survey', *Journal of Accounting Literature* (1982), pp. 154–213.

Batstone, E., 'Systems of Domination, Accommodation, and Industrial Democracy', in T. R. Burns, L. E. Karlsson and V. Rus (eds), *Work and Power: The Liberation of Work and the Control of Political Power*, Sage (1979).

Berry, A. J., Capps, T., Cooper, D., Ferguson, P., Hopper, T. and Lowe, E. A., 'Management Control in an Area of the NCB: Rationales of Accounting Practice in a Public Enterprise', *Accounting, Organizations and Society* (1985), pp. 3–28.

Birnberg, J. G. and Sadhu, K., 'The Contribution of Psychological and Cognitive Research to Managerial Accounting', in M. Bromwich and A. G. Hopwood (eds), *Research and Current Issues in Management Accounting*, Pitman (1986).

Burchell, S., Clubb, C., Hopwood, A., Hughes, J. and Nahapiet, J., 'The Roles of Accounting in Organizations and Society', *Accounting, Organizations and Society* (1980), pp. 5–27.

Burchell, S., Clubb, C. and Hopwood, A. G., 'Accounting in Its Social Context: Towards a History of Value Added in the United Kingdom', *Accounting, Organizations and Society* (1985), pp. 381–413.

Chandler, A., *Strategy and Structure*, MIT Press (1962).

Chandler, A., *The Visible Hand: The Management Revolution in American Business*, Harvard University Press (1977).

Chandler, A. and Daems, H., 'Administrative Co-ordination, Allocation and Monitoring: A Comparative Analysis of the Emergence of Accounting and Organization in the USA and Europe', *Accounting, Organizations and Society* (1979), pp. 3–20.

Clawson, D., *Bureaucracy and the Labour Process*, Monthly Review Press (1980).

Colville, I., 'Reconstructing "Behavioural Accounting"', *Accounting, Organizations and Society* (1981), pp. 119–132. 207

Cooley, M., 'Work and Time', in C. Rawlence (ed.), *About Time*, Jonathan Cape (1985).

Cooper, D., 'Organizational Aspects of Budgetary Control', in J. E. Lewis and G. Dickinson (eds), *Handbook of Financial Management*, Kluwer–Harrap (1977).

Cooper, D., 'A Social and Organizational View of Management Accounting', in M. Bromwich and A. G. Hopwood (eds), *Essays in British Accounting Research*, Pitman (1981).

Crawford, A., 'Cost Accounting, Work Control and the Development of Cost Accounting in Britain 1914–1925', paper presented to the Congress of the European Accounting Association, St Gallen, Switzerland (1984).

Dent, J., 'Organizational Research in Accounting: Perspectives, Issues and a Commentary', in M. Bromwich and A. G. Hopwood (eds), *Research and Current Issues in Management Accounting*, Pitman (1986).

DiMaggio, P. J. and Powell, W. W., 'The Iron Cage Revisited: Institutional Isomorphism and Collective Rationality in Organizational Fields', *American Sociological Review* (1983), pp. 147–160.

Earl, M. J. and Hopwood, A. G., 'From Management Information to Information Management', in H. C. Lucas, E. F. Land, T. J. Lincoln and K. Supper (eds), *The Information Systems Environment*, North-Holland (1980).

Epstein, M. J., *The Effect of Scientific Management on the Development of the Standard Cost System*, Arno Press (1978).

European Foundation for the Improvement of Living and Working Conditions, *Economic and Working Conditions: Methodological Aspects*, EFIL&WC (1982).

Flamholtz, E., *Human Resource Accounting*, Dickenson Publishing (1974).

Foucault, M., 'Orders of Discourse', *Social Science Information* (1971), pp. 7–30.

Foucault, M., *Discipline and Punish: The Birth of the Prison*, Allen Lane (1977).

Galbraith, J., *Designing Complex Organizations*, Addison-Wesley (1973).

Goold, M., 'Accounting and Strategy', in M. Bromwich and A. G. Hopwood (eds), *Research and Current Issues in Management Accounting*, Pitman (1986).

Hagg, I., Magnuson, A. and Samuelson, L. A., 'Research in Budgeting in the Nordic Countries – A Survey', unpublished Working Paper, University of Stockholm (1983).

Hannah, L., *The Rise of the Corporate Economy*, Methuen (1976).

Hayes, R. H. and Abernathy, W. J., 'Managing Our Way Out of Economic Decline', *Harvard Business Review* (1980), pp. 67–77.

Hofstede, G. and Kassem, M. S., (eds), *European Contributions to Organization Theory*, Van Gorcum (1976).

Hopwood, A. G., *An Accounting System and Management Behaviour*, Saxon House (1973).

Hopwood, A. G., 'Information Systems for Matrix Organizations', in K. Knight (ed.), *Matrix Management*, Saxon House (1977).

Hopwood, A. G., 'Towards an Organizational Perspective for the Study of Accounting and Information Systems', *Accounting, Organizations and Society* (1978), pp. 3–14.

Hopwood, A. G., 'Economic Costs and Benefits of New Forms of Work Organization', in *New Forms of Work Organizations*, Vol. 2, International Labour Office (1979a).

Hopwood, A. G., 'Criteria of Corporate Effectiveness', in M. Brodie and R. Bennett (eds), *Perspectives on Management Effectiveness*, Thames Valley Regional Management Centre (1979b).

Hopwood, A. G., 'Some Thoughts on Information and the Structural Organization of
208 Companies', *Proceedings of the 5th Annual Conference of the Association of Information Officers in the Pharmaceutical Industry* (1982).

Hopwood, A. G., 'On Trying to Study Accounting in the Contexts in Which It Operates', *Accounting, Organizations and Society* (1983), pp. 287–305.

Hopwood, A. G., 'Accounting and the Pursuit of Efficiency', in A. G. Hopwood and C. Tomkins (eds), *Issues in Public Sector Accounting*, Philip Allan (1984a).

Hopwood, A. G., 'Accounting Research and Accounting Practice: The Ambiguous Relationship Between the Two', a paper presented at the Conference on New Challenges to Management Research, Leuven (1984b).

Hopwood, A. G., 'The Tale of a Committee that Never Reported: Disagreements on Intertwining Accounting with the Social', *Accounting, Organizations and Society* (1985), pp. 361–377.

Hopwood, A. G., 'The Archaeology of Accounting Systems', *Accounting, Organizations and Society* (1987).

Hopwood, A. G., 'The Development of "Worrying" About Management Accounting', in K. B. Clark, R. H. Hayes and C. Lorenz (eds), *The Uneasy Alliance: Managing the Productivity—Technology Dilemma*, Harvard Business School Press (1985).

Hopwood, A. G. and Bromwich, M., 'Accounting Research in the United Kingdom', in A. G. Hopwood and H. Schreuder (eds), *European Contributions to Accounting Research: The Achievements of the Last Decade*, Free University of Amsterdam Press (1984).

Hopwood, A. G., Burchell, S. and Clubb, C., 'The Development of Accounting in Its International Context: Past Concerns and Emergent Issues', in A. Roberts (ed.), *A Historical and Contemporary Review of the Development of International Accounting*, Georgia State University (1980).

Horovitz, J. H., *Top Management Control in Europe*, Macmillan (1980).

Jasinski, E. J., 'Use and Misuse of Efficiency Controls', *Harvard Business Review* (1956), pp. 105–112.

Johnson, H. T., 'The Search for Gain in Markets and Firms: A Review of the Historical Emergence of Management Accounting', *Accounting, Organizations and Society* (1983), pp. 139–146.

Johnson, H. T., *The Role of Accounting History in the Education of Prospective Accountants*, University of Glasgow (1984).

Johnson, H. T., 'The Organizational Awakening in Management Accounting History', in M. Bromwich and A. G. Hopwood (eds), *Research and Current Issues in Management Accounting*, Pitman (1986).
Kaplan, R. S., 'Measuring Manufacturing Performance: A New Challenge for Managerial Accounting Research', *The Accounting Review* (1983), pp. 686–705.
Kaplan, R. S., 'Quantitative Models for Management Accounting in Today's Production Environment', in M. Bromwich and A. G. Hopwood (eds), *Research and Current Issues in Management Accounting*, Pitman (1986).
Khandwalla, P. N., 'Crisis Responses of Competing Versus Noncompeting Organizations', *Journal of Business Administration* (1978), pp. 151–178.
Landes, D. S., *Revolution in Time: Clocks and the Making of the Modern World*, Harvard University Press (1983).
Littler, C. R., *The Development of the Labour Process in Capitalist Societies*, Heinemann Educational (1982).
Loft, A., 'Towards a Critical Understanding of Accounting: The Case of Cost Accounting in the UK, 1914–1925', *Accounting, Organizations and Society* (1986).
Lukka, K., Majala, R., Paasio, A. and Pihlanto, P., 'Accounting Research in Finland', in A. G. Hopwood and H. Schreuder (eds), *European Contributions to Accounting Research: The Achievements of the Last Decade*, Free University of Amsterdam Press (1984).

McCosh, A. M., 'Management Accounting in the I.T. Age', in M. Bromwich and A. G. Hopwood (eds), *Research and Current Issues in Management Accounting*, Pitman (1986).
Madsen, V. and Polesie, T., *Human Factors in Budgeting: Judgement and Evaluation*, Pitman (1981).
Merchant, K. A., 'On the Incidence and Cause of Dysfunctional Side Effects of Control Systems', unpublished Working Paper, Graduate School of Business Administration, Harvard University (1985).
Merchant, K. A. and Simons, R., 'Research on Control in Complex Organizations: An Overview', unpublished Working Paper, Graduate School of Business Administration, Harvard University (1985).
Merkle, J. A., *Management and Ideology: The Legacy of the International Scientific Management Movement*, University of California Press (1980).
Meyer, J. W., 'On the Celebration of Rationality: Some Comments on Boland and Pondy', *Accounting, Organizations and Society* (1983), pp. 235–240.
Meyer, J. W., 'Social Environments and Organizational Accounting', *Accounting, Organizations and Society* (1986).
Meyer, J. W. and Rowan, B., 'Institutionalized Organizations: Formal Structures as Myth and Ceremony', *American Journal of Sociology* (1977), pp. 340–363.
Miller, P. and O'Leary, T., 'Accounting and the Construction of the Governable Person', *Accounting, Organizations and Society* (1987).
Olofsson, C. and Svalander, P. A., 'The Medical Services Change Over to a Poor Environment – "New Poor" Behaviour', unpublished Working Paper, University of Linkoping (1975).
Ostman, L., 'Some Impressions of Accounting Research in Scandinavia During the 1970s', in A. G. Hopwood and H. Schreuder (eds), *European Contributions to Accounting Research: The Achievements of the Last Decade*, Free University of Amsterdam Press (1984).
Otley, D., 'Management Accounting and Organization Theory: A Review of Their

Interrelationship', in R. Lister, D. Otley and R. W. Scapens (eds), *Management Accounting, Organizational Behaviour and Capital Budgeting*, Macmillan (1984).

Plowden, F., 'Management Accounting: Pressures for Changes in the Public Sector', in M. Bromwich and A. G. Hopwood (eds), *Research and Current Issues in Management Accounting*, Pitman (1986).

Pollard, S., *The Genesis of Modern Management*, Edward Arnold (1965).

Ridgway, V. F., 'Dysfunctional Consequences of Performance Measurements', *Adminis-trative Science Quarterly* (1956), pp. 240–247.

Samuelson, L. A., 'Discrepancies Between the Roles of Budgeting', *Accounting, Organizations and Society* (1986), pp. 35–46.

Scapens, R. W. and Arnold, J. A., 'Economics and Management Accounting Research', in M. Bromwich and A. G. Hopwood (eds), *Research and Current Issues in Management Accounting*, Pitman (1986).

Sheridan, A., *Michel Foucault: The Will to Truth*, Tavistock (1980).

Simmonds, K., 'Strategic Management Accounting', in D. Fanning (ed.), *Handbook of Management Accounting*, Gower Press (1983).

210 Simon, H. A., Kozmetsky, G., Guetzkow, H., and Tyndall, G., *Centralization v. Decentralization in Organizing the Controller's Department*, The Controllership Foundation (1954).

Starbuck, W. H., Greve, A. and Hedberg, B. L. T., 'Responding to Crisis', *Journal of Business Administration* (1978), pp. 111–137.

Wells, M. C., *Accounting for Common Costs*, International Center for Accounting Education and Research, University of Illinois (1978).

Whyte, W. F., *Money and Motivation*, Harper and Row (1955).

Wildvasky, A., *The Politics of the Budgetary Process*, Little, Brown and Company (1964).

# ACCOUNTING AND ORGANISATIONAL ACTION

**Anthony G. Hopwood**

Management accounting is a diverse craft. It seemingly takes different forms in not only different sectors, and even different enterprises within a sector, but also shows a diversity of arrangements and emphases across both time and space. Different historical junctures have had their different accounting priorities. Interestingly, in the context of a consideration of the cultural aspects of accounting, different cultural configurations appear to make different appeals to the accounting art, endowing it with different roles and different significances [Birnberg and Snodgrass, 1986; Horovitz,
212 1980].

However, accounting diversity, and the factors that lie behind it, largely remain hidden from the contemporary view. Educational texts and manuals of consulting practice invest heavily in the articulation of a quite homogeneous technical domain. They attribute homogeneous rationales to the accounting craft. The multitude of ways in which accounting becomes embedded in organisational forms, the diverse ways in which it can become intertwined with organisational action, and even the actual consequences of the technical art are all virtually ignored by contemporary commentaries on the accounting craft. For the rhetoric of accounting has tended to be one of intention. Emphasis has been placed on the accounts that organisations need and the technical accounting configurations that they must have. Pragmatic necessities, normative intentions, and even conceptual imperatives have mobilised the ways in which accounting is conceived and talked of in its organisational context. The actual practice of the craft, the ways in which it does, rather than might, become intertwined with organisational functioning, the actual contexts in which appeals to accounting are made, and the ways in which it becomes related to organisational action, have all tended to be ignored, seemingly confined to the domain of the uninteresting and thereby the unknown. The mission and the potential rather than the actuality of accounting have tended to monopolise attention.

Of course others have been concerned with this state of affairs. Even a few of our intellectual ancestors, like DR Scott (1931), sought to understand the wider societal pressures that put accounting into motion and that shaped not only the technical form that accounting took but also the social and organisational functions which it was called upon to serve. However, Scott's was a lonely voice, then and now, compared with the pronouncements of those who preferred to try to make accounting what it was not.

*Anthony G. Hopwood is Arthur Young Professor of International Accounting and Financial Management, London School of Economics and Political Science.*

*I am grateful for the helpful comments of Jake Birnberg and Tony Tinker.*

Subsequently a whole series of major intellects tried to interrogate the accounting actuality, to delve into its involvement with the organisational condition, and to illuminate, however partially and problematically, the organisational consequences of the imperatives that seemingly drive the application of accounting techniques. Such names as Chris Argyris [1952; 1977], Melville Dalton [1959], William Whyte [1955], and Aaron Wildavsky [1964; 1978] come to mind. Both individually and collectively they provide a rich and provocative account of the accounting condition, an account that many might have thought would have stirred the accounting imagination into investigating and accounting for its own condition. But very little of that occurred. The rhetoric of a dominant accounting mission and potential was seemingly too strong, too focused, and too embedded in the social fabric of both accounting intellectual life and its practice for such pleas and such exemplars to encourage accounting to account for itself.

Perhaps there is a little more reason to be optimistic of some small change of direction at the present time. Kaplan's pleas for us to address the actuality of the accounting condition are not going unnoticed [Kaplan, 1983]. I and others seem not to be talking in a wilderness when we seek to explicate, albeit in different ways, some of the means by which we can advance our capability to interrogate the accounting 213
condition and strive to appreciate its involvement with organisational, economic, and social affairs [Burchell et al., 1980; Burchell et al., 1985; Hopwood, 1983; 1985a]. Moreover, although I will subsequently distance myself from its conventional epistomological stance, the rise of an interest in empiricism, even if not its expression in terms of an umproblematic philosophy of positivism, has already achieved some reformulation of our conceptions of the accounting condition [Watts and Zimmerman, 1986]. If nothing else, such investigations have placed accounting in a more interdependent position with respect to other forms of information processing and wider institutional arrangements for the governance and regulation of the enterprise. They have even provided at least some basis for appreciating the institutional preconditions for some forms of accounting theorising [Watts and Zimmerman, 1979], although not, as will subsequently become clear, of the bases that might underlie theorising about accounting theorising.

It is such attempts to appreciate, explore, and indeed account for accounting that I wish to build upon and develop in the argument that follows. My remarks of necessity have to be brief. However, they will draw upon my own recent inquiries into both the factors that are implicated in accounting change [Burchell et al., 1985; Hopwood, 1987], that, in my words, make accounting what it was not, and the rationales which are associated with such mobilisations of the accounting craft [Burchell et al., 1980]. The aim in so doing is to inquire into accounting as it has come to function, to ask questions of it, indeed to interrogate it, with a view not to appreciating its technicalities in isolation but rather to appreciate its organisational functioning. Indeed my remarks constitute what one of my friends, on hearing the text, described as a "paper about understanding ourselves." I also hope that it will help some to understand both accounting and the possibilities for accounting research. For in the analysis, I seek to characterise accounting in ways that are not part of the discipline's conventional wisdom. I use conceptual frameworks and languages that do not form a part of the normal accounting discourse. I seek to probe into a few rationales for accounting development that are not a part of accounting's account of itself. In so doing I try to suggest the powerful role that knowledge plays in accounting change and I aim to provide a characterisation of some of the many ways in which accounting can become intimately involved in organisational action.

## MANAGEMENT ACCOUNTING AND THE DIVERSITY OF INFLUENCES UPON IT

Management accounting, as we now know it, bears the mark of many influences, only some of which form a part of the conventional wisdom that is associated with it.

In the United Kingdom, for instance, the government regulation of prices and profits during World War I resulted not only in a considerable increase in the accounting calculus implanted in the enterprise but also the enhanced social acceptance and legitimacy of the accounting craft and its practitioners [Loft, 1986]. And that legitimacy was to serve accounting well in the subsequent occupational struggles that were to determine which practitioners had an influential position in the control of the enterprise [Armstrong, 1985] – struggles that were resolved in very different ways in different countries. In subsequent years very different interests appealed to accounting within the enterprise. During the crisis years of the Depression it was advanced as a sign of efficient management that was acceptable in the eyes of the financial establishment [Armstrong, 1987]. The State strove to inculcate the accounting art as
214 part of its strategy to restructure British manufacturing industry, both immediately after the Second World War and thereafter. Indeed, in the context of continued economic difficulties, the economic management policies of the State continued to advance the regime of accounting calculation within enterprises. Price controls resulted in a plethora of more detailed and sophisticated costings. Wage controls resulted in the advance of accounting for productivity, for value added, and for a wider dissemination of financial information within the firm as accounting sought to transform economic motivations and orientations prevailing within the enterprise [Burchell et al., 1985].

So although management accounting conventionally is given an internal rationale, many of the residues of economic calculation that reside within the enterprise have external origins. And such a phenomenon is in no way an idiosyncrasy of the British. Early American regulatory attempts also transformed the forms of economic calculation utilised within the enterprise. Wider social and political transformations associated with the efficiency movement [Haber, 1964] and the quest for enhanced enterprise accountability [Hays, 1959] changed the bases of legitimacy underlying management practices and resulted in an enhanced concern with what came to be regarded as rational approaches to management, including forms of accounting and financial management. As in the United Kingdom, the crises of legitimacy engendered by the Depression and the Great Crash resulted in regulatory attempts that utilised accounting and provided means by which external conceptions of economic calculation could inculcate internal accounting – something that only now is starting to be made more problematic by Kaplan and others. And also, as in the UK, war, the cold war, and defence contracting have all played a role in implanting within the enterprise particular forms of economic calculation.

Although it may be difficult for those accustomed to the present practice of management accounting to disentangle such external origins from the internal rationales which are now attributed to the resultant practices, the same forces can be observed at work in other management areas, and perhaps it is easier to recognise their significance there. Consider, for example, the present condition of human resource information systems in U.S. enterprises. No longer do they merely reflect the internally recognised needs for information. In the main they reflect a mass of federal and state regulatory provisions regarding employment, plus the demands of fiscal, insurance, and all manner of other agencies. Here the external origins of the internal information flows are clearer to see. Here too, as with financial information, external circumstances not only create a demand for information but also leave an information residue that has the potential to shift and disturb internal patterns of visibility and knowledge. A potential thereby is created for a more disruptive effect.

Management accounting also has been appealed to in order to help regulate social forces which pass through the organisation rather than remain at the door. In both the United States and the United Kingdom the rise of internal economic calculation and costing was associated with the regulation of the labour force and the rise of the labour movement. Management was not faced with a disciplined, orderly work force which was tolerant of management authority and accepting of economic rationales for action. Rather, the discipline and order in the factory had to be constructed by an array of architectural forms, management practices, and organisational controls on the utilisation and specification of time. A domain for economic action had to be laboriously constructed – often, as numerous authors have illustrated [Burawoy, 1979, 1986; Clawson, 1980; Edwards, 1979], in the midst of resistances and strategies for counter-control. In striving for the control of the enterprise, management had to address both problems of social and organisational control. Accounting was appealed to for both inseparable reasons. The accounting eye provided a means for penetrating into 215
the inner workings of the organisation, constructing a strategic visibility of the economic. The aims of management could be diffused throughout the enterprise in a powerful way, economic rewards could start to become related to action, and the detailed workings of the newly visible corporate economy could be exposed to those in positions of power and authority. Not only could the enterprise thereby attempt to confront the forces of the social through accounting and other means, but also the newly ordered enterprise could itself contribute to the different functioning of the social – and it did. Seen in such terms, caution must be exercised in imposing a boundary between the enterprise and society. Society passes through the enterprise and is often transformed in the process, sometimes by accounting means.

Of course such mobilising rationales do not enter into conventional accounting dialogue, and, of course, that is my reason for emphasising them. Management accounting, as conventionally seen, is an internal organisational phenomenon. Many of the factors implicated in its emergence have been forgotten. And, as a result, there is now little appreciation of the ways in which external influences have transformed internal accounts, of the ways in which the factual residues those forces created have transformed the internal economy, and of the ways in which a selectivity thereby has entered into explanations of the accounting craft.

Be that as it may, such alternative views are extremely useful for appreciating the ways in which the accounting craft comes to occupy a different place and hold a different significance in different national cultures. Different regulatory practices of the State can make different appeals to economic calculation and result in different implantations of economic visibility in the enterprise – a phenomenon of particular importance in the U.S.A. Different appeals by the State to the practitioners of economic calculation, especially accountants, can endow them with different social legitimacies and recognition, and thereby shift some of the preconditions for the interoccupational competition for the control of the enterprise. For certainly we know from the work of Horovitz [1980] and Armstrong [1985; 1987] that there is no general approach to either enterprise control or visibility that prevails across national boundaries. Different configurations of practices are observed, different emphases are given, and different strategies are used to interrelate the economic with the noneconomic – all differences that are at least suggestive of the ways in which the cultural environment and different national institutional structures and strategies pass through enterprises and their accountings, transforming them in the process.

Perhaps even more significantly, an awareness of the wider social origins of the accounting craft can alert us to the possible ways in which both the form and significance of organisational accountings can be dependent on the precise configurations of practices oriented towards enhancing social rather than organisational control. Where the instilling of an acceptance of the legitimacy of order, discipline, and perhaps even an economic rationale for action is effectively achieved by the institutions of the family, the educational system, and the community, the factory can focus on accounting for the organisation. That prior investment in socialisation certainly could not be taken for granted in the formative days of accounting in the United States and the United Kingdom, however, and possibly still cannot. The enterprise had to address issues of both organisational and social control. An organisational order had to be explicitly forged out of the social fabric through the use of well-articulated management structures, information and control practices, and associated discourses which enhanced both their organisational and social legitimacy. Questions of discipline and the organisational management of time equally gave rise to innovations in organ-
216 isational rather than just external social practices. And the mobilisation of an economic rationale for action resulted in an ever more penetrating accounting eye as investments were made in constructing rather than merely revealing a conception of economic reality that could infuse much of organisational life.

Hardly surprisingly, in those countries where the enterprise had to address questions of both organisational and social control, there is a tendency to find more elaborated information, control, and accounting systems which have a greater significance and legitimacy. For accounting, by linking economic and social conditions, is a phenomenon that arises out of the social fabric, is infused by it, and contributes to its transformation.

## THE DIVERSE FUNCTIONS OF THE MANAGEMENT ACCOUNTING CRAFT

Already I hope to have disturbed at least some of the conceptions of a narrow functionality and instrumentality that are implicit in conventional accounting discourses. However, I do not want to ignore the very real mobilising potential that more frequently cited rationales for accounting have had. Accounting is invoked to provide an informational bridge between markets and production. It is used to orchestrate an economic rationality within the enterprise. And it is used to mobilise and monitor organisational members dispersed across hierarchical levels. My aim, however, is not to be comprehensive but rather to open up for a wider consideration the instrumentality of the accounting craft and to emphasise some of the diverse but influential arenas which have given rise to accounting as it is.

For notions of functionality are all too frequently conceived too narrowly in the accounting literature, ignoring both the wider rationales that can mobilise accounting change, and, as I briefly discuss later, the often equivocal relationship between the rationales that infuse accounting rhetoric and the actual consequences of accounting in action.

Consider for a moment the functionality of the clothes in which I stand. They not only provide a way of cushioning me from the elements in a way that is cognisant of the prevailing climatic conditions, but also they reflect cultural notions of the way in which the male body should be attired [Barthes, 1985] – and how extensively it should be attired. All too clearly, the latter notions have changed over time. Indeed I come to you attired in the garb of the 1980s and I hope that I would be reluctant to expose myself to you in the clothes of the 1950s, or '60s, or '70s. For clothes are also a cultural and symbolic phenomenon, conveying a whole host of messages about my wider relationship to the world and it to me. Although at times they have a more particular functionality – for instance, when I go climbing or hiking, or expose myself either to the heat of the southwest or the winters of the midwest – they also are involved in the management of appearances, in the creation of a symbolic conception of Hopwood, and in my occasional attempts to purchase a particular legitimacy with a particular audience.

Accounting too has a range of functionalities, many of which are also symbolic and cultural in nature, and only some of which enter into the official discourses of the craft. The techniques of accounting can be implicated in the creation and propagation of a particular significance, in the furtherance of strategic changes in language, in the articulation of a set of categories and codes that enable the wider dissemination of other information as well as accounting information itself, in the construction of quite particular conceptions of time, and, not least in significance, in attempts to enhance enterprise and organisational legitimacy [Meyer, 1986].

As far as the latter is concerned, to refer to the concerns with social accounting and 217
auditing in the socially turbulent days of the 1960s and 1970s is a little too obvious, and too distanced from the conventional practice of the accounting craft. Rather we should ponder on the impacts on accounting, particularly in the public or not-for-profit sphere, of the changes in political practice and rhetoric that accompanied the emergence of the Reagan administration in the U.S.A. and the Thatcher government in the U.K. With such sudden changes in the legitimacy of particular actions and interests, new means for justifying action were needed, new ways of demonstrating conformity to prevailing values were required, and public organisations had to clothe themselves in the newly legitimate practices of economic action and what was regarded as efficient management. As we know from the work of John Meyer of Stanford, at times such as this accounting can be endowed with a symbolic significance, helping to shape the organisation in ways that are consistent with the symbolic structures prevailing in its environment [Meyer, 1983; 1986]. Although at least initially loosely coupled to patterns of ongoing action in the organisation, and thereby facilitating the speedy consulting change assignments that so many of us have witnessed, these legitimising strategies nevertheless leave an informational residue and shift the patterns of significance and concern in the organisation. Worries start to be talked about in different ways. New experts can enter the organisational power structure. A newly created domain of economic facts can confront the politically and socially vague and nebulous. In these and other ways, the symbolic can disturb the status quo, allowing accounting sometimes to function as an agent for wider organisational transformations in the name of externally mobilised rhetorics [Hopwood, 1984].

## THE POWER OF BOTH ACCOUNTING KNOWLEDGE AND ACCOUNTING ITSELF

Hopefully I have at least created some conception of not only a diverse accounting craft but also one that is implicated in diverse rationalities and functions. Hopefully I also have created a conception of the craft that stands in some contrast to the ones that are enshrined in the texts that we use. For although some element of technical fragmentation pervades such works, they nevertheless substitute an abstract conception of accounting in the organisation for the diversity of accounting's links to organisational functioning. They also impose a very particular selectivity on the rationales that are articulated for accounting action, indeed using what rationales are given to construct a coherence for management accounting. A unity thereby is created within their pages that stands in stark contrast to the diversity of accounting in action.

Be that as it may, the world of textbook accounting is of great significance both in itself and for the wider forces that it reflects. For such texts are exemplars of our ability to talk and write accounting rather than merely to do it. They are one reflection of the enormous growth of knowledge that has occurred around accounting – a knowledge that has emerged amidst professional regulation, educational practices, enterprise standardisation and specification, state regulatory initiatives, the development of competitive consulting practices, and only more recently, academic research. As a result of developments in all of these areas we can now talk rather than merely do accounting. And we should recognise that accounting-speak can have an autonomy from accounting practice. Very different factors can influence it. It can become intertwined with other very different bodies of knowledge, such as economics, organisational behaviour, and mathematics. But even though it can change independently of accounting practice, accounting talk – accounting knowledge – can still be brought to bear to question, assess, and indeed change accounting practice. The level
218 of abstraction implicit in accounting talk facilitates just that. At times the doing of accounting can be confronted by our ability to talk accounting, and changed as a result. Indeed, although the contribution of formal research to accounting talk is relatively recent, I nevertheless think that both accounting academics and practitioners massively underestimate the impact that accounting ideas have had.

Costing practice can now be confronted with abstract notions of costliness, and changed as a result. Investments have even been made in specialised institutions for talking accounting. Bodies like the Financial Accounting Standards Board and the Accounting Standards Committee both consume and produce vast amounts of knowledge and operate on the practice of the craft by their ability to appeal to and advance discursive notions of it. In management accounting generally, the role of knowledge has been no less great. The fragmented practices can now be addressed in terms of notions of management responsibility and functions. Accounting now can be powerfully related to cognitive conceptions of decision making. The diversity of practice can be orchestrated by appeals to notions of management and organisational control that not only impose a unity on the diversity but also give priority to particular conceptions of the rationales that have made management accounting what it is.

Seen in such terms, it is accounting knowledge rather than accounting itself that has made much of my earlier conception of accounting in action a somewhat alien and unfamiliar one. For so great is the impact of our investment in quite particular accounting knowledge that we now see and understand accounting in quite specific ways; ways, moreover, whose patterns of emergence and intellectual preconditions are lost amidst the seeming obviousness of accounting as it is. Accounting no longer is just accounting. It is a more rationalised, more coherent, and apparently less social phenomenon that is observed, analysed, and changed through a lens, the making and components of which are no longer remembered.

When seen in this way, it can be appreciated that accounting knowledge has played a role in making accounting what it was not. It has not merely reflected the world in any simple positivistic sense. It has changed it. In this sense, though, it is like accounting itself. For although we conventionally think of accounting as reflecting organisational notions of control, decision making, and strategy; of reflecting the production, technological, organisational, and market circumstances of the enterprise; in fact accounting itself (along with other organisational practices, of course) has had the power to play a role in mobilising and creating the enterprise as we now know it.

Through its intertwining with notions of accountability and responsibility, accounting has played a role in the reconstitution of organisational agents and actors, enabling different configurations of organisational arrangements to exist. By extending the range of influence patterns within the enterprise, by creating different patterns of interaction and interdependence, and by enabling new forms of organisational segmentation to exist, accounting has played a positive role in both shifting the preconditions for organisational change and influencing its outcomes. By its routinisation of information flows and the ways in which it imposes a spatialisation on time, it has changed conceptions of the past, the present, and the future, contributing different saliences to each, which in turn have moderated temporal preferences and emphases, and thereby, organisational actions. Creating quite particular objectifications of the otherwise vague and abstract and particular conceptions of economic facts, accounting also has created not only a context in which the conditions exist for other organisational practices to change, but also a means by which a particular organisational visibility can either compete for or be imposed upon managerial attention; and, if such strategies succeed, perhaps even eventually exclude the visibility and significance of other ways of characterising the organisational terrain.
Moreover, as such developments occur, the transformational potential of accounting is 219
only enhanced further, as the facts created by the craft give rise to an influential language and set of categories for conceiving and changing the organisation in economic terms.

So not only am I describing a diverse accounting that serves many roles, many of which are not accounted for in accounting's account of itself – an accounting whose practice and our conceptions of it are infused by knowledge in many more ways than is conventionally appreciated – but also an accounting and a knowledge of it that does not merely sit in the enterprise, reflecting other organisational pressures and constraints, but one that has a more active potential to transform the enterprise, to make it what it was not. Accounting, from such a view, at times can be much more influential than is often presumed.

## ACCOUNTING IN ACTION

It is useful to see some of these forces in operation in a specific accounting area. For this purpose let us consider financial methods of investment appraisal – capital budgeting and the methodology of discounted cash-flow analysis.

Capital budgeting is interesting because it owes its more widespread implantation into the enterprise to the very development of financial and accounting knowledge that has just been discussed, and, in the United Kingdom at least, to the concerns of the State with the national need for efficient business management and a form of economic calculation that could recognise the financial interdependence between the enterprise and the State. Seen in such terms, it is a technique which bases its rationale on a formal and abstract economic rationality rather than on empirical appeals to its effectiveness in shaping patterns of investment in different and more strategic ways. It is grounded in an external logical obviousness rather than being infused by any understanding of organisational process and action and the ways in which it might intersect with other organisational processes and practices.

Yet even within the context of economic reasoning, possibilities exist for different ways of infusing economic investment rationalities into the enterprise. If, for example, we assume highly competitive markets, as most economic and financial theorists do, then our expectation should be that the acceptable project should have a zero net present value. Few such projects enter our texts, however, so we can only presume that the authors implicitly are assuming that particular competitive advantages prevail, if only temporarily. But if it is competitive advantage that is the source of profitability, an alternative mode of economic evaluation would be to first analyse in strategic, marketing, manufacturing, technological, or whatever terms the nature of that advantage and the means for its possible furtherance. Once such analyses had isolated any advantages, the role of a formal financial analysis would be more minimal – to check on the arithmetic, to assure that everything had been done to increase the efficiency of the project, and to ensure a compatibility with the enterprise's overall financial policies.

From what we can gather, just such an approach characterises Japanese approaches to investment analysis. A temporal priority is given to strategic rather than financial assessment. Both, of course, are compatible with a formal economic reasoning. But the two approaches can call on different bodies of knowledge, give priority to different modes of analysis, call on different experts, and create different organisational linkages and interdependencies during the evaluation process. And because of these differences, rather than their formal logical similarities, the two approaches can become intertwined with other aspects of organisational action in different ways and thereby
220 have at least the potential to have a different impact on the enterprise.

Such different intertwinings of economic rationality and organisational action are ignored by dominant bodies of knowledge, however. Despite being oriented towards changing organisational processes and consequences, they nevertheless conceive of the organisation as a vacuum, as a phenomenon that seemingly has no possibilities for more proactively influencing the investment process. Moreover, dominant views also ignore how and when evaluative technologies are used. The ways in which assessment procedures become involved with organisational politics are not considered. Yet when they function as what I have called "ammunition machines" [Earl and Hopwood, 1980], the orientation of the methods can radically change. They no longer provide an evaluation within an agreed framework but rather form part of a strategy for forging agreements on aims and objectives, striving to construct that hopefully agreed-upon framework. The organisational processes and actions associated with such different uses can be very different indeed; as can those stemming from the use of evaluative procedures which follow, rather than form, a part of the decision process, particularly for complex, uncertain, and multiple-person decision processes. In such circumstances formal evaluation is less a proactive instrument of choice than a means for rationalisation, for the construction of legitimate rationales for action, and for the mobilisation of support – all very necessary and very important processes, but ones which do not enter into the formal bodies of knowledge which give rise to the techniques that are utilised in these ways.

Such wider organisational processes are emphasised, albeit all too briefly, because they are an important part of the context in which abstract rationales for intervention in the organisation become interconnected with organisational action and they therefore play a role in shaping the ultimate instrumentalilty of the practices themselves. There is no obvious and automatic relationship between an abstract accounting or financial rhetoric and an intervention in the organisation in the name of it. Rather than being presumed, that relationship has to be painstakingly constructed, as all practitioners know but few rationalisers of practice admit. Nowhere is this clearer than in the cognitive emphasis given to investment appraisal methodologies. The stress is placed on making the right decision. Assuming that the realm of the future lies ahead, the methods serve as a telescope for observing its characteristics – and wrenching it into the present via discounting so as to enable a decision to be made as to whether the enterprise wishes to occupy that future space. But such an approach, however dominant in our formal bodies of knowledge, is partial because it ignores the action processes through which that future must be created rather than passively occupied. Perhaps that partiality is less problematic if organisational cognitions and actions are relatively independent [Brunsson, 1982]. But they might not be. The very detail of an evaluation might influence perceptions of uncertainty and risk, and thereby action. Clinical and analytical approaches to evaluation might do nothing to engender, if not more negatively disturb, the processes of commitment and enthusiasm out of which the future might be created. In these and many other ways there are very real possibilities for an interdependency between cognitions and actions, possibilities which further disturb the obviousness of the relationship between abstract rationalities and organisational praxis, and possibilities which provide further insights into the nature of the relationship between the knowledge through which we have come to know accounting and the contexts in which accounting functions.

Once again I have pointed to the partiality of emphases implicit in accounting knowledge, to the selective rationales for action, and to the under-accounting for both accounting as it is and for the ways in which it has its effects. Once again I have emphasised the extent to which very partial concerns with "shoulds" and with "oughts" 221
monopolise imagination outside of any appreciation of organisational praxis. For people who claim to be practical, applied, and pragmatic – indeed who see themselves as practical agents for change and improvement – such partialities ought to be profoundly worrying. I think it is profoundly worrying that they are not.

## SOME IMPLICATIONS FOR RESEARCH AND PRACTICE

Although the implications of my remarks for both research and practice are great, to some extent they are consistent with some current directions for change. I too look for greater concern with accounting as it is practised – a view articulated by Kaplan [1986], amongst others. I therefore am sympathetic with many aspects of empiricism within the accounting research community. We do need to observe, survey, and delve into accounting as it was and as it is. But as I hope should be clear from the emphases that I have given, I think that observation and analysis are tasks that are inevitably, of necessity, theoretically grounded and driven. We have to think as we observe. And it is that joint theoretical and empirical task that lies behind my concern to advance not just our knowledge of the bits and pieces of the accounting craft, but our understanding and appreciation of accounting as it has come to be, as it now functions, and as it might come to be. It is the emphasis on understanding, appreciation, and simple human intelligibility that I seek to stress.

From this perspective, we simply cannot just observe the world as it is. Observation is of itself a theoretical exercise. To observe we must of necessity appeal to categories, languages, conceptual interrelationships, and theories. As of now it is not just our observations that are inadequate; it is our theories also. We have pitifully few at our disposal that allow us to interrogate, question, and understand accounting in the contexts in which it operates. Our theories or the implicit bodies of knowledge that serve in their place actively mask and reduce the salience and significance of so much accounting as it is. In seeing what we think, we not only have a view that is partial but we also have few insights into its partiality.

Characterising the problem in this way, I think it is a pity that accounting is having to witness a rise of interest in positivism [Watts and Zimmerman, 1986], an epistemological stance that denies the interdependence of theory and observation, at the very time when it has been rejected by most of the human and social sciences. So many of the greatest intellects of the nineteenth and twentieth centuries have articulated philosophies that undermine the pretensions of positivism and provide alternative epistemological frameworks for guiding the human task of understanding the world in which we live. Even Popper [1976, pp. 87-88], whose strategies of falsification are appealed to in order to buttress the positivistic framework in accounting, has felt compelled not only to ask "Who killed . . . positivism?" but also to answer "I fear I must admit responsibility." Not knowing of accounting developments, Popper even went on to note that "Everyone knows nowadays that...positivism is dead."

Dead may it be, positivism has seemingly come to haunt accounting research, along with a number of other theoretical ghosts that seem to have little relationship to the wider patterns of intellectual life in many other human and social sciences.

I do not want to overemphasise this point because I am most sympathetic with the empirical questioning of accounting that has resulted from such a stance. Even so, I think that it is a pity that at the very time when accounting needs to appreciate the complexity, the social nature, and the wider consequences of the act of theorising, it seemingly moves towards adopting a perspective that is less conducive to grappling
222 with such issues. And the same could be said for that strongly articulated functionalism that pervades accounting research – a view that assumes that what is, is what should be – and our seeming inability to deal with dynamics, with process, and with action, something that is heavily reinforced by the ahistorical nature of most accounting theoretical stances.

What is needed is a much more open approach to theorising and research in general. In accounting we need to reflect more on patterns of theorising in other fields of intellectual endeavour rather than the present approach that seemingly only allows a few to innovate theoretically and that is even reluctant to allow younger researchers to push at the boundaries of our knowledge; something that would be inconceivable in most other disciplines. Research is something that is still relatively new to accounting. We are still unsure of research, unsure of intellectual questioning rather than technical propagation, and possibly because of this, invest the research life with a whole series of social and institutional constraints. Equally, and possibly because of it, we are reluctant to admit the social nature of our theorising. Research is seen as residing in a purely technical domain, like accounting itself. We are hesitant to admit its human and social bases, even the humane nature of the drive for intelligibility and understanding that lies behind it.

If only we could do more to set at least some of these constraints aside, be more self-conscious about research, be more at ease with the research life, be more appreciative of the human activity of understanding, and be more willing to see it in human terms rather than mask it in a mantle of epistemological privilege, we could start to address the prerequisites for good and sound theorising more effectively. And for me, one of those prerequisites should be a theoretical reflexivity. We should be willing to apply our own theories to ourselves. Theorists of accounting theories should be willing to at least entertain the implications of their views for their own condition. Those appealing to the primacy of supply and demand should reflect on the constraints which prevent those forces applying to their own act of theorising, so destabilising the epistemological claims of any temporary theoretical equilibrium.

I choose to emphasise these points, rather than many others which I also see as important for research progress, because I think that above all else a more self-conscious awareness of the research endeavour is a prerequisite for any significant change in accounting's ability to account for itself. If we are to see and perceive accounting differently, if we are to see it in the contexts in which it operates rather than as an exercise in formal logic, and if we are to appreciate both the diversity of the craft itself and the diversity of the rationales and forces that mobilise it, major advances in our conceptual understanding and ability to theorise are required.

For at a more practical level, what is at stake with a view that seeks to ground accounting in the organisational and social contexts out of which it emerges and in which it functions is a more adequate way for appreciating accounting as it is and as it might become. Such a view can provide an improved basis for understanding the ways in which accounting intersects with other organisational processes and practices, for appreciating how it can actively shape the organisational fabric, and for sensitising us to at least some of the ways in which accounting fails to have the consequences which were anticipated for it and has consequences which were not anticipated – all vital factors lying behind the current development of worrying about management accounting [Hopwood, 1985b], and all factors stimulating some practitioners to look at accounting in ways that increasingly are different from those used by many of their academic colleagues.

From an educational point of view, an organisationally grounded accounting could provide a basis on which management accounting textbooks could become more than 223
the bricklaying or plumbing manuals of the accounting craft. It could enable a more explicit design approach to accounting education to emerge, one that helps students to relate technique to circumstance, one that strives to encourage them to consider and appreciate the wider organisational consequences of their acts, and one that moves towards an architecture, albeit a landscape or community-oriented architecture, of accounting system design.

All too clearly a great deal more work is required before such educational, practical, and research objectives can be realised. To me, however, that work is of the greatest importance. Put simply, I think that the enhanced ability of accounting to account for itself is an essential prerequisite for our ability to direct accounting so that it might better serve organisations, and indeed society, as a whole.

## REFERENCES


Argyris, C., *The Impact of Budgets on People* (New York: The Controllership Foundation, 1952).

———, "Organizational Learning and Management Information Systems," *Accounting, Organizations and Society, 2* (1977), pp. 113-123.

Armstrong, P., "Changing Management Control Strategies: The Role of Competition Between Accountancy and Other Organizational Professions," *Accounting, Organizations and Society, 10* (1985), pp. 129-148.

———, "The Rise of Accounting Controls in British Capitalist Enterprises," *Accounting, Organizations and Society, 12* (1987).

Barthes, R., *The Fashion System* (London: Jonathan Cape, 1985).

Birnberg, J.G., and C. Snodgrass, "Culture and Control," Unpublished working paper (Graduate School of Business, University of Pittsburgh, 1986).

Brunsson, N., "The Irrationality of Action and Action Rationality: Decisions, Ideologies and Organizational Actions," *Journal of Management Studies* (January 1982), pp. 29-44.

Burawoy, M., *Manufacturing Consent: Changes in the Labor Process Under Monopoly Capitalism* (Chicago: University of Chicago Press, 1979).

———, *The Politics of Production* (London: Verso, 1986).

Burchell, S., C. Clubb, and A.G. Hopwood, "Accounting in its Social Context: Towards a History of Value Added in the United Kingdom," *Accounting, Organizations and Society, 10* (1985), pp. 381-413.

———, ———, ———, J. Hughes, and J. Nahapiet, "The Roles of Accounting in Organizations and Society," *Accounting, Organizations and Society, 5* (1980), pp. 5-27.

Clawson, D., *Bureaucracy and the Labour Process* (New York: Monthly Review Press, 1980).

Dalton, M., *Men Who Manage* (New York: John Wiley & Sons, 1959).

Earl, M., and A.G. Hopwood, "From Management Information to Information Management," in H.C. Lucas, F.F. Land, T.J. Lincoln and K. Supper (Eds.), *The Information Systems Environment* (New York: North-Holland, 1980).

Edwards, R., *Contested Terrain: The Transformation of the Workplace in the Twentieth Century* (New York: Basic Books, 1979).

Haber, S., *Efficiency and Uplift: Scientific Management in the Progressive Era 1890-1920* (Chicago: University of Chicago Press, 1964).

224 Hays, S.P., *Conservation and the Gospel of Efficiency: The Progressive Conservation Movement 1890-1920* (Boston: Harvard University Press, 1959).

Hopwood, A.G., "On Trying to Study Accounting in the Contexts in Which it Operates," *Accounting, Organizations and Society, 8* (1983), pp. 287-305.

———, "Accounting and the Pursuit of Efficiency," in A.G. Hopwood and C. Tomkins (Eds.), *Issues in Public Sector Accounting* (Oxford: Philip Allan, 1984).

———, "The Tale of a Committee that Never Reported: Disagreements on Intertwining Accounting with the Social," *Accounting, Organizations and Society, 10* (1985a), pp. 361-377.

———, "The Development of 'Worrying' About Management Accounting," in K.B. Clark, R.H. Hayes, and C. Lorenz (Eds.), *The Uneasy Alliance: Managing The Productivity - Technology Dilemma* (Boston: Harvard Business School Press, 1985b).

———, "The Archaeology of Accounting Systems," *Accounting, Organizations and Society, 12* (1987, in press).

Horovitz, J., *Top Management Control in Europe* (London: Macmillan, 1980).

Kaplan, R.S., "Measuring Manufacturing Performance: A New Challenge for Managerial Accounting Research," *The Accounting Review* (October 1983), pp. 686-705.

———, "The Role for Empirical Research in Management Accounting," *Accounting, Organizations and Society, 11* (1986), pp. 429-452.

Loft, A., "Towards a Critical Understanding of Accounting: The Case of Cost Accounting in the U.K., 1914-1925," *Accounting, Organizations and Society, 11* (1986), pp. 137-169.

Meyer, J.W., "On the Celebration of Rationality: Some Comments on Boland and Pondy," *Accounting, Organizations and Society, 8* (1983), pp. 235-240.

———, "Social Environments and Organizational Accounting," *Accounting, Organizations and Society, 11* (1986), pp. 345-356.

Popper, K., *Unended Quest; An Intellectual Autobiography* (London: Collins, 1976).

Scott, DR, *The Cultural Significance of Accounts* (New York: H. Holt, 1931; Reprinted, Houston: Scholars Book Co., 1973).

Watts, R.L. and J.L. Zimmerman, "The Demand for and Supply of Accounting Theories: The Market for Excuses," *The Accounting Review* (April 1979), pp. 273-305.

———, and ———, *Positive Accounting Theory* (Englewood Cliffs, NJ: Prentice-Hall, 1986).

Whyte, W.F., *Money and Motivation* (New York: Harper & Row, 1955).

Wildavsky, A., *The Politics of the Budgetary Process* (Boston: Little, Brown & Co., 1964).

———, "Policy Analysis is What Information Systems are Not," *Accounting, Organizations and Society*, *3* (1978), pp. 77-88.

# Accounting and the Transformation of the Public Sector

# Value For Money: Practice In Other Countries

ANTHONY G. HOPWOOD
Professor of Accounting and Financial Reporting, London Graduate School of Business Studies; Professor of Management, European Institute for Advanced Studies in Management, Brussels; American Accounting Association Distinguished International Visiting Professor in the USA 1981.

Although a great deal of attention is being given to the need for value for money auditing in the United Kingdom, far less consideration is being paid to the lessons that can be learnt from the practical exercises that have been undertaken so far, both here and elsewhere. As in so many other areas of management debate, apparently it is much easier to discuss what should be and how it should be done than what is being done, why it is being done and, perhaps most important of all, the practical consequences that have followed from it. Indeed in this area, as in others, even the most practical of people often appear reluctant to engage themselves with the intricacies of practice, preferring instead to conduct their discussions in the realms of what might be rather than in the world that is. Such preferences can have, and indeed have had, many unfortunate consequences however, not least because even the best intentions often give rise to a set of consequences that are very different from those hoped for or expected. If for no other reason than this, I think that it is of great importance to complement our discussions of what should be done in the value for money area with at least some consideration of the lessons that can be learnt from what has been done.



With such an objective in mind it is only natural that I should focus my attention on those situations where I have some first hand knowledge of current practice. Athough often useful, so much of the literature in the area nevertheless places more emphasis on the intentions lying behind action than on what actually has been achieved. For this reason alone I will concentrate my comments on developments in the USA, Canada and Sweden, ignoring the perhaps equally important experiments elsewhere. First of all, however, it is useful to consider briefly a number of the important generic issues lying behind the current discussions of value for money auditing in the UK.

## SOME ISSUES UNDERLYING THE PRESENT DEBATE

Just why has there been such a sudden emergence of interest in the concept of VFM auditing in the UK? Not too long ago it would have appeared alien to the British political scene — an imported notion from realms where management processes have a more explicit and perhaps rapidly changing vocabulary. Now, however, the idea is widely discussed. No doubt many factors are implicated in that change. I think three are of particular significance however; two of them in a more positive sense and the third playing a somewhat negative role.

First, the last few years undoubtedly have seen a growing questioning of the legitimacy of the state in both the UK and elsewhere. Increasingly both the authority of the state to intervene in certain areas of economic and social life and the adequacy of such interventions are being debated and re-examined. Rather than that authority being taken for granted, demands are growing for both a greater visibility of governmental processes and a more systematic examination of actions and achievements. The VFM debate is merely a part of this more general development.

When seen in this way it is perhaps not surprising that government audit operations are most highly developed in those countries, such as the USA, where there has been a longer tradition of suspicion of government activities, and least developed in those countries, possibly such as France and Germany, where the machinery of government has had a greater historical legitimacy. In the past the UK has occupied an intermediary position. It would appear,
230 however, that there have been pressures recently for that position to change.

Such tendencies have been reinforced by current economic circumstances, not least in respect of the pressures for economy in governmental operations and the associated demands not only for greater accountability in general but also for a greater investment in accounting, more specifically defined. For although the UK has made one of the greatest investments in accounting expertise and its practitioners, both have had relatively little involvement with the operations of central government, at least until recently. Even these current pressures are best seen in a longer historical perspective however, for accounting has tended to flourish and develop in the UK during periods of major economic difficulty. The auditing profession as we now know it was born amidst the bankruptcies that came with the great depression that characterized the latter part of the nineteenth century and auditors made their entry into the financial administration of industrial companies during the troubled times of the 1930s. Even now the intricacies of accounting do not give rise to such extensive management practices in the financial sector or central government, although the last few years have seen demands for the latter to change.

A third factor underlying the present debate is a more curious one. For despite the current pressures to change, both central and local government in the UK already have a considerable investment in and experience of financial and economic evaluation, review and audit, although only rarely has this been associated with the body of professionalized accounting practice. Be that as it may, let us not forget that the UK has pioneered in the social cost-benefit analysis of government projects and that economic analyses of policies, both proposed and realized, are not an infrequent aspect of administrative life. Moreover both the Exchequer and Audit Department and the District Audit Service have a distinguished tradition of thorough and innovative work in their respective areas. Indeed today there could well be more experience of operational and VFM audits in those organizations, in terms of both their potential and practical achievements and problems, than in the private audit sector, where notions of management and operational audit have been peculiarly slow to develop. That might well come as a surprise to many. If nothing else however, that surprise should make us realize that governmental auditors in the UK have been reluctant to discuss their activities in any meaningful way and, unlike many of their overseas colleagues, have not graced their activities with a new technical jargon. Although the absence of the latter might be very desirable, I nevertheless think that we should be given many more opportunities to examine the approaches used by those who seek to make visible the actions of others. If for no other reason than to enhance the processes of accountability in the public domain, the nature of these examinations and the standard of their scrutiny should be more widely known. The contrast with American practice is particularly striking in this respect.

## SOME COMPARATIVE EXPERIENCES

### Practice in the United States 231

A wider concern with the efficiency and effectiveness of government operations has been a part of the administrative process in the USA for much of the post-war era. Although its origins may have had more to do with assuring the political support necessary for the implementation of new and controversial programmes than with the desire for an unbiased evaluation of their consequences, repeated legislative provisions for the monitoring of achievements nevertheless have resulted in the creation of a large body of expertise in the area of policy review or 'evaluation research', as it is now known. Initially such reviews were separate from the financial compliance audits undertaken by the General Accounting Office (GAO), the US equivalent of the Exchequer and Audit Department. However with the appointment of Elmer Staats as Comptroller and Auditor General attempts started to be made at integrating compliance audits with VFM and effectiveness reviews.

To this end Staats announced a ten year programme for transforming the professional expertise of his department, aiming to supplement the traditional emphasis on accounting skills with the employment of economists, technologists, sociologists, educationalists and others who could enhance the GAO's ability to comment on both the aims and the achievements of government policy. Today almost a half of the professional staff of the GAO are non-accountants — a paradoxical result for those in the UK who expect VFM concerns to result in an enhancement of the accounting perspective!

Before commenting further on what such a reorientation of the audit task might have achieved, it is important to emphasize a number of basic differences between the UK and American contexts. First, the GAO is a part of the legislative branch of government. The Comptroller and Auditor General is an officer of Congress and a significant amount of the investigatory work undertaken by the GAO is done at the request of Congress. Second, the reorientation undertaken by the GAO was only a part of a wider attempt to increase the visibility and scrutiny of governmental operations in the USA. At the time the reforms were being introduced into the audit area, freedom of information provisions were enacted and 'sunshine' and 'sunset' legislation also strived to make governmental activities more amenable to wider observation and review. Finally, no doubt reflecting such wider concerns, the GAO itself has invested a lot of effort into making its assessments available to a wider audience. Freely available to all, the mass of reports produced are written in a popular style with titles that owe more to journalistic flair than a more cautious administrative mind.

However, the fact that all the above points differentiate the American context from that prevailing in the UK should not be used as a basis for suggesting that we cannot learn from their experiences to date. Although it might be true that wholesale copying is not in order — it rarely is — I nevertheless think that some important lessons can be gained at a more general level.

To me, by far the most significant one relates to the lack of investment by the Americans in new and explicit routines for the wider review of government operatives. Despite the length of time that they have been engaged in VFM

reviews, their approaches have remained diverse and non-standardized. The origins of their inquiries are diverse, reflecting both congressional, and thereby political interests and the agency's own longer term strategies for areas in need of audit and assessment. The disciplines, perspectives and approaches used in their investigations also are characterized by diversity. There is neither a uniform methodology nor a standard way in which their findings are reported or taken-up. Rather than bureaucratising its concerns with efficiency and effectiveness, the GAO has provided a continual series of informed, multidisciplinary and — dare one say it — ad hoc investigations into topics of concern. For me at least however, in that very ad-hocracy resides one of the most crucial bases of the agency's effectiveness. By emphasizing an informed diversity rather than attempting to routinize its concerns with efficiency and effectiveness the GAO might have enabled more of its messages to penetrate the walls of officialdom. However difficult it might be to justify such an approach in conceptual terms, it could well be that at a practical level government officials are simply less skilled at deflecting a series of sharp, well-informed but diverse assessments, than the more predictable findings of a standardized 'audit cannon'.

It should be remembered, however, that such an ad-hocracy can only work if the reviews emanate from a respected and professional source. With few routines and technical means to provide a legitimate basis for commentary, an agency using such an approach must rely heavily on the legitimacy of its institutional origins and present nexus of relationships, and the professional expertise in which it has invested so much. If for any reason these are questioned, the approach can very quickly become quite problematic.

Despite in my view achieving a great deal, the GAO nevertheless has not been immune from criticism. For one thing, it has proved difficult to maintain the legitimacy of its basis for action. With reviews of programme effectiveness almost inevitably becoming intertwined with the political questioning of the desirability of particular policies, some have accused the agency of encroaching into the political domain. Somewhat paradoxically, faced with such criticisms, immediately prior to his retirement as Comptroller and Auditor General, Elmer Staats established an institute within the GAO which has the task of improving the professional basis of, and possibly introducing some element of standardization into its evaluative approaches. However, if nothing else, such an initiative should serve to demonstrate just how elusive such methodologies are. After so much experience in the area, practice to date has remained grounded in professional skill rather than in the mysteries of technique. Perhaps more significantly, the GAO also has been accused of neglecting its more traditional audit responsibilities in the area of financial compliance and regularity.

Although such accusations undoubtedly reflect some element of political concern with the extent of 'waste, fraud and abuse' rather than 'economy and efficiency' in the executive function, they nevertheless should alert us to the fact that auditing is and must remain a multi-faceted endeavour. Although the perspectives of the past might be in need of extension, their replacement is not in order.



### The Situation in Canada

The wider review of governmental activities is a more recent concern in Canada. As in so many other countries, it has stemmed from the questionings of the accountability of public sector organizations that were articulated during the 1960s and 1970s. Unlike in the UK however, that debate resulted in quite a number of institutional innovations, of which the reform of the audit function was only one. In Canada the enactment of freedom of information legislation and the provision of numerous other mechanisms for wider public participation in the political process have resulted in a much more general enhancement of the means available for observing the state than has occurred in the UK.

Be that as it may, the wider brief given to the Auditor General's Department in relation to all three aspects of economy, efficiency and effectiveness is still of interest. In respect of economy and efficiency the brief is a direct one. The Auditor General's Department is itself responsible for appraising the adequacy of governmental operations in relation to these, albeit quite general, criteria. The brief in respect of effectiveness is an indirect one however. Being aware of the potential overlap between a questioning of effectiveness and the political consideration of policies, the enabling legislation for the department provides it with a responsibility for monitoring the adequacy of departmental and agency systems and approaches for monitoring and reviewing their own effectiveness. Unlike in the other two areas, in this one the primary emphasis is still placed on self-evaluation and democratic debate.

Both the direct and indirect responsibilities given to the Auditor General's Department have resulted in a programme of considerable change and reform — a programme that is still in process. Indeed after several years of experience, officials still speak of the 'experiment' that is 'underway'. Despite recruiting a new cadre of professional auditors from the accounting profession and elsewhere, it has taken much longer than expected to mobilize the organization so that it can serve its new objectives, to recruit and to train the relevant staff and, not least, to establish both expertise and respect in relation to its new mission. For however simple and attractive notions such as economy and efficiency, let alone effectiveness, might initially have appeared, their translation into practical terms and operational procedures has been a task of genuine and unanticipated complexity and difficulty — a lesson that should not be lost on British observers.

As might be expected, the indirect brief given to the Auditor General's Department in respect of effectiveness already is resulting in an approach very different from that adopted in the USA. Unable to investigate directly, emphasis is having to be placed on the review of system effectiveness, albeit quite widely defined. In such a context the ad-hocracy that has characterized the activities of the GAO hardly appears appropriate. In its place is developing a concern for the specification of those standards for agency management processes and procedures that it is thought are, or perhaps more accurately, should be associated with effective management.

It is too early to judge whether such an emphasis on ensuring that the use of the standard routines of efficient and effective management will result in
234 the realization of greater efficiency and effectiveness. However even at this stage I would have some personal concerns. Evidence from elsewhere suggests that the relationship between such routines and organizational performance is far more equivocal than is being presumed. Not only does their own effectiveness depend on the existence of far more subtle organizational processes than can be encapsulated in organizational manuals and reports, but also such procedures invariably have consequences that are unanticipated as well as anticipated, particularly in times of political and environmental change. In addition to influencing the direct management of the task, organizational systems and procedures can affect factors such as the locus of visibility in the organization, the perception of risk and uncertainty, the distribution of power and influence, and not least in significance at the present time, the organization's ability to respond to the new and unexpected. Although it might be possible for such questions of organizational rather than purely system design to be addressed by those guiding the administration of the Department's indirect brief, I suspect that it will take much more time, effort and not least, the lessons of experience. To be fair however, there already are some officials within the Department that share such concerns.

## Experiments in Sweden

The situation in Sweden is much more difficult to characterize not least because of the ambiguous role which government auditing plays. On the one hand, at least until recently, the machinery of the state had a high degree of social legitimacy. Athough audit was still of significance, perhaps less was expected of it as a mechanism for scrutiny and review. On the other hand, there exist numerous other ways of observing the state, not least in importance being the rights for citizens to access public information that were enshrined within the constitutional provisions of the eighteenth century state. In such a context, so different from that prevailing in the UK, it hardly is surprising that the audit task has been seen as an ambiguous one.

Nevertheless the Swedish situation is still of some interest, if only because of their traditional openness to administrative innovation and reform. Compared with many other countries, the Swedes have at least experimented with numerous technical and organizational ways of approaching the wider review of governmental activities. Equally, however, they have failed to find any easy solutions. As a result they are now investing much more effort into understanding the organizational processes of questioning and debate which an audit should stimulate rather than seeing the problem in terms of administrative technique alone.

## SOME IMPLICATIONS

Despite the importance of the VFM debate, I would venture to suggest that practical progress in the area will be slow.

One reason for this stems from the very ambiguity of the phrase, a characteristic that we should remember has a very positive value in the political arena. Everyone can agree with the need for it without knowing what they might be getting! However that very characteristic is guaranteed to make the 235
transition from political rhetoric to administrative practice far from an easy one.

More significantly in the present context, comparative experiences in the area are suggestive of a number of other implications:

(a) At present there is no readily available technology for VFM auditing. Despite the wealth of their experience, the American situation suggests that it is an area where the routinization of practice is difficult. Moreover the length and difficulty of the Canadian experimental stage confirms this observation. Although such a view contrasts with the claims of those who see it as not only 'necessary' and 'needed' but also 'straight forward' and 'obvious', perhaps the difficulties can best be appreciated by saying that it is more than likely that the evaluation of any task has at least some relationship to the simplicity or complexity of the task itself. To the extent that the relevant governmental activities are simple (which some are), we can expect speedy progress in the audit area. However, where the underlying tasks cannot be so characterized, the audit task will start to assume some of the difficulties which are inherent in the activities and policies that are being evaluated.

(b) Familiarity with experiences elsewhere should instill a greater realization of the differences between what should be done and what is said to be done, and what is done and what might be done. Unfortunately much of the literature in the area is full of normative imperatives and technical analyses. Far less attention has been given to documenting, let alone understanding, either the underlying organizational processes that sometimes enable the claims of the technical to be realized or the organizational consequences which arise when greater emphasis is placed on evaluative activities.

Such organizational analyses will not be of direct assistance to all however. Although they offer some potential to understand the processes which shape how evaluative activities are implemented and the consequences which they give rise to, they also can shed some light on the origins of the interest in new forms of organizational review. To further appreciate that evaluations can improve processes of policy formulation and decision making will not be contentious. But understandings of political interests in evaluation and the ways in which evaluations of the past can arise from conceptions of the future might be more provocative. Be that as it may, we are starting to appreciate some of the many processes by which an interest in evaluation can arise and such understandings will make it increasingly difficult to discuss the technical bases for evaluation in isolation of the nature of the interests in them — as some of the present debates already demonstrate.

(c) Both the size of the developmental task and the observed disparity between aims and achievements suggest that value for money auditing is an area where experimentation is needed. Rather than presuming what can be done, a series of specific initiatives should be encouraged and every effort made to monitor their achievements

and consequences. The latter point needs particular emphasis, not only because of the pervasiveness of the unexpected but also because experience also suggests that those who seek to review the activities of others only rarely invest in monitoring themselves. Although feedback may be said to be important, we should not forget the resistances to it!

(d) One final implication is worth emphasizing. In so many of the countries where VFM auditing is underway, its emergence often has been associated with the development of other mechanisms for increasing the visibility of governmental processes and the extent to which they are subjected to public scrutiny and review. In the UK however, attempts to gain greater value for money have been related to a very different set of political issues. Rather than being part of a debate on the democratic accountability of public institutions, British discussions have adopted a more economic stance, placing more emphasis on the need for economy rather than on accountability *per se* and on the roles which experts rather than the public might be able to play. When trying to understand the different national contexts in which auditing mechanisms operate, this difference must be borne in mind.

All too clearly the lessons which can be learnt from experiments with VFM auditing in other countries do not only reside in the technical domain. It undoubtedly is useful to contrast the insights into the complexity of the task with the often simplistic statements of what can readily be achieved. Equally significantly, however, reflections on experiences elsewhere should serve to emphasize that an interest in audit and review cannot be isolated from wider interests in the dynamics of the political process and the organizational means for their fulfillment. The technical problems in the area are real and important but the suggestions for their solution must be considered in a wider context.

# 9

# Accounting and the Pursuit of Efficiency

ANTHONY HOPWOOD



'Every society keeps the records most relevant for its major values.' (Lazarsfeld, 1959, p. 108)

Accounting for the public sector has become a major issue for both discussion and action. In the last few years both the language and the practices of accounting have entered much more frequently and forcefully into debates about the efficiency, accountability and even scope of public sector activities. Appeals are now being made to the apparent inefficiency, lack of cost effectiveness, unprofitability and waste associated with the public sector. Referring to the existing economic calculus, it is being said that we are now 'living beyond our means', supporting that which is not 'economically viable', and either unable or unwilling, to face 'the facts of economic reality'. Although there is a long history of investing in accounting mechanisms for recording, planning, controlling and making visible public sector activities, within a very short period of time indeed recent pressures for change have succeeded in challenging the adequacy of existing public accounts and management accounting practices. New demands are now being made for the practices of accounting to become even more implicated in public sector management.

Where have these pressures for change come from? What form do they take? And what are their implications? How, in other words, can we not only better understand the forces at work but also attempt to gain a more adequate appreciation of their consequences for both the technical practice of accounting and the conduct of business within the public sector?

Before focusing on these questions, however, it is useful to consider some of the ways in which existing accounting practices have become intertwined with quite substantive issues of public policy. For, like today, much of the power of the public accountings of the past derived from their ability to move beyond merely facilitating the operation of pregiven and relatively unproblematic forms of economic and financial management. Accounting has already been implicated in a more positive shaping and influencing of that which is regarded as problematic, the forms
 which public debates take and the options seemingly available for management and public action.

### Accounting and Public Policy

Accounting records provide a way of freezing the decisions of the past (Bahmueller, 1981, p.193). What was problematic and debated can become lost within the accounting archive. 'Facts' can thereby be created out of dissent and disagreement. An aura of the obvious and the unchallengeable can and does emerge out of the residues of past actions which accounting presents.

The significance of the ability of accounting to forge a domain of the factual in this way can be seen in the patterns of both relative and absolute performance of many public sector bodies. Past subsidies, allowances and provisions, decisions on transfer prices and payments, and the specific means used for their financing, play a significant role now in determining where current costs are incurred, continuing subsidies required and profits and losses both generated and shown. The relationships between past policies in the areas of defence, industrial development and regional support, all have current impacts of this type. Examples abound in the interplay between taxation, economic and social policies. For the National Coal Board, British Rail, London Transport and the Central Electricity Generating Board the patterns of present financial performance emerge out of a complex array of decisions of a social and political, as well as purely economic, nature. But those decisions give rise to accounting residues which can be and are used independently of the contexts out of which they emerged. Being 'profitable' or 'unprofitable', 'subsidised' or 'a drain on the Exchequer', can have a powerful contemporary significance. In this way accounting seems to provide a means of judiciously selecting the time-scale for comment and debate. The compelling obviousness of the present can overwhelm the contingencies of the past.

The fact that accounting, as we know it, provides a partial record of organisational choices and actions has also been of enormous importance. Organisational accounts both reflect and, in turn, influence the emphases that are given in public debates. Consequently, the economic has undoubtedly been made more visible than the social and the political, in many spheres of public life. 
Now, however, the imperatives of those economic 'facts' can be contrasted with the more questionable dictates of political ideology and social preference, illustrating, in the process, the powerful influence that the recording tools of the public domain can have.

In fact, organisational accounts laid down to orientate management action to wider ends can themselves come to serve as statements of the ends to be achieved (Ridgeway, 1956). Much of the apparatus of national income accounting emerged to aid the management of a constrained wartime economy (Seers (1976), Tomlinson (1981, pp. 129–132)). In the postwar discussions on the desirability of economic growth, however, GNP started to take on many of the attributes of being an end in itself and, in the process, had a more widespread influence on other governmental policies. The imagery of profitability and self-sufficiency has been subject to the same transformation. And, in more recent times, we have seen how actions have come to be taken in the name of such indicators as the Public Sector Borrowing Requirement – a complex and ambiguous indicator that emerged in the context of attempts to manage a constrained economy.

Accounting has also become implicated in the development of the institutional structures and linkages which today characterise the public sector. Particular forms of accounts have been used to buffer certain organisations from the dictates of government policy and intervention. 'Losses', for instance, have served as a pretext for price increases which have provided subsequent investment autonomy, sometimes on a very large scale; profits, similarly, have been used as evidence of both the granting of greater autonomy and its positive achievements. More frequently, accountings have served to tighten the relationships between different parts of the public sector. They have been used as a means of restraint; to constrain expenditures, actions and policies. The selective visibility created by organisational accountings has served to further the salience of imposed patterns of standardisation and uniformity. The information which they produce is used to monitor and evaluate the actions of others, and more frequent plans, budgets and reports can facilitate centralised control at the expense of local discretion.

All told, accounting is already centrally implicated in the institutional frameworks, language and patterns of power and influence that characterise the public sector. As a means of collecting and reporting selective patterns of information it has played a not
240 insignificant role in the construction of public organisations and policies as we now know them. There are, however, yet further pressures for public sector accounting not only to change but also to expand its sphere of influence.

**Pressures for Public Sector Accounting to Change**

The pressures for the expansion and reform of public sector accounting are numerous, diverse and even conflicting in nature. Moreover, the emphasis given to particular factors can change remarkably over time, as recent decades have illustrated. In what follows, an attempt is made to outline only some of the main forces at work in recent debates in the area.

*Changing Conceptions of the State*

One of the major factors behind the current interest in public sector accounting is the changing view of the State that has entered political discourse in recent times. The legitimacy and value of at least some State actions and prerogatives are now being questioned from the perspective of a very different ideological stance. Indeed, a new way of examining and managing the State is emerging, and accounting is being implicated in that process.

Agencies of the State are now being asked to account for their aims, actions and achievements. Many more of their activities are coming to be seen in quite explicit economic terms. Cost and efficiency rather than effectiveness are being highlighted and debated. Information on economic consequences is being demanded. 'Value for money' has now entered the vocabulary of government.

In a whole series of ways the practices of accounting are increasingly being used to infiltrate and change, rather than merely record, the activities of the State. A new economic visibility is being forged to emphasise what was previously ignored and to challenge what was previously taken for granted. Economic calculations are now being seen as a way not only of reforming the management of the State but also of influencing the priorities which are given in policy determination and decision making. Accounting is quite explicitly becoming implicated in the construction of different views of the problematic, the desirable and the possible.



### *Accounting and Economic Restraint*

Organisations tend to increase their investment in economic calculation and visibility during periods of restraint. In what has become known as 'newly poor behaviour' (Olofsson and Svalander, 1975), the constrained organisation places a renewed emphasis on costs, financial information and the calculus of economic decision making. Mechanisms for enhancing economic visibility extend further into the organisation. Financial standards, budgets and plans become both more detailed and more subject to change. The organisation overall becomes more economically orientated, more influenced by economic calculation and, somewhat paradoxically (given that very frequently the economic difficulties emanate from without rather than from within), more orientated towards the seeming dictates of its own internal economic circumstances rather than the pressures of the world at large.

Accounting in the United Kingdom has tended to flourish during just such periods of economic difficulty. The auditing profession emerged during the great depression of the latter part of the nineteenth century, and was, in many senses, a product of attempts to reform the practice of bankruptcy administration. (Only later did the profession gain the legal requirement for an audit and the

legal monopoly in its practice that together provide the basis for the auditing profession today.) At the same time, cost accounting and the elementary practices of financial control started to play a more important role in manufacturing organisations faced with a rising real cost of labour at a time of general deflation and recession. In the depression of the 1920s, cost accounting seems to have been used aggressively as a way of getting at the 'facts' of economic difficulty. Similarly, the slump of the 1930s saw a dramatic rise in the role and status of accountants in industry as members of the auditing profession started to enter the upper echelons of manufacturing industry. Accounting has also been called upon in other times of economic restraint. The practice of costing was much
242 utilised and developed in the munitions factories of the First World War. The Second World War saw investment in an internal economic calculus for government that was to provide the basis for national income accounting as we now know it. And, in the post-war period of economic restraint, it was the government that attempted to further the practices of economic management in industry in the name of enhanced international competitiveness.

During periods of economic difficulty, accounting and accountants have consistently expanded their sphere of influence in the UK. However, the relatively large British investment in the profession remains quite localised in its influence, having, until recently, much less of a presence in the service, financial and governmental sectors than in the area of manufacturing industry. Now, it seems, the current recession is providing a pretext for that to change, at least for the public sector. As the economic receives more emphasis in government, and as economic decision making itself becomes more constrained, more and more demands are being made for the type of economic calculations that accounting provides.

### *The Search for Greater Efficiency*

Continued economic restraint has given a new urgency to demands to improve the efficiency of management in the public sector. More and more accusations of waste, maladministration and inefficiency have been made. High staffing levels have been pointed out. The traditionalism and sluggishness of decision processes in the public sector is noted repeatedly. Although it is sometimes realised that the demands of public accountability and decision making in a political context can serve to limit the extent to which concepts of efficiency derived from the private sector can be applied uncritically in the public domain, there nevertheless remains a feeling that much could be done to improve resource utilisation. Efficiency remains a very real and persuasive dream.

To this end, there is a renewed interest in importing into the public sector management practices developed in the private sector. Reference is made to the valuable roles that might be served by more adequate instruments for management planning and control. Appeals are made to the potential offered by improved costing procedures, more specific criteria for resource allocation, improved management information systems, investigations of administrative efficiency and better audits (which compare actual accomplishments with both original intentions and experience elsewhere). Such improved management practices, including those related to accounting itself, are seen as being able to assist in locating the inefficiencies of the past and ensuring that better performance is achieved in the future, not least by making public sector management and employees accountable for their actions and decisions.



*Accounting and the Demand for Accountability*

Appeals to the concept of accountability pervade many discussions concerned with the advance of accounting practice in the public sector. Accounting is seen as a way of both making visible and disciplining performance so that accountability can be demanded, policed and enforced.

A major impetus to the development of financial accounting in the private sector occurred when a separate cadre of managers came to be recognised as being accountable for their actions and performance to shareholders, the legally recognised owners of business. Since then, periodic crises of confidence have resulted first, in more and more elaborate and detailed accountings of both organisational aims and achievements being demanded; and second, in the supply of such accountings by managers who have tried to maintain respect for their ability to manage the assets of others. Equally, in the public sector, accounting has been implicated with the development of notions of stewardship and accountability. Accounting information has flowed from agencies of the State to Parliament and the public at large in recognition of the emerging constitutional requirement for the former to provide an account to the latter.

In the 1960s and early 1970s there were, in many Western countries, quite major pressures to expand the concept of accountability. In the name of social performance, environmental impact and the quality of working life, attempts were made to redefine the basis of organisational accountability to include aspects of performance broader than the purely economic. Related efforts were orientated towards expanding the information provided by the organisation in order to enable assessments to be
244 made of its performance in new areas of concern. Notions of social, environmental and energy accounting and auditing were discussed and experimented upon. In the public sphere not unrelated developments were underway. Wider audiences started to demand the right to question the actions of the State. Not only was the State increasingly being asked to account for its actions and achievements, but greater demands were also being made for the right to assess public information, attend public meetings and more generally observe and interrogate the machinery of the State so that others might construct their own accounts of its performance. Concepts such as 'freedom of information' and 'the right to information' started to enter the language of political negotiation and debate.

However, in retrospect, it is interesting to note that most of these developments were much less significant in the UK than elsewhere. Here they did not result in any appreciable questioning of, let alone change in, our concepts of either accountability or accounting. Ideas of wider accountings of the social remained peripheral to UK concerns. Nor was the traditional secrecy of the State effectively challenged in the name of wider rights to public information. Accounting maintained its emphasis on the economic, and disclosure, rather than access, remained the vehicle by which information flowed. The reasons for this relative lack of debate and change in the UK are little understood. However, it is possible to point to the continual dominance of the economic over the social in the UK, the emphasis that all sides of the political spectrum have put on the primacy of the ownership of assets (be they in private or public hands), rather than on other strategies for regulating their deployment and use, and the long history of constraints on the dissemination of information which still pervade our legal, administrative and constitutional systems.

From such a perspective perhaps we should not be surprised that recent discussions of the advance of public sector accounting in the UK continue to emphasise the narrowly economic. Efficiency and value for money, rather than effectiveness, are the focuses of attention. Equally, we can note how little attention continues to be given to strategies for the wider dissemination and use of information, accounting or otherwise. Although demands for more accounting are still permeated with the rhetoric of accountability, the latter continues to have quite a constrained meaning. Indeed, many recent discussions appear to emphasise the role that account-  ing can serve in advancing accountability within the machinery of the State, rather than between it and the public at large. Administrative rather than public accountability appears to be the problem at issue.

No doubt other factors have played a role in mobilising current concern with the state of public sector accounting in the UK. On the supply side, for instance, attention could have been drawn to the increasing interest of the accountancy profession in expanding its sphere of influence and activity in all areas of the public sector. However, hopefully, sufficient has been said to demonstrate that the interest in public sector accounting is not purely a technical one. Accounting is explicitly implicated in the development of quite strategic interests and concerns. Rather than emanating from the specifics of particular accountings, deficient or otherwise, current pressures for change have stemmed from views of the role which the particular might play in mobilising more general strategic arguments.

However, such strategic interests in accounting are now attempting to grapple with questions of the particular and the specific. A rhetoric of economy, efficiency and value for money is now being used to call for a detailed concern with the specific accounting innovations that can service these wider ends.

The direction of change, from the general to the specific, has important implications for those interested in understanding and directing the practical process of accounting reform in the public sector. The generality, and indeed ambiguity, of notions such as efficiency and value for money must be recognised. For, although

the ideas appeal to the comparison of inputs and outputs, and financial resources with their consequences, the delineation of those inputs, outputs, resources and consequences remains both a practically and conceptually difficult endeavour, not least in organisations which are complex, have little tradition of financial administration and economic record keeping, and where outputs and consequences repeatedly arise in organisations different from those initiating the developments. In fact, very little is known about not only the practice of the new public accountings but also the wider impacts which might stem from such an intensification of economic visibility in the public domain. To date, accountings for efficiency and value for money have been advanced in the name of
246 their presumed potential rather than their practical possibility or actual consequences.

**On Examining the Practices of Accounting**

In order to facilitate an examination of the practical consequences of public sector accounting developments, we now consider some of the ways of examining and questioning proposals for such accounting changes. Attention is directed towards the technical practices of accounting themselves, the ways in which they are embedded in organisations, and the wider issues to which extensions of accounting give prominence and significance.

*Accounting as Technique*

Given the ambiguity which pervades such notions as 'efficiency' and 'value for money' when used in public debate, it is always important to analyse proposals for the practical assessment of these concerns carefully and precisely. Only rarely can it be presumed that there will be a direct and unproblematic relationship between the issues of concern and their measurement in practice. More frequently, there will be a gap between the policies which mobilised interest and the specific accounting practices that result from them. Accounting, in practice, invariably requires a specification of detail and a reliance on other organisational practices and procedures that make the final assessments arrived at only partially dependent on the initial interest in them. When subsequently taken up and used in decision making and policy formulation, practical accountings can, and do, have the potential to result in consequences very different from those originally envisaged for them.

Discretion often exists as to what inputs are deemed to be relevant, the costs that are assigned to the resources used, the outputs that are seen to flow from them, and their assessment in both financial and other terms. Issues of organisational interdependency will invariably arise, questions of presumed patterns of causal relationships will need to be debated, and proposals for specific valuations, weightings and assignments of priority will rarely be straightforward and unproblematic. Indeed, 
the difficulties of accounting in practice are such that it is often easy to arrive at a whole array of costs, efficiencies and value-for-money assessments. Many of these never see the light of day, however. Some are buried as a result of seemingly technical accounting choices; others fail to be recognised because of the dominance of particular organisational emphases and favoured theories of the determination of outcomes and consequences; and still others never emerge from internal discussions of 'the message to be presented'.

The ambiguous relationship between the general and the specific in the accounting area is such that attention needs to be directed to the assumptions, choices and practices that enter into the process of making practical what was previously rhetorical. Proposals for accounting change should always be interrogated in the name of the technical; for if this is not done, the consequences that such accountings have may bear only a loose relationship to those which explicitly entered into their justification and development.

### *Accounting and the Process of Organising*

Accounting has the potential to have organisational consequences beyond merely facilitating, in a technical manner, the processes of decision making and policy formulation. By making visible what was previously unknown, it can open up different areas of the organisation for examination and debate. That visibility can also transcend different levels of the organisational hierarchy. What is accounted for can thereby shape the patterns of power and

influence both within the organisation and without. Those with the power to determine what enters into the organisational accounts have the means to articulate and diffuse their values and concerns, and subsequently to monitor, observe and regulate the actions of those that are now accounted for. An expanded flow of information on organisational resources, capabilities and achievements can enable the monitoring, control and planning of organisational actions to be more readily abstracted from their execution. Management, in other words, can become more centralised. New linkages can be drawn both within and between organisations. Different and more abstract criteria can be used for resource allocation. And opportunities can be created for new specialists to
248 enter into the processes of decision making and policy formulation.

The process of organising is not invariant to the accounting of it. Different investments in accounting do have the potential to enable different decisions to be made by different people in different parts of the organisation. Only rarely, however, does an organisational questioning accompany proposals for accounting change. Without it though, an ambiguous rhetoric can enable a partially independent accounting to shape quite important features of organisational life in ways which might not have entered into its original justification.

### *Accounting and the Creation of the Significant*

The selective visibility which accounting gives to organisational actions and outcomes can play an important role in influencing what comes to be seen as problematic, possible, desirable and significant. Neither organisational participants, nor interested parties outside, can ever know the whole extent of organisational life. Direct observation can play a vital role in determining what is seen and valued. However, in organisational hierarchies and in those circumstances where geographical distance and organisational boundaries restrict what is directly visible, observation is soon supplemented and often superseded by that which is recorded. 'Information', both accounting and otherwise, then comes to play a significant role in determining what is known of the organisation and what is expected of it.

In such circumstances, those who influence what enters into the organisational accounts have a powerful and influential role. Some organisational disturbances are more likely to be seen as problematic than others. Some organisational options for change will be able to appeal more readily to supportive information and facts than others. Some criteria for the evaluation of change will likewise find it easier to relate to the partial mappings of the organisation that are incorporated into the accounting system. In these and other ways, not only can the emphasis given to different aspects of the organisation be changed, but also different values can more readily enter into decision processes and appeals can be made to different legitimacies for action. The economic, for instance, can be given more attention than the social. The internal workings of the organisation can be emphasised rather than its external context. The immediate can be given priority rather than the longer term. Accounting, by shaping the realm of the visible, can have a major impact on the significance that is attached to both organisational life as it is and the directions of change which are considered desirable. Both the organisational landscapes of the present and the future are in part, at least, a creation of the accountings that are given of them.

A very conscious attempt has been made to emphasise the need to interrogate and understand proposals for accounting change in terms different and wider than those in which they are usually presented. The ambiguity and generality of the accounting desirable needs to be confronted by an insight into the specificity of actual accounting practice. This needs to be done in terms of its precise operationalisation, the impacts that it has on organisational functioning and the emphasis that it creates in discussions and debates. Just as accounting is called upon to serve more than the merely technical, so it needs to be evaluated in commensurate terms.

### Accounting for Accounting

It is possible to examine developments in public sector accounting on numerous grounds and from a variety of different perspectives. In the discussion which follows, emphasis will be placed on just a few axes for questioning which, nevertheless, raise issues of quite widespread significance. Stemming from an appreciation of how the technical practice of accounting intermingles with the fabric of political and organisational life, the aim is to identify some issues which are worthy of consideration by a much wider audience than they attract at present.

*Accounting, Technical Practice and the Realm of Politics*

Accounting has the potential to create 'facts' out of the uncertain world of the past and even, in a planning context, the future. What was, and still is, debated and challenged can give rise to a residue of accounting calculations of what is costly, beneficial and of value. A
250 world of the seemingly precise, specific and quantitative can, in this way, emerge out of that of the contentious and the uncertain.

A calculative priority can be given to the economic rather than the social. Costs, consequences and benefits can come to be divided into the defined and known, and the imprecise and intangible. In such ways accounting can create very different maps of organisational and social functioning. Particular emphases are given. Only certain chains of reaction are made visible. Only some consequences of actions enter into the world of the precise, the known and even the knowable. In part, at least, what comes to be known of organisational reality starts to be created by the accountings of it. A different view of what is central, and what is residual and peripheral, can start to be reinforced by the ways in which the calculations of accounting intertwine with the complex functionings of organisations as we know them.

Such changes in the visible are accompanied by other changes in organisational life. Expertise in the creation of particular organisational realities starts to emerge and be rewarded. Different legitimacies can come to be attached to arguments and viewpoints, depending on the extent to which they appeal to the domain of the newly factual. Quite specific calculative procedures for decision making and resource allocation can come to be used in contexts where underlying disagreements remain.

Accounting, in other words, can become implicated in the creation of a domain where technical expertise can come to dominate political debate. By appealing to the centrality of the newly visible, be it the economic or whatever, an imperative for technical action can more readily be justified. What were previously seen to be problems of political priority can now start to be seen as requiring management guidance and expertise. We must now face the facts of the newly emerged reality. Rather than debating and arguing, we must appeal to those with expertise in the technical. Politics must stay at the door of public organisations. Within them, so it is said, planning, decision making, resource allocation and the evaluation of performance must come to be seen in management terms. The emerging domain of the technically factual and necessary must be given priority over the domain of the political.

Such attempts to restructure the sphere of legitimate political debate and action have profound consequences for the nature of the society in which we live. Is it necessary, one wonders, for politics to be thus confronted by the domain of the technical? From  what political strategies does this itself emerge? And what are the wider consequences for political and social life? Just what might be at stake in such a juxtaposition of the rhetoric of efficiency with that of democracy? Is it really necessary, one wonders, for the enhancement of the legitimacy of the technical to be gained at the expense of the legitimacy of politics?

Of course, not all changes in public sector accounting raise such fundamental questions. Indeed, accounting itself can be used to mobilise political arguments and debates. The ambiguity of technical accounting practice is such that it often has an uncertain relationship to political practice. Nevertheless, both some specific proposals for accounting change and the general emphasis which together they place on the managerial and the economic, suggest that, at times, accounting developments do need to be seen in such wider terms. Although often masked by the language of the technical and the procedural, accountings can have quite profound consequences in the political sphere.

### *Accounting, Organisational Visibility and the Centralisation of Authority*

Accounting can also become implicated in the creation of very different patterns of organisational influence and control. The selective patterns of visibility which it creates can enable the local to become known to the centre. Institutional boundaries can be made less opaque. Different patterns of local behaviour can come to be

seen, compared and more readily labelled as conforming to, or deviating from, the dictates of the centre. Equally, the preferences of the centre can more easily become known to the local. Procedures for planning, budgeting and performance assessment can serve to both disseminate and make real the demands of the centre. Constraints on local behaviour can be imposed on the basis of the calculative visibility created by accounting systems. Specific behaviours can be monitored and more readily restrained. The local can, in this way, come to be managed as a part of the centre. Organisational interrelationships can become tighter. Discretion can more readily be specified and monitored. Indeed, the local can start to enter into the plans, policies and strategies of the centre so
252 that the meaning of the distinction between the local and the centre can be radically changed.

Yet again, accounting can become implicated in the attainment of a set of consequences which extend far beyond the merely technical. Questions, therefore, can be, and perhaps should be, asked of the organisational and wider consequences of accounting developments.

Just who is made visible to whom? Are the patterns of visibility symmetrical or otherwise? Can only the centre observe the local? Or can the local also observe the centre? Equally, what emphasis is placed on the forging of a visibility within the system of public administration, as compared with the creation of an external account? In other words, just what concepts of accountability (as distinct from accounting) are implicated in the process of accounting change?

### *Accounting and the Enhancement of Organisational Legitimacy*

Accounting can also provide quite a direct basis for enhancing organisational legitimacy. Investments in rational organisational accounts and technical management procedures can be used to demonstrate to others that the organisation accepts the legitimacy of economic and technical bases for action and is seeking to further these ends. Accounts, plans, budgets and the practices of efficient management then become symbols of the organisation's commitment to efficiency both as an aim and a particular strategy of rational governance and management.

The manifestation of such accounting symbols need not result in their coupling to organisational action however (Meyer, (1979), Meyer and Rowan (1977)). The display of the rational accounts may be orientated to those who ask questions of the organisation and seek to probe into its affairs from without, rather than to those who determine from within the organisation's course of events. So, somewhat paradoxically, if the investment in accounting provides sufficient evidence of the organisation's commitment to the course of rational economic and technical action, the discretion so gained might be used to uncouple organisational actions from the accounts which are made of them. Accounting might, in such circumstances, provide the freedom for the organisation to be unaccountable. By successfully appealing to the symbols of legitimate action, accounting might enable the internal affairs of the organisation to have a looser relationship to the external accounts of them.

### *Accounting and the Routinisation of Concern*

Thus, the practices of accounting can come to be valued independently of the precise ways in which they intermingle with other organisational practices to influence the course of practical events. In any event, accounting, often stemming from more wide-ranging and ambiguous concerns, can have difficulty reflecting the specificity of both particular mobilising concerns and particular organisational phenomena, not least in the public sector. In addition, accounting can also come to function as a specialist area of activity in its own right. Technical questions of accounting can arise independently of the contexts in which it functions; accounting can be changed in the name of its own organisational bases and management rather than the wider concerns of the organisations in which it operates.

Such tendencies serve to detach accounting from the organisations in which it functions and the concerns in the name of which it was mobilised. Efficiency, for instance, can lose its force as the basis for accounting changes, to be replaced by a more procedural concern for accounting for efficiency. Similarly, plans can become more important than planning; budgets than the process of budgeting; and costing than the ascertainment of costs. A routine emphasis on accounting as procedure and technique can, at times, supersede accounting's initial concern for the issues in the name of which it was introduced and reformed.

Such a displacement of concern does not always take place. There is no imperative in this direction. Care, diligence and continual attention can result in the routines of accounting maintaining their orientation towards the purposes which they were established to serve. Accounting can continue to penetrate the organisation and change it in the name of more strategic ends.

However, the tendency for accounting over time to emphasise the procedural and the routine, to the detriment of the managerial and the strategic, has recently been recognised as a problem in the industrial sector (Kaplan, 1983). There accounting's routine

emphasis on the short-term economic has been seen to constrain the organisation's strategic vision and posture (Simmonds, 1983). Concerns have been expressed about the rigidity of the information and control practices which accounting has traditionally advanced. Accounting has been seen to emphasise the proliferation of routine techniques in the absence of a concern with the specific managerial consequences which they have. And quite active attempts are now being made in some parts of the private sector to reform accounting in the name of what it should be doing rather than what some now see as what it has done.

### *Accounting and Its Use*

Accounting developments do not always lose contact with either the organisations or the missions which they seek to serve. Similarly, accounting does not have any automatic relationship to shifts in organisational legitimacy, the location of social power and influence, and what are seen to be legitimate or illegitimate bases for political action. Moreover, even when accountings of organisational actions and achievements do become intertwined with such substantive concerns, they do not necessarily have any automatic effects. Accountings can counter accountings: those provided by one organisation can confront those made by others. The routinisation of accounting can even limit the changes in organisational power that might stem from accounting developments. The legitimacy that a particular accounting helps to establish at the organisational boundary can protect rather than necessarily disrupt the internal political processes of decision making.

The consequences of accounting are multiple, often conflicting and far from automatic. There is no imperative intrinsic to the accounting mission (Burchell *et al.*, 1980). Although accounting can have very real consequences, those consequences are created in the specific contexts in which it is made to operate. The effects of accounting are determined by the uses that are made of it, the organisational and social roles which it is made to serve, the ways in which it intersects with other organisational and social processes and practices, and the resistances which its use engenders. Rather than being either a unitary or automatic phenomenon, accounting comes to function in a variety of very different ways in very different settings. And it is those ways and settings which influence the effects that it comes to have.

However, such a contingent view of accounting and its consequences does not deny that accounting can raise quite legitimate and significant questions at levels far beyond the purely technical. If for no other reason than this, accounting developments should be examined in a wider forum. Attempts should be made in this way to account even for accounting itself.

## Accounting and That Which Happens in its Name

Throughout this discussion an attempt has been made to demonstrate that the consequences of accounting do not necessarily have a close and automatic relationship with the aims in the name of which it is introduced and changed. For one thing, the aims that are expressed on behalf of accounting are general and often ambiguous. Stemming from political and managerial rhetoric, they are rarely expressed in terms of the specific operational and pragmatic questions which accounting must address before it can give rise to its technical procedures and practices. However, that gap between the general and the specific can be a very large one. As a result, the precise operationalisation of accounting's aims can introduce quite significant elements of technical autonomy into the accounting process. These elements serve to distance the specific from the general to which it seeks to appeal. Equally significantly, accounting practices come to be enmeshed in wider organisational processes and concerns. The domain of the factual, that they create, gives rise to a visibility, emphasis and basis for governability that can enable the consequences of accounting to become both more pervasive and more independent of the original aims which might have been advanced on its behalf.

It is, therefore, always legitimate to seek to confront accounting with an analysis of the specific consequences which it has had. What has been changed in the name of accounting both within the organisation and without? What effects have attempts to increase efficiency actually had? What precisely has happened to costs, resources and outcomes? What organisational actions have been curtailed or expanded? What changes, if any, have been introduced

into the power structure of the organisation and its processes of management and governance? And how do any such precise consequences of specific accountings relate to the missions and rationales which mobilised them in the first place?

Although such an examination should not be alien to the accounting perspective, accounting itself has only rarely been accounted for. The furtherance of accounting in the public sector could, however, provide an ideal context in which to ask questions of accounting; for its use in this sector can raise questions of a wider organisational, social and even political nature. Given this, perhaps we should use the current pressures for change as a basis for starting to account for accounting and to ask questions about what is actually achieved in the pursuit of efficiency.

**References**

Bahmueller, C. E. (1981) *The National Charity Company: Jeremy Bentham's Silent Revolution*, University of California Press.

Burchell, S., Clubb, C., Hopwood, A., Hughes, J. and Nahapiet, J. (1980) 'The roles of accounting in organisations and society', *Accounting, Organisations and Society*, pp. 5–27.

Kaplan, R. S. (1983) 'Measuring manufacturing performance: A new challenge for management accounting research', *The Accounting Review*, October.

Lazarsfeld, P. F. (1959) 'Sociological reflections on business: consumers and managers', in R. A. Dahl, M. Haire and P. F. Lazarsfeld (eds), *Social Science Research on Business: Product and Potential*, Columbia University Press.

Meyer, J. (1979) *Environmental and Internal Origins of Symbolic Structure in Organisations,* Paper presented at the Seminar on Organisations as Ideological Systems, Stockholm.

Meyer, J. and Rowan, B. (1977) 'Institutionalised organisations: formal structure as myth and ceremony', *American Journal of Sociology*, September, pp. 340–363.

Olofsson, C. and Svalander, P. A. (1975) *The Medical Services Change Over to a Poor Environment*, Unpublished Working Paper, University of Linköping.

Ridgeway, V. F. (1956) 'Dysfunctional consequences of performance measurements', *Administrative Science Quarterly*, Vol. 1, pp. 240–247.

Seers, D. (1976) 'The political economy of national accounting', in A. Cairncross and M. Pur (eds), *Employment, Income Distribution and Development Strategy*, Macmillan.

Simmonds, K. (1983) 'Strategic management accounting', in D. Fanning (ed.), *Handbook of Management Accounting*, Gower Press.

Tomlinson, J. (1981) *Problems of British Economic Policy 1870–1945*, Methuen.

# Accounting and the Domain of the Public: Some Observations on Current Developments

ANTHONY G HOPWOOD



ACCOUNTING in the public sector has become a topic of widespread interest and debate. In the last few years both the language and the practice of accounting have entered much more frequently and forcefully into debates about the management, accountability and even scope of public sector activities. Appeals have been made to the apparent inefficiency, lack of cost effectiveness, and unprofitability associated with activities that reside within the public sector. Referring to the existing economic calculus, it has been said that we are 'living beyond our means', supporting that which is not 'economically viable' and either unable or unwilling to face 'the facts of economic reality'. Although there is a long history of investing in accounting mechanisms for recording, planning, controlling and making visible public sector activities, within a very short period of time recent pressures for change have succeeded in challenging the adequacy of existing public accounts and management accounting practices. New demands have been made for the practices and practitioners of accounting to become ever more implicated in public sector management.

Recognizing these developments, I nevertheless have been perplexed by the form that they have taken, the rhetoric with which they have so often been associated and, not least, the inadequacy of our means for appreciating both the factors at stake in such transformations and their implications for organizational, social and political action. Although I have been both an observer and an active participant in the area, I still have found it difficult to come to a personal view of the developments under way in public sector accounting. At times I indeed have recognized the need for a more adequate economic calculus in public sector organizations, for ways of enhancing the visibility of consequences within the public domain, and for better means of planning and control. In some instances it would be difficult not to do so. At the same time, however, I also have been aware of both the wider patterns of transformation with which the calls for enhanced accountings have been associated and the ways in which the apparently managerially specific can be associated with a wider and legitimately debatable rhetoric of economic and political change. Equally, as a person interested in the organizational and social aspects of accounting and related forms of economic calculation, I have been aware of the problematic relationship between the justifications which are often provided for accounting developments and their actual organizational and social consequences. So although I have sometimes recognized the need for change and, on occasions, participated in it, my view of current developments in public sector accounting remains a questioning and ambivalent one.

That unease and uncertainty is reflected in the title for this lecture – 'Accounting and the Domain of the Public'. It is quite deliberately a complex and ambiguous one. For although I have already referred to public sector accounting, and will continue to do so, I wanted a title that would enable me to make the area somewhat more problematic than is usually the case and in ways that also might not be the usual ones.

The title is designed to acknowledge that there is a legitimate debate over what should be regarded as public and what should be regarded as private. In part, such debates arise out of very long term processes of social development. As historians and sociologists have documented, there has been an ever growing tendency to create private spaces and private realms out of communal life. Barrington Moore (1984), for example, has provided a rich analysis of both the social location of private concerns and some of the factors involved in the emergence of public authority. Elias (1978; 1983) vividly illustrates the articulation of the sphere of the private during the Medieval and subsequent periods, illuminating in the process the ways in which such patterns of transformation created a new vision of the self. In more recent times, not least in the nineteenth and twentieth centuries, whilst the sphere of the private continued to expand, debates about the appropriate responsibilities and activities of the State have also intensified, creating, in the process, a tension between the realms of both the private and the communal and that of the public. The frontiers between them, although rarely stated, have nevertheless appeared to be in an almost continual state of flux. And, as Hirschman has documented in his fascinating volume on *Shifting Involvements: Private Interests and Public Action*, those debates have themselves been subject to a cyclical process of ebb and flow, as the public has been promoted over the private, only to be reversed and reversed again and again – a process that strikes us as a very real one as we sit in the midst of the dynamics of attempts to achieve just such a reversal.

Fascinating though such processes are, some may question their relevance for an understanding of accounting. I want to argue to the contrary, however. I want to advance the view that accounting, as an activity that is implicated in the creation of both visibilities and their boundaries, is one of the ways, but only one, in which the private is demarcated from the public, in which the concerns of the public attempt to permeate the sphere of the private, and in which private emphases can be brought to bear on public concerns. It acts as an information frontier but one which has dynamic properties, allowing some of the visibilities of one sphere of action to be known to the other, and, by so doing, enabling the practice of each to be partially reconstituted in the name of the other.

Just consider the paradox that private sector financial accounts are one of the ways in which Public Limited Companies are enabled to remain in the private sector. Consider also the outcome of the debates on the appropriate mode of accounting for public private sector companies in the nineteenth century. Resulting in a calculative schema which deducted dividends after the declaration of profit, the accounting portrayal of enterprise financial performance was seemingly compatible with a view which located the shareholders, the legal owners of the enterprise, outside of the organizational boundary. Finally consider the numerous ways in which accounting has been used to permeate the boundaries of private sector companies in the name of public interests and concerns. Taxation is an obvious example. In Sweden enterprise accounting is quite explicitly used as a calculative basis for facilitating the management of counter cyclical macro-economic policies. Even in the United Kingdom, however, the economic calculus of accounting has been used, and often transformed in the process of such usage, in order to mobilize private sector organizations to act in ways which are deemed to be in the public interest. Accounting has served as an important basis for price controls in both times of war and peace, with such a use often providing both an incentive for an expansion of the regime of detailed economic calculation in the enterprise and a basis for its wider legitimacy (Loft, 1986). Wage controls and national incomes policies also have utilized the accounting craft and provided a context for a more pervasive calculus of productivity within many enterprises (Burchell et al, 1985). Not least in significance, public concerns with the inadequacy of national economic performance have been used to encourage the more widespread use of economically rational means of investment appraisal within private enterprises. Indeed such strategies of calculative penetration are still seen to be effective by both politicians of the left and the right. On the one hand, we have concerns with social accounting and the means for a wider calculation and revelation of the costs of employment and unemployment in order to infuse the concerns of the public into the sphere of the private. On the other hand, there is a belief in the advantages that can flow from infusing economic calculations into spheres where such managerial strategies have traditionally not been emphasized. Indeed it is just such a concern that provides the context for the present discussion.

So not only is there a fluidity in our notions of the public and private but, of particular importance for the present argument, accounting has some role to play in both establishing a calculative boundary between the two at any point in time and facilitating any process of transformation as the position and legitimacy of such boundaries change over time. Given such a contribution, it is particularly appropriate to consider such issues at the present time when the legitimacy of prevailing conceptions of the public and the private is being debated and when accounting is being brought into the conduct of such debates.

From such a perspective my unease with current developments in public sector accounting becomes more understandable. For although I recognize the value which particular accounting innovations and applications can make, I nevertheless have difficulty in drawing any line between accounting as a mere facilitator of organizational action and the role which it can play in the furtherance of broader social and political initiatives, between its contribution to managing economic resources to other ends and its positive furtherance of the priority of the economic itself. Indeed I sense that no such line can be drawn. Whatever the reasoning that might lie behind even a small, incremental and seemingly technical extension of the accounting craft, it can contribute to the creation of a new visibility and establish a new economic linkage between seemingly disparate organizational actions. Even if such aims had not entered into their original justification, seemingly minor amendments to the accounting regime can, at times, nevertheless play some role in the articulation of a new organizational and social significance.



One of the important ways in which accounting can have such effects stems from its potential to create 'facts' out of the uncertain world of the past and even, in a planning context, the future. What was and still is debated and challenged can give rise to a residue of accounting calculations of what is costly, beneficial and of value. A world of the seemingly precise, specific and quantitative can in this way emerge out of that of the contentious and the uncertain. A calculative priority can be given to the economic rather than the social. Costs, consequences and benefits can come to be divided into the defined and seemingly known and the imprecise and intangible. In such ways accounting, often by a slow process of change, can and does create very different ways of organizational and social functioning. Particular emphases are given. Only certain chains of reaction are made visible. Only some consequences of action enter into the world of the precise, the known, and even, what is considered to be knowable. In part, at least, what comes to be known of organizational reality starts to be created by the accountings of it. A different view of what is central and what is peripheral can start to be reinforced by the ways in which the calculations of accounting intertwine with the complex functionings of organizations as we know them.

Such changes in visibility can sometimes be accompanied by other changes in organizational life. Expertise in the creation of particular organizational realities starts to emerge and be rewarded. Different legitimacies can come to be attached to arguments and viewpoints depending on the extent to which they appeal to the domain of the newly factual. Quite specific calculative procedures for decision making and resource allocation can come to be used in contexts where underlying disagreements remain.

Accounting, in other words, can become implicated in the creation of a domain where technical expertise can come to dominate political debate. By appealing to the centrality of the newly visible, an imperative for technical action can more readily be justified. What were previously seen to be problems of political priority can now start to be seen as requiring management guidance and expertise. We must now face the facts of the reality newly emergent. Rather than debating and arguing, we must appeal to those with expertise in the technical. Politics seemingly must stay at the door of public organizations. Within them, so it is said, planning, decision making, resource allocation and the evaluation of performance must come to be seen in technical and managerial terms. The emerging domain of the technically factual can start to claim a priority over the domain of the political, sometimes restructuring in the process what is seen to be the sphere for legitimate political debate and action.

Of course not all changes in public sector accounting raise such fundamental questions. And, as we will see, the ambiguity of accounting practices can be such that it often has an uncertain relationship to political practice. Nevertheless both some specific proposals for accounting change and the general emphasis which together they place on the managerial and the economic suggest that at times accounting developments do need to be seen in such wider terms. Although often masked by the language and rationality of the technical and the procedural, accounting can and does have quite profound consequences in the political sphere. Because of this it is always as important to consider the context of accounting use and the factors both impinging and likely to impinge upon it as it is to analyse the technical bases of any new accounting proposals. All are important for making an informed assessment.

Seen in such terms, some of my other uncertainties about the current pace of developments in the area of public sector accounting might become more understandable. For instance, I still have difficulty understanding the complex organizational and social dynamics which result in specific public sector accounting initiatives. As an outsider I have often found it difficult, and indeed still do so, to distinguish between the advance of accounting for ritualistic, legitimizing and rationalizing reasons and its advance out of a belief that it can and should engage with the detail of organizational process, to change and hopefully to improve the organization rather than to justify its status quo. Another concern is not unrelated to this. For although I am interested in the provision of intelligent information on the use of economic resources, I nevertheless do have some more fundamental worries about the appeals that so frequently seem to be made to the bureaucracy of systems and to the formality rather than the actuality of planning and organizational control and decision making. Not only can such initiatives sometimes mask either a more explicitly political or legitimizing intent to change the structures of language, meaning and significance either within the organization or without, but also, even when they strive more directly for some form of organizational improvement, they seem to ignore what I see as the very real dangers that can stem from a bureaucratization of concern rather than a more informed and nuanced attempt to disturb and redirect the factors that mobilize action within organizations.

One last concern, possibly one that may well be implicit in those already mentioned, relates to the very real degree of ambiguity that is present in many debates in the area of public sector accounting. The concept of efficiency illustrates this well. Just what is efficiency? At best it is a concept that can be subject to a wide variety of interpretations. Although it is possible to change the world in the name of efficiency, there are very real problems in relating the generality of the concept to the specific operational procedures, let alone their specific consequences in organizations, that can flow from its articulation and use. Of course that very ambiguity is a very positive factor in political discourse. It is difficult to disagree with a concern with efficiency. Who wants to be inefficient? Be that as it may, the indeterminacy of the concept can be much more problematic at the level of its organizational implementation. While not wishing to dissent from the rhetoric, I may well object to what is done in the name of it in any specific instance, either in terms of organizational procedures and practices or their organizational and social consequences. As with efficiency, the ambiguity of so many of the concepts that are appealed to as mobilizing concerns in recent debates in the public domain seemingly enables an uncoupling of the general from that which happens in its name. To me this is something worthy of very genuine debate.

At this stage in my argument I would like to extend my comments on just two of my concerns with recent developments. First, I turn to the intermingling of accounting and politics. Second, I will discuss in a little more detail some of the implications which I see as flowing from the complexity of the organizational processes associated with the advancement of both abstract concepts of efficiency and specific organizational practices, such as accounting, that go along with them.

As far as the political dimensions of accounting are concerned, I do not want to be interpreted as implying that the intermingling of accounting with political affairs is a new phenomenon. Accounting's role in creating a strategic visibility of the economic has ensured it a long history of involvement in the political area.

The very rise of notions of political accountability in the public sector resulted in the advance of both audit and accounting. Long before there was a legislative requirement for the audit of private accounts, we should remember that the municipal reform movements of the 1830s resulted in the establishment of the District Audit Service, thereby giving the public sector a longer history of expert financial scrutiny. Moreover the political debate and modernization movements that gave rise to the present central civil service also concerned themselves with questions of financial control and accountability, creating the Exchequer and Audit Department and the post of Comptroller and Auditor General.



Neither is the appeal to efficiency a new phenomenon in the public realm. In the 1870s Joseph Chamberlain justified his municipal policies not only on the grounds of pubic welfare but also on the basis of the argument that there were economies to be made by efficient municipal management which could in turn produce profits with which to subsidize rate-borne expenditures (Gyford, 1985). Later the Fabians also came to advocate both a concern with efficiency and the roles which modern methods of administration, including accounting, could play to this end. Addressing his fellow members of the Fabian Society, H G Wells said that those who would municipalize activities must also 'develop the most efficient bodies possible' (Wells (1959), quoted in Gyford, 1985). For Wells and others of his political persuasion the advance of efficiency and the utilization of the techniques associated with it were related to the achievement of an overall social efficiency rather than a concept that was orientated solely towards private gain. Perhaps in this context it should not be surprising that the authors of the first British text on cost accounting – Garkle and Fells – were founding members of the Fabian Society.

Around the turn of the century, in the midst of a period of national questioning and debate, there developed a more widespread efficiency movement that encapsulated concerns with the body and its health and reproduction and the mind and its education and training as well as the organization and its management (Searle, 1971). But although the wider ramifications of the use of the efficiency concept were to have a profound impact on social consciousness, institutions and policies, by the 1940s the concept had become increasingly associated with the realm of the economic, where it provided a basis for an interest in the achievement of economies of scale, once again considered from the perspective of national needs rather than private gains. On this basis some of the arguments for the advent of Public Corporations as the vehicles for nationalization and even the creation of the National Health Service were mobilized. Efficiency had come to infuse and influence the language of political debate and the arguments appealed to for the rationalization of action.

Even at that time, however, such concerns were not seen as unproblematic by some. Building on the essential ambiguity of the concept of efficiency, Wright Robinson, a former Lord Mayor of Manchester, said in 1948 (Robinson (1948), quoted in Gyford, 1985):

> Many . . . feel that a point has been reached in this drive when technical efficiency is being pursued without sufficient consideration being given to the long term effect on the democratic efficiency of a human society.



Such doubts did not prevent the forward march of the concern with efficiency, either at that time or subsequently. Striving to promote the efficiency of the private sector, the State advocated the increasing use of management accounting techniques and other practices of rational management. In subsequent times institutions were established to restructure the corporate economy in the name of increased efficiency and enhanced competitiveness. Mergers were seen as a means of ensuring economies of scale rather than monopoly power. Focusing increasingly on the purely economic rationale for investment, agencies of the State sought to promote the use of modern methods of economic investment appraisal.

A not dissimilar rhetoric still permeates political debate. But rather than the public trying to promote the efficiency of the private, the public realm is now itself the focus of deliberation as the practices associated with the private sector (many of which had previously been the target of public promotion) are advocated as a means of increasing the efficiency of the use made of scarce economic resources in public sector organizations.

Admittedly such an historical survey is all too brief and many significant episodes have been ignored. However, I hope that it has nevertheless illustrated how the concept of efficiency and the techniques and practices that are presumed to be associated with it have not only been intertwined with the pursuit of politics but also have been advanced from a number of very different political perspectives. So perceived, accounting can be appreciated as a phenomenon that has been caught up with and related to a wide variety of social, political and economic movements and concerns, only some of which have been articulated in the course of its furtherance and transformation. If nothing else, such an awareness should help to instill a concern with both the ambiguous and changing nature of the concept of efficiency and, thereby, an appreciation of the important role played by the management practices, such as accounting, that serve to provide a precise operationalization of its meaning and significance at any particular point in time. In some senses it is through such specific manifestations of the wider phenomenon, and their actual consequences, that we come to know in more concrete and visible terms the issues that are actually at stake.

The ambiguities associated with accounting's use also inform my difficulties in understanding the organizational dynamics which can result in public sector accounting change. To illustrate this difficulty, let me initially refer to an experience I had a number of years ago (see Hopwood, 1984).

After being privy to a series of meetings which one major public sector corporation held to evaluate and reform its management accounting systems, I became fascinated by the highly abstract notion of managerial process which underlay accounting change. Participants in the exercise dissociated themselves personally from the imperatives which they saw pushing for change. They were not so unhappy with the old information. They did not want the new information. They, it seems, accessed a wide and rich variety of formal and informal information already. They already knew what was going on. Still, however, change was contemplated and eventually agreed, not in the name of any specific practical use or user but rather in the name of a 'person' whom I came to see as residing in the (empty) middle of the table, a 'person' of some considerable significance whom I later came to describe as the person on the Clapham Omnibus. Rather than explicitly acknowledging the operative interests in a centralization of influence, an information flow that would increase the salience of economic factors and a central concern for increasing the structured component of the managerial task, the participants repeatedly referred to the decision needs of a 'person' whom they admitted had very different information desires than themselves. As a result of this experience I became fascinated with the practical interest in seemingly abstract conceptions of information use and the ways in which a rhetoric of facilitating rational decision making can mask a variety of other interests in accounting change.



Building on this example, I would like to extend my arguments relating to the ways in which accounting relates to organizational action.

As the example itself illustrates, although accounting can be appealed to in times of economic restraint, such as now, to provide information to help allocate scarce economic resources, potentially, to a variety of ends wider than the economic itself, I do not think that such a conception of the role of accounting in and of itself gives a full and fair – one might say true and fair – account of the factors implicated in the advance of accounting and the achievement of its consequences. For accounting is appealed to for reasons much wider than its particular technical enabling roles, important though at times these may be. The visibilities which it creates can play a role in mobilizing power and influence both within organizations and without.

Accounting can also play more symbolic, but none the less significant, roles. It can help to shift the patterns of organizational significance. It can facilitate the articulation of new structures of meaning. It can help to demonstrate a concern with the economic at times when economic priorities and ideologies are dominant, such as now.

Having such a diversity of origins and roles, the relationship which accounting has to action is not surprisingly subject to some degree of indeterminacy. Moreover, as organizational participants respond to new pressures and concerns, the organizational accounts are rarely completely transformed. Accountings accumulate in organizations, reflecting both the crises of the past and the concerns of the present, and those stemming from the former, creating, as they do, their own visibilities and emphases, are only rarely inconsequential. A singular rationality is almost never in play in



the accounting domain. Competing rationalities and purposes, diverse visibilities and a variety of interpretative schemas serve to disrupt any singularity that might be promulgated as an accounting mission. And, if only because of this, the organizational and social actions that rise from accounting inventions are positively and often surprisingly enacted rather than being mere reflections of any predetermined intent.

Accounting does not always achieve what it sets out to achieve. Indeed in a complex organizational setting, a concern with only the economic can never do justice to the mobilization of the diverse emphases, resources and concerns that are required to create even particular economic outcomes. Abstract notions of economic rationality have difficulty engaging with the multidimensional characteristics of organizational life. The technical, the social and the environmental need more direct management even for the fulfilment of economic aims. The time scales implicit in the conventional economic calculus often do not relate to those underlying the rhythms of competitive and technological change. And the modes of formal organization and patterns of influence engendered by the visibilities which accounting often creates might not be compatible with the responsiveness and capacity to adapt and change that modern circumstances require. The static categorizations and the normative standardizations that are implicit in the conventional accounting craft may relate uneasily to the turbulence of a particular organizational setting.

Indeed such concerns have provided the basis for the recent development of a widespread 'worrying about management accounting' in the corporate sector (Hopwood, 1985), not least in the USA. Often initiated by enterprises faced with a more competitive environment, even senior financial executives have been encouraged to ponder on the adequacy of their own craft in the name of wider corporate objectives. Studies and investigations have been commissioned. More probing questions have been posed of the accounting mentality. Attempts have been made to extend the range of organizational visibility. The accounting craft has been complemented by information on other significant aspects of organizational performance. More explicitly related to longer-term planning, accounting has been given a more strategic posture. Ad-hoc analyses and interpretations are now starting to be emphasized alongside the routinization of concern that so far has tended to characterize the accounting craft.

There are indeed some signs that accounting itself is in the process of being brought to account. It undoubtedly remains an important and influential form of organizational practice, but the obviousness of its functionality is at least starting to be questioned from a wider managerial perspective. Economic calculation is coming to be seen in more problematic terms. Accounting is increasingly being seen as something that needs to be much more proactively mobilized and consciously related to the functioning of other organizational practices if enterprise objectives are to be met.



Returning to the consideration of current developments in public sector accounting, it might appear paradoxical that so much of the conventional wisdom of accounting of the past seemingly is being transferred unproblematically to the public realm at the very time when it is being subjected to more questioning in the private sector. Of course, in part this reflects the relative lack of prior investment in quite rudimentary procedures in some public organizations. Be that as it may, the development of a wider and more questioning discourse around accounting has encouraged some people to look further than concerns with organizational level economic rationality for explanations of the upsurge in the appeals to public accounting, in fact to explanations which place less emphasis on the direct technical rationality of the craft and more on its symbolic and politically strategic properties. Indeed at the present time it is tempting to place at least some emphasis on the role of accounting in reflecting a conformity to dominant economic values and political priorities. However, although such an explanation certainly should not be dismissed, in and of itself it provides only a partial account of the symbolic nature of the appeals being made to accounting practice. Not only does it not do justice to the history of the involvement of accounting and economic conceptions of efficiency in diverse political arenas but also it fails to consider the ways in which accounting might be seen as a sign of a wider notion of sound and effective management – a long-standing and peculiarly important concern in the United Kingdom.

To enable me to take this part of my argument further, I would like to offer some elements of a short, albeit idiosyncratic Hopwoodian account of accounting in the United Kingdom – an account that some might consider consists of a number of provocative (and certainly debatable) statements and the drawing of a number of very tentative conclusions.

I am not sure how widely it is realized that the United Kingdom has one of the highest national investments in accounting in the western world. Although there admittedly are problems of definition, I nevertheless think that it can be argued that we have one of the highest, if not the highest, accountant per capita ratios of any industrialized nation. And that investment shows every sign of growing before our very eyes, consuming an ever larger proportion of our skilled human resources. In a country where only a modest proportion of the relevant age group enter higher education, over 10 per cent of all university graduates (in all subjects) have been entering the accountancy profession in recent years.

Despite such facts, we have incredibly little understanding of the factors behind the long-standing and still developing British investment in accounting expertise. The nature of our capital markets is most likely



involved in this, as is their role in the structuring of British industry through mergers and acquisition – a role which could well have implemented a distinct financial rather than business logic in the governance structures of the resultant enterprises. However, I sense that other factors are also involved, and to a brief consideration of these I now turn.

There is reason to think that economic, social and political circumstances in the United Kingdom have stimulated our urge to account. On the economic side, the country has a long history of economic problems and restraint, albeit one peppered with periods of prosperity and growth. Economic resources have been at a premium, particularly in the manufacturing sector, and pennies have been seen as having to be counted. Indeed it is in such a 'newly poor' environment (Olofsson and Svalander, 1975) that extensive investments in economic visibility and calculation take place, albeit, in this case, repeatedly so, even though it is now sensed that the resultant internal financial visibility may have an equivocal relationship, at best, to the external circumstances which lie behind the economic difficulties. Be that as it may, the urge to economize provides a fruitful environment for the growth of accounting systems and the wider acknowledgement of the expertise of the practitioners associated with them. In all probability social circumstances may have reinforced such concerns. A contentious society with continued debates over the priority to be given to the economic has resulted in a national investment in the articulation of economic rationales for action and a conception of a determining economic reality.

Enterprise management has not been able to presume the existence of a disciplined, orderly and economically orientated work force. The factory and the office have had to invest in strategies and practices for socio-economic as well as organizational control, and the means for their legitimation, and the regimes of economic visibility and calculation that accounting systems create have been tied up with such attempts to gain mastery over the social, the economic and the organizational infrastructure of the enterprise. Their effectiveness in so doing perhaps has been more problematic, however, a factor that paradoxically might well be implicated in the continued appeals for investment in the accounting craft.

Partly because of the significance of the economic and social problems endemic to Britain, there also has been a long history of direct and indirect government intervention in the economy, which continues to the present day. Having often to rely on surrogates of the corporate economy and its components, such political strategies also have utilized the economic visibility provided by accounting systems. This is true of concerns with taxation and its strategic fine-tuning, with wartime attempts to control prices and profits in the name of social equity, with the pursuit of macro-economic policies orientatated to the control of wages and prices, and with the operational development of micro-economic policies of industrial investment, industrial restructuring and regional development, and the re-orientation of management in the public sector.

Indeed we should recognize that the accountancy profession in the United Kingdom was born in the context of government regulation of and intervention in the economy, and has continued to flourish in that context. Difficulties associated with the administration of the bankruptcy laws of the State provided a powerful incentive for the formation of a professional institute. Thereafter the profession developed in the context of a market for audit services that was to become legally required, and eventually gained a legal monopoly in its provision. The role which accountants played in price and profit control during the First World War not only enhanced the legitimacy of costing, a task that previously had been deemed to be the province of clerks rather than professionals (Loft, 1986), but also increased the social prestige of accounting practitioners. Subsequently accountants were active in governmental attempts to restructure the economy in the 1920s and 1930s and in the post-war reconstruction served as agents of the State's concern with improving management expertise and practices in the private sector. Today that active involvement on the axis between State and the private sector continues. So much of the work of professional accountants resides within the interstices of State interventionist policies, not only in areas such as taxation and corporate restructuring, but also in their capacity as applied economic consultants, specialists in the compilation of economic data and intelligence.

Even though it is difficult to understand the contemporary significance of the accountancy profession in the United Kingdom without appreciating its mutual intertwining with the modern conception of the State, the profession itself also has adopted a most entrepreneurial stance. It has repeatedly done what it has not done before. It moved into industrial accounting and administration after having seen such work as too lowly. It has been an innovator in the application of office equipment and information technology. Now it is moving into general management consultancy and, of particular significance in the context of the present argument, the public sector. Such an entrepreneurial posture has no doubt been enabled by the absence of any effective competition. Lawyers in the United Kingdom have, until recently, stayed with the law. And unlike the USA or continental Europe, Britain has tended not to invest in university trained experts in economic praxis.

So accounting has continued to march forward in the United Kingdom for a variety of quite diverse reasons. Interestingly, however, our high national investment in the area has been extremely unevenly distributed, a



phenomenon which is itself little understood. Outside of immediate professional circles, accountants have tended to be concentrated in British manufacturing industry and, to some extent, local government. Until recently there were relatively few in the financial sector, not a high proportion in the service sector and a very small number indeed in central government and its agencies.

Any account of accounting needs to probe into this uneven distribution. I sense that an investigation might reveal many of the same factors operating that lay behind the expansion of accounting *per se*. Economic difficulties have been particularly severe in the manufacturing sector. State intervention also has traditionally been orientated towards manufacturing and local government. And the contention about the priority to be given to the economic has been a phenomenon associated with the manufacturing enterprise, as is illustrated by the rise of an interest in costing and economic calculation alongside the rise of a more active shop steward movement. However, I sense that even more might be at stake, not least at the present time.

So pursuing my investigation of the factors implicated in accounting elaboration and change in the public sector, I would like to advance the proposition that one significant (albeit partial) factor involved in an organization's desire to account can be a questioning of its legitimacy. When the bases of organizational action are being challenged, when prevailing views of organizational purpose are being undermined, when significant groups start to interrogate and question the organization on grounds different from those involved in its current functioning and when questions are asked of either the adequacy or appropriateness of its modes of operation, there is a tendency both for the organization to account for itself by offering a more detailed and strategically directed explanation of its rationales, modes of functioning and consequences, and, where possible, for it to invest in the symbols and practices of the newly emergent rationality, seeking at least to conform outwardly to the newly articulated expectations for its behaviour and mode of operation.

Such appeals to legitimating strategies are not unfamiliar to the accounting profession both in the United Kingdom and the USA, and no doubt elsewhere. At times when its institutions for accounting regulation have no longer had sufficient authority and legitimacy, and yet do not wish to appeal directly to the democratic mandate of the State, they have invested in the bases of alternative legitimacies. Although not becoming part of the apparatus of government, they nevertheless have tended to incorporate some of the procedural rules associated with democratic institutions, including, in the American context, a concern with due process. Recognizing the singular interest base of existing bodies, the profession has sought to widen the representative nature of the regulatory agencies, once again appealing to political notions of the legitimate bases for authority. Not least in significance, being aware of the traditional nature of professional claims to expertise, professional regulatory agencies have started to commission more modern rational analyses of the accounting craft and the technical options on their agendas.

Similar shifts in the bases of legitimacy have confronted a multitude of other organizations. Further investigation might reveal, for instance, that accounting and accountants were so appealed to by manufacturing concerns amidst the economic crises of the 1920s and 1930s and in the midst of their subsequent reconstruction. More significantly in the present context, we can today witness the questioning and probing that faces organizations in the public sector, not least on economic grounds. Questions are being asked not only of their right to exist and their rationales for action but also of the appropriateness of their organizational forms and both the efficiency and the effectiveness of their management functioning. No longer is it sufficient to claim a social, political or even macro-economic rationale. The language of political economic discourse has been brought to bear on the rationales underlying their existence within the public domain and the most detailed aspects of their functioning. As a result, many organizations are now having to account for themselves or at least shift the basis of their accounting. Rationales have to be articulated and newly stated in the emergent vocabulary. Their performance on economic grounds has to be made known. And there has to be a public demonstration of their commitment to the new ethos by an investment in the apparatus of economic management.

Hardly surprisingly, accounting itself has been appealed to in the process of such transformations, not only as a means of giving a direct account, a way of satisfying the will to disclose, but also more indirectly as a way of demonstrating a commitment to the now accepted and legitimate modes of economic functioning. As such, accounting has been appealed to as much, if not more so, for what it is rather than for what it might help the organization to become. Accounting seemingly has been seen as a manifestation of sound economic management, of appropriate organizational arrangements and of a commitment to the objective of efficiency. In the midst of the urgency to change, accounting has been provided with a symbolic rather than a technically instrumental role. It has been implicated in the management of appearances – a peculiarly important phenomenon in the British scene.

Cast in such terms it is possible to appreciate not only the haste with which new accountings have been implanted into organizations of amazing diversity but also the very possibility of so doing in such incredibly short periods of time. Although a consulting boom has been based on such speedy transformations, a phenomenon that might itself further change the nature of the accountancy profession, the speed of implementation contrasts sharply with the slow and often agonizing process of change confronting those who have sought to instil a conception of economic reasoning into the detailed management functioning of very similar organizations.

Accounting, it would appear, is being appealed to as an indicator of good management, independently of the means through which it engages with and becomes coupled to the detailed processes of organizational functioning. Within the prevailing political discourse, a value and legitimacy is seemingly being set on accounting itself. This is a phenomenon of some interest in its own right. However research has yet to confront the perplexing question of how, in the United Kingdom, what are seen to be organizational practices of the private sector, and particularly industry, can be seen to instil a legitimacy for the managerial functioning of public bodies, being drawn, as they are, from an organizational sector that itself has an equivocal record of economic performance.

The mystery is further increased when one looks at some of the more specific appeals that are being made to both accounting in particular and economic calculation in general. Once again, a paradox emerges. At few times in the past have more appeals been made to 'facts', 'economic reality' and 'the imperative of economic circumstances'. Yet it is difficult to remember a time when those very same facts and realities have been more open to management and manipulation. The unemployment statistics have been a floating phenomenon. Attempts have been made to recast the measurement of inflation and the Public Sector Borrowing Requirement, despite both seemingly having a significance as real objects for policy initiatives. Local government accounting has become a site for artistic creation and the preprivatization accounts of some of the nationalized industries have served as a source of amazement for those interested in the finer aspects of the accountant's skill. One could go on. The facts, accounts and economic statistics to which policy appeals are made seem to be increasingly seen as moveable and manageable phenomena, possibly more so than ever before. Apparently the facts are not the facts.

It would seem that in the 1980s this can be done even if people know that it is being done. Whilst newspaper headlines proclaim 'When in doubt fix the index' (*Guardian*, 21 June, 1985), 'It just goes to show that one man's statistics are another's lies' (*Guardian*, 16 October, 1985), 'How Ministers fiddle figures' (*New Society*, 28 February, 1986) and 'When people are right and statistics are wrong' (*New Statesman*, 23 May, 1986), a fact can still be used as a fact. Unlike the days of the 1970s when investments had to be made in conceptually different measurement schemas with externally accepted logics and rationales, such as inflation accounting and value added, to change conceptions of economic reality, a more direct and seemingly more confident approach is in order today at the very time when the language of the factual has become a more dominant feature of political discourse. It is almost as if some claim to know a reality hidden by the facts.

Although research has yet to grapple with all the factors implicated in the diverse and often paradoxical pressures impacting on the public sector and its accountings, their consequences are evident for all to see. The National Health Service, one of the cheapest vehicles for health care provision in the industrialized world, is under pressure to invest in more legitimate instruments of management, many of which have difficulty becoming connected with the complexities and subtleties of its specific management processes. In local government, accounting has been used as an instrument to further the influence of central government, in the process stimulating such a display of creative accounting that even the *New Statesman* (30 August, 1985) could proclaim the virtues of council accountants for their efforts in maintaining an informational buffer between the local and the central. Universities are being encouraged to adopt abstract management regimes that seemingly have little relationship to either the educational task and the generation of knowledge, or the very real changes that are needed if British higher education is to adapt to a modern era. The nationalized industries have invested in externally orientated management systems to manage their relationship with Whitehall, and when accounting started to be politicized in the National Coal Board, the official response was speedy and forceful, all too obviously, recognizing the role which a legitimate account plays in creating the pretence of a dividing line between management and politics, between the private and the public.

So although accounting has important symbolic properties and is implicated in the management of changes in legitimacy in society at large, such examples illustrate that it is more than a mere symbol. Accounting can penetrate into organizational functioning. It can create a particular visibility. It can facilitate the construction of a specific significance. It can shape the ways in which arguments can be mobilized and the information and bodies of expertise which are deemed to be relevant for their resolution. It can serve as a means for transferring power and influence, allowing what was hidden to be observed and enabling constraints to be imposed on economic action. Accounting can be an enabling craft. It can result in organizational change. Through such processes even symbolic accountings can have their effects. What might initially have been uncoupled to organizational process can start to play a more proactive role. Accounting can and does have its effects, although often ones that did not enter into its original justification.



Indeed much more effort should be devoted to knowing accounting through its effects. Rather than focusing on general rationales, more attention needs to be placed on the specific manifestations of accounting in specific organizations. The generality of the practice needs to be questioned. Instead we should become interested in the ways in which it interacts with specific decision making and control processes, its particular consequences for resource allocation and through these effects, the ways in which over time it moderates organizational action and its consequences. Accounting, in other words, should be accounted for. It should be known for what it does rather than for what it might be able to do.

That represents the main message with which I would like to conclude the analysis. It might appear simple. Indeed it is. However I think that it is one of great importance. Accounting needs to be recognized for what it is – a useful but imperfect craft that operates in highly localized and specific contexts. Compared with the abstract and highly generalized notions accompanying accounting in the past, we want more adequate ways of appreciating accounting in the specific contexts in which it operates.

Adequately formulated, such knowledge would help us to recognize the wider pressures impacting on accounting and the accountancy profession. It would help us to disentangle the conflicting pressures that I am sure will be of greater intensity and concern in the years ahead. By looking at accounting in action, such a way of appreciating accounting will not blind us to the broader organizational, social and political consequences of the craft. Rather, the insights into the uses made of it, the ways in which it relates to organizational action and the means through which it moderates organizational processes and structures, and has its effects, will help us to see accounting as it is rather than as it often accounts for itself.

It is my view that such understandings are necessary if the positive enabling properties of accounting are to be realized. For although they have